Born in Cefn Cribwr, Wales, Lloyd Llewellyn-Jones is Professor of Ancient History at Cardiff University and Director of the Ancient Iran Program for the British Institute of Persian Studies.

He has previously taught at Edinburgh University, where he was Professor of Ancient Iranian and Greek History. He has spent extensive time in Iran, and is a specialist in the histories and cultures of Persia, the Near East, and Greece.

He has also appeared on the BBC, Channel 4, in *The Times* and other media outlets. His previous books include *King and Court in Ancient Persia*, *Ctesias' History of Persia*, *The Culture of Animals in Antiquity*, and *Designs on the Past: How Hollywood Created the Ancient World*.

Lloyd Llewellyn-Jones

PERSIANS

The Age of the Great Kings

WILDFIRE

First published in 2022 by
WILDFIRE
an imprint of HEADLINE PUBLISHING GROUP

First published in paperback in 2023 by
WILDFIRE
an imprint of HEADLINE PUBLISHING GROUP

3

Cataloguing in Publication Data is available from the British Library

ISBN 9 781 4722 7732 9

Epigraph calligraphy by Farnaz Moshenpour
Map and family tree artwork by Tim Peters
Line drawings by Kateryna Kyslitska

All translations are the author's own, except those taken from
the IVP edition of The Bible

Designed and typeset by EM&EN
Printed and bound in Great Britain by Clays Ltd, Elcograf S.p.A.

HEADLINE PUBLISHING GROUP
An Hachette UK Company
Carmelite House
50 Victoria Embankment
London EC4Y 0DZ

www.headline.co.uk
www.hachette.co.uk

آئینه سکندر جام می است بنگر

تا بر تو عرضه دارد احوال ملک دارا

A bowl of wine is the Mirror of Alexander –
Look, it displays the state of King Darius' realm to us.

– Hafez

To my students, past and present,
for joining me on the journey back to Persia.

Contents

Part Three: High Empire

Illustrations

Line Drawings

1. A Greek hoplite prepares to violate a Persian soldier. 'Eurymedon Vase', Attic red-figure *oinochoe*, a wine jug attributed to the circle of the Triptolemos Painter, *c.*460 BCE. Museum für Kunst und Gewerbe, Hamburg.

2. Cyrus I of Anshan defeats his enemies. Seal impression (PFS 93*).

3. Winged and crowned *apkallu* (guardian) from the gateway into the garden-palace of Cyrus the Great at Pasargadae.

4. The Bisitun Relief, a pictorial imagining of the victory of Darius the Great.

5. The Great King, in his guise as a Persian 'hero', kills a mythical monster (part lion, part eagle, part scorpion) representing the chaos of '*drauga*' (the Lie). From a door jamb of the Hall of a Hundred Columns, Persepolis.

6. Seal impression of Parnakka (PFS 9).

7. Seal impression of Zishshawish (PFS 83*).

8. Second seal impression of Parnakka (PFS 16*).

9. Second seal impression of Zishshawish (PFS 11).

10. Gold daric showing an image of a Great King armed with a bow and arrow and a spear, 460 BCE. Metropolitan Museum of Art (Public Domain).

11. Impression of a cylinder seal depicting a female audience scene. Possibly from Susa, *c.*490 BCE. Louvre, Paris.

12. Impression from a seal belonging to Rashda, the chief steward of the household of Irdabama, the mother of Darius the Great (PFS 535).

13. Impression of a seal belonging to Artystone (PFS 38).

14. Impression of a seal belonging to Shalamana, chief steward to Artystone (PFS 535).

15. Detail taken from the so-called 'Treasury Relief' at Persepolis; the Great King and crown prince are shown in royal audience.

Colour Plates

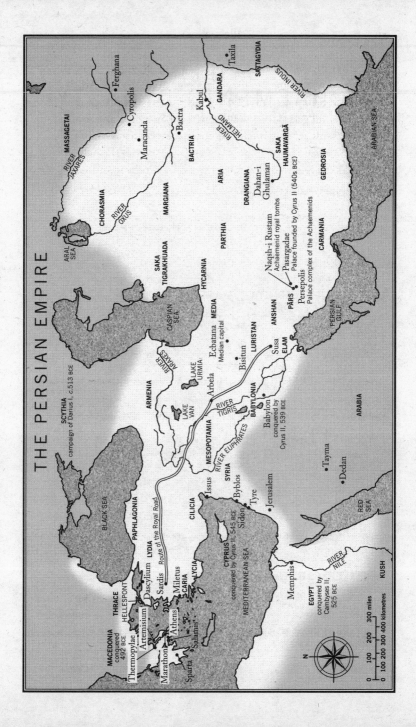

THE PERSIAN EMPIRE

SCYTHIA
campaign of Darius I, c.513 BCE

MASSAGETAI

•Ferghana

•Cyropolis

RIVER JAXARTES

Taxila

SATTAGYDIA

RIVER INDUS

Kabul

GANDARA

CHORASMIA

RIVER OXUS

•Bactra

Maracanda

BACTRIA

ARIA

HELMAND RIVER

DRANGIANA

Dahan-i Ghulaman

SAKA HAUMAVARGĀ

GEDROSIA

ARABIAN SEA

ARAL SEA

SAKA TIGRAKHUADA

MARGIANA

PARTHIA

Naqsh-i Rustam
Achaemenid royal tombs

Pasargadae
Palace founded by Cyrus II (540s BCE)

CARMANIA

HYCARNIA

CASPIAN SEA

MEDIA

Ecbatana
Median capital

ANSHAN

PĀRS

Persepolis
Palace complex of the Achaemenids

PERSIAN GULF

ARMENIA

RIVER ARAXES

LAKE URMIA

Bistun

Arbela

LURISTAN

Susa

ELAM

LAKE VAN

RIVER TIGRIS

MESOPOTAMIA

RIVER EUPHRATES

BABYLONIA

Babylon
conquered by Cyrus II, 539 BCE

ARABIA

•Tayma

•Dedan

BLACK SEA

PAPHLAGONIA

THRACE

MACEDONIA
conquered 492 BCE

HELLESPONT

Dascylium

Sardis

LYDIA   Route of the Royal Road

Miletus

CARIA

LYCIA

Thermopylae

Artemisium

Marathon

Athens

Salamis

Sparta

CILICIA

Issus

SYRIA

Byblos

Sidon

Tyre

•Jerusalem

CYPRUS
conquered by Cyrus II, 545 BCE

MEDITERRANEAN SEA

RED SEA

RIVER NILE

Memphis•

EGYPT
conquered by Cambyses II, 525 BCE

KUSH

0 100 200   300 miles
0 100 200 300 400 kilometres

N

THE
ACHAEMENID DYNASTY

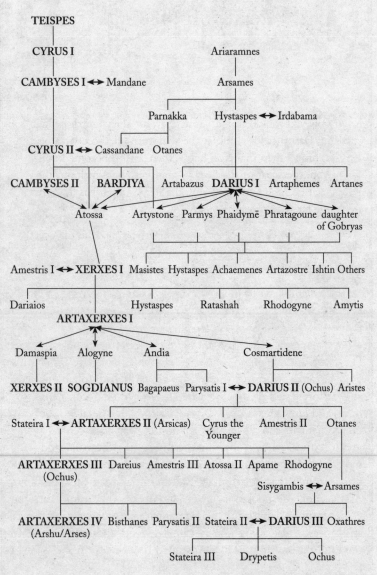

Prologue

Persepolis 488 BCE

> If now you should think: 'How many are the countries which King Darius held?', look at the sculptures of those who bear the throne, then shall you know, then shall it become known to you: the spear of the Persian man has gone forth far; then shall it become known to you: the Persian man has delivered battle far indeed from Persia.

> Inscription from the tomb façade of Darius the Great

At the *Nowruz* festival in the spring of 488 BCE, the time in which the Persians celebrated their New Year with feasting, partying, and gift-giving, Darius, Great King, King of Kings, King of All Lands, the Achaemenid, sat on his throne in the heart of his palace-city of Persepolis and magnanimously received the homage of his empire. Huge bronze trumpets ripped the air with triumphant fanfares and an orchestra of drums, cymbals, and *sistra*, accompanied by harps and lyres, created a rhythmic march which heralded the commencement of the glittering ceremonies that were central to the joyful festival. Foreign diplomats had travelled from far and wide to Persepolis in order to bring Darius their tribute: from Libya they came, from Pakistan, from the southern Eurasian Steppe, Egypt, Asia Minor, Mesopotamia, Syria, and India; they came carrying gold, turquoise, lapis lazuli, wool tapestries, silk coats, cotton tunics, and spices, and leading horses, camels, sheep, and even lions into the lofty throne room. They prostrated themselves on the floor in abject humility in front of the Great King, grasped the hem of his robe, and loyally kissed his feet.

Darius the Great took enormous satisfaction in surveying his empire in this way, as ambassadors and diplomats paraded before him, one delegation following another in strict formation, displaying the bounty of so many far-off lands. He must have smiled at his success, for he was indeed a mighty king, the unrivalled ruler of the Seven Climes. The evidence of his prowess was right there, marching before his eyes. So what if squalid little Greece had avoided capture and remained out of reach? There would be other opportunities to bring that wretched outpost of civilisation under heel. Besides, proof of the success of his empire-building was parading before him, and if evidence were needed of its good order and efficiency, Darius only had to observe the spectacular – and very well-disciplined – presentation ceremony in which his subject peoples so readily participated. For they were not humiliated slaves, thrust to the ground in oppression and trembling in terror before their overlord, but willing partners in a glorious imperial enterprise. They enthusiastically offered Darius their loyalty, their service, and their tribute. Or so he chose to believe.

The diplomatic gift-giving ceremony was so intrinsic to his understanding of empire that Darius had it represented in painted stone reliefs on the staircases which led up to his massive throne hall at Persepolis, the so-called *Apadana*. At nearby Naqsh-i Rustam, on the façade of his rock-face tomb, which he had commissioned in preparedness for the day when it would inevitably be needed, Darius had his artists sculpt a variation on the same theme. He was shown in the act of worshipping his divine protector, the god Ahuramazda, standing on a throne platform (a *takht*, as it was known in Persian) which was raised high above the heads of representatives of the different peoples of the empire in a joyous act of reciprocal collaboration. It was a visual celebration of the diversity of Darius' empire. An inscription carved into the rock in Old Persian cuneiform lettering invited the viewer to count the figures who represented the various geographical regions which made up the empire (each one clothed in 'national costume' to make the

point clearer). To make sure that none were missed, the artist carefully labelled each of them:

> This is the Persian; this is the Mede; this the Elamite; this is
> the Parthian; this is the Areian; this is the Bactrian; this is the
> Sogdian; this is the Chorasmian; this is the Drangianian; this
> is the Arachosian; this is the Sattagydian; this is the Gandaran;
> this is the Indian; this is the drug-drinking Saca; this is the
> Pointed-Hat Saca; this is the Babylonian; this is the Assyrian;
> this is the Arab; this is the Egyptian; this is the Armenian; this
> is the Cappadocian; this is the Sardian; this is the Ionian; this is
> the Scythian from across the sea; this is the Thracian; this is the
> sun-hat-wearing Ionian; this is the Libyan; this is the Nubian.
> This is the man from Maka. This is the Carian. (DNe)

The royal rhetoric propounded on Darius' tomb emphasised
the notion that all conquered nations were united in service to
him, the Great King, a warrior king whose 'spear has gone forth far',
whose laws they obeyed, and whose majesty they upheld. Darius
the Great was thusly lauded not only as the 'Great King' and 'King
of Kings', but also 'King of countries containing all kinds of men',
'King of many countries', as well as 'King in this great earth far and
wide'. All subject peoples were put under Darius' rule and he made
it clear that he would tolerate no trouble or brook no resistance:
'What I said to them,' he stated with gravitas, 'that they did, as was
my desire.' Yet by projecting an image of harmonious cooperation,
Darius propounded that his empire worked best when it pulled
together and was unified in purpose. The empire functioned well
when all the peoples he ruled bought into his notion of 'family'.
When they cooperated, they unequivocally benefited from the
security of a *Pax Persica* – a 'Persian Peace'.

In the Nowruz celebrations of 488 BCE, when the 62-year-old
Darius sat upon his throne and received the ambassadors' homage
and accepted their much-valued gifts, he was accompanied by his
son and chosen successor, Xerxes. This young man, good-looking,
independently minded, and pious, had already served in the
empire's administration as a satrap, or regional governor, in Parthia,

where he had honed his skills as a bureaucrat (there was nothing Darius admired more than a good record-keeper) and as a judge. Aged thirty, Xerxes was now back at court at his father's side and was functioning as the Achaemenid heir-elect. He was not Darius' eldest son, however; nor was he even a second son. No, for Darius had many sons who were much older than Xerxes. These men had been born to the numerous women of his harem, but Xerxes was the first boy born to Darius after he had ascended Persia's throne and so it was fitting that the Achaemenid empire should pass to him, the first royal baby born into the purple. Besides, through his esteemed and clever mother, Atossa, Xerxes carried the blood of Cyrus the Great in his veins; this alone qualified him, more than any of his brothers, for the kingship. Darius was confident that the Achaemenid line would flourish under Xerxes, whose own principal consort, Amestris, had already borne a brood of healthy boys and who herself was to prove to be a contentious dynastic matriarch. In the spring of 488 BCE the Achaemenid family's future was secure.

Introduction

This is a history of ancient Persia. It is unlike other histories of Persia (not that there have been many). This history uses genuine, indigenous, ancient Persian sources to tell a very different story from the one we might be familiar with, the one moulded around ancient Greek accounts. This story is told by the Persians themselves. It is Persia's inside story. It is the Persian Version of Persia's history.

What emerges is new. Far from being the barbarians of the Greek imagination, the Persians emerge here as culturally and socially sophisticated, economically strong, militarily powerful, and intellectually gifted. The Persian Version (a phrase I borrow from the title of a 1945 'conflict poem' by Robert Graves) grounds us in a new reality. It provides us with an original, sometimes startling, understanding of Persia's place in antiquity and highlights Iran's contribution to world civilisation.

In this book, we will travel through time and space, plotting the rise, spread, and consolidation of the Persian empire from its modest beginnings as a tribal society in south-western Iran to the time it dominated the earth as history's first great superpower. We will examine the lives of its monarchs, the Great Kings of Persia, the autocratic rulers of the mighty Achaemenid family, and explore the way in which dynastic politics affected the governance of the empire at large. As we encounter a rich panoply of memorable characters – kings, queens, eunuchs, soldiers, prisoners, tax-collectors, and concubines – we will pause to explore the world they inhabited: their religious ideas, their political thoughts, their territorial aspirations. We will discover how and where they lived, what they ate, how they dressed, what they thought, and how they died. This book is both a political history of ancient Iran's first great empire and a socio-cultural exploration of the world of the Persians.

The creation of the Persian empire made possible the first significant and continuous contact between East and West and prepared the ground for the later empires of antiquity. Its importance in the conception of what a successful world-empire should be cannot be overstated. The Persian empire opened up, for the first time in history, an international dialogue, for, by and large, the Persians were enlightened despots. They employed a surprisingly *laissez-faire* attitude towards their imperial authority. Unlike the Romans or the British who were to follow them as enthusiastic imperialists, the Persians had no desire to impose their language upon conquered peoples. British settlers, soldiers, merchants, and administrators carried the Queen's English to every continent and forced it on captive nations. From Britannia to Syria, the Romans employed Latin as the language of business, finance, and law and order; to be anybody in the Roman empire, Latin was required. The Persians never forced their language on subject peoples. They preferred to utilise local languages for their decrees and they employed Aramaic as a form of *lingua franca* throughout the imperial territories to help facilitate effective – unbiased – communication. In the realm of religion, too, the Persian kings were careful to appear as active upholders of local cults, if only to ensure control of the wealthy sanctuaries and the adherence of powerful priesthoods. Even in small administrative regions, the Persians granted temple privileges and acknowledged the support their local gods had given them. Nor was a Persian 'look' imposed upon the architecture of the empire in the way that, under the Romans and the British, a visual brand was employed across their realms. This remarkably modern and enlightened mindset can be summed up by a single Old Persian word that Darius the Great used to describe his empire: *vispazanānām* – 'multicultural'.

Ancient Persian imperial inscriptions delight in emphasising the diversity of the empire (although they always privilege Persia at its heart). As an inscription of Darius puts it, 'this is the kingdom which I hold, from the Saka who live beyond Sogdiana, from there all the way as far as Ethiopia, from India, from there all the way as far as Sparda' (DPh). Another text, found at Persepolis, demarcates Persia as the centre of the world, but shows that the empire was bestowed on Darius as a gift by Ahuramazda, 'the Wise Lord', the chief deity of the Persian pantheon, who entrusted the king with this most precious present:

> Ahuramazda is a great god. He made Darius king and gave to King Darius the kingship of this wide earth with many lands in it – Persia, Media, and the other lands of other tongues, of the mountains and the plains, of this side of the ocean and the far side of the ocean, and of this side of the desert and the far side of the desert. (DPg)

Darius and his successors controlled an empire which stretched out of Persia to the Mediterranean Sea in the west, and to India in the east. It extended south to the Gulf of Oman and far north into southern Russia. The empire encompassed Ethiopia and Libya, northern Greece and Asia Minor, Afghanistan, and the Punjab up to the Indus River. It was rich in countless farmlands. Barley, dates, lentils, and wheat were grown, and the lands of the empire groaned with precious materials – copper, lead, gold, silver, and lapis lazuli. There was no kingdom on earth to rival its wealth.

The Persians ruled the largest of all ancient-world empires. All more remarkable then is its rise to greatness. It ascended out of a minuscule tribal territory in what is now the modern province of Fārs in south-west Iran. In the Old Persian language, the area was known as 'Pārs' or 'Pārsa'. This was later heard by the ancient Greeks as 'Persis' and it is that name which has come down to us as 'Persia'. The ruling family of the Persian empire, the focus of this book, was the Achaemenids, who took their name from an eponymous founder, 'Achaemenes', an alleged ancestor of both Cyrus the Great and Darius the Great. 'Achaemenes' was also a Greek rendering of a Persian name: 'Haxāmanish', which in turn was derived from the Old Persian words *haxā-*, 'friend', and *manah*, 'thinking power'. Formed of a patronymic, the dynasty was known to the speakers of Old Persian as 'Haxāmanishiya' – 'Achaemenids'.

Throughout this study, personal names will be encountered in their Latinised forms (the exception is for individuals known only through Persian sources; an appendix of names appears at the end of this book). This is an expedient, if not necessarily happy, solution to the question of finding a way to refer to our history's principal players. After centuries of familiarisation, we are more at home with 'Darius' (the Latinised version of the ancient Greek 'Dareîos'), than the genuine Old Persian 'Dārayavaush'. This is a pity, because Persian names were rich with meaning and acted as powerful statements, designed to reflect the nature and status of their bearers. Moreover, important Persian customs and values were reflected in personal names too, giving us a good insight into the Persian mindset. Dārayavaush, for instance, means 'holding firm the good', a reflection of his kingly role for certain. Xerxes' true name was Xshayarshā, meaning 'ruling over heroes', while the four kings known to the Greeks and Romans as 'Artaxerxes' bore the Persian name Artaxshaça – 'whose rule is ordained by Truth'. Cyrus was always Kūrush – 'humiliator of the enemy', an interesting moniker for a king whose reputation has been built on justice, tolerance, and kindness.

The process of the Latinisation of Persian names is highly suggestive of the way in which Persia's history has been appropriated by, and then written from, a wholly Western perspective. That we speak of a 'Darius' and not of a 'Dārayavaush' is a sad indictment of the corrupting process of Western historiography and the crushing of a genuine Persian cultural distinctiveness.

Names and naming are important when it comes to Persian history. Take the name 'Persia' itself. Its use can be highly controversial. What was once known in the West as 'Persia' is now 'Iran' (or the Islamic Republic of Iran, to give the country its correct title). In today's West, and in parts of the Middle East, Iran is often viewed as a pariah state, a war-mongering troublemaker in the most unstable region of the world. Iran is conceived of as the avowed enemy of the West and of American imperialism especially. For Westerners, Iran is the harbinger of Middle Eastern terrorism and the byword for social oppression. 'Iran' has become a dirty word. Through its association with the Islamic regime which governs the modern nation state, Iranian culture is demeaned and condemned too. The Iranians are well aware of how their image is being played out to the world through news headlines, TV documentaries, magazine articles, and the ubiquitous presence of social media platforms. Many Iranians have pride in the name of their country, but are embarrassed by the connotations it has accumulated since the Islamic Revolution of 1979. Feelings regarding the terms 'Iran' and 'Persia' are in a constant state of flux, and in everyday discourse these two words often overlap and might be used synonymously. Among the post-1979 émigrés who have settled in America or Europe, it has become usual to use 'Persia' to denote a 'better' place and time and a more sophisticated cultural identity than what is now being offered by the government of the Islamic Republic. It might be thought that a simple formula – 'Persia' for the pre-Islamic period and 'Iran' for the Islamic era – would be a pragmatic solution to the problem of terminology. But no, such a simplistic labelling does not suffice.

It was on 28 December 1934 that a British minister in Tehran, Sir Hughe Montgomery Knatchbull-Hugessen, wrote to George Rendel, the Head of the Eastern Department of Britain's Foreign Office, to say that 'We have just received an absurd note from the Persian Government.' He expounded: 'it is asking us to speak of "Iran" and "Iranian" instead of "Persia" and "Persians".' Having mulled over the request, Rendel was compelled to write back to Knatchbull-Hugessen: 'I understand the person originally responsible for this is Herodotus, who, not being able to foresee the sensitivities of the modern Persian, was insufficiently polite in his references to this country.'

During the Nowruz celebrations in March 1935, Reza Shah, the first ruler of the short-lived Pahlavi dynasty (1922–79), declared that the antiquated word 'Persia' should cease to be used in reference to the country he ruled. He opted instead to adopt the word 'Iran'. Reza Shah was aware that, in the Western imagination, 'Persia' had remained, since the time of Herodotus, synonymous with images of

decadence, luxury, and a certain backwardness of thought. Western
travellers to Persia expanded on the old image and crafted in their
reports and memoirs a fantastical land of mystery, dark shadows,
places of intrigue, despotic rulers, enslaved women, and wealth
beyond imagination. Reza Shah knew about the clichés. He wrote
that, 'Whenever the word "Persia" is spoken or written, it immediately recalls to foreigners the weakness, ignorance, misery, lack of
independence, disorderly condition, and incapacity which marked
the last century of Persian history.'

In 1935 the Shah had no word to describe the Western appropriation of his country's image, for it was not until 1978 that the
Palestinian born scholar Edward Said famously broached a theory
that Reza Shah might have been able to use: 'Orientalism'. This
idea describes a method by which Western imperialist discourse has
represented the 'colonies' and cultures of the Middle Eastern world
in a way that would justify and support the West's colonial enterprise. Put more succinctly, Orientalism is an idiosyncratic means
of representing 'Otherness'. 'The Orient' was almost a European
invention, and has been, since antiquity, a place of romance, exotic
beings, haunting memories and landscapes, remarkable experiences.
Reza Shah recognised that the connotations of the word 'Persia',
derived from a Greek term, undermined Iran's potential within the
modern world. 'Iran' derives from the Middle Persian ērān, which
was used to refer to the Iranian peoples and, by extension, to their
empire itself. The peoples and places outside of Iran, such as Greeks
and Romans, were called anērān ('not-Iran'). Reza Shah thought
'Iran' a fitting title for his country, a name rooted to the land, the
history, and the people.

So, what word should we use – 'Persia' or 'Iran'? 'Persia' can be
used to describe the realms ruled by a number of monarchs, beginning with Cyrus II in the sixth century BCE. Since that name refers
to a specific land in the south-west of the Iranian plateau which
was the homeland of the Achaemenid tribe, it describes, in a very
narrow sense, the Achaemenid empire too. So, what about 'Iran'?
This too is an acceptable term. From the perspectives of ethnicity,
geography, and history, there has been, since time immemorial, a

'Greater Iran' which extends from southern Russia, the Ukraine, and the Danube Basin, right across the Caucasus Mountains, the Caspian, and towards the vast plains of Central Asia and the rugged region of north-west India. In this discourse, the Achaemenid empire ('Persia' in the narrowest sense) is, to all intents and purposes, a proxy for this 'Greater Iran'. Both 'Iran' and 'Persia' will be used throughout this book. No judgement is passed on either word.

*

If the Persian empire was such a world-dominating, era-defining entity, then why have the ancient Persians not been given the place in history they warrant? This oddity can be partly explained by the fact that until the early nineteenth century nobody had access to any genuine Achaemenid-period textual sources. It was Henry Rawlinson of the East India Company who in 1832 deduced that the Old Persian cuneiform language was a phonetic script and successfully deciphered it. In 1837 he finished his copy of the Bisitun Inscription, a long text commissioned by Darius the Great, and sent a translation of its opening paragraphs to the Royal Asiatic Society. But the second part did not appear until 1849 and the uptake of Old Persian among scholars was slow. True, the decipherment of Old Persian was the key that was needed to crack the codes of Elamite, Babylonian, and ultimately Akkadian (the language of the Assyrians), and scholarship quickly turned its attention to the rich literary and epigraphic heritage of Mesopotamia, leaving Persian studies to lag behind pitifully. Meanwhile the scholarly discipline of Assyriology blossomed and flourished.

As a consequence, the Persian empire only entered into the Western historical consciousness through two diverse outside sources: the Hebrew Bible ('Old Testament') and the works of classical Greek and Roman authors. By and large, the biblical texts championed the Persians. It was the Great Kings of Persia who freed the Jews from their Babylonian exile and allowed them to return home to build a new (second) temple in Jerusalem on the site of King Solomon's original place of worship. In the Bible, the Persians are God's servants, a cooperative and supportive superpower championing the Jewish right to a homeland. The classical authors, however, depict Persia in an almost wholly negative light. The Great Kings are shown as lustful, capricious, mad tyrants, and the empire is regarded as an oppressive challenge to the Greek ideals of 'freedom' (whatever that meant). The Greeks represent the Persians as cowardly, scheming, effeminate, vindictive, and dishonourable. They are the epitome of barbarianism.

The Persians and their vast empire exerted a remarkable hold over the Greek imagination. The Greeks were obsessed with their powerful eastern neighbours. Greek art contains an endless catalogue of images of the Persians, showing them as pampered despots and defeated soldiers, and Greek literature overflows with details about all kinds of diverse Persian exotica. There are references to Persian-sounding (but fake) names, references to tribute, to law, truth-telling, hard drinking, and gold. The Greeks speak of citrus fruit, camels, horses, peacocks, roosters, lion-hunting, gardens, and road systems measured in *parasangs*. They tell of great wealth, pride, hauteur, and a luxurious lifestyle exemplified by expensive clothes and textiles, fine food and drink, luxurious tableware, fans and fly-whisks, and ivory furniture. There are queens, concubines, harems, and eunuchs, impalement, crucifixion, and many hideous forms of drawn-out torture. This limitless directory of 'Persianisms' helped to mould Greek self-identity, although it said very little about the reality of Persian life. Athenian society during the classical age was self-crafted to be a mirror image to Persian civilisation. The Athenians, it seems, were best aware of their 'Athenianness' when they imagined looking back at themselves through Persian eyes. In the fifth book of his *Histories*, for instance, Herodotus described King Darius' reaction to the burning of Sardis, a Persian-held city, during the Athenian-abetted Ionian revolt. Paying little mind to the Ionians themselves, the Persian king was focused, from the start, says Herodotus, on the Athenians:

> Darius asked who the Athenians were, and after getting his answer he called for his bow. After taking it and loading an arrow, he shot it up towards heaven, and as it flew into the

sky, he exclaimed: 'O Zeus, may it be granted to me to take vengeance on the Athenians.' When he had said these things, he commanded one of his attendants to remind him three times whenever a meal was put before him, 'Sire, remember the Athenians.'

Only a Greek – and a pro-Athenian one at that – could have composed such a scene. It is very unlikely that Darius ever gave *much* thought to the far-off Athenians; he had far more important things on his mind, like Scythia and India. But the story informs us very clearly of the Athenians' sense of puffed-up pride and inflated self-importance. To visualise themselves as the Great King's nerve-wracking nemesis gave the Athenians a sense of worth.

Herodotus took this idea further. According to him, it was the memory of Athens' support of the Ionian Revolt that motivated the Persian campaigns against Greece in 490 and 480 BCE. The latter expedition is particularly notable because even though Xerxes had by this time succeeded his father as monarch, Herodotus continued to emphasise the depth to which Athens penetrated into Darius' memory. It was the latter invasion which was the focus of Aeschylus' great tragic drama *Persians* of 472 BCE, in which Xerxes is characterised as a monstrous tyrant who attempts to crush the freedoms enjoyed by Athens and the Greek city states. The subsequent fortuitous repulsion of the overwhelming forces of the Achaemenid despots became something to celebrate in poetry, drama, art, and in new narrative histories, such as that which was crafted by Herodotus.

On closer examination, Herodotus' Xerxes is a character of intense complexity. His blustering brutality alternates with child-like sulkiness and unexpected, mawkish, explosions of tears. One of the most significant and unexpected incidents in the *Histories*, which has the sensitive subtlety of truly great fiction writing, comes when Xerxes, reviewing the armada of ships he has amassed for the invasion of Greece, breaks down and weeps genuine tears. He is 'overcome' (as Herodotus explains) 'by pity because he ponderd the brevity of human existence' and finds it all too upsetting. For a despot, whose casual indifference to humanity is highlighted throughout the *Histories,* to have such empathy towards the certainty of death is a remarkable psychological invention on the part of Herodotus. The nightmare of a psychopathic leader (one minute up, the next down) at the head of a brutally centralised authoritarian state has become an image that has unsettled liberal democrats ever since Herodotus first created it. But it has very little to do with the *real* Xerxes of the 'Persian Version'.

That is not to say that Herodotus' view of Persian history should be completely written off as a bunch of concocted morality tales. No; Herodotus was, after all, born a subject of the Persians – his home town of Halicarnassus was part of the Persian empire – and he must have had some understanding of how (parts of) the empire worked. He certainly recorded Persian stories that were circulating during his lifetime and it is possible to extract from the *Histories* genuine, informative, and illuminating Persian materials. This process has to be handled carefully though. Herodotus' chief agenda was to hold up that mirror to the Persians. The reflection which came back showed the Persians to be the converse – the very antithesis – of the Greeks. The Persians were the ultimate 'Other'.

There were further Greek authors writing at roughly the same time as Herodotus. Some of their works were enriched by more direct engagement with the Persians. Xenophon, for instance, had marched from Greece to Babylon as part of a mercenary army in the pay of Prince Cyrus the Younger in 401 BCE. His works, the *Anabasis* ('The Expedition') and *Cyropaedia* ('The Education of Cyrus'), are useful first-hand accounts of a soldier's view of the Persians, although Xenophon too could not help but give a somewhat pejorative reading of his subject matter. Of more direct use are the writings of Ctesias of Cindus, a Greek doctor who served as a royal physician at the heart of the Persian court during the reign of Artaxerxes II. For seventeen years Ctesias was stationed in close proximity to the royal family and learned to speak Persian. He conversed with Achaemenid nobility and gathered first-hand accounts of their family histories and dynastic traditions. His mammoth bestseller, the *Persika* ('Persian Things', which sadly survives now only in fragments), presented a unique history of Persia from an insider's point of view. Ctesias transmitted stories, fables, and legends which were being told, recited, and performed within the halls of Persia's elite. Once thought by scholars as little more than a spinner of tall-tales, Ctesias is now recognised for making an important contribution to our understanding of how 'history' was approached by the Persians.

From around 550 BCE to the age of Alexander the Great in the 330s BCE, each successive generation of Greeks had its own particular way of reconfirming, as needed, Hellenic identity against the ever-changing yet ever-present Persian threat. The Greek obsession with the Persians focused on minimising their credibility as a super-power. Denigration of the Persians – by vilification or lampooning – was intended to cauterise the wounds of anguish and fear provoked by the threats and realities of being neighbours of an empire whose territorial ambitions were very real and which showed no sign of ever abating. In order to increase Greek morale, a series of what might be termed 'cathartic' images were created on stage, in sculpture, and in the other arts. These disparaged, degraded, and belittled the Persians and confirmed Greek (especially Athenian) pre-eminence. One such object is a red-figured wine-jug dated to the mid-460s BCE. Known as the 'Eurymedon Vase', it shows a humiliated Persian soldier bending forward from the waist. His backside is offered up to a grubby Athenian squaddie who stands with his erect penis in his hand, rushing forward in order to penetrate the Persian's rear. The painted rape scene (for that's what it is) was created as a 'commemorative issue' at the time the Athenians celebrated a

Figure 1. A Greek hoplite prepares to violate a Persian soldier. 'Eurymedon Vase', Attic red-figure *oinochoe*, a wine jug attributed to the circle of the Triptolemos Painter, c.460 BCE.

victory over Persian forces at the battle of the River Eurymedon in
Asia Minor in 467 BCE. It was used at some kind of drinking party,
probably a soldiers' get-together. As the jug was passed around a
group of hoplites – the Greek equivalent of GIs – so the wine flowed
and the dirty jokes began to fly. So too was the Persian on the vase
manhandled from soldier to soldier. As each drinker gripped the
jug, he replayed the drama of the scene: 'Now I am Eurymedon',
he boasted. 'Look at me, buggering this Persian!' The vase image is
a perceptive visualisation of soldiers' humour, although it is highly
likely that the scene reflected a lived reality. After all, the post-battle
rape of defeated soldiers has never been just a drinking-game fantasy.
The Eurymedon vase was an expression of the Athenian zeitgeist
of the 460s BCE. It was a well-aimed joke on recent unexpected but
fortuitous political and military events which demonstrated the
natural superiority of the Greeks over the barbarian Persians.

Where does this image of a humiliated, defeated, defunct Persia
take us? It takes us directly to the era of the European Enlightenment, when intellectuals began to theorise as to why the West had
become so dominant in the world order and had been so successful
in the spread of white civilisation. They came up with a radical
theory: European superiority came not from Christianity, as had
previously been thought throughout the Middle Ages and Renaissance, but from a cultural tradition that began in ancient Greece.
The Greeks, they stipulated, invented freedom and rationality. Rome
then spread these precious gifts across Europe in a series of civilis-
ing imperial conquests. Other cultures on the fringes of Greece
and Rome were barbaric and the worst and most threatening of
all barbarians were the Persians, with their quest for world domination. This was contrary to the natural order of white supremacy.
The concept was given voice by Charles-Louis de Montesquieu in
his *Persian Letters* of 1721: 'Liberty', he wrote, 'was intended for the
genius of European races, and slavery for that of the Asiatics.' The
Scottish historian John Gillies expanded on this thought in 1787,
maintaining that the Persians 'enslaved the Greeks of Asia Minor
and for the first time, threatened Europe with the terrors of Asiatic
despotism'. Across the decades and into new centuries, it became

the 'White Man's Burden' (as Rudyard Kipling put it) to spread the benefits of freedom-giving Hellenic culture all over the globe, for the betterment of all races and to keep the barbarian at bay.

In September 1889 George Nathaniel Curzon, a young British Member of Parliament with a big destiny, began a three-month tour of Persia (his sole visit to the country). As he strolled around Persepolis, he was moved by what he encountered, regarding the ruins as a 'solemn lesson of the ages'. The 'lesson' of course was one of *hubris* – the Persians, he certified, were unable to understand that they 'did not have the qualities needed to maintain an empire', nor to govern it effectively. Persia's long decline and fall were inevitable, Curzon opined, but it needed a Greek of Alexander's stature to bring about its predestined end. Curzon noted in his stately two-volume work *Persia and the Persian Question* (often regarded as history's longest job application; the post was the coveted job of Viceroy of India) that he found Persian and Indian resistance to Western colonialisation baffling: 'the normal Asiatic would sooner be misgoverned by Asiatics than well governed by Europeans', he wrote, somewhat bewildered.

Curzon was a successful product of the *locus classicus* of a distinctly *British* form of philhellenism: the English elite public-school system. These all-male institutions, factories of privilege, where senior judges, top civil servants, and Foreign Office diplomats were conveyor-belt manufactured, traditionally embedded Classics at the core of their curricula. Ancient Greek language and literature were considered the cornerstones of education and Greek was used to inculcate the next generation of Britain's imperial administrators. Significantly, knowledge of Greek language and history circulated only among this most privileged of Britain's (mostly male) elite. Winston Churchill famously said that he would allow schoolboys to 'learn Latin as an honour, and Greek as a treat'. Yet sitting behind this familiar *bon mot* was Churchill's commitment to the use of the Classics as a means of social distancing. It was a powerful device which could be relied upon to keep the classes well apart and, by extension, add to the processes of empire-building by initiating only the top brass of society into its mysteries. The classicist

H. D. F. Kitto, himself a product of the British public-education system and the author of a (still bestselling) 1951 introduction to Greek history, invited his readers 'to accept ... as a reasonable statement of fact' that the Greeks 'had a totally new conception of what human life was for, and showed for the first time what the human mind was for'.

What has emerged from this long legacy of imperialised philhellenism is a series of damaging premises and a harmful conclusion – that classical Greece was an exceptional moment in world history and that the West has unquestionably benefited from being the heir to Greek culture. That legacy has shaped national histories. Writing in 1867, the British philosopher and political economist John Stuart Mill claimed that, 'even as an event in British history', the battle of Marathon, fought between the Greeks and the Persians in 490 BCE, 'is more important than the battle of Hastings'. He declared that 'the true ancestors of the European nations are not those from whose blood they are sprung, but those from whom they derive the richest portion of their inheritance'. Westerners saw themselves as the direct heirs of the miracle of Greek civilisation. It was logical for them to thereby affirm that Western culture must be exceptional too. By deduction, cultures deprived of the legacy of classical Hellenism had to be lesser civilisations in terms of rational thought and governance, unity of purpose, intelligence, and ambition. The old Greek image of a decadent and despotic Persia was repurposed to represent the inadequacies and inabilities of all non-Europeans.

This perverse understanding of a hierarchy of cultural competence is still propounded. An eminent German scholar of the Greco-Roman world, Hermann Bengston, for example, has rooted his academic career in promoting this hackneyed myth of Western superiority. He recently found the compulsion to write that:

> The ramifications of the Greek triumph over the Persians are almost incalculable. By repulsing the assault of the East, the Hellenes charted the political and cultural development of the West. With the triumphant struggle for liberty by the Greeks,

Europe was first born, both as a concept and as a reality. The freedom which permitted Greek culture to rise to the classical models in art, drama, philosophy and historiography, Europe owes to those who fought at Salamis and Plataea. If we regard ourselves today as free-thinking people, it is the Greeks who created the condition for this.

We can add to this the voice of Andrew Bayliss, a historian at Birmingham University, who in 2020, on the anniversary of the Battle of Thermopylae, fought in 480 BCE between Xerxes' Persians and the combined forces of the Greek city states, advocated that:

Thermopylae's greatest legacy was the so-called 'Golden Age' . . . Had the Persians succeeded in permanently destroying Athens they would have snuffed out the fledgling Athenian democracy, and we would not today marvel at the magnificence of the Parthenon on the Athenian acropolis, or be able to read the great works of literature by the like of . . . Thucydides . . ., Aeschylus, Sophocles, Euripides, Aristophanes . . . and Plato. None of this would have been possible without the inspiration that [the Spartan king] Leonidas and his men provided in their stand for freedom.

These sentiments are as flawed as they are spurious. The Persians were never out to destroy 'democracy' (whatever 'democracy' means in its ancient context). In fact, many Ionian Greek city states continued to practise 'democracy' under Persian rule – after all, the Persians recognised the Ionian Greeks' dislike of autocratic tyrants and they happily replaced them with democracies. Had the Achaemenids brought the mainland Greeks into their empire, they doubtless would have tolerated democracy there as well. They might even have encouraged it. A Persian victory over Sparta – the most oppressive freedom-denying slave state of antiquity – would have been a win for liberty. It would have put an end to Sparta's terrorist-like hold over the rest of Greece. The idea that the Persians inhibited and held back Europe's cultural development is absurd.

Since the era of the Greco-Persian Wars, the Persians themselves have been at the receiving end of a historiographic smear campaign in which they have been cast as the tyrannical oppressors of the free world. The Western intellectual commitment to the promotion of its own supposed singularity and superiority has been very damaging for the study of Persia's history. It is time to rectify the long-standing injurious distortion that the Persians have suffered by giving ear to a genuine ancient Persian voice.

*

How, then, can we access the Persian Version when it seems that the source materials work against us? After all, the Persians never wrote narrative history in the way that the Greeks did. There was no Persian Version of Herodotus, Thucydides, or Xenophon. Does that mean that the Persians had no sense of their past? Did they not contemplate their place in the progress of history? The absence of a historical narrative does not equate to the idea that the Persians did not understand or respond to their history. The Persians knew their history, but they chose to remember it differently. The Persian past was transmitted through songs, poetry, fables, and legends. It was a performed history.

A notable feature of the rich oral culture of the ancient Near East in general was a positive *dislike* for exact facts or specific dates. Persians, Babylonians, and Assyrians comprehended their past in terms of their myths, especially creation stories, and the grand tales of gods, heroes, and kings. Kingship as a manifestation of divine will stood at the centre of the Near Eastern concept of historical progression, and the actual details of historical events were of less interest than the *pattern* by which the past was explained in relation to mythic events. 'History' was the result of the activities of the gods who set events in motion. The ancient pursuit of a coherent pattern in understanding history meant that a sense of 'what really happened' in 'history' was gained only in light of the outcome of events. Hindsight was the defining factor in the Near Eastern understanding of the historical process. For the Persians, the history of their empire was set in motion by the gods. Their quest for territory was successful because Ahuramazda had ordained it should be so. So, can we find a *bone fide* Persian record of the Persian past? The answer to that question is a simple 'yes'.

The Persian Version is everywhere. We cannot pick and choose our sources, so while materials may not be found in one continuous narrative format, Persia's insider history can be pieced together from diverse and scattered sources. It has taken historians of the ancient world a long time to recognise that the Persians can be approached from their own indigenous materials. Now that we have recognised this, the Persians can be liberated from the classical tradition.

Persian history is an enormous jigsaw puzzle which requires patient assemblage and some clear-headed collaboration. Some pieces are missing, and there are gaps around the edges, but, on the whole, the picture which is emerging from the real Persian evidence is illuminating. It is also a tremendously exciting field of exploration in which a dizzying assortment of sources can be – and will be – encountered.

Let us start with the language of ancient Persia. The Achaemenid Persians spoke an early form of modern Farsi (or 'New Persian') called 'Old Persian'. It was written in cuneiform script, the old, time-honoured Mesopotamian form of wedge-shaped writing. In written form, it could either be pressed into wet tablets of clay or carved into hard surfaces, such as stone, lapis lazuli, alabaster, and even silver and gold. It was a language used for the composition of public, official, and royal statements, and virtually all the surviving Old Persian texts have been found inscribed onto buildings and other royal monuments. They are often accompanied by a translation of the same text into another language – Akkadian, Egyptian, or Elamite. The Old Persian inscriptions tend to be repetitive in character, propounding royal ideology and promoting imperial power. One exception, the so-called Bisitun Inscription of Darius I, is inscribed on a rock face overlooking the main highway between the Mesopotamian plain and Ecbatana (modern Hamadan) in Media. It provides more of a narrative history of Darius' accession to the throne, as we will go on to explore. The repetitive inscriptions reiterate ideological statements and they are important sources for our understanding of how the Achaemenid kings saw themselves. The Old Persian texts proclaim the heroic and militaristic qualities of the monarchs and place their successes within the shadow of Ahuramazda, the great god of the Achaemenids. Other cuneiform texts in Elamite and Akkadian strengthen our knowledge of Persian history, and Egypt too has also offered up information on Persian rule in localised hieroglyphic and demotic texts. Inscriptions written in Greek, Lydian, and Phrygian attest to the geographic spread of the empire and to the diversity of languages spoken within its borders.

The most widespread of all the tongues of the Persian empire though was not Old Persian, but Aramaic. This ancient Semitic language had been widely in use throughout the Near East in the eighth century BCE and had been employed by the Assyrians as an effective method of international communication. The Persians used it as a language of diplomacy and administration, so that it served the same purpose as Latin would later do in the Middle Ages by becoming the *lingua franca* of the Persian empire. All educated men, diplomats, and scribes were well-versed in Aramaic, and its efficacy as a bureaucratic tool can be seen in the fact that the language was still functioning in the Near East well into the Hellenistic period and beyond (Aramaic was the language which Jesus of Nazareth spoke in Roman-occupied Judaea of the first century BCE). Aramaic was easy to read and write (it was a fluid cursive script) and it could be scribbled in ink onto papyrus, wood, pot sherds, bone, or other easily portable surfaces. For this reason, Achaemenid-period Aramaic documents have been discovered as far afield as southern Egypt and eastern Bactria (modern Tajikistan and Uzbekistan). It was a truly universal language.

Our understanding of the cuneiform languages of the Near East means that we have access to materials unique to Persia. Digging at Persepolis in the 1930s, archaeologists unearthed a trove of documents which were written and stored at the centre of the Achaemenid bureaucracy. Known as the Persepolis Treasury texts and the Persepolis Fortification tablets (after their places of discovery), some 30,000 baked-clay tablets were unearthed, dating to between 492 and 458 BCE – that is, from late in the reign of Darius I into the early years of king Artaxerxes I. Most were written in Elamite cuneiform, the language of the Persian chancellery, and dealt with economic transactions (mainly food rations), although a couple of them are in Aramaic, Phrygian, Old Persian, and even Greek. Both the Elamite and the Aramaic tablets carry the impressions of cylinder seals (usually of one or two seals but sometimes more) which were stamped into the wet clay. The tablets and the seals provide a remarkable insight into life and work at Persepolis and its immediate environs in the fifth century BCE, providing a Who's Who of people living and working in and around the palace and evidence for the functioning of the administrative system. They record all sorts of food rations to workers (men, women, and children), priests and religious authorities (some of which was used for sacrifice), to the Persian nobility, and to the royal family. The tablet collection is an incredibly rich database for understanding the complex bureaucracy of the Achaemenid administration, highlighting taxation methods, storage systems, landholdings, diet, settlement organisation, and travel routes – the intimate materials of Persian life completely unrecognised in the Greek sources.

Archaeology is a major field in contemporary studies of ancient Iran. Fieldwork undertaken in Iran since the 1930s has cast much-needed light on the material culture of the Achaemenid period, with excavations at Persepolis, Pasargadae, Susa, and Ecbatana – the great imperial centres – taking much of the attention. The archaeological exploration of the imperial territories has been less systematic, although more attention is now being given to Achaemenid-period archaeological levels at places like Sardis and Dascylium in Turkey, as well as sites in the Levant and Central Asia. Recent excavations in Georgia are unearthing evidence of close contact between the Persian heartlands and this peripheral area of the empire, and in recent years Egyptologists have turned with increasing enthusiasm to the remains of Egypt's Persian dynasty, uncovering previously unknown sites in the Nile Delta and the Kharga oasis. As the archaeologists uncover and evaluate more evidence for the diversity of life in the imperial provinces, so our picture of the nature of the Persian empire increases.

Exploration of Achaemenid art, emerging from the archaeology, confirms that it was an eclectic mix of styles and motifs drawn from different parts of the empire, fused together to produce a distinctive and harmonious 'Persian' look. Egyptian and Assyrian motifs (like winged discs and winged genii, pediment designs, and even methods for depicting the human figure) were frequently melded together, so that Achaemenid art can be said to reflect in material form both the diversity and the unity of the empire as a whole. The art of the Achaemenid empire served a primary purpose: it confirmed the royal ideology of the unity of the empire and promoted the image of the monarch. In a way, all Achaemenid art was royal art, since the motifs created for the glorification of the king are found time and again in almost all Persian material artefacts. These range from vast rock-cut sculptures – such as those found at Bisitun or the tombs of the kings at Naqsh-i Rustam and Persepolis – to minuscule engravings found on gemstones and seals.

*

Using the rich assortment of source materials in order to understand the Persian Version of Iran's ancient past can only be a good thing. But we must recognise that this approach too has its problems and pitfalls. The sources created inside Iran, by and for the Persians and their subject peoples, are not free of hyperbole, bias, or falsehoods. Beneath every indigenous Persian source – text, image, or artefact – there lies an imperial agenda. The Persian Version of history projects its own variety of historical spin.

Thus, on the surface, Darius' royal inscriptions stress that all is good throughout his empire:

> I am Darius the Great King, King of Kings, King of all Nations, King of this Earth, the son of Hystaspes, an Achaemenid. King Darius says: when Ahuramazda made me king of this earth, by the grace of Ahuramazda, I made everything orderly. (DSz)

But was all as 'orderly' as he insists? Was the empire really a land of harmony? A land of plenty? The imperial territories were a contiguous land mass, true, and, on the surface, the empire certainly benefited from the unity of the Persian system (roads were excellent and communication infrastructures were very advanced and served the empire well, as we will see in more detail later). Yet the Persian empire was unnervingly vulnerable at its frontiers, which were, geographically, very far removed from the imperial heartland in Iran. The borderlands and outlying hinterlands were frequently the sites of rebellion against the monarch or his governors. Moreover, the empire's population, huge as it was, was mainly composed of peasants, illiterate, unskilled, and eking out a living through subsistence farming. Most people lived in abject poverty and their meagre plots of land contributed little to the wealth of the empire. Nor did the vast stretches of land comprised of inhospitable, barren deserts, salt lakes, windswept tundra, or rocky mountain faces bring anything to the empire's benefit. Uninhabitable, ill-suited to transport, and certainly non-profitable, these territories were an undiscardable burden to the Persian empire as a whole.

It is crucial that we recognise from the outset that Darius, like all Persia's Great Kings, was in the business of spin-doctoring. He ran a well-organised and effective propaganda campaign and commissioned inscriptions and images less to inform than to persuade. Darius the Great was an adroit propagandist. On the walls of his palaces at Persepolis, Susa, and Babylon, he cleverly commissioned a picture of the world as it never was in actuality. The Persian empire was created – as all empires are – through military conquest. The realities of building and keeping an empire, even one as (on the surface) tolerant as Persia's, meant doing some pretty horrific things. Bloodshed and violence are the hallmarks of any forced occupation, of any kind of imperial enterprise, and in this respect the Persians were not exempt from committing atrocities as part of the process. Soldiers trained to kill willingly committed extreme violence in the name of Persian imperialism. The Persians could prove to be merciless when crossed or challenged, and rebellious subjects and states were treated with ruthless suppression. Whole populations were uprooted from their homelands and deported to different locales across the empire. Their cities, towns, and holy shrines were burned and destroyed. Looting and the gratuitous destruction of livestock was commonplace, as was the taking of hostages, children, and female prisoners, often raped and sold as slaves. There was torture and mutilation: hair torn from the heads of prisoners, beards ripped out of the skin, the gouging out of eyes, the lopping off of noses, the slitting off of ears, the beatings, the sodomy, the countless violations. Whole populations were put to the sword.

Yet while news of this violent Persian military expansion was striking terror into the hearts of people throughout the Near East and the Mediterranean, at Persepolis and the other palatial sites, artists from across the empire were creating fantasies in limestone, gold, and marble for Darius. Elegantly sculpted and painted propaganda advanced his vision of imperial harmony. The paradox between the actuality of empire-building and the art and rhetoric of the *Pax Persica* cannot be ignored. But to give the Persians their due, even to have *conceived* of an empire which ran to this harmonious ideal was something unparalleled in the ancient world. The Assyrians and Romans never reached that level of self-awareness. Nor did the British. The dream of a Persian Peace stands as a tottering tribute to the ancient Persian mindset.

The Achaemenids reigned supreme over their empire. They had no contemporary peers and there were no contenders to their territorial ambitions. Despite (as we will explore) internal revolts, frontier problems, succession struggles, murders, and even regicides, the Achaemenid empire held on to its enormous territories and diverse subject populations for more than two centuries. The Persian empire never underwent a slow process of decline and eventual collapse, nor did it follow any familiar 'Rise and Fall' scenario that might be construed for other empires. When its end came, with the conquests of Alexander of Macedon in the late 330s BCE, it was swift and totally unexpected. Darius III, the final Achaemenid Great King, ruled an empire that was as functional, wealthy, and secure as it had been 150 years earlier.

The question which inevitably arises of these facts, therefore, is not why did the Persian empire come to an end, but rather how did it stay successful for so long? There is one fundamental answer to that question: the Achaemenid family never lost its exclusive hold on the kingship. The Persian empire never had to contend with opposing dynasts who put the unity of the state in danger. The Achaemenids ran their empire as a family business which, under careful management, matured, stabilised, and returned dividends over time. Each king passed on to his chosen male successor the skills needed for good rulership. The dynasty's women carefully guarded the purity of the bloodline and maintained the efficacy of a royal breeding programme by producing sons to serve as satraps and army officers, and daughters to marry into elite Persian families or to be brides to foreign princes. Therefore, the vitality of the foundation period of the empire under Cyrus the Great and Cambyses II never gave way to stagnation or terminal decline, but was kept buoyant through repeated imperial consolidation. There were rebellions within the imperial house, it is true, but they focused only on who should sit on the throne as the head of the Achaemenid family 'firm', not on establishing separatist states.

The Achaemenids were a family of kings. The king was a glorified version of a family father. They referred to themselves as a *vith*, which is an Old Persian word meaning 'dynasty', 'house', and 'household'. Like all royal dynasties, the Achaemenids very often amplified the everyday troubles of family life. They presented all sorts of human desires, failings, and strengths, albeit in exaggerated form. Among dynastic relatives, rivalry was far more common than affection, and hostility was a lot more familiar than love. Such experiences had a consequence on the maintenance of the Persian empire at large, as this book will show. At the centre of our study is the powerful, monolithic concept of 'dynasty' itself. We will explore the history of ancient Persia through the prism of the Achaemenid family because it was the kings' character traits, together with the ways in which they interacted with their family – parents, wives and concubines, sons, daughters, and siblings – and the larger circle of the Persian elite that defined the way in which the empire worked.

The minutiae of family dynamics could have a profound, sometimes grave, impact on the maintenance and success of the empire
as a whole. What happened within the family, and how events
played out in the private quarters of the royal palaces, ultimately
resonated throughout the whole imperial sphere.

*

This book tells the history of the Persians from the time of their
arrival on the Iranian plateau, around 1000 BCE, to the moment in
330 BCE when their great empire was captured, held, and garrotted
by the forceful hand of Alexander of Macedon. This will be a story
of empire-building, and imperial ambition. It is also the story of
one of the great dysfunctional families of history. The Achaemenids
easily outmatched the familial sagas of the Yorkists and Lancastri-
ans of Shakespeare's imagination, the Borgias of the Vatican, or
the Romanovs of Russia. The story of the Achaemenids is an epic
soap opera of naked ambition, betrayal, revenge, and murder – to
all intents and purposes, their history is Robert Graves's *I, Claudius*
in a Middle Eastern setting. Today the study of the Achaemenid
dynasty and its empire is expanding and flourishing as never before.
Textual studies of indigenous Persian sources continue to appear,
and the archaeology of the empire is still producing unexpected
finds which constantly force scholarship to rethink and remould
our definitions of empire. This is a good time to explore the world
of the Persians.

PART ONE

ESTABLISHING
EMPIRE

Who were the Persians? How did they set about creating an empire and why did they do it? In this, the first part of our investigation into the world of the ancient Persians, our attention will be on narrative history. We shall cover some 900 years in all, beginning with the origins of the Persians in Central Asia and their subsequent migration into the Iranian plateau. Moving steadily west and finally settling in the south-west of Iran, the nomadic Persians, divided into tribes ruled by what we might call *khāns* (a traditional title given to clan chiefs and officials in Central Asia), found themselves brushing up against some ancient indigenous peoples, including the culturally sophisticated, sedentary, city-living Elamites. Elam was one of the most significant of Mesopotamian societies and had strong cultural links to the great players of the Near Eastern world – the Babylonians and the Assyrians. Sources prove that, over the years, the Persians and the Elamites cemented a binding relationship and that Elam became an important ally of the early Persians, especially in the area of Anshan, a fertile region of the lower Zagros Mountains ruled by a powerful tribe under the leadership of a man named Teispes. So strong was this cultural bond that the Persians began to look to Elam as a model of successful power.

Other Eurasian peoples moved into Iran at the same time as the Persians. These included the Medes, first cousins to the Persians, certainly, but more warlike and territorially ambitious (at least in the early days) than the Persians. The *khānates* (or tribes) of the Medes occupied the north-west of Iran, abutting against the mighty Assyrians of northern Iraq. A period of hostilities between the

Medes and the Assyrians came to a head in 614 BCE, when the Median tribes, united under the rule of King Cyaxares, joined in alliance with Assyria's southern enemy, Babylon, and sacked the Assyrian capital of Nineveh. As Assyria fell, Median hegemony grew. Soon Cyaxares annexed former Assyrian territories and expanded Median control over peoples living to the west, up the natural border of the Hylas River in Anatolia. Cyaxares then looked south, to Anshan and to the Persians. He saw there rich territory, ripe for conquest.

In Part One of this study, we explore what happened when these two tribal peoples clashed, and we study evidence to show how the Persians began to fight back, consolidate their powers, and, ultimately, turn the Median supremacy on its head. We will look at the remarkable rise to power of Cyrus the Great and examine his methods of conquest and settlement, and we will end our narrative at the point when Egypt – wealthy, ancient, sophisticated Egypt – was subsumed into Persia's expanding empire by Cyrus' son, the much-maligned Cambyses II. Part I is the story of the foundation of Persian identity and the birth of Persian imperialism. It describes the events which led to Persia becoming the world's first superpower.

1

The Medes and the Persians

Some 5,000 years ago, nomadic tribal peoples from Central Eurasia settled on the Iranian plateau. They were pastoral migrants whose main occupation was cattle-rearing. Cattle were the centre of their world, their most valuable possessions, and, as the ultimate life-sustainers, their protection and care were an almost religious duty. The nomads who herded their cattle into common pens or cow-sheds belonged to the same *gotra*, a very ancient term meaning 'descent from a common ancestor'. In other words, the nomads primarily identified themselves in tribes or ancestral clans and it was tribal order which brought a sense of harmony to their fragile existence. Cattle-raiders were despised. They were forces of evil who disrupted the order of life and shattered tribal confidence, and so they were pursued, punished, and killed. The Eurasian migrants could be warlike when so prompted.

The migratory nomads identified themselves as *arya*, 'Aryans', an ethnic language label for groups of people who circulated in the geographic region known as *Āryāvarta* – 'Abode of the Aryans' – a vast topographical area which stretched for thousands of miles throughout Central Asia. Many philologists agree that *arya* originally meant 'hospitable', 'noble', 'household', or 'lord', words that all emphasise the communality and hierarchical structures of nomadic communities. The word (and the concept) 'Aryan' has nothing to do with race. Today we tend to marginalise the term because of its sinister connection to extreme fascist ideology. The Nazis hijacked 'Aryan' in the late 1920s and, as a gross perversion, used it as a sinister ethnic concept which expressed Caucasian, specifically Germanic, racial superiority. 'Aryan' has meaning *only* as a linguistic idiom. 'Aryan' forms the etymological source of the name 'Iran'.

These Aryans – or Proto-Iranians, as they are more familiarly called now – spoke Old Avestan, the oldest preserved language of the Iranian sub-branch of the Indo-European family, and the sister language of Sanskrit. It was the direct ancestor of Old Persian. Especially close semantic similarities can be found in the ancient languages of Avestan and Sanskrit, a demonstration of the common origins of the Aryans of Iran and India. Consider this word-list and notice the common sound-values:

English	Avestan	Sanskrit
horse	*aspa*	*asva*
cattle	*pasu*	*pasu*
cow	*gav*	*go*
earth	*bumi*	*bhumi*
man	*nar*	*nar*
woman	*jani*	*jani*
brother	*brater*	*bhrata*
son	*puthra*	*putra*
daughter	*dugedar*	*duhitar*
army	*haena*	*sena*

The earliest datable evidence for an Old Avestan-speaking branch of Proto-Iranians dates to about 1300 BCE, about the time that these Aryan peoples began to move south, away from their traditional homelands in Central Asia. As they did so, the mass migration split, with some settling in India and others in Iran. India plays a crucial role in the Aryan story and is intricately linked to our growing knowledge of the nomadic migrations, particularly so in the religious ideologies that underpinned later Iranian and Indian cultures. The holy prayers, hymns, and rituals contained in the *Avesta*, the sacred teachings of the early Iranian Aryans, find ready reflection in the *Rig-Veda*, the most important compendium of religious teachings in the early Indian world. The *Avesta* and the *Rig-Veda* emerged from a common ancestor.

Based on linguistic analysis we know that these early settlers were part of the family of Indo-European speakers. The Avestan and the Sanskrit spoken by those early Aryans finds reflection in many other languages, including Greek, Latin, English, French, Welsh, and a staggering 440 others. Any speaker of a contemporary European language who is intent on learning modern Persian should take heart in knowing that the language is quite straightforward. They will soon encounter familiar vocabulary and find that words and sounds are shared across time and space by this user-friendly linguistic family:

> *pedar* (father; Latin *pater*); *mader* (mother; Spanish *madre*)
> *dokhtar* (daughter; German *tochter*); *bardar* (brother; Welsh *brawd*)
> *mordan* (to die; French *mourir*); *bordan* (to carry; Spanish *portar*)
> *nārānge* (orange; Spanish *naranja*); *div* (devil; Italian *diavolo*)

All in all, there are around 265 Persian cognate words that work this way.

Like all other major population movements past and present, the impetus for the Aryan migration was a matter of survival. Climate change, overpopulation, and a lack of resources in ancestral homelands, combined with the military ambitions of warlords and kings, created a perfect storm of discontent and forced people to migrate. The relocation of the Proto-Iranians happened in at least three successive stages or phases, with each movement taking on a very different character. The first type of migration was represented by the slow infiltration into Iran of cattle-breeding families who voluntarily uprooted themselves from their ancestral lands and made the laborious journey into the Iranian plateau. These people had no masterplan but were content to wander until they found a space for themselves which offered safety and good animal grazing. In general, they established friendly relations with the local populations and offered no threat to the sedentary societies in whose territories they resided.

The second type of migration was a mass exodus of tribes headed by a well-organised army of warriors. During this second wave of migration, many thousands of people moved simultaneously in vast columns of human life and trundled slowly, mile after mile, step after step, into Iran. Their scouts and warriors cleared the paths of any hostile resistance. Most people went on foot, carrying bundles on their backs; they led mules and donkeys weighed down with everything needed to set up home. Camels portered the tents and the carpets that would provide accommodation, and there were huge carts too, pulled by powerful, lumbering long-horned oxen, piled precariously high with food and provisions, bronze cauldrons and wooden chests. On top were perched young infants, too young to walk, and happy for the opportunity to hitch a ride and a nap. The older children were tasked with herding the animals – goats, sheep, and cattle, as well as young foals – and to keep them at a safe distance from the many perils of the journey: the ravines and rock-falls and rivers, as well as the lions, leopards, foxes, and wolves which were commonplace throughout Eurasia and Iran. Everywhere there was the sound of tinkling, ringing, and clanging bronze bells tied around the animals' necks, creating a moveable pastoral symphony. To help them with their herding duties the children were aided by dogs – the tall, powerfully muscled mastiff-types whose names – 'Expeller of evil', 'Catcher of the enemy', 'Don't think, bite!', 'Bitter of his foe!', or 'Loud is his bark!' – belied the fact that with the youngsters they were soft and playful and soppy.

Finally, the last phase of the migration was characterised by the massive movements of the equestrian nomads. It must have been quite a spectacle to behold as thousands and thousands of horse-men and their steeds thundered across the terrain. These peoples lived in the saddle. They had no buildings, nor did they have need for them for their lives were spent on horseback. It is clear that the Proto-Iranians could be a bellicose lot and we must resist being swayed into thinking that they were eco-friendly pastoral pacifists. The Steppe horsemen who entered into Iran were fierce. Their tribes and clans clashed violently and fought constantly, particularly when drought or snow ruined the pastures and killed many of their livestock, so that the raiding of other tribes' animals became a necessity. The *Avesta* provides us with a rich vocabulary of the fight-ing techniques and weaponry available to them, including: army (*spāda*), battle line (*rasman*), archers (*thanwani*), bowstrings made from gazelle gut (*jīyā*), quivers with room for thirty arrows (*akana*), slings (*fradakhshanā*) and sling-stones (*asan fradakhshanā*), as well as helmets (*sārawāra*), belts (*kamara*), horse saddles (*upari-spāta*), horse whips (*ashtra*), and swift battle horses (*arwant*). It was their mastery of the horse and, via the use of the bronze bit, their ability to form cavalry units freed from cumbersome chariots that allowed the early Proto-Iranians to move swiftly to occupy new territories.

The Eurasian horse nomads and their Persian descendants were masters at shooting with bows and arrows from horseback. Their main technique was to shoot a volley of arrows while galloping at a breakneck pace straight towards the enemy and, at the last moment, to do a pivot turn while continuing to shoot arrows back over their horses' rumps as they galloped off. Only a well-balanced rider with substantial experience and horse knowledge could execute such a strategy, especially when this remarkable feat was achieved without a saddle or stirrups. With only reins and the grip of the thighs a good horseman could control the horse's movement and even shoot several arrows at the same moment, all in a line and aimed at the enemy with pinpoint precision. This so-called 'Parthian shot' (as it later became known) was enabled through the use of a small, versatile composite bow. A technological *tour-de-force*, the bow was a compact little killing machine. It revolutionised cavalry warfare and played no small part in the Eurasian takeover of Iran and in the subsequent building of a Persian empire.

Warrior aristocrats distinguished themselves through the possession of horses. As an obvious symbol of status and wealth, horses were closely connected to tribal ideology and to the model warrior image. The importance of horses among the nobility is especially evidenced by the fact that many nobles bore names compounded with the Old Persian word for 'horse', *aspa* – such as Vištāspa ('possessing racing horses'), Satāspa ('having hundreds of horses'), and Aspabāra ('borne by a horse').

Taking a course to the east following the Oxus River, some of these horsemen emigrants settled in the oases of the hill country – these became what was called in Old Persian the *Baḥtriš* (Bactrians) and the *Suguda* (Sogdians). Others wandered further south, hugging the mountains and hills of what is now the border between Iran and Afghanistan – these were the *Harahuvatiš* (Arachosians), the *Haraiva* (Areians), and the *Zranka* (Drangians). The final group of peoples entered onto the Iranian plateau proper, setting up bases in the north-east – the *Parthava* (Parthians); the central northern area near the Elburz Mountains – the *Māda* (Medes); and within the western Zagros Mountains – the *Pārsa* (Persians).

Of course, humans had been settled on the Iranian plateau long before the Eurasian tribes made their entry there. People were already living in Iran as early as 10,000 BCE. By 6,000 BCE they had created successful agricultural communities and small townships which developed into well-defended walled cities, typical of Near Eastern settlements in Mesopotamia. There were Kassites, who had settled in the green river valleys of the Zagros, and the Uxians, who controlled the Zagros lowlands close to Susa; there were Lullubians in south-eastern Kurdistan, Gutians, who inhabited the snow-capped high Zagros range, Manneans in north-eastern Kurdistan, and Hurrians in the craggy northern Zagros near Lake Urmia.

The most important and culturally influential of the sedentary peoples of the plateau were the Elamites, who lived in the vast flat plains of the south-west of Iran. The Elamites were a distinguished and venerable people. They had occupied the area of the lower Zagros from as early as 3,000 BCE, which made them one of the longest-lasting and most culturally significant peoples of Mesopotamia. They had their own language and employed their own form of cuneiform script, although, curiously, the Elamite language had no linguistic relatives in the Mesopotamian region. Our knowledge of Elamite vocabulary and grammar is not terribly developed, and in many respects Elam is the Mesopotamian civilisation still awaiting discovery.

The Elamites were master builders. Their greatest architectural wonder is situated near Elam's great walled capital of Susa (modern Sush on the Iran-Iraq border): the magnificent ziggurat of Choga Zanbil (Dur-Untash, or City of Untash, in Elamite), a towering 53-metre-high step-pyramid temple complex dated to 1250 BCE.

This is where the gods of the Elamite pantheon were worshipped in numerous sanctuaries. Set amid sacred groves planted with divine trees, the hallowed site included a royal quarter, where three monumental palaces have been unearthed. The ziggurat itself was thought of as the earthly abode of Inshushinak, the bull-god of Susa, a deity much beloved by the Elamite king Untaš Napiriša, whose masterpiece Choga Zanbil truly was. Today it stands as the best-preserved ziggurat in existence, a monument to Elamite ingenuity and political might.

Throughout their history, the Elamites had fought fiercely for their autonomy. They witnessed many aggressive incursions from the Babylonians and the Assyrians but, at times, they had ruled much of the fertile crescent themselves, plaguing Babylonia with raids and guerrilla-style attacks. Elam refused to kowtow to the authority of the last great Assyrian ruler, Ashurbanipal, and the city of Susa was reduced to rubble as a consequence. But with the fall of Assyria in 612 BCE, Elamite culture witnessed a remarkable revival and Susa was lovingly rebuilt, glazed brick on glazed brick. Elam was an important player in the history and culture of Mesopotamia. It was a centre of Mesopotamian thought and identity although it mustered its own ambitions for self-identity and independence.

The sedentary indigenous peoples of Iran welcomed the early Eurasian nomads with extraordinary equanimity, and, by and large, the two groups worked harmoniously together. It quickly became apparent that the nomadic lifestyle had advantages over that of famers and urbanites. Their portable wealth – the precious livestock herds and flocks which they maintained with such devoted care – could be gathered together quickly and moved elsewhere in the face of attack or the threat of violence. At times of war, however, farmers simply endured the destruction of their crops while urban settlers contended with brutal military sieges, the inevitable demolition of walls, the plundering of goods, and the taking of lives. In peacetime, nomads exchanged wool and meat for farmers' grain and vegetables, but when harvests failed, the nomads could live self-sufficiently on their meat and dairy products and, in exchange for food, they forced farmers and metropolitans to provide them with other desirable commodities such as gold, iron, incense, spices, lapis lazuli, turquoise, and even women. From this advantageous position the nomads operated a lucrative protection racket which quickly developed into a kind of tribute-taxation system.

The most successful of the Eurasian peoples who settled on the Iranian plateau were the Medes and the Persians. In the popular imagination, these two Iranian peoples are often moulded into one, as though they were, in every way, a single unit. This was not the case. Although they shared a common DNA and many cultural norms and values, the Medes and the Persians had distinctly idiosyncratic identities, and found themselves operating in radically separate geopolitical contexts, which resulted in the formation of two very different mindsets. To understand the way in which the Medes and the Persians developed their identities we need to examine the formative histories of these key players in Iran's early civilization and discover how their worlds became intertwined.

*

The many tribes that made up the Medes settled in, and ruled over, a huge swathe of land in the north of Iran, some 14,000 square miles of mountains and valleys wedged between the southern Black Sea and the Caspian Sea. They moved about these difficult spaces, endlessly driving their flocks of sheep and goats and herds of cattle and horses to find good grazing, trying always to avoid the bad weather, which could be apocalyptic. The Medes were expert horse-breeders. The stocky, hardy little horses they bred thrived well in the alfalfa-rich pastures of Media. The premium horses were bred in the area of Nisaea, and these magnificent little steeds, universally regarded as the nimblest of beasts, became celebrated for their bravery and tenacity. An official writing from far-off China was impressed enough to note that Chinese horses could never rival those of Nisaea. He commented on the fact that they excelled in climbing up and down mountains and crossing ravines and torrents They were, he confirmed, the perfect animals for life in the mountains.

The Medes had little knowledge of the world beyond the immediate pressing concerns of nomadic life. Alongside horse-breeding, they raised and tended their sheep, goats, and cattle for meat and milk and for the dung which they dried and used as fuel for burning. The animals provided them with the wool and cowhide which they used for clothes, tents, horse-bridles and other trappings, as well as carpets. They simply herded the animals around the broad valleys and the steep ravines. Each mountain valley had its own tribe, ruled by a *khān* (tribal leader) who, when not moving with his flocks, stopped in a small stone fortified residence surrounded by domestic tents and animal pens. One of these *khāns* was Cyaxares, whose lands were located around Ecbatana, today the city of Hamadan, about four hours' drive west of Tehran. Here he and his tribe dwelt in colourful tents, or *gers*, portable yurt-like structures that were so central to nomadic life. The Medes never built cities and had no interest in sedentary living; instead, when Cyaxares resided at Ecbatana, his tribe accompanied him and established themselves across the plain in tents and pavilions made from textiles. The tents sprawled out endlessly across the landscape towards the distant horizons.

The Medes relished congregating together. They enjoyed feasting, music, gambling with dice, horse-racing, hunting, singing, and storytelling. No doubt Cyaxares knew something about his ancestry through the storytelling of the bards, those singer-historians who carried the memory of the past within them, turning journeys, skirmishes, and weddings into epic tales of quest, war, and romance. If Cyaxares knew anything of his Eurasian heritage, it would have come down to him in epic verse performed at a campfire.

Cyaxares was a formidable leader. A born warrior, he made certain that his tribe was well-prepared for action. Under his leadership, they had successfully repelled the incursion of Scythian forces into Median territory, although Cyaxares had employed some underhanded ways of ensuring their defeat. He invited a number of the Scythian chieftains to a banquet, at which he made them drunk and then systematically murdered them. By 625 BCE, Cyaxares had removed Scythians from Median lands while learning new fighting techniques from them. With his tribal army reorganised on Scythian precedents, Cyaxares turned it into a lethal striking force.

By the time Cyaxares died in 584 BCE, he had made Media a wealthy and powerful kingdom. By the standards of the day, the Medes were not really empire-builders and they never moved fully to kingship. But they did successfully operate a system of chiefdom-leadership which encouraged a tradition of tribal alliances and congregational authority. Astyages, Cyaxares' son, succeeded to his father's position as nominal 'King of Media' without contest and took the reins of power, determined to maintain and expand the boundaries of Media. Astyages' Iranian name was, suitably, Rishti Vaiga – 'spear-hurler'.

*

The Persians are first attested in history in the records of Shalmaneser III, the powerful king of Assyria (modern northern Iraq; 859–824 BCE), who claimed to have received tribute from twenty-seven *khāns* of the *Parsuwash* – 'men from the land of *Pārsa*'. The name *Pārsa* derives from the old Indo-Iranian word *Pārćwa*, meaning 'rib', so that, etymologically, the Persians were the 'people of the land of the rib', which surely must be a reference to the great ribcage of mountains which formed the mighty Zagros range in whose shadow the Persians had come to settle. In modern-day Iran, the same area is known as Fārs Province – originally it was known as 'Pārs' – although the ancient land of the *Pārsa* people was probably much smaller than the large and thriving modern-day province.

In the north of Iran, the Medes had successfully expanded their territories through military prowess, but in the south the Persians faced a very different situation. When they settled into the area of Pārs, between 1200 and 1000 BCE, the Persians had butted up against the Elamites, who were known to them as *Uja* or *Huja*. A large part of Pārs was inhabited by an Elamite population at the time of the arrival of the Persians. This could have led to aggression, but warfare was not on the cards. An extended period of peaceful and cooperative cohabitation in the land developed between the two peoples. Current archaeological investigations increasingly yield evidence for this, particularly in the rich finds from a late Neo-Elamite elite tomb burial at Arjan (*c.* 650–630 BCE), situated in the vicinity of modern Behbahan, on the eastern boundary of Khuzestan Province. The tomb was discovered in 1982 and, inside, archaeologists unearthed a series of unique artistic masterpieces of superior quality. There were gold and silver bowls and beakers, bracelets, a fine dagger, a ceremonial ring, a candelabrum, and even cotton textiles (the first to be found in the Near East), studded with fine gold appliqués. Stylistically the objects revealed Assyrian and Phoenician artistic influences, but it is clear that all the products were the creation of a single local workshop and confirm that there was an 'Arjan school' of craftsmen who were bringing the remnants of the old Elamite civilisation to mix with the newly settled population of Persians.

A particularly strong cultural bond between the Persian tribes and the Elamites emerged in an area of lowland Elam called Anshan (Old Persian, *Yanzhan*). Centred at the site of modern-day Tol-e Malyan, twenty-nine miles north of Shiraz and twenty-seven miles west of Persepolis in the Ramjerd plain, Anshan extended into the tribal areas of Persia. Indeed, so integrated were these two lands that, in the sources, 'Anshan' and 'Pārsa' can be taken as synonyms. The evidence suggests that Persian settlers established an important power centre in Anshan under the rulership of a *khān* named Teispes, of whom we know no more than that he bore an Iranian name (Tishpish) and was said to be the king of Anshan, and therefore was later regarded as the ancestral father of the Anshanite or Teispid dynasty. As *khāns* of Anshan, the early Persian rulers were easily pulled into the culturally dominant orbit of the sophisticated Elamites, and it is certain that a geopolitical interdependency emerged between Elam and southern Iran during the seventh and early sixth centuries BCE. There can be little doubt that the Elamites form the 'missing link' in the chain of Persian ideological development; that is to say, the way in which the Persians developed as a distinct culture. The Persians were the true heirs of the Elamites.

An Assyrian inscription dating to the late 640s BCE, which recounts the destruction of Susa by Ashurbanipal of Assyria, mentions a king of Persia named Kurash. Through chronological comparison, he can be recognised as Cyrus I of Anshan – the grandfather of Cyrus the Great, the famous founder of the Persian empire. The Assyrian king claimed that 'Cyrus [I] the king of Persia heard about my strength. He became aware of the might that I yielded ... He implored my lordship.' To curry favour with Ashurbanipal, Cyrus sent his son, Arukku, to Nineveh as proof of his obedience to Assyria. Arukku spent several years living as a royal hostage – a 'guest of the king' – far from home in Assyria. This was a common form of 'royal exchange' throughout the ancient Near East, and it was a system which was intended to make vassal states more loyal to the central authority. It was hoped that by educating Prince Arukku in the ways of Assyria, he could safely be returned home to Persia thoroughly Assyrianised, where he would rule as a loyal suppliant of his Assyrian master. Nothing more is heard of Arukku, and if he did receive an Assyrian-style education, then it served no purpose in Persia. The prince probably died in Nineveh.

In the period *c.* 650–610 BCE, Cyrus I was, at one and the same time, both king of Anshan and the tribal overlord, or *khān*, of the Pasargadae people. There were several tribal chiefs alongside Cyrus who bore the title *Khshayathia Parsaiy*, 'King in Persia', but to judge from Ashurbanipal's inscription, which seems to acknowledge Cyrus as the *only* king in Persia, the Assyrians misunderstood the title to connote sovereignty over the entire territory of Persia. Herodotus got closer to the reality of the situation for, even as an outsider looking in, he understood that the nomadic people of Iran were part of a huge and complex network of tribes. He noted that within Persia there were three major tribes (Greek, *genea*): the Pasargadae (Old Persian, *Pathragada* – 'Wielder of heavy clubs'), the Maspians (Old Persian, *Ma-aspa* – 'With horses'), and the Maraphians (Old Persian, *Ma-arafa* – 'With chariots'). Herodotus noted that 'Of all the tribes the Pasargadae are the most eminent for they contain the clan [*phratria*] ... from which spring the ... kings.' Although Herodotus used a Greek vocabulary to designate the groups and hierarchies of the tribes, it is possible to recognise in his terminology a genuine Iranian social structure. All Iranian tribes were based on the norm of the patrilineal family (Old Persian, taumā). A group of families constituted a clan (Old Persian, *vith* – this can also be translated as 'household' or 'dynasty'); the clans were grouped into a tribe (Old Iranian, *zantu*) that was defined both genealogically (through blood kin) and spatially (through land acquisition). Every tribe and each clan had its own territory under the leadership of a tribal *khān* (Old Iranian *zantupati*), such as Cyrus I.

A fascinating little cylinder seal, whose imprint can be seen on a clay tablet found at Persepolis, places Cyrus I squarely in his historical context. It bears a unique inscription, written in Elamite cuneiform: 'Kurush of Anshan, son of Tishpish'. At the centre of the scene is Cyrus I, the horseback warrior, raising his lance and riding his horse over the corpses of two enemies who lie spread-eagled on the ground. A third opponent, standing before Cyrus, is speared and killed. Cyrus I regarded himself principally as a hardy horseback warrior.

Sadly, we know next to nothing about Cambyses I, the son of Cyrus I, although he too was king of Anshan and *khān* of the Parsargadae (*c.* 600–559 BCE). No references to him from his lifetime exist, and he only emerges in later inscriptions dating to the reign of his son Cyrus the Great. In one such inscription discovered at Ur in southern Mesopotamia, Cyrus the Great stated that he was the 'son of Cambyses, king of the land of Anshan', while pressed into building bricks from Uruk is the statement that Cyrus was the 'son of Cambyses, mighty king.' His rule saw the build-up of

Figure 2. Cyrus I of Anshan defeats his enemies. Seal impression.

tensions between Persia and Media as Astyages the Mede began an aggressive land-grab policy aimed at Persian and Babylonian-held territories.

The Medes had entered Persia under Cyaxares when, in the 620s BCE, he was attempting to build tribal alliances for his campaign against Assyria. Once they had appeared in Persia, the Medes never really left. With each military success, the Medes felt powerful enough to extract tribute out of their Persian neighbours, as well as from the Hycarnians, Saka, and Parthians. From thereon, the Persians were obliged to acknowledge Median supremacy. Under Astyages of Media, land-grabbing campaigns resulted in the Medes storming into the north of Syria (around the present-day Syrian–Turkish border), which was part of Babylon's empire, and they took control of the great religious centres of Arbela and Harran. The Medes destroyed shrines and deported hundreds of prisoners. A stele discovered in Babylon relays details of the devastation they wrought:

> The king of the Medes, unafraid, destroyed the temples of all the gods . . . and the towns with sanctuaries in the territory of Akkad . . .; he destroyed every one of their cults, devastating their cult-centres like a flood. The king of Babylon, to whom sacrilege is an abomination, did not raise his hand against the cults of any of the gods, but he left his hair unkempt and slept on the ground.

The Babylonian king, Nebuchadnezzar, went into formal royal mourning for the destruction of the shrines. In response to the annihilation, and to prevent the Medes from entering deeper into Mesopotamia, the Babylonians built a wall – some 100 feet high at sections – between the rivers Tigris and Euphrates. It was a tangible expression of the Cold War mentality which existed between the two states.

Sitting in Jerusalem, and feeling the threat of Babylonian invasion, the prophet Jeremiah visualised with a certain glee Babylon's inevitable fall at the hands of the merciless Medes. He cried out a warning to Mesopotamia:

Look! A great army is coming from the north . . . They are armed with bows and spears. They are cruel and show no mercy. As they ride forward on horses, they sound like a roaring sea. They are coming in battle formation, planning to destroy you, Babylon. The king of Babylon is weak with fright. The earth will shake with the shout, 'Babylon has been taken!' . . . This is what the Lord says: 'I will stir up a destroyer against Babylon. Foreigners will come and winnow her, blowing her away as chaff'.

It looked as though a war between Astyages of Media and Nebuchadnezzar was inevitable. Both rulers recognised that warfare was a costly business, but Babylon's treasury was full from the spoils taken from Assyria, and Media's resources had just been nicely replenished from the spoils from Harran and Arbela. Astyages further pressed his subordinates to supply him with men and finances. Persia was especially squeezed to provide support, although Astyages quickly recognised that, in his bond with Elam – itself a foothold into lower Mesopotamia – the king of Anshan needed to be treated differently, and certainly more deferentially. To that end, around 598 BCE, Astyages gave Cambyses I of Anshan, the tribal chief, one of his daughters, Princess Mandane, as a wife. Through this marriage, Astyages and Cambyses entered into a contract of mutual fidelity. Cambyses came out the greatest beneficiary: his familial bond with the king of the Medes gave him a certain authority over the other Persian chieftains, and, to all intents and purposes, with his wedding to Mandane, Cambyses became, among the powerful *khāns*, the undisputed *primus inter pares*.

2

See, the Conqu'ring Hero Comes

Prince Cyrus, destined to become Cyrus the Great, the son of Cambyses I of Anshan and Mandane of Media, was born between 600 and 590 BCE. We cannot be certain of the date or even the place of his birth. No historical records exist of his childhood, his youth, or his ascendancy to power, although, to be sure, in the years, decades, and centuries following his death, legends of his nativity and infancy were celebrated in story and song. Classical writers said that every Persian schoolboy was taught Cyrus' birth-story and how he fought against the Medes. But, in terms of hard historical fact, sources for his early life are not forthcoming. What can be said with some authority, however, is that at his birth the infant Cyrus was the heir to the throne of Anshan and to the chiefdom of the Pasargadae, the most powerful of the Persian tribes. Through his mother, he was an heir to the ever-expanding kingdom of Astyages' Medes.

The young Prince Cyrus was the apple of his mother's eye. It was Mandane who raised him within the tents and wagons assigned to the women and infants of the tribe. The first five years of Cyrus' life were spent at Mandane's side and she cared for each of his needs as, like all of the tribe's women, she spun wool, wove cloth, churned milk, and baked bread (at this early stage in Persia's history, queens were not exempt from physical labour, although all that changed with time). Until they turned six years old, Persian boys were raised among the women and girls and they barely saw their fathers or had any other adult male company, so the strong empathy created between mothers and sons became a defining feature of their subsequent adult lives. In societies which valued gender segregation, sons tended to fill the voids in their mothers' lives created by husbands who were literally or emotionally absent or preoccupied; Persian women trained their sons to replace the older, adored, men and as a consequence they bonded with them very deeply.

The infant Cyrus had been passed around from woman to woman, from one set of loving arms to another, because each of the tribe's womenfolk took turns looking after the children; they were all 'aunties', regardless of an actual blood connection. He had nursed from any number of them and had shared the breast milk of all of the tribe's nursing mothers – as was expected. But as Mandane's eldest son, the first boy to leave her womb, he was special and was considered by everyone in the tribe to embody the honour and future success of his family. One day Cyrus, son of Mandane, would be responsible not just for his mother's welfare, but for that of all the Persians.

When Cyrus was an infant, Mandane had delighted in singing Median nursery rhymes to him, and it was through his mother that Cyrus quickly grasped the dialect of the Medes and thereafter spoke it throughout his life as easily as he did the Persian tongue. Mandane told him about life in the highlands of Media and captivated him with the legends of the Medes: there was the story of Zāl, the white-haired baby who was abandoned by his father on the slopes of the Elburz Mountains and was nursed to adulthood by a great magical bird who nested in the snowy peaks of Mount Damavand. There was the tale of Sindokht – 'the daughter of China' – whose cleverness, wise counsel, and beauty made her a model of womanhood. And there were the stories of the devils (*divs*) of Mazandaran, that no-go area somewhere to the north – or was it the east? – which was filled with wickedness and lawlessness.

Mandane instilled in Cyrus a profound sense of belonging to the mountainous world of the north and she stressed to him, whenever the occasion arose, that, through her own blood, he was an heir to Astyages' throne (regardless of how many other children or grandchildren might have been born to the Median king's wives and concubines). She made a point too of reminding Cyrus that while his own father, Cambyses, also had a profusion of wives and children, it was he and only he who was heir to both the Persians and the Medes. This incontrovertible fact alone put Cyrus in a very privileged position.

Finally, the day came for Cyrus to be taken away from the women's tents. There was no choice, there was no discussion, and perhaps he cried as, clinging on to Mandane's veil with his soft little hands, he was passed into the arms of his father. His hair was cropped and he was thrust into the brooding society of the menfolk, and into the rough-and-tumble world of horses, hunting, and warfare, and of finding faults, punishments, and the flexing of muscles. It must have come as a shock to Cyrus, as to every Persian boy, to experience so swift and resolute a departure from all the comforts he had known. But Cambyses I doted on his son too and he carefully nurtured him through the years of Cyrus' childhood and adolescence as the boy mastered the skills needed for leadership. Like all Persian boys who emerged from the woman's world, Cyrus was taught to ride a horse, shoot a bow, and to tell the truth – and in each of these valuable life principles Cambyses proved himself to be a patient but dogmatically focused master. Although Cambyses himself never gained a reputation for military excellence, later stories spoke of his determination to imbue his son with the qualities of good warrior kingship: 'Cyrus was preeminent among all men of his time in bravery and sagacity and other virtues; for his father had raised him after the manner of kings and had made him zealous to emulate the highest achievements,' said Diodorus Siculus, the Greek historian. Cambyses was proud to see how quickly Cyrus learned his lessons and honed the crafts of kingship.

Quiet, unassuming, Cambyses died in 559 BCE and Cyrus grieved for him deeply. The funerary rituals for the revered monarch were carried out with full pomp and, as the news of his passing spread among the tribes, the whole of Persia went into mourning. Cyrus and his male kin shaved their hair and donned sackcloth, while Mandane and the women threw off their veils, scattered ashes over their heads, slashed their cheeks with their finger-nails, and let out the prescribed bloodcurdling ritual wails of lamentation: 'O, my husband! O my glory! O! That ruler! Ah! That man!' Her screams were repeated ceaselessly, accompanied by rhythmical drumming and the lamentations of professional wailing women, a guild of well-paid mourning-diehards who were experts at causing a scene.

Cyrus had a deep respect for his father and he honoured him with the full rites of mourning. He must also have felt liberated from his father's moderating influence, though. Yet custom demanded that an official mourning period be observed and so Cyrus waited for five months before he had himself invested as king. This ceremony took place on the beautiful plain of Pasargadae, at the heart of his ancestral tribal lands. In the springtime Pasargadae, surrounded by low rolling hills, was verdant and blooming with red and purple poppies which carpeted the ground in rich and complex interwoven patterns. The pomegranate trees were bursting with fruit and the fresh blue skies were cloudless and seemingly endless in their vastness. In the late fourth century BCE the Greek historian Hieronymus of Cardia described central Persia as a veritable nirvana:

> High land, blessed with a healthy climate and full of the fruits appropriate to the season. There were glens heavily wooded and shady cultivated trees of various kinds in parks, and also naturally converging glades and hills of trees of every sort, and streams of water, so that travellers lingered with delight in places pleasantly inviting repose. Also, there was an abundance of cattle of every kind . . . Those who inhabited the country were the most warlike of the Persians, every man being a bowman and a slinger, and in density of population, too, this country surpassed all others.

In that place of bounty, so obviously blessed by the gods, Cyrus was initiated as Persia's king and *khān* in a ceremony so loaded with ancient Eurasian symbolism that even the priests could not quite explain some of the more arcane rites. In the presence of the clergy, and through their agency, Cyrus was transformed from heir-designate to monarch and he symbolically took on a new royal 'body' by wearing a dynastic heirloom – the cowhide *gaunaka* or long-sleeved coat that had once belonged to his ancestor Teispes (although it was perhaps much older even than that). Cyrus then ate a simple meal of sweet dates and pistachio nuts and drank a dish of *airag*, or thick, sour, fermented mare's milk – the humble subsistence foodstuffs of the Eurasian nomads. Humility was the hallmark of this sacred ritual, and through his participation in the rituals Cyrus was drawn back to his Steppe identity and to the simple nomadic roots of his people.

*

At the time of his investiture, Cyrus was in his thirties, a man in the prime of life. His complexion was browned by the sun and the wind, his skin was taut, although around his eyes there were deep furrowed lines, paler than the rest of his face, the result of habitually squinting into the sun, attempting to spot his falcon as she mounted the skies before swooping low to the earth to make a precision kill. His dark eyes were shaded beneath thick, unforgiving eyebrows. The black *kohl*, a watery mascara which he liberally smeared above and below his eyelashes, added to the lustre of his gaze. He was lean and good-looking in that way that Persian men are uniquely handsome. He wore a heavy, colourful, woven tunic of good thick wool, padded for insulation and belted at the waist. Over this was a floor-length *gaunaka*, which was lined with a shaggy sheep's fleece and decorated with appliquéd golden rosettes and felt horses' heads. His hands were calloused and hard, the result of three decades of clutching the rawhide of horses' reins, of gripping the wooden shafts of spears, and of stretching the gut-string of the bow. When an infant, as soon as he could grip, he had been given reins to hold and horses to ride. He did not wear gloves but the flaring cuffs of the over-long sleeves of his coat reached past the tips of his fingers, affording them some protection from the biting wind; 'horse-hoof cuffs', they were called. When riding horses in the harsh winter, he pulled the reins up inside the sleeves to have warmth without compromising his sensitive control over the horse. The most notable characteristic of his outfit – like all nomadic clothing – was its bulk, as it was made for insulation and comfort, and the fleecy *gaunaka* was always big enough to enclose within it a lamb or a kid or some other precious thing that needed shielding.

He wore woollen trousers – colourful baggy britches which hung low and gaped open at the crotch but tapered tight at the ankle, to be tucked into thick leather boots which reached to the knee and were lined with fox fur. Over his trousers were leather chaps, softened by age, but indispensable for horseback riding. As kings went, he was perhaps not the most sartorially elegant of rulers. He did not have the voluminous purple and gold robes of the king of Babylon, nor his chic little fez. He wore a felt cap lined with hare-skin – it was more practical than any fez anyway, and it kept the chill winds out efficiently. His long black hair was abundantly thick and tamed into a low chignon at the nape of his neck, and he wore a beard that was long, full, and very bushy. Remnants of his latest meal of goat's cheese and a flat bread still hung in it. He was not the kingliest-looking of kings, but for his people he was the epitome of a warrior, a fine specimen of manhood and the only ruler they desired; he was their chieftain, their *khān*, and their king. They were ferociously loyal to him.

Cyrus' clothing was ideally suited to a people dependent upon horses for transportation, warfare, and status display. The tailored coats and tunics of the Persians afforded the wearer flexible movement, warmth, padding, and protection. The trousers and leather chaps prevented the thighs from chafing – an irritation which inevitably came from endless bareback horse-riding. In fact, it was Iranian nomads such as the Persians and the Medes who first introduced trouser-wearing to the world. Before they appeared in Iran, no society west of the Zagros Mountains had ever encountered leg coverings. Throughout Mesopotamia, the Aegean, the Levant, and Egypt, clothing was made of simple wrap-around, sari-like cloth which was just draped, belted, or pinned around the body. These garments required no cutting, shaping, or sewing. In sharp contrast, Iranian costume accentuated the body through tailored fabrics which were sewn together to create shapes.

In 2008, a complete set of ancient Iranian clothes was discovered in the Chehrabad salt mine in the north of Iran, some 210 miles north-west of Tehran, when workmen quite literally stumbled over an ancient corpse. The auto-mummified male body found there had been perfectly preserved by the salt in which it had been buried. On careful scholarly examination it was dated to around 500 BCE. DNA analysis revealed that the boy – for he could have been no more than sixteen when he died – came from the Tehran-Qazvin plain and that he had been crushed to death by a huge falling salt seam that pinned him to the ground as he was trying to collect salt, deep underground, in a dark, cramped shaft. His mummy is the stuff of a Grand-Guignol spectacle and yet, compellingly, there is, in the details of his preservation, something touchingly human about him still. On the day he died, he was wearing his usual clothing (no specialised garments were worn when gathering salt): a long-sleeved beige wool tunic and a pair of baggy trousers of soft light-brown wool with a drawstring waist and red piping at the seams. The inside and outside seams of the voluminous trousers ('harem pants' by any other name) were not stitched closed, so that the bare tissue of the thighs is easily visible. 'Salt Man 4', as he was forensically registered by the archaeologists, was wearing garments common to all Iranian horsemen, because around 500 BCE, this was the standard dress of the male nomads of the Iranian plateau. For the peoples of the West, encountering trouser-wearing Persians for the first time was to prove to be an uncomfortably disconcerting experience. For the Greeks it was tinged with trauma. Herodotus noted that the Athenians 'were the first of all Greeks to *endure* the sight of Persian clothing' – an extreme reaction, perhaps, but one which tells us much about Greek conceptions of their strange, powerful, but alien enemy. But for the male nomadic settlers of Iran, like poor 'Salt Man 4', trousers were the hallmark of an old and sophisticated culture, the garment which articulated most clearly their horseman heritage and their Eurasian origins. And trousers were destined to conquer the world.

*

The decades of Cyrus' childhood and adolescence had been tough on Persia. In the north of Iran, as Astyages of Media edged ever closer towards war with Nebuchadnezzar of Babylon, so too was Persia, in the south of the Iranian plateau, pulled into the orbit of the territorial ambitions of the Medes. Astyages knew that a war against Babylon would be costly and so he pressed his dependent subjects for soldiers and finances and focused his particular attention on Persia for special support. The Persians had little interest in aligning with their northern Median cousins – if their loyalty was to anyone, then it was to the southern state of Elam – but they paid lip service to Astyages' ambition nonetheless and duly offered him homage in the form of gifts of tribute.

This was not enough for Astyages. He was after substantial financial backing. His troops began to encroach deeper into Persian territory. He established checkpoints on the roads in and out of the land and insisted that all travel between Media and Persia needed documented justification (a bewildering mandate for nomads). A Median governor was stationed in Persia to supervise the regular collection of taxes from the Persian tribes. The swift colonisation of the south of Iran looked curiously like a Median reworking of the Assyrian method of empire-building, and the Persians found Astyages' claim on their land to be both unnatural and intolerable. They pushed against his aggressive expansionism.

In Media too, Astyages extended his power over all the tribal *khāns*, removing their autonomy and developing a Mesopotamian-style absolute kingship in which he ruled alone. He surrounded himself with an ever-increasing system of elaborate court ritual and complex bureaucratic administration, through which he intended to remove himself from public view by crafting a kind of 'mystique of monarchy' which had served the kings of Mesopotamia well for millennia. But this abstract style of governance was alien to the hands-on nomadic tribal way of life and, unsurprisingly, Astyages' nobles reacted badly to it. Some of them went so far as to ally themselves with Cyrus of Persia, in whom they saw a more measured – traditional – form of leadership. One Median grandee, Harpagus, took pains to win Cyrus' favour by conspiring with other Median nobles to offer their loyalty to Cyrus. A letter from Harpagus was smuggled into Persia through the Median border checks sewn inside the body of a hare. 'Son of Cambyses', Harpagus wrote, 'the gods watch over you. Persuade the Persians to revolt and march against the Medes, for the Median nobility will be the first to desert Astyages and to join you.'

Astyages' spies were everywhere and it was not long before the king began to hear of insurrection in the heartlands of Persia. Indeed, a legend tells of how one night in his palace at Ecbatana, Astyages summoned a concubine to entertain him. She performed a song for his amusement: 'Although the lion had the wild boar in his power', she sang, 'he let him go into his lair; he has become mightier there and will give the lion much grief.' 'What is this wild boar?' the king asked. Smiling, the concubine replied, 'Cyrus the Persian.'

To counter the threat of rebellion, Astyages found it prudent to make alliances with some influential Median families, chief among them that of the nobleman Spitamas, who was brought into the immediate royal circle through his marriage to a daughter of Astyages named Amytis. Her dowry was nothing less than Media itself. This was a cleverly calculated move on the part of Astyages: through marriage to Amytis, Spitamas became the presumptive successor of his father-in-law, while Cyrus' claim on Media as Astyages' grandson (Mandane and Amytis were sisters or half-sisters) was instantaneously weakened as a consequence.

That Cyrus' thoughts naturally turned to seizing by force what he had been denied through blood was not surprising. He whipped up the support of the Persian tribes by expanding his influence over the Mardians, the Sagartians, as well as the tribes of the Panthialaei, Derusiaei, and Carmanians. He also negotiated the aid of the Dahae and Derbices, two powerful members of the Saka confederation. As he went about establishing his authority across all of Persia, so too he was joined by influential *khāns*: there was Oebaras, a very capable general who brought a cold efficacy to any mission he undertook, and Pharnaspes 'the Red', a man who had enjoyed considerable authority by working closely with the Anshanite dynasty and as a consequence was one of Persia's wealthiest nobles. Cyrus harnessed Pharnaspes' talents, wealth, and loyalty by marrying his daughter, Cassandane, a woman who, for the remainder of her life, remained Cyrus' great love. She bore him several children, including two imperial heirs, Cambyses (named for his grandfather) and Bardiya, and two daughters, Atossa and Artystone.

Pharnaspes and Cassandane were members of a venerable old Persian clan known as the Achaemenids, which had probably settled in the country surrounding Persepolis as early as 900 BCE. They enjoyed a renowned ancestry. Their dynastic founder, Achaemenes, was something of a legend, reportedly having been reared when a little child by an eagle on a mountaintop in the Zagros – a local variation, clearly, of the Median tale of Zal and the magical bird. That Cyrus managed to garner the support of the Achaemenids, and even marry a daughter of that ancient house, was a major coup for his mission against Astyages. Cyrus' children shared Teispid and Achaemenid blood, giving them an enviable Persian pedigree. Cyrus' connection to the Achaemenids was further solidified when their most important prince and *khān*, Arsames, together with his young and energetic son, Hystaspes, also pledged their support and loyalty to Cyrus and the Teispids of Anshan. With them came the fealty of all the Achaemenids en masse.

In just five years, the tribes of Persia had united under the banner of Cyrus of Anshan and recognised him as their liege lord and king. During a vast tribal gathering at Pasargadae, Cyrus addressed his allies with stirring, prophetic words: 'Men of Persia', he pronounced, 'listen to me. I am the man destined to undertake your liberation and it is my belief that you are a match for the Medes in war as in everything else. It is the truth I tell you. Do not delay, but fling off the yoke of Astyages at once!'

Throughout the time when he was wooing, cajoling, and pressuring the Persian tribes to unite under his leadership, Cyrus, the master multitasker, was also negotiating with the new king of Babylon, Nabonidus, to enter into an alliance with him against Astyages, their common enemy. It was a difficult process given that Nabonidus, one of history's great eccentrics, found it close to impossible to find the head space for politics. A genuine religious fanatic, Nabonidus took the throne of Babylon after the boy king Labashi-Marduk, Nebuchadnezzar II's successor, had been murdered in a conspiracy only nine months after his coronation. It is not known whether Nabonidus played a role in his death, but he was chosen as the new king of Babylon soon afterwards in spite of being, at best, only a collateral member of the royal family. An Aramean from Harran in North Syria, Nabonidus was the son of Nabu-balatşu-iqbi, a 'wise prince and governor', and Adad-Guppi, an influential votary of the god Sin, who had long served as a priestess and was a zealous devotee of the moon-god. The extraordinary 104-year life of this éminence grise was recorded in a posthumous autobiographical set of inscriptions erected in the courtyard of Sin's temple in which she boasted of how Sin had visited her in a dream and predicted Nabonidus' glorious kingship. Consequently, on his ascent to power, her son devoted his life to the erecting of temples and the performance of rituals in honour of the god who had raised him so high. He even turned the temple of Marduk in Babylon into a sanctuary for Sin. That act led to unrest throughout Babylonia.

Nevertheless, Cyrus was able to harness Nabonidus' fanaticism to a good end, encouraging the king to send troops into Harran to liberate the temple from the Medes who had occupied the holy city for a generation. However, before Nabonidus' forces reached Harran, in 553 BCE Astyages pulled his troops out of Syria and called them back to Media to prepare, no doubt, for action against Persia. To celebrate the return of Harran into Babylonian hands, Nabonidus commissioned an inscription, preserved on a fired-clay cylinder, which recounts a dream Nabonidus experienced wherein the gods of Babylonia commanded him to restore the temple of Sin in Harran and which, remarkably, predicted Cyrus' victory over Media:

> The *Umman-manda* [Babylonian shorthand for 'barbarian Medes'] and the kings who march at his side are no more. Marduk will cause Cyrus, king of Anshan, his little servant, to advance against him [Astyages] with his small army. He will overthrow the wide extending *Umman-manda*; he will capture Astyages, the king of the *Umman-manda*, and take him in bonds to his own land.

For two years between 553 and 551 BCE, Cyrus and his troops pushed ever further into Median territory, determinedly marching towards Ecbatana. They were joined by Harpagus, who made good his promise to support Cyrus, and by many other Median nobles who had defected to Cyrus' side and brought him troops. The Persians were soon joined by the Hycarnians, Parthians, and the Saka, who rose against Astyages in support of Cyrus too. However, the mountainous terrain of Media proved to be an obstacle to their progress and the harsh winters limited the campaigning season to just six months. In the spring of 550 BCE Cyrus' army was back in the Persian homeland, camped around Pasargadae, and trying to regroup for another assault on Media. This is when Astyages struck.

The Median invasion of Persia was intended to put an end to Cyrus' uprising once and for all. The Persians struggled to cope with the sheer number of the enemy, who, well-fed, well-rested, and well-supplied, attacked in wave after wave, and they began to retreat into the mountains behind Pasargadae. The Persian soldiers were stopped in their tracks when their womenfolk opened their robes, flashed their genitals, and shouted out to them, 'Where are you off to, you quitters?! Do you want to crawl back in where you came from?' It is because of this that, in subsequent decades, when the king of Persia travelled to Pasargadae, he reportedly always presented gifts of gold to the brave local women.

The Battle of Pasargadae, one of the most consequential events in Iran's history, lasted for two full days. Both sides fought long, vigorously, and courageously. But mustering the strength for one final push forward, the Persians and their allies managed to charge against the Median battle line, which collapsed in a chaotic heap. The Persians had taken the battlefield, and suddenly Astyages found himself deserted as his leading generals mutinied and surrendered to Cyrus. The cuneiform Babylonian Chronicle picks up the events:

> The army rebelled against Astyages and he was taken prisoner. They handed him over to Cyrus ... Cyrus marched to Ecbatana, the royal city. The silver, gold, goods, and property he carried off as booty from Ecbatana, he took them to Anshan.

Ensconced in Ecbatana within the opulent royal tent made of strong, coarse red cloth but ornamented inside with brocade and beautiful hand-painted silk, the victorious Cyrus sat on his grandfather's throne and held his sceptre as he received the homage of the Median chiefs and their tribes, who hailed him as 'king of the Medes and the Persians'. Cyrus decided that in peace the Medes were to be on an equal footing with the Persians. Thereafter, throughout the Achaemenid period, Medes were routinely appointed to high office at the Persian court. Foreigners tended to make no distinction between 'the Medes and the Persians', and, indeed, for the Greeks the word 'Mede' was often the only term used to describe both.

Cyrus rewarded Hystaspes, Oebares, and his Achaemenid supporters extravagantly. He magnanimously received emissaries from Hyrcania, Parthia, and Saka, who prostrated themselves at his feet and offered Cyrus the allegiance which had once belonged to Astyages. The defeated king was paraded in chains in front of his former subjects before being carted off to Anshan where he was again put on display to the gratification of the Persian populace. The ancient sources all agree that Astyages was treated with remarkable clemency, although the details of his last years differ. Herodotus wrote that Cyrus kept Astyages at his court for the remainder of his life, while the Greek historian Ctesias, who got his account from stories he heard in Persia, insisted that he was made a governor of a province of Parthia and was later murdered by Oebares, who always regarded him as a political opponent. The events of Astyages' death are, sadly, unknown. His son-in-law, Spitamas, however, did not survive Cyrus' occupation of Ecbatana – he was quickly liquidated alongside his children, Spitaces and Megabernes, Cyrus' cousins. Their mother, Amytis, Cyrus' aunt, suddenly found herself to be a childless widow, but as a princess of Media she nevertheless still had political potential. Realising that she might be snatched up and married by any rogue Mede who harboured ambitions of rulership, Cyrus married her himself and incorporated her into his ever-expanding harem. When she arrived in Persia at the side of her new husband, Amytis was reunited with Mandane, who was, at one and the same time, both her elder sister and her mother-in-law. Such were the consequences of dynastic marriage policies.

*

The fall of Astyages of Media had a profound impact upon Near Eastern politics. For the Babylonians it meant a reprieve from invasion. Nabonidus left Babylon and went to reside at the rich desert oasis of Temâ in Arabia, where he might worship Sin without the distractions of state affairs. His decade-long spiritual retreat (553–543 BCE) saw the beautification of the oasis with a full royal complex, most of which has come to light during recent excavations. In his absence, Nabonidus' son Belshazzar ruled from Babylon.

Meanwhile in Lydia, the kingdom that stretched from the Aegean coast of Asia Minor to the Hylas River in central Anatolia, Astyages' defeat was lamented by Croesus, his brother-in-law, who had succeeded to the Lydian throne in 560 BCE. Croesus ruled from his sophisticated acropolis city of Sardis, his army dominated western Anatolia, and his vast wealth, mainly acquired as plunder from the Greek city states, was proverbial even in antiquity. It was Croesus who first created a two-part coinage system in which coins of pure gold and pure silver (at a fixed proportion of three to forty) replaced the single coin of white gold. And it was Croesus whose gifts to the oracle of Apollo at Delphi numbered some 117 gold ingots, a pure gold mixing bowl (and another of silver), a gold statue of a lion, another of a woman, and countless trinkets. It was Croesus too who funded construction of the great Temple of Artemis at Ephesus, one of the Seven Wonders of the ancient world. In short, Croesus was unspeakably rich, vulgarly wealthy, and, like a latter-day Russian oligarch, had absolutely no qualms about putting his affluence on conspicuous, ostentatious display.

The wealth of Lydia was a draw to Cyrus, of course, but the Persian king was far more interested in stamping out any remnants of Median resistance which may have lodged in Croesus' kingdom. He was also motivated by the prospect of territorial expansion and the benefits which might come from Croesus' overthrow. For his part, Herodotus reported, Croesus too 'had a craving to extend his territories and prepared an expedition in Cappadocia, sure of success in bringing down the power of Cyrus and the Persians'. The treasure he had gifted to Delphi's temple was used to solicit an answer from the famous prophetess of Apollo through whom the god spoke his oracles in riddles. Croesus asked the god whether or not he should go to war against the Persians. The oracle replied, 'If Croesus goes to war, he will destroy a great empire' (or so Herodotus recorded). Delighted by this answer, and without pausing to consider its deliberately ambiguous meaning, in the autumn of 547 BCE Croesus crossed the Hylas River, entering what was now Persian-ruled territory.

Cyrus countered swiftly and his troops confronted Croesus at Pteria (probably the area of the ancient city of Hattusa at the south end of the Budaközü Plain). There a ferocious but indecisive battle was fought. Croesus withdrew and disbanded his army, which was mainly composed of well-paid mercenaries. He had not anticipated that Cyrus would campaign in the freezing depths of the Anatolian highlands in winter. But that is precisely what Cyrus did. His hardy warriors, wrapped in their cowhide and sheepskin coats and trousers, pushed through the deep snows and biting winds on their hardy little Nisean horses, their camping equipment and arms carried on camel-back, all in pursuit of the Lydian soldiers. Croesus was surprised by Cyrus' sudden arrival at the plain of Thumbra near Sardis, where their troops met again in battle. By mounting his cavalry on the baggage camels, whose scent spooked the Lydian horses so badly that they refused to charge, Cyrus butchered Croesus' cavalry in the field. Croesus escaped and took refuge in the heavily fortified acropolis above Sardis, from where he sent desperate pleas to his allies on the Ionian coast. But within a fortnight, in late December 547 BCE, the siege was broken and the Lydian king was captured.

The fate of Croesus became the subject of diverse traditions. Writing many decades later, Herodotus reported that Cyrus spared Croesus' life, brought him to court in Persia, and valued him as a royal advisor. Ctesias said that Cyrus gave the defeated king a large city, Barnene, near Ecbatana, which he was allowed to rule as a semi-independent fiefdom. In another tradition, however, which has more of a ring of truth about it, Croesus followed the practice of many fallen kings and chose self-immolation, burning to death alongside his wife, daughters, and servants on a huge funerary pyre.

Certainly, the Greek poet Bacchylides, Croesus' contemporary, believed that the king underwent the rituals of a mass suicide, and in a victory ode which he penned shortly afterwards, he vividly described Croesus' self-immolation (although at its climax the king is carried off to heaven on the command of the gods):

> When he had come to that unexpected day, Croesus had no intention of waiting any longer for the tears of slavery. He had a pyre built before his bronze-walled courtyard, and he mounted the pyre with his dear wife and his daughters with beautiful tresses; they were weeping inconsolably . . . He bid the slave with the delicate step to kindle the wooden structure. His daughters cried out, and threw their arms out towards their mother; for death is most hateful to mortals when it is right before their eyes. But when the flashing force of terrible fire began to shoot through the wood, Zeus set a dark rain-cloud over it, and began to quench the golden flame.

However, a fragmentary cuneiform text from Babylon provides conclusive evidence that Croesus did indeed die at Sardis early in 546 BCE:

> In the month Nisanu, Cyrus, king of Parsu [Persia], mustered his army and crossed the Tigris below Arbela. In the month Ajaru, he marched to the land of Luud-du [Lydia]. He killed its king, took his possessions, [and] stationed his own garrison [there].

When Sardis fell, the Ionian coastal cities fell too. They quickly accepted Persian hegemony, sued for peace, and offered their tribute to Cyrus, who allowed them to keep a vestige of self-governance. From thereon in, each Ionian city was ruled by a local Greek who was chosen and supervised by a Persian superior. Any revolts, such as that led by a Lydian named Pactyes, whom Cyrus had commissioned to gather tribute from the coastal cities, were dealt with ruthlessly – this was not the time for clemency. Harpagus, Cyrus' most important Median ally, was put in charge of all the Persian forces in Asia Minor and ruled there in Cyrus' name, endowed with the impressive title 'Generalissimo of the Sea'. It was a label he took to heart as, over the next four years, he systematically subdued city after city along the coastline of Asia Minor, 'turning upside down and bringing into subjugation every nation without exception', wrote Herodotus.

With Harpagus in charge of the west, Cyrus' focus was drawn back east and his eye fell on Babylonia, with its vassal territories of Syria, Judah and Israel, Phoenicia, and parts of Arabia. The Neo-Babylonian empire had been locked in a crisis of government since Nabonidus' self-imposed exile in Arabia. In a rare moment of clarity, the king had returned to Babylon in the seventeenth year of his reign to find the city in disarray, its temples neglected, and its cult rituals left unperformed. The relationship between Babylon and its ruler was not propitious, but when Nabonidus heard of Cyrus' imminent arrival in Babylonia, he proved to be a better leader than anyone predicted. He mustered his troops and marched them north under the leadership of his son, Belshazzar, who stationed them close to the walled city of Opis, on the banks of the River Tigris, just fifty miles from Babylon.

In September 539 BCE Cyrus entered Babylonia and made straight for Opis. He was intercepted on his journey by a venerable Babylonian nobleman named Ugbrau, who governed a vast territory at the northern frontiers of Babylonia and who was opposed to Nabonidus' erratic rulership. On the spot he offered the services of his troops and his complete loyalty to Cyrus. A pact was made between the two leaders and Ugbrau's soldiers led the Persians towards Opis. The battle in front of the city's walls was short-lived but brutal. The Babylonian troops were cut to pieces and many others deserted the field, only to be killed as they fled. The desecration continued within the city itself as the Persian invaders burst through its walls, killing men, women, and children in a frenzied bloodbath that was clearly intended as a punitive attempt to make an example of a city so intent on resisting the Persians. An immense haul of booty was taken from Opis as the bodies of the dead, including that of Prince Belshazzar, were piled up in the streets and left to rot in the hot sunshine. Next to fall to the Persians, on 6 October, was the old city of Sippar. It was taken without battle. Cyrus then sent Ugbrau on to Babylon, where he met the shattered remnants of Nabonidus' army within striking distance of the city. The Babylonian soldiers quickly took sanctuary inside Babylon as Nabonidus, having no hope of defending his capital, fled and made his escape south to Borsippa.

*

On 12 October 539 BCE the mighty gates of Babylon swung open and the army of Cyrus of Persia made its way in stately procession, unhindered and unopposed, to the heart of the city, and moved towards the towering ziggurat of the god Marduk. Cyrus was mounted on a fine white stallion and at his side was his twenty-year-old son, Cambyses, who had joined Cyrus for his first experience of conquest (it was important for Cambyses to get training in the niceties of empire-building). Cyrus was attended by his old friend Oebaras, and the newcomer Ugbrau, whose presence alongside the conqueror must have rankled deeply with the Babylonians. For them, Ugbrau was a hated collaborator and a traitor to Babylon and her gods.

If there were no conspicuous scenes of jubilation from the Babylonians, there was no resistance either. There was just an eerie silence punctuated by the rhythmical tramping of the feet of Cyrus' soldiers and the clip-clop of horses' hooves and the occasional neigh or snort. Having heard the reports of the massacre at Opis, the Babylonians decided to keep their own counsel and show no resistance to the Persians as they processed into the ancient city. Cyrus had instructed his army that there was to be no looting, and no disorder, yet even so, for the Babylonians the sight of an occupying force, even an apparently passive one, was overwhelming. But what a prize for Cyrus Babylon was!

Babylon, 'the Jewel of Cities', with its broad avenues, its palaces, temples, and gardens, its public squares and marketplaces, and its houses packed tightly together in meandering streets, was unrivalled in the ancient world for its size and splendour. It was antiquity's only metropolis, teeming with life. Throughout its long and often violent history it had been attacked and destroyed many times, but after each desecration the city re-emerged anew from the ruins looking more magnificent than before. In the decades that preceded the Persian occupation, Babylon had been given a new lease of life by King Nebopolassar and his son Nebuchadnezzar, both of whom lavished resources on its glorification. Massive fortification walls sprang up, affording the city ample protection, and Nebuchadnezzar constructed a deep moat within the walls of Babylon so that an inner fortress city, a triangular island containing the old town and the venerated temple of Marduk, was given added protection. But it was with the building of the so-called Northern and Southern Summer Palaces that Nebuchadnezzar's Babylon took on a particular splendour. The façades of his royal residences were richly ornamented with lapis-coloured bricks, glazed so highly that they shone like mirrors in the sunshine. And everywhere, everywhere, were the images of prowling lions, trotting bulls, and striding dragons – a mythical menagerie encoding Babylonian royal power. And at the north-east corner of the great southern palace there were the renowned Hanging Gardens, one of the Seven Wonders of the ancient world, built – it was later said – by Nebuchadnezzar for his Median queen, Amytis, to remind her of the mountains of her Iranian homeland.

Decades of emulating the Assyrian policy of plundering and demanding tribute of defeated rulers saw Babylon's treasury swell with loot. It contained the rich spoils that had once graced the temple of Yahweh at Jerusalem – the silver censers and the gold furnishings, the ceremonial washing bowl known as the 'Molten Sea', as well as the tapestries, hangings, and carpets. In a bid to add to his collection of Judaean ephemera, in 597 BCE Nebuchadnezzar deported its king himself, Jehoiachin of Judah, and no fewer than 10,000 of his subjects into Babylonia. The effects of the Babylonian exile were profound and far-reaching. The exile transformed the Judeans into Jews. From being just one of many captive peoples, they emerged as the People of the Book. From one of many nations doomed for destruction, they transformed into history's perpetual survivor. In this process Cyrus of Persia was to play a significant role.

Cyrus and his men marched down Babylon's great Processional Way. Decorated with 120 moulded glazed-brick lions (the symbol of the goddess Ishtar), the grand avenue ran along the eastern side of the Southern Palace. It was known locally (now ironically) as *Aibur-shabu*, 'the enemy shall never pass', and it was used chiefly for parading the statues of the gods during the great New Year Festival, the annual renewal of divine cosmic protection that was so central to Babylon's religious and social framework. But where the gods had been carried, now rode Cyrus. He passed through the massive Ishtar Gate – sparklingly vivid blue and gold, and ornamented with bulls and dragons, the sacred symbols of Adad and Marduk – and penetrated ever deeper into the city until he stood at the base of the Esagila, the temple and dwelling place of the city-god Marduk, Babylon's sacred heart. Built at the top of the towering ziggurat was an inner cella where the god himself resided. Nebuchadnezzar declared that he had 'covered its wall with sparkling gold and caused it to shine like the sun', and it was in this inner sanctum that Cyrus was welcomed by the chief priests and by the city's councillors as they prostrated themselves before him and kissed his feet, brushing their beards into the dust beneath them. 'I took up my lordly abode in the royal palace', Cyrus recalled (blanking the reality), 'amidst rejoicing and happiness.'

Cyrus understood the importance of cultivating a good public image and worked closely with the priests and nobles of Babylon to solidify the appearance of his legitimate rulership of Babylonia. It might be thought that a regime change of this kind would have necessitated the overhaul of the government, with old officers of state being replaced by men drawn from the victorious administration. Yet cuneiform documents from this formative period of the Persian invasion reveal that, remarkably, Cyrus did not change the bureaucratic system at all, but let it run its familiar course. Documents prove that priesthoods, bureaucratic administrators, tax officials, and bankers retained their offices without interruption, allowing Babylon to maintain without rupture its economic, civic, and religious functions despite the psychologically traumatic upheaval of conquest. A Persian of venerable lineage, Gobryas, *khān* of the Patischorian tribe of Pārs, was installed as the satrap (governor) of Babylonia. He worked alongside Nabonidus' former chief administrator, Nabu-ahhe-bullit, to get an understanding of how the city functioned, and he was responsible for overseeing the peaceful transference of power within the territories of the former Babylonian empire. To that end Gobryas summoned the chieftains, governors, and princes of north Arabia, Syria, Judah, Israel, and the Levant to a great durbar, or ceremonial parade, at Babylon, where, at a carefully staged *diwan*, or ceremony of presentation, they paid homage to Cyrus as their undisputed overlord, swore their allegiance to him – and to Cambyses, his son – and proffered their diplomatic gifts. Cyrus cannot have failed to see in this assembly of dignitaries the physical proof of his successful empire-building. Later, he recalled that 'all the kings, who sit on thrones, from all parts of the world, from the Upper Sea to the Lower Sea, who dwell in distant regions, all the kings of Amurru, who dwell in tents, brought their heavy tribute to me and kissed my feet in Babylon'. He must have been delighted, in particular, to have received the submission of ambassadors from the wealthy city states of Phoenicia – Tyre, Sidon, and Byblos – with their merchant fleets ready to set sail and open up new trade routes. Their shipbuilders were capable of making Persia a great sea power too.

It was during this great meeting of the luminaries of the Near East that Nabonidus, who had been captured at Borsippa, was executed. Later stories (like those told of Croesus) suggested that a magnanimous Cyrus allowed him to live and that he was permitted to enjoy a comfortable retirement in Persia. This is unlikely. Cyrus was a shrewd politician and knew that the security of his fledgling empire and his newly founded dynasty, barely embedded yet into government, had more chance of survival without the presence of rival claimants or their loyalists. The execution of Nabonidus was the only option. His name and titles were hacked from all public monuments and the history of his reign was overwritten.

The victory Cyrus was enjoying was tarnished when, just eight days after the entry into Babylon, Oebaras died of a sudden stroke. Then, three months later, Cyrus' beloved wife, Cassandane, died too. He was bereft. The period between 20 and 26 March 538 BCE was a time of state mourning when, the cuneiform documents record, 'all the people went around with their hair dishevelled' as the queen was laid to rest.

But in Babylon the work of legitimisation continued. Cyrus began rebuilding the dilapidated city walls which had been so badly neglected throughout Nabonidus' reign and in doing so he crafted a public image of responsible kingship. As his workers patched up and reconstructed bits of the run-down fortifications, they unearthed an old Akkadian text which roused Cyrus' interest: 'I saw within the great wall of Babylon', he recalled, 'an inscription with the name of Ashurbanipal, a king who preceded me.' In the seventh century BCE, King Ashurbanipal of Assyria had been the most powerful man on earth and for nearly forty years he ruled a vast warlike empire. Cyrus proudly saw himself as the true heir to the Assyrian king and aligned himself with Ashurbanipal to legitimise his occupation of Babylon.

*

The events of October 539 BCE, and of the months that followed, are chronicled in the so-called Cyrus Cylinder. It is the greatest PR document from antiquity. It is a masterpiece of propaganda, a brilliant revisionist take on the events that led to the Persian occupation of Babylon, and a bold and audacious overwriting of historical fact. The imposition of a new narrative is expounded in the Cyrus Cylinder, where the conquest and subjugation of Babylon is written up as the city's liberation.

The Cylinder, an unprepossessing heavy lump of clay densely packed with cuneiform wedges, takes pride of place in the British Museum's Rahim Irvani Gallery of Ancient Iran. It is the sole survivor of many such cylinders created en masse on the order of Cyrus the Great. The king, working alongside the priests and scholars of Babylon, was determined to craft an image of himself as an old-style, naturalised Babylonian monarch. The Cylinder is modelled on standard royal Babylonian cylinder inscriptions which were intended to be buried in the foundations of building structures.

The Cyrus Cylinder was found in the city wall of Babylon but copies were made for wide dissemination – on clay tablets and papyrus – and through public proclamation.

The text villainises Nabonidus for his impiety towards the Babylonian gods, (especially long-suffering Marduk) and claims that he had imposed harsh corvée labour service on the city's population (a blatant lie). The heartfelt lamentations of the Babylonians were heard by the gods. Marduk, the Cylinder states, looked around for a champion to restore order over chaos and, recognising both his virtue and his bravery, chose Cyrus of Anshan and declared him to be the king of the world. In the words of the Babylonian scribes, 'Marduk took him by the hand, he called for dominion over the totality of the world, and he named his name – Cyrus of Anshan . . . Marduk, the great lord, who cares for his people, looked with pleasure at his good deeds and his righteous heart.' Marduk then ordered Cyrus to march on Babylon, which, the Cylinder states, he entered without a fight. The people of Babylon, it goes on to proclaim, joyfully accepted Cyrus' rule, grateful to be liberated from the darkness of Nabonidus' tyranny. From this point on, the text is written as if Cyrus himself is speaking and he presents himself as a faithful worshipper of Marduk whose only aim was to bring peace to Babylon:

> I, Cyrus, king of the universe, mighty king, king of Babylon, king of Sumer and Akkad, king of the four quarters of the world . . ., eternal seed of kingship, whose reign was loved by Bel and Nabu and whose kingship they wanted to please their hearts – when I had entered Babylon peacefully, I set up, with acclamation and rejoicing, the seat of lordship in the palace of the ruler. Marduk, the great lord, gave me Babylon and daily I cared for his worship. The city of Babylon and all its cult-centres I maintained in well-being. The inhabitants of Babylon, I allowed to find rest from their exhaustion, their servitude I relieved. Marduk, the great lord, rejoiced at my good deeds. Me, Cyrus, the king, who worships him, and Cambyses, my very own son, as well as all my troops, he blessed mercifully. In well-being we walk happily before him.

Lest we become swayed by the persuasive propaganda and begin to regard Cyrus as an acolyte to Marduk and other gods of Babylon, we need to remember that in other proclamations issued at the same time as the Cylinder's text was doing the rounds, Cyrus was also fashioning himself as a servant of the Hebrew god and a benefactor of the Jews. In 538 BCE he decreed that the temple in Jerusalem should be rebuilt at his own expense and that the treasures plundered from the sacred sanctuary by Nebuchadnezzar should be returned to the house of God. The captive Jews (like all other foreign deportees) were free to go home. In 537 BCE more than 40,000 of them undertook what they declared to be the 'Second Exodus' and joyfully trekked back to Jerusalem and to the land flowing with milk and honey. This is why in the Hebrew Bible Cyrus became regarded as a servant of Yahweh, the one selected by the invisible God to bring His chosen people out of bondage. Thus, the prophets of the exile lauded Cyrus as God's instrument of liberation. A prophet we know as Trito-Isaiah was particularly enthusiastic. He recorded God's jubilation at finding so worthy a champion as Cyrus:

> 'Behold my servant, whom I uphold,
> my chosen one in whom I delight,
> I have bestowed my spirit upon him,
> and he will make justice shine upon the nations . . .
> I have taken you [Cyrus] by the hand and formed you;
> to be a light to all peoples . . .'
> Thus says Yahweh, who says to Cyrus:
> 'You shall be my shepherd
> to carry out all my purpose,
> so that Jerusalem may be rebuilt
> and the foundations of the temple may be laid.'
> Thus says the Lord to Cyrus, the Anointed One,
> Cyrus whom he has taken by the hand
> to subdue nations before him and undo the might of kings.

For his generosity to the Jews Cyrus received no less an accolade than the title *meshiach* – 'Messiah', or 'Anointed One' – an expression which exilic Jews used when they spoke of a God-sent saviour or redeemer. It was a profoundly theological title that spoke of Cyrus' ratification as a legitimate king appointed and protected by God. In the Psalms, the Anointed One is an idealised, semi-mythical leader, a warrior whom God champions and protects:

> Now I know that God will give victory
> to His Anointed,
> will answer him from His heavenly sanctuary
> with the mighty victories of His right arm.

The parallels with Marduk's championship of Cyrus are clear, and it is feasible to think that the Babylonian scribes and the Hebrew prophets drew on a common image of Cyrus as a champion of the gods. While the bestowal of the messianic title did not elevate Cyrus to any form of divine status, his recognition as a figure of theological importance was singularly unique: in all of the bible, he is the only gentile to receive that most lofty of titles. While Yahweh acknowledged that Cyrus did not recognise His divine authority, He was still moved enough by the Persian king's virtue to make him a Messiah for the Hebrews. In the end, as Trito-Isaiah put it, he commanded Cyrus to 'rebuild Jerusalem and set my people free'.

It is doubtful that Cyrus acted under divine authority to release the Jews from their Mesopotamian prison. More likely than not, he acted pragmatically to reduce tension in Babylon and throughout the empire. By embracing the appearance of (what we might call) religious tolerance and authorising the Jewish population to leave Babylon of their own free will, Cyrus dealt with the practical problem of over-population within Babylonia. His repopulation of Jerusalem and its surroundings was a smart move (although it must be remembered that many Jews stayed in Babylonia and established an important cultural centre there which lasted for many hundreds of years). And yet, hand in hand with the Babylonialised Cyrus of the Cylinder, the portrayal of the king in the Hebrew Bible has played an important part in the creation of his image as a liberal, tolerant peacemaker who somehow marks a break between the barbaric and forbidding rule of the Assyrian and Babylonian tyrant kings and a new form of enlightened rulership. The Cyrus Cylinder has been dubbed the 'first declaration of human rights' and Cyrus has been praised as the original advocate of decent humane principles as well as a supporter of abolition and civic freedoms. In truth, there is nothing in the text of the Cyrus Cylinder that suggests the concept of human rights. In fact, this progressive idea was entirely unknown in antiquity and was completely alien to Cyrus' world.

It is important to recognise Cyrus for what he was: a gifted and successful military leader and an adroit political manipulator, unquestionably. But he was also an ambitious warlord and ruthless imperialist. His empire was founded on bloodshed, as all empires invariably are. The fact that slavery, imprisonment, battle, murder, execution, and mass extermination were inevitable consequences of his – and his successors' – territorial ambitions goes to prove that in their pursuit of land the Persians were not out of step with the Assyrians, for whom they had a curious respect. The Persian empire was not built on virgin territory. In every one of the places that Cyrus seized, he encountered resistance from local populations who were rooted to their lands. In fact, Media, Lydia, and Babylonia were wrestled from the clutches of other ambitious colonial powers that were already on their own journey of self-aggrandisement. The expansion of the Persian empire was a military exercise. It was a sneaky political game too, for in the initial phases of empire-building the Persians benefited inextricably from ingratiating themselves with collaborators and other treacherous persons. The initial opposition to Cyrus' conquests continued off and on, and in varying ways, throughout the Achaemenid era, in almost every colonised territory. To retain control, the Persians established empire-wide systems of management, ranging from the sophisticated to the brutal.

The benign view of Cyrus as a poster boy for free-thinking pacifism does harm to the historical figure who fought his way, knee-deep in gore, throughout the Middle East, slashing and stabbing a path to world domination. The sobriquet 'the Great' loses its cogency if we imagine him otherwise. Cyrus was a resourceful and shrewd trailblazer, who understood the importance of mollifying conquered peoples through the superficial championship of religious traditions and alignment with past rulers. He was also capable of transmitting his dominance through pitiless expressions of force and proclamations of cultural pre-eminence; in this respect, he could be coldly Machiavellian. To provide a definitive example: when, at the great temple of Marduk on the fourth day of Nisannu (27 March) 538 BCE, Cyrus oversaw the investiture of his son, Cambyses, as king of Babylon (a glorified vice-regent really), Cyrus opted to wear a cotton, fringe-decorated Elamite robe. This had been the type of garment worn by the rulers of Susa, Babylon's great enemy for many centuries. The explicit reference in the cuneiform sources to the king's Elamite dress, worn during a Babylonian religious ceremony, seems to allude to the idea that Cyrus was not the universally accepted and celebrated liberator portrayed by his propagandists. His public appearance in Elamite costume must have caused consternation among even the most Persian-friendly Babylonian elites, for, at this most sacred and most public of ceremonies, Cyrus' garments sent a stinging message: Babylon was now ruled by a foreign power, and he, Cyrus of Anshan, ruler of Persia, was King of the World.

3

The Many Deaths – and Births – of Cyrus the Great

Early in the spring of 530 BCE Cyrus was enjoying the simple delights of his garden-palace at Pasargadae, where he was taking in the magical fragrance of a myriad of blossoms. He sat in the shaded portico of his elegant little pavilion of stone and wood. A wide awning, colourfully woven, was attached to the building, and this protected him from the glare of the sun and effectively extended the palace into the garden and drew the garden back into the palace. The whole edifice was an expression of Cyrus' life. The well-worked stones were a nod to the sophistication of the urban world – Susa, Sardis, and Babylon – which he had made his own; the billowing tent-like awning, with its tasselled fringe dancing in the cooling breeze, was a vestige of his nomadic self. As he looked out across the plain from his throne portico, Cyrus could just make out in the heat haze the colourful tent city which accompanied him wherever he went.

It was rare for him to be home in the Persian heartlands of his youth. In the last two decades he had spent most of his time on horseback in far-flung places acquiring lucrative territory. But, for now, Cyrus was pleased to be at Pasargadae. Spring was the right time to be there and he was delighted to see how, over the years, his fine garden had matured with tall cypress trees running in straight avenues alongside bubbling streams which passed through endless stone water channels and little pools. Flowerbeds burst with the colour of exotic flora imported from each part of the empire, and every now and then Cyrus saw the red flash of a rooster's coxcomb as the haughty bird strutted through the garden, its feathers shimmering black-blue-gold. Cyrus had a dozen cockerels, an unexpected gift of the Indian ambassador. *Bas-bas* they were called in Persian. They were angry and aggressive and Cyrus was shown by the ambassador how, in India, they were trained and used for sport. Consequently, he and his best friends wagered fortunes on cockfights. But this particular cockerel did not fight. He was allowed to wander the gardens of Pasargadae and service the fat brown hens who gave Cyrus eggs on a daily basis – a new phenomenon for a society that knew only the seasonal hatchings of geese, swans, and ducks. His chickens were precious birds and Cyrus entrusted them to the safe keeping of their own warden, the Master of the *bas-bas*.

The transformation of the palace and gardens of Pasargadae had begun shortly after Cyrus conquered Lydia. He was impressed by the grandeur of the architecture of Sardis and the other Ionian cities, and so Greek stonemasons were sent to Pārs to mastermind the creation of the first stone buildings in Persia. Judging from the archaeology, there had been no permanent settlement at Pasargadae before Cyrus' decision to build there, even though the site had functioned as an important tribal meeting place for centuries. The Medes had known of it and, during their occupation of Persia, Pasargadae had been a garrison post that was known by the Median name *Badrakatash*. But for the Persians it was *Pāthra-gadā* – 'the place of those who wield solid clubs'. Cyrus had decided that his new empire deserved – and needed – a focal point for ceremonial purposes, and although Pasargadae was never intended to be a palatial complex of the size of Persepolis, it was planned to be a focal point of a new-found form of Persian kingship.

Located some fifty-five miles north of Shiraz in the Dasht-e Morghab ('plain of the water bird'), close to the Pulvar River on what was a busy caravan route running between Ecbatana and the Persian Gulf, Pasargadae sits over 2,000 feet above sea level. Today it is a quiet and remote archaeological site which requires much imagination from the tourists who visit. Its ruins are sparse and scattered and it is a difficult place to comprehend. In fact, the full extent of this enormous, sprawling imperial site is yet to be completely understood, although the official palaces, built in stone and decorated in marble, have been well-documented and studied. Now only a few broken columns and some cracked flagstones mark out the place of Cyrus' elegant palace-pavilion. A once glorious monumental gateway stands close by the pavilion ruins. It was the only entrance portal in the entire palatial complex but its former grandeur is now indicated by a single standing door jamb decorated with a high-relief sculpture. It is of a four-winged male figure wearing an Elamite garment and an elaborate Egyptian-style crown – a towering Folies-Bergère confection of ostrich plumes, falcon feathers, and twisted rams' horns. For centuries this curious hybrid figure has been identified as a portrait of Cyrus the Great himself, but that is simply not the case. Its angel-like wings show it to be an Assyrian-style guardian spirit known as an *apkallu*.

This sort of angelic being was commonly represented on the walls and door jambs of Neo-Assyrian palaces, where it functioned as a divine superintendent or a kind of celestial bouncer charged with keeping heavenly riff-raff from entering the palace and preventing cosmic undesirables from bringing harm or mischief to its occupants. Transferred to Pasargadae and given a Persian makeover, the winged *apkallu* figure (formerly one of a pair) was a regal but formidable *djinn* who functioned as part of Pasargadae's defence system. The *apkallu* protected Cyrus from any malevolent force.

Figure 3. Winged and crowned apkallu (guardian) from the gateway into the garden-palace of Cyrus the Great at Pasargadae.

The gateway stood in splendid isolation. It had no associated wall because, unlike other palace sites throughout the Near East, Pasargadae had no fortifications to encircle it, so confident was Cyrus of the invulnerability of the place, located as it was deep in the Persian homeland. The absence of defences only strengthened the symbolic power of the gate as both a magical and a ceremonial portal through which foreign diplomats, suppliants, and tribute-bearers processed to greet their king. Pasargadae was not totally without its defences, however, for overlooking the complex from a high mound was a great fortified platform known as the *Tall-e Takht* – 'Hill of the Throne'. Under the later Achaemenids, the hillside developed into a sprawling citadel with substantial mud-brick defences which was used as a military garrison.

Close to the gateway, and built to serve as the principal public setting for Cyrus and his court, was 'Palace S' (a sadly flat and unim-aginative archaeological label). It was composed of a rectangular columned hypostyle hall laid out with two rows of four columns, and four doorways that led out to a portico which enveloped the building. The decorative scheme inside the palace (such as sur-vives) was drawn from Assyrian and Babylonian motifs, carved in high relief and painted. They showed bulls, improbably standing upright on two legs and tottering in procession. And there were priests, swathed in curious fish-skin cloaks and trout's-head masks. The colourful Assyrian-style stone reliefs, rich in detail if bizarre in theme, were set against the plain, elegant Greek stonework of the columns and porticoes. The architecture and décor were a curious amalgam of styles and, aesthetically speaking, it should not have worked. Yet it did. The Persians created a unique art form that was a curious but holistic blend of Mesopotamian, Egyptian, and Greek styles. When pulled together, they resulted in something visually appealing, harmonious, and distinctively 'Persian'. At Pasargadae this idiosyncratic merging of styles is best reflected in the unique architecture of the tomb of Cyrus the Great.

Set well apart from the palaces, the mausoleum of Cyrus stands in a remote position on the Murghab plain, a mile from the cere-monial centre of Pasargadae. Lord Curzon once rhapsodised that its walls 'gleam like a white patch on a sombre landscape'. The tomb was the first building to be erected at Pasargadae and consists of two distinctive elements. First, a rectangular burial chamber with a steep-pitched gable roof of a type found in the Ionian architectural funerary tradition. Second, a stepped base that was meant to evoke a Mesopotamian ziggurat – specifically, perhaps, the great Elamite structure at Chogha Zanbil near Susa, which was certainly still visible, if no longer functioning, in Cyrus' lifetime. Examination of the tomb's stonework confirms that Lydians were actively involved in the construction of the grave, although the overall dramatic visual effect of the monument was shaped by its curious but successful juxtaposition of Anatolian and Mesopotamian elements. The characteristics of Achaemenid art and architecture were therefore already defined and established in Cyrus' burial monument even before his palaces were built.

Pasargadae's chief jewel, however, was its formal garden. An expansive area of rich cultivation linked the gateway and the palaces together into a single, unified whole. The layout of lush green spaces interspersed with palaces, pavilions, and audience halls became a defining feature of Persian garden design. Dressed-stone water channels unified the garden through a carefully planned geometric layout by creating an elegant fourfold design, or *chahar bagh*. This distinctive feature was destined to become a major characteristic of garden design throughout the Islamic world from Samarkand to Seville. Through the intricacy of its *chahar bagh* design, the garden of Pasargadae became a living reflection of the royal title Cyrus emphasised in his Babylonian Cylinder: 'I am Cyrus . . . king of the four quarters of the world.'

The Old Persian word for 'garden(s)' was *paridaida*. The Hebrews heard it as *pardes* and the Greeks transcribed it as *paradeisos* – whence comes the English 'paradise'. Strictly speaking, a 'paradise' was a walled green space with clear demarcations between the cultivated and tamed 'within' and the untamed and uncivilised 'without', a concept that can be found in the Bible's book of Genesis. When Jewish priests and scribes, working in Persian-occupied Jerusalem and Babylonia, depicted the Garden of Eden, the locale of the 'garden of God', they modelled it on a Persian paradise.

Throughout the empire, the carefully cultivated gardens and parks were living symbols of Persian dominance. Kings and princes boasted of their achievements as gardeners: 'I made great works: I built houses and planted vineyards for myself; I made myself gardens and parks and planted in them all kinds of trees. I made myself pools from which to water the forest of growing trees.' The royal parks were empires-in-miniature, exotic garden symbols of the monarch's control of a huge territory. Cyrus and the later Achaemenid kings enriched their *paridaida* with foreign shrubs and fruit trees, and grafters were employed to prune precious grapevines in Lebanon and replant them in Persian soil. The desire to create and maintain a beautiful flourishing garden was a Persian art form, an obsession which the pedestrian Greeks never understood. For an Athenian, a garden was a place to grow radishes.

The idea that the king was capable of creating fertile gardens which displayed both symmetry and order was a powerful statement of monarchic authority. The planning and creation of Pasargadae was therefore an enormous and important enterprise. Its successful completion demonstrated the presence of a developed administrative structure which dealt with the logistics of so monumental an undertaking. All in all, Pasargadae demonstrated Cyrus' sophisticated appreciation of the trappings of kingship and it remained an important royal ceremonial centre throughout the empire's existence. It was the location for the investiture of every new Persian king, who was ritually linked there with the founder of the Persian empire.

A spectacular archaeological discovery was made in 2015 at a site in Fārs province known as Tol-e Ajori ('Hill of Bricks'), located near Firuzi village in very close proximity to Persepolis. There, a Joint Iranian–Italian Archaeological Mission unearthed the remains of a huge gateway. It was square in shape, thirty metres long on each side, with walls ten metres thick, and decorated with colourful glazed-brick panels with figurative designs. Around the gate, excavators unearthed small pavilions and found, as at Pasargadae, clear traces of perfectly planned formal gardens. Intriguingly, studies of the bricks have revealed striking iconographical similarities with panels from Nebuchadnezzar's buildings in Babylon, particularly the figural imagery of fantastic beasts found on the famous Ishtar

Gate. The massive gateway, with its blue-glazed brick coating, was once a near copy of that famous structure. When compared with other architectural structures in Achaemenid Pārs, in plan, in building, and in decoration, the gate structure was absolutely unique.

The monumental Babylonian-style gateway was surely the work of Cyrus. In fact, the attribution of the building to him seems to be confirmed through the finding of a brick fragment containing the beginning of a cuneiform inscription painted in the glaze on which is part of the Akkadian word *sharru*, 'king'. The discovery of King Cyrus' gateway so close to Persepolis means that the history of that latter key Achaemenid site has undergone radical revision in recent years. What was thought to have been virgin territory, untouched before Darius I started to build there in *c.* 518 BCE, can now be viewed as having been a flourishing royal centre well before that time. The gateway might have started taking shape, if Cyrus had sent Babylonian craftsmen to Pārs, as early as 538 BCE, shortly after the conquest of Babylon itself, thereby predating Darius' palatial structures by at least two decades. But why did Cyrus choose to build so conspicuously foreign a structure in the centre of Persia? The building work at Pasargadae demonstrates how Cyrus was keen to incorporate the visual 'look' of his freshly conquered territories into a new canon of 'Persian' style. But while, at Pasargadae, the architecture was predominantly Lydian in form, he chose the more overtly grandiose splendour of Babylonian constructions to stamp his mark on the landscape of Persepolis. More than likely, Cyrus aimed to create there a new Babylon, a Persian city that would outshine the former Mother of All Cities. His ambition was to realign the central axis of his four-cornered empire towards Pārs itself by placing Persia at the centre of civilisation. His unexpected death in battle brought that masterplan to an abrupt end.

*

In 530 BCE Cyrus was at Pasargadae for the purpose of launching a new military campaign. He had decided to venture far into the north-east, to go well beyond the River Araxes on the lower Oxus, and conquer the troublesome Massagetai. These were a Scythian people who inhabited the great plain wedged between the Caspian Sea and the Aral Sea. They had begun to make forays over the empire's north-eastern frontier, although they caused little long-term damage beyond some light pillaging. Nevertheless, Cyrus decided that a robust and decisive action against them was needed and that he, personally, would lead the campaign to crush them – an overreaction, it must be conceded, to what was merely cattle-rustling. It is hard to justify Cyrus' bellicose attitude towards the Massagetai or to see him as anything other than an aggressor in his mission to bring them to heel. But even after his successes in the west, his territorial desires had yet to be satisfied.

Keen to settle the royal succession before he departed for war, Cyrus summoned his two sons to meet him at Pasargadae. Cambyses, who arrived quickly from Sippar in Babylonia, was formally named as his successor and was instructed to serve as regent during Cyrus' time in the east. The younger son, Prince Bardiya, was given an enormous territory in Central Asia by way of compensation for missing out on the throne. The gift was further sweetened when Cyrus declared that Bardiya's lands were exempt from taxation and that any tribute raised there was his to keep.

It was possibly at this juncture that Cambyses, now the official heir to the throne, undertook a series of marriages. First, he married Phaidymē, the daughter of Otanes, a mighty *khān*, and reputedly the wealthiest man in Persia. Then, significantly, he wed his full-blood sister, Atossa, the daughter of Cyrus and Mandane, and took a half-sister, Rhoxane, as a consort too (the concept of 'incest' was of no importance when building a dynasty). These marriages were the first attestation of the importance the dynasty laid on endogamy – the notion of marrying within a specific social group or caste. It was to be employed by the Achaemenids throughout their tenure as Persia's royal house. Achaemenid kings generally made marriage alliances with the daughters or sisters of great Persian *khāns* or married within the family itself by taking cousins, nieces, sisters, and half-sisters as wives.

With his legacy settled, Cyrus' army started out from Pasargadae at the end of spring 530 BCE. Cambyses accompanied his father as far as the Jaxartes River and returned home to Persia to take up the duties of regent and heir-designate. Meanwhile, Cyrus and his troops marched on east.

Details of the final years of Cyrus' life are hard to piece together. His eastern campaign is especially problematic since much of it blurs into legend. Facts lose their cogency in Herodotus' narrative, the principal surviving source for Cyrus' final military operation. He tells a very odd story. Having marched into Massagetai territory, Herodotus says, Cyrus set up camp, ordering his men to cook and lay out food, to light fires, and spread carpets and rugs on the ground, just as would be done at a sumptuous banquet. Cyrus withdrew most of his men into the surrounding hills and left only a small detachment behind. Like moths to a flame, the Massagetai quickly gathered at the abandoned camp, plundering the Persians' goods, eating their food, and drinking their wine until, with shouts and yells, the Persians suddenly galloped back to their tents, slaughtering the half-drunk barbarians and taking their leaders captive. These included Prince Spargapses, the son of Queen Tomyris, the female, Amazon-like ruler of the Massagetai. Dishonoured and deeply ashamed after being captured by such a cheap trick, the young prince begged to be unchained. Cyrus consented. On his release, Spargapses promptly killed himself.

A grief-stricken Tomyris, incandescent with anger, strapped on her armour, mounted her charger and galloped towards the Persian forces with such ferocity that her own troops barely kept pace with her. The sky darkened as volley after volley of arrows flew thick and fast overhead. Tomyris plunged deep into the midst of the battle. Spears, daggers, scimitars, and lances clashed and slashed, ripped, and tore, and rivers of blood flowed through the valley and stained the rocks red. The two armies fought all day and the combat was brutal. By the time it was finished, Cyrus was dead. A triumphant Tomyris let forth an ululation of joy mixed with lamentation as she lashed Cyrus' corpse to her horse and dragged it back to her camp. She hacked off his noble head and, gripping it by the bloody strands of hair, addressed the Persian king: 'Bloodthirsty Cyrus, so insatiate of blood', she said, 'I will give you your fill.' With that, she plunged the decapitated trophy into a wineskin filled with human gore.

There were numerous accounts of Cyrus' death in circulation in the years following his demise. The story of Tomyris, Herodotus insisted, was the most probable. Is it to be trusted? Well, the names Tomyris and Spargapses are certainly Iranian in origin, and it is probable that Herodotus drew on genuine Persian traditions which maintained that Cyrus died in battle against a warrior queen of the east. But the way in which Herodotus moulded that story was motivated by his Greek view of the Persian enemy. After all, in writing his *Histories*, Herodotus was not pursuing forensic facts. No, his concern was with composing an elegant *logos*, a form of historical 'dialogue', which can be seen to run throughout the entire work. The topic was the overreaching imperial ambitions of the kings of Persia. Herodotus was writing not so much a history as a lesson in morality: 'know your limits.'

The *real* events surrounding the death of Cyrus the Great are unknown. There are no Persian textual sources which describe it and legends are all that are left. Even these come down to us from the Greek tradition and are highly contradictory. Xenophon's Cyrus dies in bed, his sons gathered around him as he divides up his kingdom. Ctesias' Cyrus is wounded while fighting against the Saka, but manages to get home to Persia for another moving deathbed scene. It stands to reason that the historical Cyrus could not die in bed and on the battlefield. The three Greek versions of Cyrus' end do contain kernels of genuine Persian stories, though, each of which functioned as a a form of propaganda for the original transmitters of the tales. Cyrus was too important a figure in Persia's history to be forgotten and, soon after his death, stories of his birth, life, and passing entered into folklore, then legend, and finally into myth. With every retelling, his story took on a new slant.

This is why there were multiple stories of Cyrus' birth and childhood circulating throughout the Persian empire for generations. Given Persia's long and noble history of producing fine poetry and song it is logical to suppose that Cyrus figured as an important hero in their narratives. The Achaemenids prized poetry as much as they prized their horses, and a popular tradition for Cyrus-stories told through verse quickly developed. There were even songs about the heroic deeds of Cyrus the Great. Writing almost 150 years after Cyrus' death, Xenophon noted that 'Cyrus is still celebrated to this day by the Persians in story and in song as the most handsome and generous of men, devoted to wisdom yet ambitious; he endured all kinds of danger and faced hardship in order to gain renown.'

In antiquity, nativity stories of great leaders played an effective part in the dissemination of their image. It is not beyond belief to suppose that some leaders, like Cyrus himself, may have encouraged the composition and broadcasting of remarkable birth-stories or anecdotes of extraordinary childhoods. These might serve as useful propaganda. In one such story, Cyrus' birth was heralded in a series of dream-omens which haunted the sleep of his Median grandfather, King Astyages. In his slumber he dreamed that a grapevine was growing out of the genitals of his daughter, Mandane. These sprouting tendrils spread across the whole of Asia. They crept into every valley and climbed up to each mountaintop. In another, far worse, night terror, Astyages saw Mandane urinate with such force that she flooded the entire Asian continent. The priests interpreted the two dreams and warned Astyages that Mandane's son, soon to be born, would become the most powerful ruler on earth, superseding Astyages himself in glory and honour. Terrified of the future, as soon as Mandane gave birth, the king ordered his henchman, no less a person than Harpagus, to take the baby Cyrus into the wilderness and kill him. But Harpagus, moved by the baby's innocent cries, found it impossible to kill the child and abandoned him on a mountainside in the hope that he would be found by peasants. Which is precisely what happened next. Cyrus grew to adolescence safe in the home of a loving old shepherd and his wife until they told him of his parentage. As he reached adulthood, he reclaimed his rightful place as Media's king. The story, rich in detail and packed with popular folk and fairy tale motifs, was no doubt composed in Media to justify Cyrus' conquest of the Medes and the overthrow of Astyages (here portrayed as a monstrous villain in the manner of other infant-killers such as Zeus, Herod, and the pharaoh of the biblical Exodus story). As a deft work of propaganda, the story justified the Perso-Median *Anschluss*.

Other stories originated in different parts of Iran and projected other lines of propaganda. In one, Cyrus' Median blood was completely ignored. Instead, he was reckoned to be the son of a poor Persian man named Atradates, a robber, and his wife Argoste, a lowly goatherd. In spite of his modest beginnings, and thanks to the goodwill of an important eunuch who worked at the Median court, Cyrus rose through the ranks of royal servants to become a member of Astyages' inner circle. Destined for great things, Cyrus overthrew Astyages and established his own dynasty in Media by marrying the Median princess Amytis. In this tale, originating, perhaps, in Pārs itself, Cyrus was a Persian-born son of the soil, a hardy Persian who through intelligence and ambition overthrew the tyranny of the Medes and set Persia on its path to empire. Yet another birth-story, allegedly disseminated as official propaganda by Cyrus' family, was that, as a baby born at Astyages' court, he had indeed been abandoned and left to die on a mountainside, but that he had been saved by a dog. The bitch had recently birthed puppies, and lovingly suckled him and saved his life. This infancy narrative, so closely resembling the Romulus and Remus tale, was said to have appealed to the Persians because of its mythic quality – for if anyone deserved a miracle-story it was Cyrus.

*

The 'Father of the Persians' was buried with due ceremony within his vaulted tomb at Pasargadae, his body laid on a couch of gold and covered with a Babylonian tapestry. A sleeved *gaunaka*, several pairs of trousers, and numerous colourful robes together with necklaces, bracelets, and earrings of semi-precious stones set in gold were interred alongside the king, to clothe him in the next life. Cambyses initiated a cult for his dead father, overseen by priests who served at the tomb. They made certain that Cyrus' soul was honoured with the sacrifice of a white horse every month.

Cyrus had been an extraordinary ruler. He was both a remarkable military mastermind and a pragmatic politician. In just two decades he took his tiny Persian kingdom to world domination. Territories that were geographically and culturally disparate found themselves ruled through his uniting authority. The widely circulated propaganda of his religious piety and benevolent states-manship (derived largely from the Babylonian cylinder, the Hebrew Bible, and Greek historians), combined with the heroic tales of his birth and accession to power, helps to explain the preservation of his reputation as a just and compassionate monarch. The legends and traditions that have flourished around the figure of Cyrus may have muted his darker, less attractive, side. After all, legends have a power to create their own truths. But whatever way we look at them, Cyrus' achievements were, and remain, astonishing.

4

The Sceptre of Egypt

Cambyses, Cyrus' eldest son and the sole heir to his empire, has got a very bad press. The familiar story, repeated time and again, insists that when compared with his august and judicious father, Cambyses was a crazed despot who ruled badly and behaved worse. 'I have no doubt', wrote Herodotus scathingly, 'that Cambyses was completely out of his mind.'

A cocktail of iniquities punctuates the story of Cambyses, although one tale about his many incompetences as a ruler has been especially persuasive. When priests at the oracle of the temple of Amun in the Siwa Oasis, far west of the Nile, criticised the king, Cambyses decided that they would be punished for their insubordination. He sent 50,000 soldiers marching across the Sahara Desert to put the troublesome priests to death, but they never reached the oasis. Just seven days into their arduous march, Herodotus explained, 'a wind arose from the south, powerful and deadly, bringing with it vast columns of whirling sand, which entirely covered up the troops and caused them to disappear completely when an enormous sandstorm erupted'. Some 2,500 years later, enthusiasts claim to have found the place in the western Sahara where Cambyses' army met its fate. There is little chance of that being the case since it was highly improbable that 50,000 men would be sent across so formidable a desert simply to slaughter a handful of mouthy prelates. Herodotus' passion for tall tales sits behind his story of Cambyses' lost army. No other ancient author makes even a passing reference to it. In fact, Herodotus spins the whole story of Cambyses in Egypt into a moralistic fable that mixes a little fact with a large dollop of fiction. The Cambyses of the *Histories* is compelling but bogus Herodotean caricature. To get a better understanding of the second Persian king, we have to look well beyond the Greek accounts. When we do so, Cambyses emerges as a successful king and a very able warrior too. It was Cambyses, after all, who conquered Egypt, bringing the richest country in the world, with its deep legacy of civilisation and its limitless supply of grain, into the orbit of the Persian empire.

*

After Cambyses had observed the correct mourning period for his dead father at Pasargadae, he and his entourage returned to Babylonia, set up court at Uruk, and began planning a campaign which would lead to Egypt's defeat. The new king was aided by Prexaspes, his right-hand man, and a young and gifted courtier named Darius, son of Hystaspes the Achaemenid. At the age of twenty-two, Darius was proving himself to be a loyal and trustworthy companion, so much so, in fact, that Cambyses gave him the privileged position of *Arshtibara*, 'Spear-Bearer', one of the high offices at court.

In 526 BCE a Greek mercenary soldier named Phanes of Halicarnassus was brought into this inner circle with the sole purpose of relaying to the king information about Egypt and her fighting capabilities. Phanes, who had served the pharaoh Amasis for several years before falling out of royal favour, instructed Cambyses in the ways of the Egyptians, drawing attention to their effective military tactics and to their many weaknesses. Phanes recommended that Cambyses lead his army into Egypt from across the Sinai Desert. To do this he suggested the Great King cut a deal with the chiefs of Arabia and ask for safe passage for his troops to cross the desert, which was under the rule of Arab tribes. He also advised that Cambyses solicit the Arabs to supply the Persian troops with water and food on their journey. The Arabs gladly obliged, and for their services to the Persian crown thereafter they became allies of the Persians, but never their subjects.

The Twenty-Sixth Dynasty of Egypt, the so-called Saite dynasty (664–525 BCE), took its name from the city of Sais in the Nile Delta.

It had been established as the capital of Egypt during this remarkable period in Egypt's long and venerable history, an era which witnessed a cultural and artistic revival of the traditional pharaonic arts, a veritable renaissance of Egyptian culture. Sais' glory lay in its magnificent temples and sanctuaries. For here the goddess Neith and the god Ptah, two deities of deep antiquity, were worshipped with lavish rituals. Sais was the religious and political powerhouse of a dynasty which had blossomed under the careful rulership of Amasis II. The splendour of its sanctuaries was testament to the economic growth that Egypt enjoyed in this era, as commerce flourished and trading treaties and political pacts were made with wealthy Mediterranean rulers, such as the kings of Cyprus and of Samos.

After a long reign of some forty-four years, Amasis II died in 526 BCE. Taking advantage of the ritual mourning period and the preparation to settle Amasis' son, Psammetichus III, onto the throne, Cambyses ramped up his plans for an Egyptian campaign. He augmented his Persian troops with paid mercenary soldiers from Babylonia and Asia Minor and by commissioning the naval forces of Phoenicia and Caria to join his expedition. It was typical of the Persians to use this type of recruitment system; from the empire's inception to its final sharp demise, this was the method used by all Great Kings. Soldiers, cavalrymen, and sailors came from every part of the empire, bringing with them their diverse weapons and fighting styles. They joined the ranks of Cambyses' army under the command of Persian officials (although the highest command was not necessarily always given to a Persian, but to the best strategist available, regardless of ethnicity). The Old Persian word for 'army' or 'fighting force' was *kāra*. It had a more generic meaning of 'people'. In the word is the recognition that the divergent peoples of the empire who fought alongside the Persian-born soldiers formed the core of the army. Regardless of ethnic origin, the Persian soldiery was a unified whole.

In the spring of 525 BCE Cambyses' armada of ships rendezvoused at Akko on the Palestinian coast and made its way along the shore to the Nile delta, just as his army marched across the Sinai desert, aided by the Arabs. The land and sea forces met at the Egyptian frontier town of Pelusium, long thought of as the gateway to Egypt. It was here that the captain of the Egyptian ships, a very able man named Udjahorresnet – having no intention of blocking the Persian advance – surrendered the Egyptian fleet and defected to Cambyses. A short, bloody battle at Pelusium ended in victory for the Persians. The remnants of the Egyptian army fled south and took refuge in the city of Memphis, with its huge defensive white walls. Cambyses' forces followed in pursuit, his ships sailing down the Nile, since Memphis could only effectively be taken from the water. The city fell without much of a struggle but many Egyptians were butchered or taken as prisoners of war, including Psammetichus III who, although initially treated respectfully by his Persian captors, tried to rebel against Cambyses and was executed. Much of the portable wealth of Memphis was sent back to Persia to bolster the royal treasury, and some 6,000 Egyptians were deported to Susa to work as slaves, labourers, administrators, artists, and architects. Memphis itself became the headquarters of a Persian garrison and the administrative centre of the Persian occupation of Egypt. By the summer of 525 BCE, the whole of Egypt, from the Nile Delta to the cataracts at Aswan, had been brought under Persian rule. Even the chieftains of Libya, the Greeks of Cyrene, and the tribes of the Western Desert submitted to Cambyses and sent him their tribute.

*

Udjahorresnet, the turncoat who aided Cambyses in Egypt's submission, is a fascinating figure. He is known to us from a simple green basalt statue that seems incongruously out of place in the crazy baroque splendour of the Vatican Museum, where it is displayed. It is a masterpiece of Late Period Egyptian sculpture and is properly regarded as the most important historical document in the Pope's extensive Egyptian collection. Headless now, Udjahorresnet holds a *naos* (shrine) bearing the image of the Egyptian god Osiris in his hands. He has his official titles engraved into the folds of his bath-towel-style robe. These tell us that he was designated as chief physician, treasurer of the king of Lower Egypt, chief priest of the goddess Neith, and commander of the king's fleet – an impressive set of credentials, it must be confessed, covering as they do the bureaucratic, spiritual, medical, and military needs of the nation. An autobiographical text covers the rest of the statue. It tells how Udjahorresnet was the personal physician to the pharaoh Amasis and a minister to young Psammetichus III. He was also responsible for the royal navy and the safeguarding of Egypt's Mediterranean coastline. In succinct language, devoid of elaboration, the statue's inscription describes how,

> The Great King of all Foreign Lands, Cambyses, came to Egypt, bringing the foreigners of every foreign country with him. When he had taken possession of the entire country, they settled themselves down therein, and he was made great sovereign of Egypt and Great King of all Foreign Lands. His Majesty appointed me his Chief Physician and caused me to stay with him in my quality of Companion and Director of the Palace.

Udjahorresnet depicts Cambyses acting respectfully towards Egyptian tradition and in doing so he presents an image of the Persian occupation quite at odds with that in the Greek sources. The Egyptian official found Cambyses to be an admirable and ambitious ruler. Although he is silent on the matter, it is probable that Udjahorresnet abandoned his position in the court of young King Psammetichus early on and had defected to the Persians as soon as he recognised the inevitability of Cambyses' invasion. Udjahorresnet threw in his lot with Cambyses because he clearly saw that Egypt's future (and his own standing) would be in Persian hands. He was the first and most influential Egyptian to collaborate with the Persians in their bid for Egypt's throne. His role in conveying Egyptian military secrets, and his expertise in showing the Persians how to bypass obstacles to their invasion, brought him significant rewards.

How might we understand Udjahorresnet's actions? What compelled him to collaborate with the Persians? Much depends on how one chooses to define 'collaboration'. Primo Levi, author and Holocaust survivor, once wrote of a 'grey zone' in which collaboration operates, meaning that there are different degrees and varieties of collaboration. These might range from 'heart and soul' collaboration – a conviction and belief in the same ideologies and aims of the enemy, a meeting of minds, as it were – to complete submission. Submission recognises outright the political and military superiority of the enemy. Taking a forgiving viewpoint, it can be argued that Udjahorresnet wanted to protect Egypt and avert disaster. He might have regarded himself as a 'shield' collaborator. Thus, he retained a handle on Egyptian affairs for the 'greater good' of his country. Conversely, it is possible that he played a double-game, a kind of manipulative and tactical collaboration with Cambyses. Udjahorresnet offered the Persians the intelligence they needed and the support they desired, in return for advancement within the enemy government. In his autobiography, Uadjhorrosnet presents himself as a saviour. He shelters the Egyptians from the chaos of war, and claims that 'I have protected the inhabitants from the very large troubles which had come over the whole country and which had not yet existed before in this country, and I defended the meek against the powerful; I saved those who were afraid.'

For his services to the Persian crown, Cambyses loaded Udjahorresnet with accolades and gifts. The Egyptian was quick to stress his new-found favour with the foreign ruler: 'I was honoured by all my masters for all my life. They gave me golden ornaments and all kinds of useful things.' A close examination of his statue reveals Udjahorresnet to be wearing Persian-style golden bracelets, his proud reward for a conspicuously flamboyant life of collaboration. Udjahorresnet retained his position as Egyptian attaché to the Persian Great King for many years, and no doubt died a very wealthy man. Whether he was loved or loathed by his compatriots is impossible to say.

*

In August 525 BCE Cambyses was crowned as Egypt's pharaoh in a splendid ceremony held at Sais. There, in the temple of Neith, he received the *pschent*, the double crown of Egypt, a combination of the white crown of Upper Egypt (the *hedjet*) and the red crown of Lower Egypt (the *deshret*). The double crown demarcated him as the Lord of the Two Lands. As the living embodiment of the god Horus and the founder of a new dynasty, Cambyses was honoured with pharaonic-style names, drawn up for him by none other than Udjahorresnet. He was Meswty-Re, 'the Horus who unites the Two Lands, born of Re, Cambyses, may he live!' It is Udjahorresnet who provides the details of what Cambyses did next, never failing, though, to insert himself into the narrative:

> The king of Upper and Lower Egypt Cambyses came to Sais. His Majesty came to the temple of Neith in person. Like all kings before, he prostrated himself before Her Majesty, Neith. Like all good kings, he made a large sacrifice of all good things to great Neith, mother of the god, and to all great gods of Sais. His Majesty did this because I had informed His Majesty about the greatness of Her Majesty, the goddess, who is the mother of Re himself.

From thereon in, in his relief depictions, Cambyses had himself shown in Egyptian costume, proffering gifts and offerings to Egypt's many gods. Cambyses even went as far as to give himself a new – Egyptian – parentage. It was circulated throughout Egypt that although he was undoubtedly the son of Cyrus, Cambyses' mother was not the Median noblewoman Cassandane, but an Egyptian princess named Nitetis, the daughter of the pharaoh Apries, who had reigned before Amasis II, who was depicted now as a traitorous usurper. It seems that the majority of Egyptians were willing to buy into the story that Cambyses was Egypt's legitimate king and no conquering foreigner. Even Herodotus had to concede that 'the Egyptians regard Cambyses as their very own.'

It is clear to see how Cambyses, like his father Cyrus before him in Babylon, appealed to the local population through the use of pageantry, religious ceremonial, and ostentatious propaganda. Just like his father, Cambyses permitted the Egyptians freedom to worship, to trade and barter, and to work without hindrance or harassment. Egyptian legal and administrative documents attest to the fact that after the invasion of Egypt, life quickly got back to normal for the locals and that Persian rule did not significantly change the rhythms of daily life. There were some incidents of Persians plundering Egyptian religious sanctuaries, but Cambyses acted quickly to control and stop these and always recompensed for the damage done to the temples.

Pleased with the settlement of Egypt, Cambyses decided to campaign south, beyond Aswan, the city traditionally regarded as Egypt's border. He determined to push into Nubia – modern Ethiopia, or Kush as it was known to the Persians – a place long exploited by the colonising Egyptians for its rich reserves of gold (*nebu* in Egyptian). En route south he visited the temple of the ram-headed god Khnum on the fortified Nilotic island of Elephantine and recruited many Jewish and other Semitic settlers into the rank and file of his army. With these welcome reinforcements, Cambyses marched into Kush and quickly conquered the northern territories that ran along the border of Egypt, beyond the Nile's First Cataract. Then he headed even deeper into the territory, moving towards the Second Cataract and further still. There are indications to suggest that the Persians pushed very deep inland: several Roman authors posited that the locals still spoke of a place called the 'Storehouse of Cambyses' near the Third Cataract. While it is possible that Cambyses did reach this point on the Nile, it is very unlikely that he ever got as far south as Meroe, the fabled capital of the kingdom of Napata, and, according to Herodotus, 'the mother city of all Ethiopia'. Sadly, there is no evidence to support the Roman legend that Meroe was so named by Cambyses, in honour of a sister who bore that name.

Cambyses resided in Ethiopia long enough for the region to settle into the rhythms of Persian rule before returning to Memphis. In his absence, there had been several disturbances against the Persian occupation, but these had been efficiently quelled by the authorities, acting under the instructions of Udjahorresnet. Classical authors insisted that the period following his return from Ethiopia was the time when Cambyses' reign descended into an orgy of unbridled violence. The king, it was said, desecrated the corpse of an earlier pharaoh, stripping it of its mummification bandages and exposing its decayed flesh and organs to the light; he had mocked Egyptian gods, rituals, and sacred ceremonies, beaten priests, and ransacked temples. One story has him shoot a boy through the heart with an arrow as target practice, and another tells how he kicked his pregnant wife to death. Perhaps there are slivers of truth lurking somewhere in the background of these stories, but it is impossible to be sure. It would be wrong to think of Cambyses as anything less than an autocrat though. Maybe he had a tendency, when compared to his father, to overcompensate and edge towards fierceness. Certainly, in later Persian tradition he was remembered as an authoritarian. But much of the criticism was pure slander, as the story of the Apis Bull confirms.

Among numerous deities worshipped within the temples of Memphis, the creator god Ptah held the place of honour. It was believed that Ptah manifested himself in a living bovine form, a visible earthly manifestation of his presence that commanded uttermost religious and socio-political respect. This so-called Apis Bull was venerated as an avatar of Ptah, and upon its natural death the bull was assimilated into the god of the underworld, Osiris, as Apis-Osiris. A search then began to find a new Apis Bull: it was identified through particular markings on its flank. Once found, the new Apis Bull was installed in a fine paddock and given a harem of heifers with which to mate. Thereafter, until his death, the animal lived a life of luxury and was worshipped as Ptah incarnate. According to Herodotus, so crazed was Cambyses that he attacked, stabbed, and killed this most sacred of animals, causing widespread panic throughout Egypt.

Egyptian sources give a very different perspective. They demonstrate how Cambyses treated the Apis Bull with grave respect, as might be expected of a pharaoh. A limestone relief found at Saqqara reveals how Cambyses adopted the prerogatives of the ancient Egyptian kings during the preparations for the burial of an Apis Bull which died in the spring of 525 BCE, one year after the Persian conquest. In theory, only through the presence of the legitimate king could the burial of the Apis Bull be completed and we know that Cambyses himself was thus present during the burial in November of 524 BCE and at the installation of the next divine bull soon afterwards, very likely early in 523 BCE. It would appear that Cambyses behaved impeccably in honouring the ancient rites of Egypt, and in this regard he was guided by his father's style of rulership. There was no hint of upheaval among the Egyptians when early in 522 BCE, after three years in Egypt, Cambyses decided to return to Persia.

*

It was pragmatism that took Cambyses out of Egypt. Rumours of treason had been filtering back from Persia for some months and it is *possible* (but far from certain) that Cambyses commissioned his close companion Darius, the son of Hystaspes, to travel back to Persia to root out the truth from all the scaremongering. It seems that the king's younger brother, Bardiya, who had proved himself to be an able and effective governor in Central Asia, had returned to Persia, ostensibly to quell some minor insurrections which had arisen because of Cambyses' protracted absence. Bardiya had done a good job in restoring order in Persia and in reconfirming his family's hold on the dynastic heartlands. Indeed, it seems that Bardiya quickly accrued a popular following among the Persian *khāns* and from the populace at large too. They actively championed his right to be their king. And why not? Bardiya was an impressive man, fit for kingship. He was tall, handsome, and athletic – the only man in Persia, it was said, who could draw the huge Ethiopian bow. His physical prowess had earned him a suitable nickname: Tanyox-arkes, 'Strong-Body'. It is possible that Bardiya was championed by members of his family, including his sister, Atossa, who was married to Cambyses. She might have seen in her youngest brother a more worthy candidate for the Persian throne.

With reports of treason and usurpation running rife, Cambyses departed from Egypt at the head of the core of his army. They travelled up the so-called King's Highway which hugged the coast of the Levant. Meanwhile, on 11 March 522 BCE Bardiya ascended the throne and proclaimed himself king. By April, as cuneiform documents from Babylon prove, subjects in Mesopotamia were acknowledging his rule. The news must have quickly reached

Cambyses, who had arrived in Syria at around the same time. The empire held its breath. What would happen? An outbreak of civil war? Would the empire split? Would the gargantuan efforts of Cyrus prove to have been in vain?

Suddenly, the dangerous matter was resolved. While in Syria, one morning, mounting his horse in haste, keen to get home and quell his brother's ambitions, Cambyses accidentally stabbed himself in the thigh with a dagger which hung from his belt. The wound was deep, almost to the bone, but was expertly cared for by one of his Egyptian physicians. The king felt comfortable enough to ride on towards Persia. But a few days later, by the time Cambyses had arrived at Aleppo, the wound had turned gangrenous and loss of blood to his leg had turned his body tissue rancid; putrefaction quickly set in. Within a week, convulsed in fever and drowning in sweat, Cambyses II died.

*

He was never a hero to his people, but neither was he the madman conjured up by his detractors – especially Herodotus. Yet Cambyses had not only kept his father's empire together, he had significantly added to it with the conquest of wealthy, fertile Egypt. Had he not been caught between the two giants of Persian history, Cyrus the Great and Darius the Great, Cambyses might now be better remembered for playing a significant part in Persia's history. But as it is, at least his reputation has been saved thanks to the privileging of Egyptian sources which reveal him to have been a ruler of real worth.

5

The Truth and the Lie

Cambyses II died without heirs. For the first time in three decades of empire-building the Persians faced the conundrum of what should happen following the death of a childless king. The solution had already appeared in the form of the king's brother, Bardiya, who (if a little precociously) took up the reins of government as the only legitimate successor to Persia's throne. It was an uncontested move, and Babylonian documents prove that, as far as the Mesopotamians were concerned, Cambyses was succeeded peacefully and legitimately by Bardiya. Throughout the empire there was a general acquiescence to this pragmatic solution and Bardiya underwent the rituals of accession at Pasargadae. He took as a wife Cambyses' sister-widow, his own full sister, Atossa, as a mark of his inheritance. He then moved the court north to Ecbatana to spend the hot summer in the cool of the mountains.

Having successfully courted popular opinion thus far, Bardiya made his first foolish move when, in an attempt (no doubt) to stamp his authority over the Persian tribes, he began to confiscate the pastures, herds, and properties of the *khāns*. It was a bid to limit their power. This had been the policy unsuccessfully attempted by Astyages of Media some fifty years earlier and it had made him unpopular among the Median chieftains, who had bristled with discontent. The fallout for Bardiya was much more catastrophic.

The army which had accompanied Cambyses to Egypt now returned to Persia. But they were leaderless and entirely without commission, and therefore restless. With the soldiers came the war-hardened Persian nobility, whose bloodlust showed no sign of abating – after thirty years of warfare they were still twitching for more action. Their loyalty towards the crown was severely tested by Bardiya's humiliation of their ancestral privileges, and as a consequence they channelled their unified indignation towards him. Conspiring with one another they looked for ways to overthrow his rule and to champion a different *khān* as Persia's king.

The tribal structure of Persian society had lost none of its potency during the reigns of Cyrus and Cambyses, and the *khāns* were as powerful as they had ever been. Over many generations their families had intermarried and all shared common blood through grandchildren, nieces, nephews, and cousins. Even interfamilial marriages were seen as advantageous, especially the well-established uncle–niece unions which were common to all tribes. Such marriages were political affairs and bonded the tribes in a rich nexus of intermingled DNA. Having ascended to the supreme position of monarch, both Cyrus and Cambyses depended upon the support of tribes in south-western Persia, and in exchange for their loyalty the kings had rewarded them appropriately with marriage alliances for their offspring. These were lucrative matches which brought economic privileges, including the acquisition of estates and fiefdoms, to tribal chiefs. Bardiya himself had been a willing participant in this process when he took as wife Phaidymē, the daughter of the nobleman Otanes. This was the girl's second marriage into the royal house. She had already been married to Cambyses II in a union that had been arranged by Cyrus and Otanes, two old saddle buddies who saw nothing but good coming from the wedding of their offspring. Otanes was the most respected of all the *khāns* and took precedence over his peers. He wielded the most clout and had more influence on the ruling family than any other *khān*. He had served the house of Cyrus very well and very profitably. With Cambyses dead, Otanes saw to it that the widowed Phaidymē became consort to the new king, her former brother-in-law, so that the bond of allegiance that had been established between Otanes and Cyrus would remain active. In spite of this, as Bardiya began to diminish tribal authority, the *khāns* turned together in order to oust him. It was Otanes himself, the new king's father-in-law, who took the initiative to bring Bardiya down.

Otanes gathered around him six other likeminded nobles. All were intent on plotting to rid themselves of Bardiya. Among them were Intaphernes, an influential courtier and successful general, Hydarnes and his close friend Aspathines, and Megabyzus the Elder. Of special importance to the group was Gobryas, Cyrus' good friend and the long-standing governor of Babylon. He rode back to Persia at the news of Bardiya's accession in order to gauge the rapidly developing situation in the homeland. He brought with him into this inner circle of conspirators Darius, son of Hystaspes.

Darius was in his late twenties. He had shown himself to be an able soldier and a gifted courtier. He had been among the first of Cambyses' aides to know about Bardiya's rebellion and it is probable that of all Cambyses' court, it was Darius who knew more than anyone else about the details of Bardiya's usurpation and accession. Darius was also close to Gobryas. In fact, he was Gobryas' son-in-law, having married one of the old *khān*'s daughters, and now Gobryas was grandfather to Darius' three healthy sons. Darius' marriage to the daughter of Gobryas was not a love match though; it was the result of careful, economic negotiations between Gobryas and his peer, Hystaspes, Darius' father. Hystaspes took the union between the two tribes even closer when he gave one of his daughters, Radushdukya, to Gobryas as a wife, making him Darius' father-in-law and brother-in-law simultaneously.

At first Darius was not the most influential of the conspirators and he was certainly not the highest-ranking of the Gang of Seven. He was not even the leader of his own tribe – both his father, Hystaspes (who was at that point the governor of Parthia), and his grandfather, Arsames, were alive and headed the Achaemenid clan. It is certain, however, that the two of them had ceaselessly promoted and supported Darius' career at the side of both Cyrus (Darius had been his quiver-bearer) and Cambyses (Darius was the king's lance-bearer). So it cannot be claimed that Darius was a self-made man; he had benefited from the nepotistic ambitions of his family elders and, latterly, of Gobryas too. Together they had bestowed upon Darius an enviable sense of self-belief and an unlimited taste for personal ambition which, when combined with his personal charisma, must have been a spellbinding combination. It certainly made him into a natural leader, for people were undeniably drawn to him. Little wonder then that no sooner had he been brought into the Gang of Seven than he began to lead it. He would show himself to be a ruthless operator.

Together, the Seven set in motion a revolution that was to have a dramatic impact on the dynastic history of Persia. It was to be a turning point in world history too. In September 522 BCE the Gang of Seven and their tribal forces arrived at Ecbatana, expecting to find Bardiya there. However, the king, the entire court, and much of the army had begun to move south, towards Isfahan at the centre of Iran, en route to settle in warmer climes, but on 29 September, the troops of the Seven met and clashed with Bardiya's forces near a fortress named Sikayauvatish in Media. The Seven emerged victorious from the battle, although the king himself was not found on the field but was rumoured to be within the fortress itself. The Seven fought their way into Sikayauvatish and overwhelmed the few bodyguards who were assigned to look after the king, and they swiftly moved towards the royal apartments at the heart of the fortified complex. There they encountered Bagapates, the king's chief steward, eunuch, and keeper of the keys, who quickly sided with the (armed and winning) conspirators. Later, Ctesias of Cnidus recorded what happened: 'With Bagapates' assistance, the Seven entered the palace and found the king in bed with a Babylonian concubine. When the king saw them, he jumped up. And when he found none of his weapons, he smashed a golden chair to pieces and fought using one of its legs.' In spite of the heroics, Bardiya was quickly overwhelmed and blow upon blow rained down on him from the Seven. With the last son of Cyrus lying dead on the floor, all eyes turned in expectation towards Darius. One question hung in the air: who should be king now?

The Gang of Seven had come together for the sole purpose of eliminating Bardiya. A deep sense of solidarity existed between them. So it is impossible that the question of succession had never arisen. It had probably been settled already because, following Cambyses' death, it was Darius alone who had managed to hold and control certain contingents of the Persian and Median army that had fought in Egypt. From the word go, Darius had been planning a violent coup, and it was Darius who stood to inherit the throne.

In his *Persika*, Ctesias recorded a Persian memory of what transpired next: 'Of the Seven', he wrote, 'it was Darius who became king because – in accordance with what they had agreed with each other – his horse was the first to neigh when the sun rose.' This curious statement suggests that Darius' accession to the throne was confirmed, supernaturally, through the rituals of hippomancy, or divination through the behaviour of horses. The horse, after all, was thought by the Persians to possess remarkable magical abilities, and Persian priests believed that horses could see and communicate with the spirits of the ancestral dead. For these reasons, the animal came to play an important role in certain forms of religious ritual. Ctesias noted, however, that in Darius' case, some sort of 'scheme or trick' had been employed to fool the priests and the Seven into accepting his prominence. Herodotus observed too that Darius cheated his way to the throne by misusing the horse rituals. Purportedly, when the Seven assembled on horseback to watch the sun rise on the horizon and to listen out for the first horse to whinny, Darius' groom made Darius' stallion neigh by letting it sniff his hand which he had earlier used to rub the vulva of a mare in heat. The horse's neigh was accompanied by lightning and a thunderstorm. The other nobles were quickly swayed to agree that Darius was now king indeed and that he enjoyed nothing less than the mandate of heaven.

*

Darius' own account of these events is carved deep into a rock face, high on Bisitun Mountain. The cliff on which it is carved is situated at the foot of the Zagros range in the Kermanshah region of Iran, some sixty-five miles west of Hamadan on the ancient caravan route which ran to Babylon. Darius knew the precipitous rock as

Bagastana, meaning 'the place of the gods', for it was a holy site, replete with an elegant garden and a lagoon – still enjoyed by the numerous Iranian families who come to the site as tourists. Carved into the sheer face of the mountain, Darius' idiosyncratic version of the events which led him to the throne of Persia is placed more than 200 feet above ground. It was a determined measure to prevent vandals or dissenters from causing it damage. The inscription (all 1,200 lines) is written in three cuneiform languages – Old Persian, Akkadian, and Elamite – and was carved into the smoothed rock with chisels. It tells of Darius' many triumphs and consecrates his victories to the gods. The inscription is the very *ipsissima verba* of Darius, so much so that each section of the text starts the same way: 'Thus says Darius the king . . .'

Darius' Bisitun account of his accession was a masterful compilation of fake news. It was a rich melange of untruths, spin, and pure bravado. Darius the Great was antiquity's most confident, bold, and successful propagandist. Utterly cynical, he seems to have believed only in the self-justification of his own power and its preservation and if, as is often claimed, propaganda is indeed the art of persuasion, then Darius must be credited as being a master of the craft.

According to Darius' version of events, even before Cambyses had departed on his Egyptian campaign, he had become aware of his younger brother's ambition for the throne and he had Bardiya executed, although the prince's death was kept a secret. As Darius insisted: 'When Cambyses slew Bardiya, the people did not know that Bardiya was slain. Then Cambyses went to Egypt and the people became hostile, and the Lie multiplied in the land, even in Persia and Media, and in the other provinces.'

In Darius' understanding, 'The Lie' (Old Persian, *Drauga*) was directly connected with the notion of revolt against the established, legitimate power and was identified by him with rebelliousness and ungodliness. To be a Liar was to be a traitor and a heretic. *Drauga* was the opposite of *Arta* or 'Truth', a rich theological concept which meant order, justice, stability, and allegiance. To be Truthful was to be loyal to the crown and faithful to god. In the binary world of Persian theological thought, *Drauga* and *Arta* were polar opposites. The Lie was implicitly the opposite of the Truth and both the Truth and the Lie were interlocked in a nexus of cosmic power struggles. Both terms belonged equally to the political and the religious domains, which were inseparable in the Persian mind. In spite of the many falsehoods that permeate the Bisitun Inscription, Darius always presents himself as a man who does not lie and who has never lied. As he states, 'Ahuramazda brought me help, and all the other gods, all that there are, because I was not wicked, nor was I a liar.'

If Darius did not 'lie' as such, then he certainly championed the dissemination of an elaborate series of alternative facts. His inscription is littered with idiosyncrasies, discrepancies, and ambiguities at the most crucial points of the narrative. He insisted that while Cambyses was away from Persia, conquering Egypt, a certain man, a Magus (priest) named Gaumâta, raised a rebellion on the border between Elam and Persia and began to call himself Bardiya and to masquerade as the king's (dead) brother. Amazingly the wicked Gaumâta happened to be the dead prince's doppelgänger and was so adept at impersonating Bardiya that he easily assembled a following of devoted acolytes and supporters. Anybody who questioned his identity was quickly terminated. Very soon after, at the time of Cambyses' death, the pretender took the throne. In Darius' own words:

> There was no man, either Persian or Mede or of our own family, who took the kingdom from Gaumâta, the Magus. The people feared him exceedingly, for he slew many who had known the real Bardiya. This is the reason why he slew them: 'That they may not know that I am not Bardiya, the son of Cyrus.' There was none who dared to act against Gaumâta, the Magus, until I came. Then I prayed to Ahuramazda; Ahuramazda brought me help. On the tenth day of the month Bâgayâdish [29 September] I, with a few men, slew that Gaumâta, the Magus, and the chief men who were his followers. At the stronghold called Sikayauvatish, in the district called Nisaea in Media, I slew him; I dispossessed him of the kingdom.

According to Darius, it was Darius, and Darius alone, who emerged as champion. It was Darius who had the courage to crush the pretender Gaumâta, a wicked follower of the Lie who had terrorised the Persians and kept them servile. In working up his version of events, Darius deliberately suppressed naming the six noblemen conspirators who had worked alongside him, referencing them merely as 'a few men', thereby undermining the critical roles they had played in the coup d'état against the real Bardiya.

The whole of the Gaumâta story rings false. The clandestine murder of Bardiya by his brother Cambyses, unknown to anyone but Darius, was nothing but a contrivance, especially when set within the contradictory scenario that people *knew* of the pretender, but were too frightened to call him out. Darius' account of Gaumâta's elimination, given its enormity, was curiously brief and puzzlingly cursory. He kept the details of the event veiled in secrecy by emphasising his role as Persia's saviour. The identity of his adversary, however, was not open to scrutiny, a fact which can only mean one thing: there was no Gaumâta. The man Darius killed was Bardiya, son of Cyrus, brother of Cambyses, and Persia's legitimate king. All the time, the real traitor, the follower of the Lie, was Darius himself.

To counter the truth that Darius was a usurper and a murderer, further alternative facts were added to the Bisitun narrative. These came in the form of a genealogy in which Darius enthusiastically advanced his family's god-given right to rule. By doing this he restated his own legitimation as Persia's king:

> King Darius says: My father is Hystaspes; the father of Hystaspes was Arsames; the father of Arsames was Ariaramnes; the father of Ariaramnes was Teispes; the father of Teispes was Achaemenes. King Darius says: That is why we are called Achaemenids; from deep in the past, we have been noble; from deep in the past has our dynasty been royal. King Darius says: Eight of my dynasty were kings before me; I am the ninth. Nine in succession we have been kings.

Darius remains vague about the details of his claim to the throne. According to his genealogy, the only member of his family tree who was a Persian king was Teispes, whose name appears in Cyrus the Great's ancestry as the first king of Anshan. According to Darius, Teispes was the son of Achaemenes. Significantly, Cyrus had made no reference to Achaemenes in his own list of royal ancestors and it is clear that Darius was trying to forge bogus links between his own family and the line of Cyrus. Yet, given his emphasis on his direct descent from the rightful royal family, he neglected to name *any* of his royal ancestors. At best, it is *possible* that Darius might have been a member of an extended Achaemenid clan which shared some common blood with Cyrus' dynasty, but *if* this was indeed the case, then the connection between Darius' family and Cyrus' lineage was a very distant one and Darius' claim on the kingship was extremely spurious.

*

In his bid for power, Darius married all the available royal women of the line of Cyrus the Great and incorporated them into his harem. It already contained high-ranking women such as Gobryas' (unnamed) daughter, as well as Phaidymē, the daughter of Otanes, and Phratagoune, daughter of Artanes. New and important marriages were made with Atossa, Cyrus' daughter and the sister-wife to both Cambyses and Bardiya, together with her sister, Artystone (another of Cyrus' girls), and with Parmys, the young daughter of Bardiya (and therefore a granddaughter of Cyrus the Great). Each of these unions helped to secure Darius legitimisation as Persia's king. In marrying his predecessors' women, Darius avoided any potential difficulties that might occur if these women had married outside their clan and produced children who, as descendants of Cyrus, would have had a better claim to the throne than Darius himself. How the women of Cyrus' dynasty regarded Darius' usurpation of power, or even if they went willingly to his bed, is impossible to know, but it is hard to imagine that a woman like Atossa, whose political acumen was so well developed, could ever have bought into the whole Gaumâta story. As the sister-wife of Bardiya she must have known the real events that surrounded his murder. So why did she marry Darius? Out of fear? That is doubtful. It must have been apparent to Atossa and her female kin that their family's bloodline and their own potential fecundity made them key political agents in a world in which women were otherwise without direct power. By allying themselves with Darius the royal women could potentially wield some personal clout at court while keeping the blood of Cyrus and the Teispids of Anshan flowing. Their fecundity made them powerful; their wombs were dynastic bargaining chips.

If there were opponents prepared to challenge the factuality of Darius' ancestry or the process by which he overthrew the imposter 'Gaumâta', then they were quickly silenced when he played his trump card – religious fervour. 'By the grace of Ahuramazda I became king', he professed, 'Ahuramazda granted me the kingdom.' Darius' victories, he ceaselessly emphasised, were the result of his relationship with the greatest of the gods of Persia, for it was Ahuramazda who had chosen Darius to be king. With god on his side, Darius had the valour and the aptitude to cleanse Persia of the chaos of the Lie which under Cambyses and Bardiya had infested Persia like a plague and it was through the championship of Ahuramazda that the Achaemenids had now emerged as the legitimate ruling house.

One question awaits an answer. In addition to Bardiya, did Darius kill Cambyses II too? It has been postulated that, in Egypt, Cambyses was poisoned – perhaps by disgruntled priests or Egyptian nationalist zealots – but the poison worked slowly and the king suffered greatly but did not die. When word reached Persia of Cambyses' sickness, Bardiya took his chance to seize the throne and, on hearing the news, Cambyses in turn rushed back home. En route, in Syria, Cambyses was poisoned again. As has been noted, the official story told of how he cut his thigh with his knife, but it has been suggested that the dagger had been rubbed with a fatal poison, administered by no less a person than Darius, Cambyses' own spear-bearer. Of course, that can never be proved, but an intriguing line in the Bisitun inscription is a matter of puzzlement. Darius tells how Cambyses 'died his own death', a strange turn of phrase to say the least, and one that can be interpreted in several ways. It might suggest that Cambyses committed suicide ('at his own hand') or that he died a death befitting him ('in accordance with divine judgement'). It also reads as though Darius had something to hide. Perhaps Darius had even more to conceal than is traditionally thought – a double regicide would be a real accomplishment, even among the feuding Achaemenids. But *did* Darius kill Cambyses? The jury is out.

*

There is no rest for the wicked, and following his seizure of the throne, Darius was overwhelmed with troubles. The year 522 BCE was to be his *annus horribilis*, for his moment of triumph as Persia's new king was astonishingly brief. Before he had time to settle into the role, Darius was being challenged for the crown. When Bardiya was murdered, almost the whole empire broke out in an orgy of revolt against the assassin usurper Darius. The empire was embroiled in a vicious civil war and it took Darius over a year to suppress it effectively. The year of rebellions presented the greatest existential threat to Persian primacy since Cyrus' conquests a generation earlier. The fullest ancient account of these events is to be found in Darius' Bisitun Inscription, which gives a somewhat formulaic overview of no fewer than thirteen insurrections which occurred between 522 and 519 BCE.

Elam was the first region to rebel and to be brought to heel. It was followed by a longer, much drawn-out campaign against Nidintu-Bēl, a Bablyonian upstart who, on 3 October 522 BCE, proclaimed himself Nebuchadnezzar III, King of Babylon and King of Lands. Darius himself led the campaign against the Babylonian insurgents and on 13 December a battle took place on the banks of the River Tigris which necessitated the Persians to cross the river on inflated skins, leather boats, camels, and horses. Five days later Darius won a victory at the site of Zazana on the Euphrates River when part of the Babylonian army was thrown into the water and drowned. Nidintu-Bēl fled to Babylon but was soon captured. Then the Babylonians got their first taste of Darius' revenge and the mighty walls of Babylon dripped blood as the strong battlements were festooned with the grisly trophies of war – some forty-nine decapitated human heads, potent war trophies that confirmed the victory of King Darius. At the main city gate, the rebellious ringleader,

Nidintu-Bēl, naked, beaten, and bloodied, was positioned on top of a long, sharpened, wooden stake that entered his lower torso between the legs and passed directly through his rectum. Impaled this way, he suffered a protracted, agonising death that lasted for many days. Nidintu-Bēl's stake was set up high above ground in the most exposed place in Babylon, guaranteeing high visibility to the terrified audience of cowering Babylonians.

It was while Darius was engaged in a punitive expedition through Babylonia, which lasted for three months, that he received the disquieting news that rebellions were erupting all over the empire. 'While I was at Babylon', Darius recalled, 'the provinces became rebellious from me.' He ordered grand-scale manoeuvres on all fronts, often at great distances from each other, and he relied on loyal generals to carry out his orders. He sent commands to his satrap in Arachosia (in modern-day southern Afghanistan) to attack the troops sent there by a man named Vahyazdata, who had taken power in Persia by claiming to be, of all people, Bardiya. At the end of December 522 BCE, his lieutenant, Vaumisa, won a battle in Assyria over Armenian rebels, and, in early January 521 BCE, the Persian officer Vidarna – hastily dispatched from Babylon – achieved yet another victory in Media.

Darius left Babylon in mid-January 521, having decided to establish his headquarters in Media. Here his officers were meeting with major, and unrelenting, difficulties. A Median rebel named Fravartish had achieved considerable success there and was aggressively extending his power into Parthia-Hyrcania. It was Hystaspes, the father of Darius, who was sent to deal with this particular problem and he quickly conquered Fravartish's partisans in Parthia-Hyrcania while Darius himself faced the Median chief in person. He gained a victory on 8 May 521 BCE. Following this success, Darius set himself up at Ecbatana, where the rebellious Median king was brought before him. Darius recorded the gory events that followed:

> They captured that Fravartish and the soldiers who were with him and sent them to me. Then I cut off his nose, his two ears, his tongue and blinded one of his eyes. He was held in fetters

at my palace entrance; all the people saw him. I impaled him
at Ecbatana. And the men who were his foremost followers,
those I hanged at Ecbatana in the fortress.

For month upon month Darius coordinated military operations on several fronts. In Armenia rebellion dragged on into June
521 BCE, but in July the Sagartian rebellion was crushed and the
last few outbreaks of revolt in Parthia-Hyrcania were finally put
down. At the same time, Vahyazdata halted the uprising in Persia
too. Darius, who had made his way back to Persia, was not able to
relax his labours though, because in August 521 BCE a second revolt
erupted in Babylon, this time under the leadership of a pretender
named Arkha, who took the title of Nebuchadnezzar IV. Early in
September, Darius sent Hydarnes at the head of an army to Babylon
and by the end of November Arkha had been executed and the
uprising neutralised. Finally, in December an uprising led by Frada
of Margiana (in the valley of the Murghab River in Afghanistan)
was stopped by Darius' man Dadarsi, who brought it to a definitive
and violent end.

It was at this point that Darius ordered the inscription to
be carved on the mountain at Bisitun where he could proudly
declare: 'This is what I did by the favour of Ahuramazda in one
and the same year after I became king. These nine kings I took
prisoner within these battles.' The text of the Bisitun Inscription
was translated into numerous other languages and was quickly
disseminated throughout the empire, where it could be read or proclaimed as the definitive history of Darius' right to rule. Fragments
of the text have been discovered in Babylon and at Elephantine in
Egypt, where they were written on papyrus in Aramaic in a unique
'commemorative edition', produced one hundred years after the
original text.

To commemorate his victories, Darius commissioned artists
to carve a raised-relief on the smooth surface of the rock face
of Bisitun Mountain. The sculpture depicts Darius, dressed in a
Persian court robe and wearing a crenelated diadem on his head,
holding a bow in his left hand. His right hand is held up to the

Figure 4. The Bisitun Relief, a pictorial imagining of the victory of
Darius the Great.

level of his face with the palm outward in a gesture of reverence,
for Darius pays homage to the god Ahuramazda, who hovers above
him. The god raises his hand in a gesture of command, signalling
that Darius, his champion, has been given the divine authority to
rule. Darius' titulature is inscribed above his head: 'I am Darius
the Great King, King of Kings, King in Persia, King of Countries
[*dahydva*], son of Hystaspes, grandson of Arsames, an Achaemenid'.
In front of him, lassoed together by ropes strung around their
necks, their hands tied tightly behind their backs, eight humiliated
rebel leaders, whom Darius titled Liar-Kings, are depicted. Each is
dressed in 'national costume' and is identified by short inscriptions
which name them: 'This is Nidintu-Bêl, the Babylonian who lied';
'This is Fravartish the Mede who lied.' Each Liar-King is shown
on a smaller scale than Darius, whose body dominates the scene.
A special place was reserved for one of the Liar-Kings though, for,
lying on his back, his arms stretched in the air in desperate supplication, is the figure of 'Gaumâta', the invented 'usurper' concocted
by Darius, who shows him no mercy. He stands over him and places
his foot on Gaumâta's chest – the pose resonates victory.

In the two years between the killing of Bardiya and the erection
of the Bisitun inscription late in 520 BCE, Darius had subdued an
agitated empire, tottering on the verge of fragmentation. He had

fashioned it into an obedient, if chastised, entity. His great inscription put his subjects on notice: Darius tolerated no opposition. That is why, when in 519 BCE the king of the Central Asian Saka tribe, Skunkha, rebelled against Persia, Darius himself led an army which decimated the tribal forces. Skunkha was taken prisoner (he was probably executed shortly afterwards) and was replaced by a *khān* whom Darius considered more 'Persia-friendly'. After his victory Darius returned to Ecbatana and ordered his artists to include Skunkha on the relief as the last in line of the Liar-Kings, where his tall pointed hat, typical of some Saka peoples, made him clearly identifiable. The addition of Skunkha to the relief necessitated a rewriting of the narrative of the campaigns, however, and so new inscriptions were set up too. Darius ended the inscription with a flourish – a piece of sage advice to the Persian kings who would one day follow him:

> Whosoever helped my family, him I favoured; he who was hostile, him I destroyed. King Darius says: You who may be king hereafter, whosoever is a liar or a rebel, or is an enemy, punish him!

*

Having settled his empire and his own august place within it, Darius launched a campaign of expansion of his borders. He added north-west India to his realm (although the exact date and circumstances of this major acquisition are a blank). He consolidated Persia's most western frontiers in the Aegean Sea and across the Dardanelles at the Hellespont into Thrace, and he made an alliance with the royal family of Macedon. But all was not well in the western provinces. In 598 BCE, supported by Eretria and Athens, several cities in Ionia on the western coast of Asia Minor (as well as parts of Cyprus) rebelled against the Persian occupation. Ionian forces sacked Sardis, the great Persian stronghold, and set it aflame. Although the Persians quickly countered the attack. Nevertheless, it took them four years of intense fighting both on land and by sea to establish a sense of peace in the region. The final act of the uprising

– a punitive attack on Eretria and Athens – ended badly for the Persians at the Battle of Marathon in 490 BCE. However, Darius lost no territories during the whole protracted debacle – a testament to Persian staying-power.

The Battle of Marathon became an advantageous propaganda opportunity for the Athenians and it provided them with material enough to launch legends that would sustain them for centuries to come. In truth, for Darius the Ionian Revolt (as it has become known in Western eulogistic histories) was an inopportune and costly border skirmish on the peripheries of the Persian empire. The revolt's major effect was on the plans Darius had drawn up for an extensive campaign of conquest in wealthy, sophisticated India which had to be aborted in order to shift Persian military resources to the far west to put down the Greek insurgencies. If it had not been for the Ionian Revolt, much of the Indian subcontinent, with all of its riches, could have been turned into a lucrative Persian territory.

Egypt had been under Persian control since its conquest by Cambyses and it does not seem to have been heavily involved in the rebellions of 522–521 BCE when Darius had seized the throne. Nonetheless, Darius felt it important that the Egyptians recognise his kingship too. He invested heavily in the country and had his royal image and kingly titulature propagated extensively in the temples and holy sites of the land. Like Cambyses, Darius saw to the interment of an Apis Bull and was depicted on a large stone stele in the act of worshipping this mysterious bovine divinity. He went further than Cambyses though in spreading his image as a divine pharaoh too when, at Hibis in the Kharga Oasis in north-western Egypt, he built an elegant temple. He dedicated it to the Theban triad of Amun, the most important ancient Egyptian deity, Mut, the mother goddess, and Khonsu, the god of the moon, in their local manifestations as 'Lords of Hibis'. Today it still stands as the largest and best-preserved temple in the Kharga Oasis area, much admired for the colourful relief sculptures which adorn its walls, many of them showing Darius in pharaonic guise, performing Egyptian rituals. In one striking scene he is depicted suckling at the breast of the goddess Mut, ingesting her milk which bestowed upon him the legitimacy of Egyptian kingship. Darius also took an Egyptian regnal name: he was 'The Good God, Beloved of Amun-Re, Lord of Hibis, the Great God, Strong of Arm, Darius-Meri-Amun, Beloved of Amun, He who was caused to resemble Re.' Close to one of Darius' inscribed cartouches archaeologists discovered the name of the mastermind behind this PR triumph. It was none other than Udjahorresnet. Having loyally served one Persian king, he was happy to minister to his usurper. His autobiography makes it clear that after Cambyses' death he had trekked to Susa (his name was found on an alabaster storage jar unearthed there) and had been welcomed to Persia by Darius. The cunning old Egyptian recollected that:

> His Majesty the king of Upper and Lower Egypt Darius (may he live forever!) sent me back to Egypt, while His Majesty was in Elam, having become Great King of all foreign countries and great sovereign of Egypt, ordering me to restore the Houses of Life [temples] after they had been ruined. The foreigners carried me from country to country until we reached Egypt, as per the orders of the Lord of the Two Lands.

It may have been Udjahorresnet who oversaw the creation of a pair of over-life-size statues of Darius which were erected at the temple of Re in Heliopolis, today a suburb of Cairo. Sadly, only one of the pair survives. It was found at Susa, having been shipped there during the reign of Xerxes. The surviving statue conveys an important message because, although sculpted in a traditional Egyptian style, Darius is shown wearing Persian dress. The stylised folds of the garment are covered with incised inscriptions in Old Persian, Elamite, and Akkadian. They stress Persia's supremacy over conquered Egypt: 'This is the statue of stone, which Darius the king ordered to be made in Egypt, so that whoever sees it in time to come will know that the Persian man holds Egypt. I am Darius, Great King, King of Kings, King of Countries, King on this Great Earth, son of Hystaspes, an Achaemenid' (DSab). The base of the statue is carved with pharaonic emblems representing the unity of

Upper and Lower Egypt, and depictions of all the peoples of the empire who were subject to Persia. Reminiscent of the pictures of the throne-bearers on Darius' tomb, these stone carvings show the conquered peoples (identified in Egyptian hieroglyphs) lifting Darius aloft, high above their heads, in an attitude of joyful unity. Egyptian hieroglyphic inscriptions declare Darius to be *both* a pious warrior pharaoh *and* a foreign conqueror king:

> The Perfect God, acting with his own hands, who inspires fear in the heart of humanity, who commands prestige in the eyes of all who see him, he whose power has conquered each of the Two Lands and who acts in accordance with divine orders, son of Re who has placed him on his throne in order to complete what he has begun here below. He has ordered him to conquer each of the Two Lands and the goddess Neith has given him the bow she holds, to throw back all his enemies, so that he may be effective in repelling those who rebel against him. The King of Upper and Lower Egypt, Lord of the Two Lands, the Great King, King of Kings, Supreme Lord of the Earth in its Totality, Son of the God's Father, Hystaspes, an Achaemenid, who has appeared as king of Upper and Lower Egypt on the seat where Horus reigns over the living, like Re, at the head of the gods, eternally. Re says, 'I give you all life and strength, stability, health and joy. I give you all countries of the plain and all countries of the mountains, united under your sandals' (DSac).

The most obvious evidence for Persia's hold over Egypt, however, was manifest in the Egyptian landscape itself. Around 500 BCE Darius sliced through the earth and dug a canal to connect the Nile to the Red Sea. He thereby opened lucrative shipping and trade routes around the Arabian Gulf and on to India. To commemorate this mammoth undertaking, he erected four monumental stele on the banks of the canal, each inscribed in hieroglyphs and cuneiform, and each incorporating a mixture of Persian and Egyptian artistic motifs. The inscriptions gave no doubt as to Darius' supremacy over the world:

King Darius proclaims: I am a Persian; from Persia, I seized Egypt. I ordered this canal to be dug, from a river called Nile, which flows in Egypt, to the sea which goes to Persia. So, this canal was dug as I had ordered, and ships went from Egypt through this canal to Persia, as was my desire (DZc).

Less impressive was Darius' attempt to conquer the nomadic tribes of Scythia, who inhabited vast swathes of land stretching north of the Black Sea from Central Asia to Eastern Europe. These hardy warrior peoples, a fractious lot, regularly raided Persian territories and brought chaos to the lives of the sedentary peoples they attacked. Darius considered them to be acolytes of the Lie and spreaders of its seditious savagery. As the upholder of the Truth, he decided he would put them in their place and yoke them to his rule. In 515 BCE, Darius and his troops crossed the Bosphorus, bridged the River Danube, and marched headlong into southern Russia, destroying every Scythian camp and settlement they encountered. They burned crops and slaughtered livestock as they went, yet, ultimately, they failed to annex any territory. No matter how hard they tried, Darius' forces could not hold on to the land and the Scythians ran amok around them. When the vicious Russian winter set in, Darius called a halt to the campaign, turned around, and headed back to Persia. In later centuries, the fighting forces of Napoleon's *Grande Armée* and Hitler's Operation Barbarossa were to encounter the savagery and brutality of winter in the Ukraine. But Darius' men were perhaps the first invaders to experience its cruelty. Disillusioned, hungry, tired, and frostbitten to their bones, they dragged themselves home. Unsurprisingly, the Scythian campaign is not alluded to in any of Darius' inscriptions, and had not Herodotus mentioned it in his *Histories*, it would have passed from memory altogether since Darius had no compulsion to recall his failed crusade to bring Truth to the barbarian followers of the Lie.

*

Succeed or fail, it was important for Darius to project an image of himself as a warrior. Kings had to fight to maintain order and it was

Figure 5. The Great King, in his guise as a Persian 'hero', kills a mythical monster (part lion, part eagle, part scorpion) representing the chaos of '*drauga*' (the Lie). From a door jamb of the Hall of a Hundred Columns, Persepolis.

the ruler's obligation to uphold Truth and dispel the Lie. In purely visual terms, this ideology is expressed many times in wall reliefs which depict the king in the guise of a 'Persian Hero', a kind of 'everyman' figure, where he is seen slaughtering a lion or a hybrid monster which represents the essence of that chaos. The inscription on the façade of Darius' tomb confirms that his empire was won and maintained by military prowess: 'the spear of a Persian man has gone far', he states, 'it shall become known to you that a Persian man has delivered battle far indeed from Persia' (DNa). He goes on to emphasise that it was the strength of his body, alongside his natural acumen for warfare, which led to his success:

This is my ability, that my body is strong. As a fighter I am a good fighter. At once my intelligence stands in its place, whether I see a rebel or not. Both by intelligence and by command at that time I regard myself as superior to panic, when I see a rebel just as when I do not see one. I am furious in the strength of my revenge with both hands and both feet. As a horseman I am a good horseman. As a bowman I am a good bowman, both on foot and on horseback. As a spearman I am a good spearman, both on foot and on horseback (DNa).

Central to the ideology of the tomb inscription is Darius' brute force. Darius stresses that he is strong enough to endure the hardships of campaigning on horseback and on the march. His arms have the strength to draw the bow and wield the lance. These

talents, he emphasises, come *directly* from Ahuramazda: 'These are
the skills which Ahuramazda has bestowed upon me and I have
had the strength to bear them' (DNa). Near Eastern monarchs
frequently suggested that there was a special connection between
their weapons and the deities they served for, after all, it was the
gods who made powerful the royal weapons and who imbued the
royal body with strength enough to wield them. At Darius' insist-
ence, in his inscription Ahuramazda is portrayed as the god who
empowers the king with martial valour.

Darius' bow is clearly visible in the Bisitun relief. Its appearance
strengthens the notion that force had played a major role in the
victory of *Arta* over *Drauga*. It is the strength of Darius the warrior
king, which he ultimately derives from his god, that is eulogised
on the monument. Here the relief sculpture depicts a victorious
Darius. He stands in sharp contrast to the humiliated bodies of
his enemies paraded before him. The texts which accompany the
scene tell how each of the defeated rebels was pursued, captured,
and finally executed. Notable is the fact that Darius himself is
never represented (in text or image) being pursued or hounded
by the rebels himself. While the narrative account given at Bisitun
demonstrates that his grip on power was challenged and tested, he
is never shown weakened, let alone fleeing his enemies. Instead,
superman-like, Darius charges across his realm (or sends a proxy
to do so), quelling rebellion after rebellion, enacting his just and
premeditated revenge on the fleeing and captured traitors. Subsequently, in the relief, as the rebel leaders fall before Darius, they
offer him their necks. For it is they, not he, who are men of violence; it is they who are followers of the Lie. The moral ambiguity
of warfare and internal strife vanishes in the face of the legitimate
Great King of Persia. The enemy bodies are justifiably abused,
mutilated, and wiped out. The Great King holds them in chains
by their necks, steps on their bellies, and then orders their death.
The image advertised the fact that Darius was the undisputed
King of All Lands.

*

What kind of man was Darius the Persian? He was motivated by overwhelming ambition, that is clear. His drive was relentless and his efficiency was startling. Darius was a man who knew what he wanted. Much more can be learned of him from his own personal credo which he had carved into his tomb façade at Naqsh-i Rustam, close to Persepolis. He asks its readers to 'make known what kind of man you are', and goes to some length to articulate his own conception of self: 'I am not hot-tempered. When I feel anger rising, I keep that under control by my thinking power. I control firmly my impulses' (DNb). Darius liked to portray himself as a rational and considered monarch who never acted in haste or in panic. It was his sheer force of personality that guaranteed that his subjects received the benefits of his considered and learned judgements. An incident which occurred early in Darius' reign, however, casts serious doubt on the king's ability to act impartially and calmly. It demonstrates how Darius' desire for personal power sometimes took him to dark places. The case of Intaphernes acts as a litmus test of Darius' claim to be an upholder of *Arta*.

One of Persia's great *khāns*, Intaphernes was a man of spectacularly high standing. He had been one of the Gang of Seven in the revolt against Bardiya and he had supported Darius' accession to the throne when, in 521 BCE, he went as a general at the head of an army to eliminate one of the men who had usurped the throne of Babylon. Intaphernes was the second man in the empire, and Darius listed him first among those he called his 'followers'. In spite of this, shortly after his accession, Darius had Intaphernes executed. The charge was treason.

According to Herodotus, who was probably reiterating a well-known Persian account (possibly originating with the family of Intaphernes itself), Intaphernes had entered the royal palace at Susa wishing to enjoy a private audience with Darius. It had been agreed between the Seven that those who had engineered the coup d'état had free access to the king without being formally presented unless, it was stipulated, the king happened to be having sex with one of his wives or concubines at the time. Intaphernes thought it was acceptable for him to go to the king without being announced.

But the palace chamberlain and the eunuch messenger thought otherwise and refused him leave to pass into the domestic interior of the palace. They told him that the king was, at the time, in bed with one of his women. Intaphernes suspected them of lying, and in anger he drew his dagger and sliced off their noses and cut off their ears. He then attached the grisly trophies to his horse's bridle, which he tied around the necks of the mutilated retainers.

In this hideous state, the shellshocked servants presented themselves to Darius and rattled off the events that had occurred. Fearing that all six nobles had conspired in this act and that another coup was at hand, Darius sent for each of them. He carefully questioned them, individually, about their thoughts on Intaphernes. When he had ascertained, and was satisfied, that Intaphernes had acted without their knowledge and that a power struggle was not imminent, he had Intaphernes arrested. His children and all his male relatives were taken into custody too. Darius was convinced that Intaphernes had conspired with his family and that they intended to remove him from the throne and found a new dynasty. Shortly afterwards, they were all condemned to death. At this juncture, Herodotus tells a curious story: while they awaited execution, Intaphernes' wife began to loiter at the gate of the palace, weeping and lamenting loudly and generally making a nuisance of herself. Her persistent wailing, day after day, persuaded Darius to take pity on her and he sent a messenger to her to say, 'Woman, Darius the king grants that you may save one of your relatives from imprisonment; whichever one you decide to select.' She thought for a moment and replied, 'If the king is really granting me one life from all those who are imprisoned, I choose my brother.' Darius was surprised by this and sent his messenger back to her: 'Woman, the king wants to know: what was your reasoning in passing over your own husband and children to pick your brother to be the one who survives, since he is for sure more of a stranger to you than your children, and less beloved to you than your husband?' And she, without hesitation, answered the king's question. 'Majesty', she said, 'I may, god willing, have another husband and bear more children, even if I lose those I have now. But with my mother and father already dead, I will never have another brother. That is the reason for my answer.' Darius thought the woman had responded wisely, and was so moved by her words that he released not only the brother she had pleaded for, but her eldest son as well. He executed all the others. Intaphernes was shown no mercy.

The detailed account of Intaphernes' wife is moving and sympathetic, but the author offers no explanation as to why her husband was killed. Why, for instance, did Darius act so quickly to have Intaphernes arrested and executed? Could it be that Darius' royal authority was still tentative and that he was not yet totally sure of his power? His fellow regicides were obviously a potential danger. The story suggests that Intaphernes was flaunting his insubordination by violating rules of protocol. It is probable that Darius took this as an excuse to rid himself of a powerful *khān* who had come uncomfortably close to his throne. The Intaphernes affair puts an end to any pretence that Darius ruled as a *primus inter pares* and heralds the fact that Darius now started to reign as a real autocrat. Any initial privileges which the co-conspirators had enjoyed were quickly revoked by Darius; no longer were they exempt from the rules of court protocol. As for the law of the land, that now bowed to Darius too.

PART TWO

BEING PERSIAN

Part Two pauses the narrative history that we have been following and examines instead the workings of the Persian empire. It explores the people and the protocols of the royal court, the dynastic heart of the empire, and the thought-processes of the Persians themselves. With Darius securely on the throne, this is a good point to stop and take stock. Questions need to be asked: how did the Persians run an empire so huge and so ungainly? Where did the Great Kings live? How many wives could they have? Did they worship many gods? This is the right time to address these questions and to raise many more besides.

This is the moment, then, where we explore the 'hows' and the 'whys' of being Persian. This is the chance to get to know the systems of Achaemenid governance, palace-building, and a very curious Persian phenomenon indeed: royal nomadism. We shall follow the Great Kings as they traversed the realm in vast horse-drawn convoys of human life, setting up temporary camps and sleeping in tents the size of fortresses. We will examine the central role women played in the royal family and question how they fitted into the ideology of the dynasty, and, with some trepidation, we'll step into the political hothouse of the king's court. There we will participate in ceremonial acts of state, ranging from royal audiences and banquets to gambling and hunting – for everything was potentially a ceremony to the Persian king. We shall contemplate evidence for the lives of slaves and we will further expound on the significance of religion – the worship of the gods, and the function of priests – in the world of the Persians. We will take the opportunity to find out about the deities that the Great Kings worshipped so ardently and the cults they promoted so energetically. It is time to look at life in ancient Persia.

6

When Bureaucrats Ruled the World

How do you govern an empire the size of Darius' and ensure that power in the centre is properly deployed at the edges? You need clear laws and a solid bureaucracy. Moreover, administrators all over the empire need to be able to demonstrate that they have the authority of the ruler. Darius and the Achaemenid kings who succeeded him conceived of themselves as defenders and champions of law and justice. They had been invested with authority by the god Ahuramazda himself, and as Great Kings by the grace of the god they were put on the throne to ensure that justice prevailed throughout the empire. The Old Persian term for the divine commandment, as well as the royal one, is *dāta*. It is one of the keywords of the Achaemenid royal inscriptions; it means, to all intents and purposes, 'law'. This word became the hallmark of the Achaemenid civic order because *dāta* was nothing more than the requirement of loyalty (*Arta*) to the monarch. The term *dāta* was borrowed by countless non-Iranian languages across the empire: in Babylon, for instance, the king's law was known as *dātu sha sharri*, and in the Hebrew Bible the term *dāta* appears in the books of Esther, Daniel, and Ezra, confirming them to have been composed in the Persian period.

Darius was particularly interested in legal codes that had been formed across his empire in what he called 'the olden days'. Mesopotamia had a long and noble legacy of law-giving, stemming from the great Hammurabi of Babylon who around 1745 BCE codified a collection of 282 rules, established standards for commercial interactions, and set fines and punishments to meet the requirements of justice. Egypt too had established laws which had been in operation

for millennia and, indeed, the verso side of a papyrus document
known as the Egyptian Demotic Chronicle contains the copy of a
decree from King Darius written in 519 BCE:

> Darius made the chiefs of the whole earth obey him because
> of his greatness of heart. He wrote [to] his satrap in Egypt in
> Year 3, saying: Have them bring to me the scholars [. . .] They
> are to write the law of Egypt from olden days [. . .] The law
> [. . .] of the temples and the people, have them brought here . . .
> He wrote matters [. . .] in the manner [?] of the law of Egypt.
> They wrote a copy on papyrus in Assyrian [Aramaic] writing
> and in documentary [demotic] writing. It was completed
> before him. They wrote in his presence; nothing was left out.

*

The laws of the Achaemenid empire reflect continuity with the
ancient legal traditions of Mesopotamia and Egypt, while being
both creative and flexible enough to attend to changing circumstances and new apprehensions.

Darius and the Achaemenid kings were not above the law.
Rather, they were an integral part of it. They decided legal cases
mostly in accordance with local circumstances on a case-by-case
basis. The shrewd and diplomatic nature of their decisions, which
often featured rewards more than punishments, resulted in a reputation for virtuousness. Darius emphasised his role as a fair judge
in an inscription found on his tomb. Having the reputation for
impartiality obviously mattered to him:

> What is right, that is my desire. To the man following the
> Lie I am not friendly . . . The man who co-operates, for him,
> according to the co-operation, thus I care for him; who does
> harm, according to the harm done, thus I punish him. It is not
> my desire that a man should do harm; moreover that [is] not
> my desire: if he should do harm, he should not be punished.
> What a man says about another man, that does not convince
> me, until I have heard the statement of both. What a man

1: Darius the Great worships Ahuramazda in front of a fire altar. He is lifted up on a takht (throne bench), supported by representatives of the empire. Tomb of Darius I at Naqsh-i Rustam

2: Huge cruciform-shaped royal tombs carved into the rock face at Naqsh-i Rustam

3: The modest remains of Cyrus' magnificent garden-palace at Pasargadae

4: Sculpted stone flowers and plants depicted on the walls of Persepolis remind us of the Persian obsession for gardens and gardening.

5: The Cyrus Cylinder: antiquity's most egregious PR exercise

6: Glazed bricks adorn Babylon's Ishtar Gate, built by Nebuchadnezzar II. Dragons and bulls strut and snort and protect the sacred city.

7: The vast spectacle that is Persepolis easily ranks among the greatest ruins of antiquity.

8: Carved high into the rock face at Mount Bisitun are the inscription and relief which record Darius I's version of his accession to the throne. His account is a masterpiece of alternative facts.

9: Enormous human-headed winged bulls stand guard at Xerxes' magnificent Gate of All Nations at Persepolis.

achieves or brings according to his powers, by that I become satisfied, and it is very much my desire; and I am pleased and give generously to loyal men (DNb).

Among the peoples of the ancient world (with the exception of obdurate Greece), the Persian kings were characterised as fair and wise. Judicial administration was ultimately under the authority of the king, and texts document his supervisory role. Although the king rarely adjudicated individual cases, he did rely on judges and officials to do so in his name. Ordinary judges were appointed from among the Persian nobility (often for life) and it was their task to arbitrate on any cases that came before them and to legislate as required.

We are fortunate in having at our disposal large archives of law codes and the records of trials and other judicial cases. Many of these come from Mesopotamia, especially Babylonia, which had a very old, tried and tested system of recording legal testimonials and civic court cases. Through the minutiae of these cuneiform texts, written on wet clay and allowed to bake in the sun until hard, we have a good understanding of how the Great King's laws affected the Mesopotamian provinces of the Persian empire. A very fine example from Babylonia is a rich dossier of legal documents focusing on a rather shifty character named Gimillu. His case is worth pursuing.

Gimillu, son of Innin-shuma-ibni, lived in the city of Uruk in Babylonia. He was a thief and petty criminal, a conman, and a thug. He was also a surprisingly good entrepreneur. He had been stealing and cheating since his youth and even as an adolescent he had achieved notoriety with a criminal record for theft and fraud, all of which had been chronicled in neat cuneiform script on mud-brick tablets that were kept in the city's judicial archive. His youthful penchant was for sheep-stealing and light embezzlement. In spite of his police record, by the time he was in his thirties Gimillu had got himself a job in Uruk's great Eanna Temple, the most prestigious religious compound in the city. He had an official, if unique, position in the temple. It was a cosy middle-management role in which, ironically, he tracked down and arrested sheep- and cattle-rustlers and other temple thieves. The job required him to report directly to the royal authorities in Babylon. It just so happened that Gimillu entered the temple's bureaucracy at the moment when Cyrus the Great and the Persians had occupied Mesopotamia. Gimillu thus found himself communicating with the Persian elite and with Babylon's satrap, the Persian nobleman Gobryas.

Gimillu was in post at the temple for less than a year before he was on trial for embezzling cattle and other temple property. It transpired that Gimillu had demanded protection 'money' from a temple shepherd in the form of one sheep, forty bushels of barley, and six bushels of dates (enough to feed a large family for two months). In September 538 BCE he was tried before the high officials of Uruk, and so numerous were his misdemeanours that it took four scribes to keep up with writing the testimonia as witness after witness denounced him as a criminal. Gimillu acted for himself in court and the surviving records show him to be a real chancer. 'I took the ewe-lamb, yes', he admitted upon cross-examination, adding the caveat, 'but I left two sheep behind for the festival! I took *that* sheep, I confess, yes, but I left behind the goat.' The court found him guilty as charged and pronounced that restitution must be paid for every item stolen on the ratio of sixty animals for every one that he stole. All in all, the fine equated to 92 cows, 302 sheep, and 10 shekels of silver. Straightaway, Gimillu appealed to the Persian satrap in Babylon, claiming that the High Court in Uruk had acted unfairly. But Gobryas upheld the court's decision and Gimillu was forced to pay the fine. However, the satrap allowed Gimillu to retain his temple job. No doubt, Gimillu had flattered and bribed his way through the satrapal court and smarmed and kowtowed sufficiently for Gobryas to reinstate his temple position.

Back in post, Gimillu continued with his crimes and misde-meanours. Later, in the reign of Cambyses, he was promoted to the office of Chief Farmer, where he found all sorts of opportunities for further scams. One of his government contracts stipulated that, in this new role, he should receive 200 oxen which were requisitioned to work the irrigation machines on the temple's lands. Additionally, the same contract provided Gimillu with a thousand *kur* of seed barley which were to be used to feed the animals, as well as enough raw iron to make the water wheels and the cattle harnesses. With these commodities Gimillu was contracted to provide the temple with 10,000 *kur* of barley and 12,000 *kur* of dates each year. Come the first harvest, however, Gimillu had come nowhere near to producing his allotted measure but instead of admitting that he had failed to meet his contract, he audaciously demanded more support from the temple employers. Another 600 oxen were needed, he claimed, as well as 400 peasants to work the fields. It is clear from the court records that he was siphoning off agricultural profits for himself. Yet somehow, with the backing of officials of the Persian regime (who must have received heavy backhanders in order to turn a blind eye), Gimillu managed to remain in office for twenty years. He grew to be an enormously wealthy man, swindling and abusing the Eanna Temple as he did so.

Gimillu's ignoble career came to an end in 520 BCE, the second year of the reign of Darius I. The monarch was singularly obsessed with the enforcement of the law and no case was too small or too far away for his personal scrutiny. It was Gimillu's singular bad fortune to hit the peak of his corruption at the moment history's greatest royal bureaucrat took the throne. In one stroke, Gimillu lost his job, his livelihood, and his freedom (if not his life). In 520 BCE, he simply vanishes forever from the official records. That was the style of Darius' justice.

Gimillu's story is fascinating. He is one of the few people from antiquity for whom we have records created as the events happened. His story opens up a window into the here-and-now of the ancient Persian world as we follow snippets of ancient history on a moment-by-moment basis. After his fall, and once the dust had settled, the Eanna Temple undertook major administrative reforms in order to ensure that opportunities for larceny and embezzlement were severely curbed. Gimillu's court files – comprising over a hundred cuneiform tablets – were carefully archived and the temple authorities looked forward to a more honest future. Such major reforms as those undertaken by the Eanna Temple were, in fact, one small part of a more sweeping imperial intervention scheme instigated on the orders of Darius the Great, whose word was, indeed, law.

*

Persian courtiers needed to be bureaucrats. Darius' court was both the household of the extended royal family and the central organ of the entire state administration. The Achaemenids revelled in administrative red tape (a love affair they shared with their Assyrian and Elamite forebears).

At some point around 500 BCE, a group of administrators working at Persepolis found themselves in a bureaucratic tizzy. Their superior officer, Parnakka, the director of the Persepolis civil service, had come to realise that important account documents which he was expecting to read had not arrived on his desk. It had become known to the administrators that the courier who was responsible for bringing the clay tablets to the director's office had quit his job. Moreover, he had travelled north, perhaps to his family home, and was putting his old job behind him. Unfortunately, when he left, the important – perhaps sensitive – documents were still in his charge. There was panic – heads were certain to roll. The administrators tried to clear up the mess: one civil servant, a man named Shak-shah-banush, dictated a letter to a scribe, who dashed it down in Elamite cuneiform onto a wet clay tablet and sent it on to Mirinzana, in the next office. 'Tell your supervisor', it said (effectively passing the buck on to middle management), 'that a sealed document concerning the fact that the accountants are not delivering the accounts was sent forth to the director, Parnakka. The man who carried that tablet, that delivery man, fled and went off.' The memo was followed by an instruction:

> Seize that man! Send him forth to Media. In Media he will be interrogated [literally, 'his oil will have its squeezing']. Furthermore, when this has been done and you send forth a tablet

from yourself to Parnakka, then write on that tablet the name
of the man who was guilty of carrying the tablet away and send
it back. This is what Parnakka has ordered. Formerly the name
of that man was not written! (PFa 28)

The Persians were as susceptible to bureaucratic bungling as
any other society.

It is a wondrous thing that this level of detail survives in the
Persian archaeological record. In fact, from sites as wide apart as
Aswan in Egypt to Bactra in Afghanistan, surviving administrative
documents (in these cases written on clay, papyrus, wood, and strips
of bone) testify to the tight administrative grip the Achaemenid
kings had over their empire. Nothing was too trivial to be logged.
The number of nails needed to repair a wooden boat in Upper
Egypt or the fact that a plague of locusts meant that a mud-brick
wall could not be built in Bactria – each and every case was individually recorded, signed off, reported to the central administration
in Persia, and methodically filed away.

Discovered in the 1930s in the northern fortified walls of
Persepolis and in the Treasury building that sits at the centre
of the palace, some 30,000 tablets, whole and fragmentary, were
unearthed by archaeologists. Known by their place of discovery as
the Persepolis Fortification tablets (PFs) and the Persepolis Treasury tablets (PTs), these unique written documents are a snapshot
of daily life in and around Fārs and eastern Elam. Altogether, the
Persepolis texts record around 750 place names – cities, towns
and villages, provinces, and districts – between Susa in Elam and
Persepolis. Their focus was chiefly on distribution of foodstuffs,
the management of flocks, and the provisioning of workers and
travellers. The Fortification tablets were drafted between the thir-
teenth and the twenty-eighth regnal years of Darius I, i.e. from
509 to 494 BCE, while the Treasury tablets cover the thirtieth year
of the reign of Darius I to the seventh year of the reign of King
Artaxerxes I (i.e. 492–458 BCE). The Fortification tablets record the
transportation of various food and drink commodities from one
place to another, and also register the distribution of products to

the 'workers' (Old Persian, *kurtash*) and to state officials, as well as fodder for livestock and poultry. The Treasury tablets record the issue of silver and foodstuffs to workmen of the royal economy in Persepolis and its suburbs. These magnificent collections of administrative tablets from Persepolis made up merely a tiny percentage of Achaemenid documentation which, sadly, has not survived to the present day.

During Darius' reign, one courtier in particular stands head and shoulders above all others in respect of his role in the Achaemenid administration. We have met him already. His name was Parnakka. He was known, grandly, as a 'son of the royal house', that is to say, he was an Achaemenid prince, very probably an uncle to King Darius. He was the director of the civil service and the chief overseer of the entire Persepolis administrative system as well as of Fārs province more generally. He seems to have had free and open access to the king and was therefore a man of great authority. He is frequently cited in the Persepolis tablets receiving his orders directly from Darius. It was Parnakka's duty to oversee the distribution of foodstuffs and other goods from the royal storerooms, and it was he who conveyed the king's orders in writing.

Working under Parnakka was a man named Zishshawish who was also responsible for recording and issuing rations. He sometimes deputised for Parnakka, but he was usually seen working alongside the royal prince as his chief aide. Between them, Parnakka and Zishshawish supervised numerous storeroom managers and rations operatives, as well as a whole range of officers in charge of provisions. These men looked after the departments of wine, beer, fruit, grain, livestock, poultry, and numerous other food and drink supplies. Parnakka and Zishshawish worked alongside the head scribe and his vast workforce of secretaries and translators; basic to the Persian administrative system was a highly trained civil service composed of men recruited on the principle of merit. The head of royal messengers and his army of staff, together with the chief treasurer, reported directly to Parnakka. Scribes and secretaries drew up the many records on which the bureaucracy depended and which were omnipresent in the administrative system. A typical administrative tablet which passed through the hands of administrative staff reads like this:

> 130 litres of barley from the possessions of Amavarta have been received by Barîk-El as his rations. Given in the town of Ithema, in the twenty-first year of Darius in the month Shibar [November/December 501 BCE] (PF 798).

In other words, in this case, a ration of barley, received by Barîk-El (a Phoenician name incidentally), was provided to him as a payment in kind for a service (we are not told what) he had undertaken for Darius. A Persian civil servant named Amavarta had issued that ration from the stock of barley that was under his administration. Finally, the location of the transaction – the town of Ithema – and the date of the transaction were recorded. There are thousands of texts which follow this pattern, although some tablets contain information about the issue of passports, orders for payments of precious metals to the chief treasurer, as well as the contracting and dispatching of judges, accountants, caravans, and teams of country labourers around the empire.

To make the processing of documentation more straightforward, every bureaucrat possessed his own cylinder seal, usually made of semi-precious stones. It was a visible emblem of office that could be carried and shown to everyone. It acted like a warrant, or a sheriff's badge, giving officers of the empire the stamp of power. The seal would be applied to all official documents, pressed into a wet clay tablet to leave its imprint as a kind of 'signature'. A seal, or rather its impression, conveyed the authority of its owners and the seal imprints could sanction action and expenditure. While a seal remained with the owner, clay tablets imprinted with the seals of civil servants and officers of state could travel far and wide. It is possible to locate tablets created in Persepolis in far-off Kandahar, Sardis, Bactra, Damascus, and many other distant clerical centres. Every seal was inscribed with a bespoke image and each image was unique to one owner, which makes it possible to trace an individual's 'signature' throughout the whole archive of documents, and to pinpoint his role in the administration.

Figure 6.
Seal impression of
Parnakka.

Figure 7.
Seal impression of
Zishshawish.

Figure 8.
Second seal impression
of Parnakka.

Figure 9.
Second seal impression of
Zishshawish.

As director of the civil service, Parnakka owned a very fine seal indeed. It was an antique Assyrian-made piece depicting a warrior grasping a somewhat confused ostrich by the neck and brandishing a sword. Zishshawish too had a smart seal design. It showed a winged cow suckling her calf, enjoying the protection of a four-winged daemon. Whenever civil servants saw the ostrich or the cow figures imprinted into a clay tablet, they recognised the owners of the seals immediately, and jumped to action. Like house or car keys, cylinder seals were apt to get lost and needed to be replaced. When Parnakka mislaid his ostrich-design seal he had it replaced with one showing a warrior throttling two lions, and quickly issued a memo to his team stating that 'The seal that used to be mine is now lost. As a substitute, I now use the seal that can be seen in this letter' (PF 2067 and 2068). As a matter of security, Zishshawish was therefore forced to abandon his regular seal and to use a new design too. Fortuitously his loyalty to the crown was rewarded when King Darius gifted Zishshawish a brand-new seal representing the king himself standing in a date grove in front of a fire altar in the presence of Ahuramazda.

The central administration of the Persian empire did not operate out of Persepolis, however. The administrative heart of the Great Kings' realm was located at Susa. A man-made canal connected this great Elamite site to the Persian Gulf and the River Tigris, and roads to Ecbatana, Babylon, and Persepolis radiated out from the city's bureaucratic offices. Orders emanated from Susa to all provinces of the empire and reports from far and wide came back to the civil servants who manned the offices there. Susa was a hotbed of officialdom: it was there that high-ranking satraps rubbed shoulders with courtiers, and low-paid civil servants got glimpses of foreign diplomats on ambassadorial embassies. All life converged at Susa for the purpose of imperial business and the major chancelleries of state were bursting with civil servants, and scribes engaged in writing, sealing, posting, and archiving thousands upon thousands of administrative clay tablets and other documents. Susa was the hub of the empire's bureaucracy, but similar, smaller offices were to be found at Persepolis, Ecbatana, Babylon, Memphis, Bactra, Sardis, and all the other important urban centres of the realm. Red tape encircled the Persian world.

*

The higher administration of the Achaemenid empire was in the hands of a group of men drawn exclusively from the noblest echelons of the Persian aristocracy, very often from within the royal family itself. These men were known as satraps (Old Persian, *xshaçapāvan*, meaning 'Protector of the Province' or 'Guardian of the Kingdom'), a title which had existed under the Medes but was given a more imperial flavour by Darius. The satraps enjoyed the privilege of being the Great King's representatives within the empire at large, and they were responsible for the collection of taxes and tribute, for raising armed forces when occasion required, and for the administration of local justice. At a regional level, satraps were also required to make all governmental decisions. Nevertheless, for matters of international importance, satraps were compelled to consult the king and his chief ministers. As a representative of the king, satraps were obliged to keep court and maintain ceremonials based on that of the royal court at the heart of the empire. They represented the king by proxy, imitated his behaviour, and emulated his taste.

Being a satrap was a hazardous business, for he was dependent on the king's good favour. He had to temper his behaviour carefully. The satrapal provincial courts were carefully scrutinised by the central authorities for any signs of self-aggrandisement or hints of potential treason. The survival of letters sent between the satrap Arshama in Egypt and the Great King in Persia at the beginning of the fourth century BCE demonstrates that even when absent from the imperial centre, nobles in the service of the king kept up a steady dialogue with the central authority in Iran and had to justify every decision which they took while acting as the Great King's representative.

Under Darius I the imperial satrapies numbered around thirty-six. That figure was in a constant state of flux, dependent upon military expansion and administrative reforms. The province of Babylonia provides a good example of the shifts which might occur in satrapal structures. In 535 BCE Cyrus the Great had created a vast single satrapy out of the whole of Mesopotamia and the lands that made up the former Neo-Babylonian empire – Judah, Israel, Phoenicia, and Syria. But by March 520 BCE Darius had divided the satrapy into two parts, each a more governable size. They were known as Mesopotamia and Beyond-the-River (Akkadian, *Eber-Nāri*). The latter comprised the countries of the Levant which had formerly been the territories of the Neo-Babylonian empire before its fall to Cyrus the Great. In 516 BCE Beyond-the-River was further subdivided into three administrative territories: Phoenicia, Judah and Samaria, and the Arabian tribes. The Phoenician cities of Tyre, Sidon, Byblos, and Aradus were vassal states ruled by hereditary local kings who struck their own silver coins and whose power was limited by the Persian satrap. Judah and Samaria enjoyed considerable internal autonomy and its governors included Sheshbazzar and Zerubbabel under Cyrus and Darius I and the biblical Nehemiah under King Artaxerxes I. From the second half of the fifth century BCE, the province of Samaria was governed by a Samaritan leader named Sanballat and his descendants, while the Arabian tribes who inhabited the area between Egypt and the Euphrates were ruled by their chieftains. Under Darius, Asia Minor was split into four satrapies, but, some twenty years later, by Xerxes' reign, it was divided into seven provinces. Darius also broke up the vast satrapy of Media and carved out of it the new province of Armenia and, in due course, Xerxes divided Armenia itself into halves, each run by separate satraps. Finally, under Xerxes' reforms, Hycarnia was separated from Parthia and Gandara was split from Bactria.

Each satrapy covered an extensive area and was ruled from a capital (which also acted as an administrative centre) where the satrap had a palace. Egypt's satrapal capital was the city of Memphis; in Syria it was Damascus; and in Ionia it was Sardis. These regional capitals were used to store taxes which were paid in both coin and kind, the latter including foodstuffs used to maintain the vast satrapal court and its dependants. Taxation payments in precious goods and metals were widely employed too. The satraps' palaces were also hubs of provincial administration. Here royal orders were received from the central authority in Persia. Royal decrees, identifiable by the king's seal, have been found as far afield as Nippur in Babylonia, Samaria in Syria, Artashat in Armenia, and at Elephantine in Upper Egypt, although the biggest hoard of royal seals was discovered at Daskyleion in northern Anatolia. The north-westernmost Achaemenian provincial capital, Daskyleion, was probably the seat of the enigmatic satrapy called in Darius the Great's Bisitun inscription *tyaiy drayahya*, or 'those Scythians who are beside the sea'. Its prominence during the Achaemenid era was determined not only by the geographical position it held (it dominated the strategically and commercially important region of Hellespontine Phrygia) but also by the fact that most of the satraps of the province were senior members of the imperial family.

The Persian satrapal system depended very much on cooperation with local power-holders, and the satraps frequently repurposed existing, well-established, regional practices in their governance. The satraps also relied on a healthy interaction with local elites, and the kings and princes who had traditionally held lands before the Persian occupation were carefully coerced into cooperating with their conquerors by becoming governors. The Persians worked hard to maintain good relations with indigenous nobility. In part, marriages between Persians and locals helped bring about a sense of shared belonging, and although we have very little information about the wives of satraps (let alone those of lesser-ranking Persian commanders and officials), there certainly were marriages between Persians and local women and between local elites and Persian women. These alliances gave the local elites a foothold in the Persian honour system. In addition, satraps took local subject women as concubines. Pharnabazus, satrap of Phrygia, for instance, kept a palace full of concubines at Sardis. These women afforded important links between the satrap and local families, and good politicians recognised that concubines could have an unofficial political influence, since they had the intimate ear of the satrap.

Persians often employed individuals who were familiar with localised government to work with or for them – the Egyptian nobleman Udjahorresnet, as has been seen, is a case in point. The satrap Pharnabazus made particularly effective use of the local rulers of Dardanus, an ancient city in the Troad on the Biga Peninsula in the north-western part of Anatolia, and his story proves that an effective working relationship between the Persian rulers and the subjected elites could be fruitful. When Zenis, the loyal, long-serving, pro-Persian client king of Dardanus, died, Pharnabazus planned to bestow the governance of the area on someone beyond Zenis' bloodline; there were many good candidates. But Zenis' wife, Mania, petitioned Pharnabazus to bestow the province on her since, she argued, she had assisted her husband in all his work and knew the job better than anyone else. The satrap took the unusual step of appointing the widowed Mania to the post and thereby kept the power within Zenis' family. Pharnabazus was delighted to find that Mania paid the tribute into the satrapal treasury just as regularly as her husband had done. The advantage of employing local elites to defend Persian interests was clear. Other hereditary rulers, such as the Dorian kings of Cos, the kings and princes of Cilicia, Paphlagonia, Tyre, Sidon, and Byblos, and the Carian rulers of Halicarnassus in Asia Minor, found that working alongside the Persians was more profitable than antagonising them. Interestingly, Cyprus was never held by a satrap. Instead, the local rulers of the island's city states governed themselves and reported directly to the Great King.

It was an important obligation of the satraps to send the best produce of their provinces to the Great King. In taking possession of these gifts the Persian monarch reconfirmed his domination over the empire. Perhaps the most symbolic of all these gifts given to – or demanded by – the king was that of earth and water. The formal offering of the two elements (probably presented to the monarch in physical form – a silver jar of water and a golden dish of earth, for instance) represented a country's unconditional surrender to Persia. It placed the Achaemenid king in the role of life-giver to his new subjects because he was considered to hold exclusive control over the natural forces that sustained life. That the king himself always travelled with his own drinking water which had been sourced from a Persian river is a reflection of the same process. The water of the Choaspes River near Susa linked the king with his homeland no matter where he might be in the empire. The offering or partaking of certain foods and drinks too became another emblematic expression of imperial ideology. Xerxes particularly enjoyed eating the 'first-fruits' that were sent to him from every district of the empire, but did not think it right for kings to eat or drink anything which came from beyond the borders of the empire. When a eunuch brought him, among the rest of the dessert dishes, some Athenian dried figs, the king asked where they came from. When he heard the answer, he immediately had the fruit taken away. Herodotus claimed that the eunuch did this on purpose, to goad Xerxes about his failed expedition against Attica.

*

It was under the Achaemenid rulers that the world experienced its first use of coinage. It began in Lydia on the west coast of Asia Minor around 650 BCE, and thereafter the western satrapies were always associated with minted coins. The first examples were made from an alloy of gold and silver called electrum, but at Sardis King Croesus introduced a coinage in gold and silver, called 'croeseids' after him. After Cyrus had conquered Lydia, the Persian administration continued to mint gold and silver coins like those Croesus had made at Sardis. Under Darius the first truly Persian coins were struck, sometime around 515 BCE. They were minted in gold and were named 'darics' (not necessarily after the king), and in silver, named 'sigloi'. Coins in both metals bore the image of a generic Great King, recognisable by his crown, his court robe, and his bow and spear.

Figure 10. Gold daric showing an image of a Great King armed with a bow and arrow and a spear, 460 BCE.

Like the earlier gold and silver croeseids, these coins were minted exclusively at Sardis. Later, mints were established in other cities of Asia Minor, with some, such as the mint at Tarsus, becoming important distribution centres. Persian coinage circulated predominantly in the western satrapies and had little impact in the Persian heartlands or the eastern empire, but studies of western coinage types show a high degree of independence among the communities who minted them. Since coins were issued in several different satrapies (and semi-independent communities such as the city states of Cyprus), they provide a varied picture of what levels of freedom some satraps or governors enjoyed. The satrap Pharnabazus, for instance, who operated in north-western Asia Minor, minted coins with his name on them. They appear to have been struck at Cyzicus, located on the southern coast of the Sea of Marmara (the coins bear the symbol of a tunny fish, the signifier of Cyzicus). The coins do not depict a Great King at all but bear a portrait of Pharnabazus himself, one of the first instances of the portrayal of a living individual in the position on a coin that was normally reserved for the depiction of a monarch or a divinity.

*

The smooth running of the Persian empire was facilitated by an excellent infrastructure, the most sophisticated of any ancient civilisation. First-rate roads connected the main satrapal centres of the empire with the imperial core, thereby allowing Darius a way to maintain control over his conquered provinces. The most important of these highways was the Royal Road, which ran for a staggering 2,400 kilometres. A major branch connected Susa to the cities of Kirkuk, Nineveh, Edessa, Hattusa, and Sardis in Lydia, which was a journey of ninety days on foot; it took ninety-three days to reach the Mediterranean coast at Ephesus. Another road from Susa, the eastern branch, was connected to Persepolis and Ecbatana and thence went onwards to Bactra and Pashwar. Yet another branch of this road steered west and crossed the foothills of the Zagros mountains, went east of the Tigris and Euphrates rivers, through Cilicia and Cappadocia and ended at Sardis, while an alternative route led into Phrygia. One more highway connected Persepolis to Egypt via Damascus and Jerusalem. The roads were all designed to interconnect with rivers, canals, and trails, as well as ports and anchorages for sea travel. Together they made the Persian transportation system the wonder of the age.

Most of the roads were unpaved, although traces of cobblestones placed on top of a low embankment have been unearthed at Gordion and Sardis in Asia Minor, suggesting that as the roads reached the outskirts of cities they were demarcated more clearly. The roads at Gordion and Sardis date to Darius' reign and were constructed some 5–7 metres in width and, in places, were faced with an elegant kerbing of dressed stone. At Gordion, the road was 6.25 metres wide, with a packed gravel surface and kerbstones and a ridge down the middle dividing it into two lanes. Archaeologists have also uncovered a rock-cut road segment at Madakeh in southwest Iran, which was part of the Persepolis-to-Susa road; it has a width of five metres. The roads were measured in six-kilometre intervals known as *parasangs*, and road stations were set up around every twenty-eight kilometres of the route to accommodate weary travellers.

Similarly to the great medieval caravanserais of the Silk Road, the Persian way stations were composed of rectangular mud-brick and stone buildings with multiple rooms around a large courtyard affording accommodation for humans and pack animals alike. It is estimated that around 112 way stations existed on the main branch between Susa and Sardis alone, but there were many hundreds more set up on alternative roads. When the Greek soldier-philosopher Xenophon passed through the satrapy of Babylonia around 401 BCE, he stayed in a number of way stations. He called them *hippon*, 'of horses' in Greek, which suggests that the buildings also included stable blocks. A large way station comprised a five-room stone building, and a courtyard has been excavated near the site of Kuh-e Qale, close to the main Persepolis–Susa road. It is known to have been a major artery for royal traffic and is a fine example of 'high-end' accommodation. With its finely worked columns and porticoes, it is far more luxurious than the average travellers' inns.

Expensive luxury goods such as fine glass and imported stone have been found at Kuh-e Qale, leading archaeologists to the conclusion that this particular way station was for the use of the super-rich. More modest way stations have been found near Germabad and Madakeh on the Persepolis–Susa road, and others have been located near Pasargadae and between Susa and Ecbatana. These smaller way stations were also the offices of road maintenance crews, the gangs of workmen known as 'road counters' who ensured that the roads were well-kept. Besides keeping the roads clean of vegetation and debris, one of their more unusual tasks was to make certain that the roads were clear of scorpions and snakes.

A fast and efficient postal relay system called in Old Persian *pirradazish* ('express runner') connected the major cities of the empire. It was the Persian Version of today's high-speed broadband and was very efficient. Fast communication was the order of the day as the Persian bureaucracy demanded an efficacious and reliable communications channel. The result was that the Persians created the earliest form of the Pony Express. Herodotus was its biggest fan:

> There is nothing mortal that is faster than the system that the Persians have devised for sending messages. Apparently, they have horses and men posted at intervals along the route, the same number in total as the overall length in days of the journey, with a fresh horse and rider for every day of travel. Whatever the conditions—it may be snowing, raining, blazing hot, or dark—they never fail to complete their assigned journey in the fastest possible time. The first man passes his instructions on to the second, the second to the third, and so on.

When compared to the somewhat sluggish speed of communication in the later Roman empire, whose provinces were largely interconnected by the Mediterranean Sea, the level of fast and efficient connectivity in the Achaemenid empire is noteworthy. No society came close to matching its competence until the modern age.

Useful information about the Royal Road system comes from the Persepolis Fortification tablets, which record the disbursement of travellers' rations or provisions along the way, describing both

their destinations and points of origin. The 'travel ration' texts attest
to the systematic criss-crossing of vast swathes of the empire by
men and women on state business (delivering messages, money, or
goods) or conducting private affairs (honouring work contracts or
attending religious ceremonies). The texts record the food rations
which individuals received on their journeys. Three tablets confirm
that individuals undertook journeys of enormous breadth – from
India to Susa, Sardis to Persepolis and, strikingly, from Susa to
Kandahar in Afghanistan:

> 11 BAN of flour Abbatema received. He carried a sealed docu-
> ment of the king and went forth from India. He went to Susa.
> 2nd month, 23rd year of Darius' reign (PF 1318).

> 4.65 BAN of flour Dauma received and went forth from Sardis.
> He went to Persepolis. 9th month. 27th year of Darius' reign
> (PF 1404).

> A woman went from Susa to Kandahar. She carried a sealed
> document of the king, and she received it. Zishandush is her
> trained guide. 22nd year. 2nd month of Darius' reign (PF 1550).

One document from Susa, written on the orders of Arshama,
the satrap of Egypt, shows the latter issuing passports and ration
books for a travelling party of his servants, including his household
steward, an Egyptian named Nakhtor. They were travelling from
Babylonia and were heading home to Egypt. The text reads:

> This is to introduce my official, Nakhtor by name. He is on his
> way to Egypt. You are to issue him daily provisions from my
> estates in your respective provinces as follows:

> White flour – 2 cups

> Fine flour – 3 cups

> Wine or beer – 2 cups [. . .]

> For his retinue (10 men in total), for each one daily:

> Flour – 1 cup, plus sufficient fodder for his horses.

> You are to issue too provisions for two Cilicians and one

artisan (three in all), my servants who are accompanying him to Egypt:

Flour – 1 cup daily per man.

Issue these provisions, each official in turn, along the route from province to province, until he arrives in Egypt. If he stops at any place for more than one day, do not give him extra provisions for the additional days.

All roads were guarded and policed. They were kept safe for private individual travel by highway patrols stationed at regular points on all thoroughfares. Traffic police had the right to stop and search any lone traveller or caravan. Brigands, highwaymen, and beggars met with heavy punishments, and their missing eyes or limbs were warnings to all potential thieves and petty criminals who thought to defy the good order of Darius' law. The Great King policed his realm carefully, and throughout the empire he maintained a tight network of spies. Known as the 'King's Ears', they reported back to the central authority any hint of rebellion in the satrapies or any flicker of insurrection in the provinces. A court official bearing the curious title 'The King's Eye' (Old Persian, *Spasaka*) was in charge of the intelligence-gathering and reported directly (and perhaps on a daily basis) to the Great King himself. One Greek author, Aristotle of Stagira, was most impressed by the efficiency of the Persian spy system, writing that:

> The king himself, they say, lived in Susa or Ecbatana, invisible to all, in a marvellous palace. Outside [the palace doors] the leaders and most eminent men were drawn up in order, some called 'guards' and the 'king's eyes and ears', so that the king himself might see everything and hear everything.

Hidden from view within his palace, from where he dispensed his laws and edicts, and surrounded by well-armed guards and rings of spies and informers, Darius the Great oversaw the efficacious, no-nonsense governance of his realm. Autocracy, it transpires, was Darius' chief goal. He achieved it with single-minded determination.

7

A Court under Canvas

Monarchs like to travel. When they travel, they do so in style. But why do monarchs travel at all? They have comfortable and secure palaces to meet both their daily requirements and the needs of state. So why take to the road? Monarchs travel because they must. They journey to meet fellow kings and queens or state leaders and to play their role on the international stage; they travel in order to witness the internal workings of their kingdoms and to play an equally important role in the dramas of domestic policy. They travel to show themselves to their subjects as manifestations of power and control or to boost their popularity. Many modern heads of state even go as far as to 'press the flesh' of their admirers – shaking hands and offering pleasantries – in a convivial manner that would have been alien to the majority of absolute rulers of past societies. In the Achaemenid period, the Persian Great Kings travelled extensively to fulfil the needs of national and international diplomacy, to fulfil religious or cultural duties, to lead armies into battle, and to participate in the lives of their subjects. They were usually accompanied on their journeys by the majority of the royal court as well as by a huge military force, so that, in effect, when the Great King journeyed across the empire, the state itself was in transit: as went the royal house, so went the empire.

The Great King and his court used the empire's sophisticated road system to traverse the realm not just for the pragmatic reasons of state, but also to satisfy a deep-set instinct in the Persian psyche. For the Achaemenids retained the nomadic lifestyle of their Eurasian ancestors. The desire to move from one place to another never left them. The regular progression of the royal court around and across the empire can be thought of as a nomadic migration on a par with the relocation patterns typical of itinerant peoples. In Iran the traditional migration movements of nomadic groups (each with its own deep-set tribal and family affiliations) have always been connected with clearly defined routes and destinations. Nomads ensure the productiveness of their livelihood through the welfare of their herds of sheep and goats, and they follow the weather patterns which produce the best grazing pasture on the land. In essence the royal court of Persia maintained this old, tried-and-tested nomadic practice. The court, too, moved around Iran following the weather patterns. In the stifling heat of summer, the court resided in the north of the Iranian plateau, in the cool mountains of Ecbatana. It journeyed to balmy Babylon and Susa for the winter months and went to Persepolis and Pasargadae for the freshness of the spring. But come the hot summer, the cycle started again with the court's relocation to Ecbatana.

*

The logistics of the court shifting locations like this required enormous organisation and colossal resources. Many thousands of people would have been affected by, or were responsible for, the move. The peripatetic royal court was, to all intents and purposes, a movable city. Virtually the whole royal establishment, the household as well as officials, shifted with the Great King. Alongside him went his personal staff, scribes, and record-keepers, as well as the royal treasury. His harem moved with him as well, as did his artists, musicians, dancers, and animal-keepers with their great numbers of livestock. Priests, astrologers, and seers accompanied the king. The armed forces moved with him too, along with all those who depended on the court and the army. Countless camp-followers, several times as numerous as the army, herded their animals alongside the royal retinue. With a cortège so vast, movement was painfully slow. The journey between Susa and Ecbatana alone could take over two months to complete since the court covered no more than ten kilometres each day, with an average travel time of seven or eight hours of marching during daylight.

Daylight was not wasted. When dawn came, the Persian court began its progress after a signal – a blast of noise from a bronze horn – was trumpeted from the king's tent. The order of the line of march was dictated by tradition. In front of the entire cavalcade went the priests, walking on foot and carrying silver fire altars and chanting traditional hymns; they were followed by over 300 young men in scarlet cloaks, acting as an honorary escort. Then came the horse-drawn chariot consecrated to the god Ahuramazda. It was followed by a white stallion, sacred to the god, which was called the Horse of the Sun. Golden sceptres and white robes adorned the horseriders who accompanied the god's chariot. Not far behind were ten carts of ritual paraphernalia, and these were followed by a cavalry, variously armed. Next in line were the Immortals, an elite corps of the imperial army, numbering, allegedly, 10,000 men. No other group looked so good. These soldiers, the pride of Persia, wore golden necklaces, uniforms interwoven with gold, and long-sleeved tunics actually studded with precious stones. Following the Immortals, after a short interval, marched 15,000 of the king's kinsmen; they were conspicuous more for luxury than the ability to fight. The next column comprised the servants of the royal wardrobe who preceded the royal chariot on which rode the king himself. Seated high above all others, he spent the journey doing a variety of activities. He might greet the populace as he passed by villages and hamlets, or he might busy himself with the official paperwork of state – the administration of the empire continued uninterrupted as the court trekked on. One charming Greek vignette depicts the some-what bored monarch sitting in his slow-moving chariot whittling a piece of wood to help pass the hours.

The king's chariot was followed by 10,000 spearmen carrying lances chased with silver and tipped with gold, and to the right and left of the monarch were 200 of his royal relatives, mounted on horseback. At the end of the column came 30,000 foot soldiers, followed by 400 of the king's horses. Next, at a distance of about one mile from the main unit, came the entourage of the royal women, travelling within *harmamaxae*. These luxuriously furnished covered carriages (deluxe versions of the prairie wagons of the

American West) were for the king's mother and the royal consorts. They were followed by a throng of the women of the queens' households, who rode on horseback. There followed fifteen more covered wagons in which rode the king's children, their nurses, and eunuchs. Afterwards came the 300 carriages of the royal concubines. It was punishable by death to cross the path of the *harmamaxae* in which any of the royal women were transported, and as they passed through the countryside, the royal ladies were assiduously guarded. Behind the carriages of the concubines were 600 mules and 300 camels, transporting the king's treasury. A guard of archers was in close attendance to protect the wealth. After this column rode the women of the king's relatives and friends, and hordes of camp-followers and servants. Finally, bringing up the rear were light-armed troops with their respective leaders. The march ended when, stage by stage, the court arrived at the overnight camp which had been set up in advance by a huge team of outriders. They worked throughout the day to ensure that the ground was prepared and that the kitchens had hot food ready for the many thousands of travellers. As unhurried as it was, the whole event nevertheless operated with military precision.

Thousands of animals facilitated the court's migrations. They pulled wagons, chariots, and carriages and carried people and commodities on their backs. Some 100,000 horses and 200,000 other animals, including donkeys, mules and oxen, were employed to shift the court. The horse, an animal intimately connected with Persian life, was the main mode of court transport, although the camel played an important part in the operations too. The Old Persian word for camel, *usha* or *ushtra*, often occurs as a component in personal names (most markedly Zarathushtra, 'he who manages camels') which testifies to their importance in Persian society. Images of Bactrian camels in Achaemenid art are unmistakable and copious, for, at Persepolis, they are included in the representations of several delegations from north-eastern Iran, whereas single-humped dromedaries are depicted only with the Arab delegation. Swift dromedary camels were important sources of meat, milk, and hair, although they were not engaged in heavy hauling. In fact, none of the Persepolis camels are portrayed as draft animals. But post-Achaemenid period sources give explicit references to camel-drawn carts, and one Achaemenid seal image shows the Great King in a chariot pulled by a team of dromedaries. Both species of camels were used by the Persian cavalry and it is clear that Darius I had employed camel troops (*ushabari*) in his campaign against the rebellious Babylonians. Large herds of camels belonging to the Great King are attested in the Persepolis tablets too. They were herded back and forth between Persepolis and Susa, and artists sometimes depicted the Great King riding a camel. One small seal actually shows the Great King spearing a lion while seated on a dromedary, suggesting that camels were used in hunting expeditions too.

*

In the open landscape, after a day's travelling, the imperial procession finally came to a halt and unpacked. Herodotus records that the Persian troops marching with Xerxes when he invaded Greece in 480 BCE had the task of dismantling, transporting, and reassembling the royal tent when they reached a new camp, and it is easy to imagine that the tents of the other royals and nobles were erected by teams of servants at the same time. Having slept in numerous Persian camps during his time in the east, Xenophon was always impressed by the efficiency with which a camp was established:

> I will comment on how orderly the operation to pack up the baggage train was carried out, vast though it was, and I will note how quickly they reached the place they were heading for. For wherever the king encamps, all his entourage follow him onto the land with their tents, whether it be summer or winter. Cyrus had made the rule that his tent should be pitched facing the east; and then he determined, first how far from the royal pavilion the spearmen of the guard should have their tent. Then he assigned a place on the right for the bakers, and on the left for the cooks, on the right for the horses, and the left for the remainder of the pack animals. Everyone knew his place – things were so well-organised. And when

they came to repacking, everyone knew he had to pack what he used and others packed the animals, so that the baggage men all came at the same time to collect the things they were supposed to carry, and at the same time load up the animals with the baggage. The time required for taking down a single tent is the same for all people. In order to be completely ready at the right time, everyone has a specific job to do. Therefore, the time required to do any job is equitable. Just as the servants in charge of provisions had a set place in the camp, so too the soldiers of every troop knew exactly where to encamp – and all this meant that the task was undertaken with no hint of friction.

Systematically arranged to reflect hierarchical and defensive concerns, the royal camp was constructed with the Great King's tent at the centre of the complex, facing towards the east. It was colourfully decorated with distinguishing heraldic devices, banners, and flags. Standing at the centre of the camp, the king's tent was the symbol of royal authority itself and inside the tent the king carried out the same rituals and duties that he followed inside the palaces: he sat in council, listened to debates, judged crimes, passed laws, ate fine food, listened to music, heard stories, and slept with his women. When the court went travelling, the royal tent became the centre of empire. It was a colossal structure, made from colourfully woven textiles and leather panels which were supported from a framework of columns thirty feet high, gilded and studded with jewels. In all respects, the king's tent was a collapsible version of a stone palace – it was large enough for a hundred couches and was decorated sumptuously and magnificently with expensive draperies and fine linens. Rectangular in shape, it had a high circular canopy at the centre, which Greeks called an *Ouranos* ('heaven'). 'In Persia', wrote one astounded Athenian, 'the royal tents and courts have circular ceilings, like skies'. Underfoot there were Tyrian purple carpets and crimson rugs interwoven with gold. The entire enclosure was surrounded with rich linen curtains woven with gold and silver thread; even the curtain rods were overlaid with gold and silver.

As a mark of favour and as a display of royal largess, the Great King might bestow a fine tent on a favoured courtier as a gift. Often the tent came richly furnished with couches, textiles, gold plate, and servants. The Athenian exile Themistocles, for example, was given the reward of a splendidly ornate tent by Artaxerxes I, one 'of extraordinary beauty and size'. With it, said Plutarch, were 'a silver-footed bedstead, rich coverings, and a slave to spread them'. The royal tent was a visible emblem of imperial authority – so much so, in fact, that during war the enemy capture of a royal tent was a symbol of the collapse of monarchic authority itself, as Alexander of Macedon came to fully appreciate once he had moved into the tent which had previously belonged to Darius III, the last Achaemenid ruler.

In the royal camp, once the tents had been erected, the work began of feeding the court – an immense and costly undertaking. Provisions were required for hundreds of thousands of people. As the Great King travelled throughout his realm – sometimes to the far edges of the empire in his expansionist pursuit of territory – so the cities, towns, and villages he passed by were expected to meet the needs of the army and court. Like a swarm of locusts, the court could easily strip bare the surrounding countryside of its produce. When Xerxes trundled through Thrace on his campaign into Greece, the villages of the Thracians were stripped of their crops. Food and drink were provided for Xerxes himself and all who dined with him. He was accommodated in a magnificent tent which the Thracians had created and had erected in his honour. For the rest of the army, the Thracians were required to provide only food. When they had eaten their fill, the soldiers passed the night sleeping in the open air. But come dawn, the army tore down the splendid royal tent and marched off with all the movables, leaving nothing behind. Megacreon of Abdera, who witnessed the scene, advised the stunned villagers to gather at the temple and thank the gods profoundly for the fact that it was Xerxes' custom to take a meal only once a day. Otherwise, they would have been commanded to furnish a breakfast similar to the dinner!

8

Constructing Majesty

The Achaemenid monarchs were well-honed nomads, but they were also enthusiastic builders. Dynastic and imperial structures were their speciality. Between them, over a period of two centuries, the Great Kings erected architectural wonders – fortresses, royal residences, and rock-cut tombs – on an impressively grandiose scale. Several Great Kings proudly alluded to their construction projects in their official inscriptions, often in an attempt to demonstrate dynastic longevity. The exhaustive planning and creation of stone structures became symbols of royal supremacy and imperial harmony. An inscription set up by Darius at Persepolis, for instance, states, 'On this terrace, where this fortified palace [Old Persian, *halmarrash*] was built, there no palace had been built before; by the favour of Ahuramazda, I built this palace. And it was Ahuramazda's desire, and the desire of all the gods who are, that this palace should be built' (DPf).

Drawing on the rich resources and the gargantuan labour force of their vast empire, the Achaemenid kings built prodigiously and lavishly throughout the realm. The chief palatial sites, crafted from fine stone, mud brick, glazed brick, and wood, were clustered in the ancient ancestral regions of Pārs (at Pasargadae and Persepolis), Media (at Ecbatana) and Elam (at Susa), or in areas of early conquest (Babylonia). Achaemenid royal residences tended to be built on top of earlier areas of older habitation, stressing Persian hegemony over the past itself.

Little remains of the once-famed Achaemenid residence at Ecbatana near Hamadan, and much controversy surrounds even its archaeological location, but it must have once afforded quite a spectacle. Polybius, a Greek historian of the Hellenistic age, wrote that 'it conveyed a high idea of the wealth of its founders', and he suggested that the woodwork was all of cedar and cypress, although no part of it was left exposed since even the rafters, the compartments of the ceiling, and the columns in the porches and colonnades were plated with either silver or gold. 'Most of the precious metals were stripped off in the invasion of Alexander and his Macedonians', he confirmed.

Following the conquest of Babylon in 539 BCE, the Persians began construction of a large ceremonial palace next to the old residence of Nebuchadnezzar II (a clear political statement to their Babylonian subjects). Little remains of it today and only a hypothetical reconstruction of its once august appearance can be attempted. There is evidence for the use of Achaemenid-style column bases and bull capitals, and at least part of the palace was decorated with fine glazed brickwork which shared motifs with examples found at Susa. In fact, the influence of Babylonian culture on Achaemenid art and architecture is apparent in various remains, such as the use of terraced platforms in palace construction, wall decoration, and repoussé technique in metal work. A Persian-style pavilion, with an *Apadana*, or throne hall, and a columned portico, was built on the west side of the former palace of Nebuchadnezzar, and a large stone platform, a Persian-style *takht* – the quintessential Achaemenid architectural structure – excavated close to the old Babylonian palace suggests that the Achaemenid rulers might have constructed a brand-new palace, in Persian style.

There is no evidence of Cyrus or Cambyses having been active at the ancient site of Susa. It was only Darius, once his power was consolidated, who opted to use Susa as one of his royal residences. There is a good possibility that Darius had been born in the city and, as one of its proud sons, he was keen to reactivate its glorious past, when it was the wealthy capital of mighty Elam. He envisaged Susa as a suitable site for the display of a new-found Achaemenid power, and so he built lavishly there. In an inscription he set up in the heart of the city, he boasted of having reconstructed Susa's dilapidated fortifications, noting that 'constructions that had previously been put out of place, I put in place. The wall was fallen from age. Before this unrepaired wall I built another, to serve from that time into the future' (DSe). Archaeological excavations show that Darius did indeed radically change the topography of old Susa. He levelled the top of the acropolis, the hill which sat at the city's centre, to a height of fifteen metres above the plain below, so that his building constructions could be seen from far and wide. Access into the royal city was through a monumental gateway built on the eastern side of the acropolis. A great square pavilion, the colossal gate dominated the landscape and even overshadowed the palace of Darius, which was approached via a passage through the gate itself, which, in turn, was flanked by two statues of Darius, much larger than life-size.

The king's residential palace at Susa was organised around three large courtyards, each embellished in enamelled brick depicting lions, royal guards, and flowering plants. The royal apartments were made difficult to access with labyrinthine corridors and zigzag passages, affording the king some privacy and security. Behind the king's private suite was a series of rooms for the immediate members of the royal family. Finally, to the north, projecting out from the other buildings, was the *Apadana*, a vast square construction twenty metres high, with a central hall of columns and a portico on each of the three open sides with two rows of six columns and stairways which led up to the flat roof. Erected on a high terrace and open on three sides, the *Apadana* would have been an imposing structure, visible from far off across the plains of Elam. A glimpse of the beauty of the Achaemenid palace at Susa can be gleaned from scenes in the biblical book of Esther, the action of which unfolds in the royal halls and gardens: 'The royal garden had hangings of white and blue linen, fastened with cords of white linen and purple material to silver rings on marble pillars. There were couches of gold and silver on a mosaic pavement of porphyry, marble, mother-of-pearl and other costly stones'.

Darius was justifiably proud of his newly built palace at Susa. He commissioned the creation of a series of finely carved cuneiform inscriptions to testify to the multi-ethnic labour of love which went into its construction. Found buried under the doorways into the *Apadana*, the so-called Susa Foundation Charters are multilingual statements. They provide valuable information about the construction of the palace complex. It had long been the tradition in Mesopotamia to bury a foundation tablet under the thresholds of palaces to invoke the protection of the gods. The Achaemenid kings enthusiastically upheld this custom, since similar texts were discovered at the *Apadana* at Persepolis too. Darius' inscriptions spoke of the fine timbers, stone, and precious materials which went into constructing the palace, and they emphasised the geographical span of Darius' empire which allowed such diverse and rare materials to be used. The Charters told of the ethnic mix of workers who had come to Susa from far-off lands to work on the completion of the palace. In the texts, Darius spoke of how his palace had its foundations built on solid ground and how his workers had dug forty cubits down into the earth in order to reach base rock and how they filled the foundations with rubble, packed tightly to form a secure base for a palace that would last for eternity. He continued:

> This palace which I built at Susa, from afar its ornamentation was brought . . . The sun-dried brick was moulded, the Babylonian people performed these tasks. The cedar timber, this was brought from a place named Lebanon. The Assyrian people brought it to Babylon; from Babylon the Carians and the Greeks brought it to Susa. The *yakâ*-timber was brought from Gandara and from Carmania. The gold was brought from Lydia and from Bactria, which here was wrought. The precious stone lapis lazuli and carnelian which was wrought here, this was brought from Sogdiana. The precious stone turquoise, this was brought from Chorasmia, which was wrought here. The silver and the ebony were brought from Egypt. The ornamentation with which the wall was adorned, that from Greece was brought. The ivory which was wrought here, was brought from Nubia and from India and from Arachosia.

The stone columns which were here wrought, a village named Abirâdu, in Elam – from there were brought. The stone-cutters who wrought the stone, those were Greeks and Lydians. The goldsmiths who wrought the gold, those were Medes and Egyptians. The men who wrought the wood, those were Lydians and Egyptians. The men who wrought the baked brick, those were Babylonians. The men who adorned the wall, those were Medes and Egyptians. Darius the king says: At Susa a very excellent work was ordered, a very excellent work was brought to completion (DSf).

The Susa Charters list no fewer than sixteen regions of the empire that furnished raw materials or labour to Darius' building project; eight more countries provided the talented craftsmen. Sardians worked stone and wood; Egyptians worked wood and created the palace reliefs; Medes worked gold and crafted palace reliefs. Some of the workmen were common hard-labourers: Babylonians who did the foundation work; Syrians, Ionians, and Carians who transported lumber from Lebanon to Babylon and on to Susa. The Susa Charters also show how foreign workers tended to be kept together, corralled into units, as they constructed certain parts of the palace.

The presence of so many foreign workers at Susa was a direct response to the young empire's need to mark its existence in stone. For the first time in their history, the Persians yearned to build palaces, governmental centres, and all the necessary infrastructures of a ruling state. Building was undertaken on a massive scale, exploiting the unparalleled reaches of the gigantic empire. The Susa Charters show how manpower and specialist workers were urgently needed in Persia to build on an extraordinary super-scale, and the huge territory that Darius and his predecessors had conquered allowed the Persians to prioritise foreign techniques of building and decorating. All in all, Darius' palace at Susa was a masterpiece of multinational design and international manufacture.

*

Best known of all the ancient Persian sites is Persepolis, whose magnificent, haunting ruins rest at the foot of Kuh-e Rahmat ('Mountain of Mercy') some 500 kilometres east of Susa and fifty kilometres north of Shiraz. Persepolis lies in the heart of Pārs and is located in a remote region in the mountains, making travel there difficult in the rainy season of the Persian winter. Its isolated location kept it a secret from the outside world (no Greek source speaks of it until the Alexander historians) and it was the safest city in the empire. Persepolis was by far the largest and most spectacular of the Achaemenid palaces and today it is the most stunning of antiquity's ruins. It is a magical place, an evocative ruin of unsurpassed beauty and grandeur, and ranks highly among the greatest archaeological sites of the world. It simply has no equivalent.

The first excavations at Persepolis took place in the 1890s but it was not until Ernst Herzfeld and his team from the University of Chicago started to dig there in 1931 that a systematic uncovering of the ruins began. Numerous palace structures, tombs, administrative buildings, and fortifications have been unearthed over the last ninety years, and excavations at the site continue – there is still much to find. The very recent excavation of Cyrus the Great's Babylonian-style gateway at Tol-e Ajori, very near to Persepolis, has rewritten the history of the site, which was once thought to have been uncharted territory chosen by Darius for a brand-new building enterprise. Instead of incorporating Cyrus' structure into the design of his palace, however, Darius had it torn down. It was a decisive act of one-upmanship that tells us much about Darius' ambivalent relationship to his great predecessor. For while Darius claimed to have been Cyrus' blood kin, he clearly found the physical presence of Cyrus' monumental building perturbing, and it was jealousy that seems to have driven him to demolish the gate and to build next to it, on a cleared plain in the Marv Dasht, an enormous platform terrace which dwarfed Cyrus' gateway and from which Darius could literally look down on Persia's founding father. Incidentally, at Pasargadae Darius also interfered with Cyrus' building works by carving trilingual cuneiform inscriptions into the stonework. The texts bogusly announce in the voice of the late Great King, 'I am Cyrus the king, an Achaemenid.'

The structures at Persepolis were chiefly built by Darius I (starting around 518 BCE), Xerxes, and Artaxerxes I, but the site was still being expanded up to 330 BCE, when it was destroyed by Alexander of Macedon. Throughout its history Persepolis functioned as a royal building site as generation upon generation of Achaemenid kings added their marks to the palatial complex. Persepolis is located in an active earthquake zone and suffered many damaging tremors, and so the kings frequently undertook restoration projects and repair jobs. In fact, at the time Alexander reached Persepolis, Darius III was undertaking an extensive rebuild in order to fix damage caused by a recent earthquake.

There is no scholarly consensus about the aims of Darius in building the palace, and the basic function of Persepolis is still much debated. It was a ceremonial centre, clearly, but was it ever meant to be inhabited? One school of thought, with much to recommend it, suggests that the palace was primarily a site for celebrating Nowruz, the Persian New Year festival. This idea has found traction from the time of Herzfeld's excavations even though some scholars completely repudiate that Nowruz was celebrated in the Achaemenid period at all. Other experts have seen Persepolis as a temple-like religious centre and not a living palace, although the presence in the site of the huge bureaucracy overseeing and recording the day-to-day economic manoeuvres seriously challenges this notion. For yet other scholars though, Persepolis was the ultimate illustration of royal power as well as an important political, economic, and administrative presence. This is perhaps the best way to regard the palace, although the case for considering Persepolis as the site of the Nowruz festival should not be dismissed lightly. The remarkably elegant images of tribute-bearers from across the empire carved into two regal staircases at the palace's throne hall certainly suggest their participation in some kind of imperial celebration, and a Nowruz festivity fits the bill nicely.

The same palatial configuration found at Susa is repeated at Persepolis. The palace was built on a fifteen-metres-high platform terrace (fortified and criss-crossed with drainage channels) 300 metres wide and 455 metres long. Its cut-limestone building blocks were taken from a nearby quarry, but some dark-grey limestone, which was used for decorative stonework, was moved there from forty kilometres away. Persepolis was a gargantuan effort of human craftsmanship and muscle, and Darius was rightly proud of the work he had undertaken there, and recorded his pleasure in an inscription on the site: 'I built it, I completed it, beautified and made it solid, exactly as I determined' (DPf).

The palace was originally entered by a modest portal which Darius had built at the south of the platform, but, around a decade after Darius' death, Xerxes shifted the entrance to the west of the terrace and constructed a monumental (and very elegant) double-flighted staircase, whose steps were shallow enough to be comfortably ascended by horses and other animals. This might endorse the theory that the palace was used for a great gift-giving festival in which animals were presented to the king (the *Apadana* reliefs show goats, sheep, rams, horses, bulls, camels, lions, and even an African okapi being presented to the ruler). At the top of the staircase stood Xerxes' mighty portal known as the 'Gate of All Nations', which was flanked by monumental stone bulls and human-headed winged bulls modelled on Assyrian *lamassu* sculptures. Official access to the palace was via this gateway (although Darius' gate at the southern end of the terrace was also maintained).

The enormous terrace was essentially divided into two areas: a public space (the outer court) for group gatherings, parades, and state occasions, and a more private area (the inner court) catering to certain ceremonial events as well as residential and administrative needs. The largest and most imposing part of public area was the magnificent audience hall or *Apadana* which, with a height of nearly twenty-two metres, stood on a podium three metres higher than the huge open courtyard that surrounded it to the north and east. It consisted of an immense square hall with thirty-six columns supporting an enormous roof of cedar wood. It had three porticoes (each with twelve columns) on the north, west, and east sides, four four-storey corner towers, and a series of storage and guardrooms on the south. It is estimated that the *Apadana* could hold around 10,000 people. The Achaemenid architects were able to use a minimal number of astonishingly slender columns to support open-air roofs. Columns were topped with elaborate capitals; typical was the double-bull capital where, resting on double volutes, the forequarters of two kneeling bulls, placed back-to-back, extend their coupled necks and their twin heads directly under the intersections of the cedar beams of the ceiling. The *Apadana*'s thick mud-brick walls were faced with glazed tiles of elegant greens, blues, and oranges in patterns of rosettes and palm trees. This was the main locale of the most important royal ceremonies, and entering into the darkened hallows of this majestic hall must have been an awesome experience for any diplomat, courtier, or suppliant. The *Apadana* was the centre of majesty and was designed primarily to be a showplace for the receptions and festivals of the Great Kings.

Other official buildings included the magnificent 'Hundred Column Hall', an immense banqueting vestibule (or an alternative throne hall), and the Tripylon or 'Central Palace', a small but lavishly ornamented structure with three doorways and four columns, which may have served as a council chamber. The jambs of the eastern doorway show foreign throne-bearers lifting high the Great King. This might be a purely symbolic image, but it has been suggested that this may reflect an actual court ceremony in which, at some great festival at Persepolis, twenty-eight courtiers representing subject nations of the empire lifted the royal dais supporting the king and prince, and carried them into the main hall of the Tripylon, where they received the guests.

The buildings of the inner court, situated to the rear of the *Apadana*, were made up of Darius' *taçara* (literally, 'suite of rooms') and Xerxes' *hadish* (literally, 'seat of power'). The two small palaces were used as 'private' residences by the kings and incorporated dining areas and even bathrooms. Other 'palaces' were located in this area, including the so-called Palace H, perhaps originally built by Artaxerxes I, and the completely destroyed Palace G (dating, maybe, to Artaxerxes III). Xerxes' palace was connected to the royal harem by two grand, well-worked flights of stairs, which must have been utilised by the king when he required direct access to the rooms below. The harem was allocated as living quarters for some of the royal family; it was hidden by high fortifications and well-guarded by the military. It was the most secure and private space on the royal terrace.

The managerial heart of the palace was based in the private part of the terrace too. The Treasury was located there. It contained not only the vast wealth of Persepolis brought to the palace by foreign dignitaries, satraps, and an unending herd of middlemen, but it also housed the state bureaucracy's army of scribes, secretaries, and other administrative personnel. It was here that the biggest number of archival documents relating to the running of the empire were discovered.

At the foot of the terrace platform, to the south, were gathered several mud-brick and stone pavilions (Buildings A-H), including one (Building H) with a sunken stone bath, which might well have served as a royal dwelling place. The royal platform was flanked on the south and north by two valleys planted with fine gardens and enclosed within fortified walls. The many thousands of courtiers, bureaucrats, and servants who accompanied the Great King at Persepolis were lodged in tents, large and small, which constituted a veritable city under canvas and stretched for many miles around the royal terrace.

Perhaps the most striking feature of Persepolis is the profusion of finely carved stone reliefs, which seem to cover every available inch of space. Once brightly painted and even embellished with precious-metal overlays, the reliefs are now bleached of colour and stripped of ornament. Yet their beauty and elegance, made most apparent in the formulaic regularity of their subject matter and detail, are a wonder of artistic creativity and planning. Armed guards, court dignitaries, foreign ambassadors, a menagerie of animals, and a host of magical creatures jostle for space on the palace walls, but all of them take second place to the many images of the Great King which dominate the scenes. He is shown calmly walking from one room to another, eyes fixed on the middle distance; he holds a long sceptre and is followed by two courtiers (always depicted on a smaller scale), one of whom holds a parasol above the king's head while the other holds a fly-whisk (some examples show a folded towel-like strip of linen or else an unguent pot). Sometimes the king is more active and is depicted slaying real or mythic animals, his sword plunging into the belly of the monster. Occasionally the monarch strangles a lion in the crook of his left arm. In these combat scenes, where the wild beasts represent chaos, disorder, and the Lie, it is possible that the king represents 'every man' and takes on the form of 'the Persian hero' restoring order to his country.

Certain artistic themes are notable by their absence: in the whole of Persepolis there is not one representation of the king engaged in warfare or the hunt. Yet we know both to have been integral components of Achaemenid kingship and its ideology; neither is the king represented feasting or drinking. Hunting scenes, feasting scenes, and war scenes are all represented in the minor arts (especially seal images), but for some reason they do not enter into the repertoire of official monumental Achaemenid iconography. Why is that? We must remember that the art of Persepolis was not created to be a quasi-photographic reflection of reality. Though it does capture elements of reality, Persian art does so in order to transform it and make it inspiring. Persepolitan art should be read as an ideological discourse on the theme of royalty and imperial might, organised around evocative images of the power of the Great King himself.

9

Slavery by Another Name

The elegant royal palaces, the impressive fortresses, the high city walls, and the well-kept road stations and pavilions of the Persian empire did not build themselves. The edifices from Iranian antiquity which so impress us today with their overwhelming beauty and sheer scale were constructed by labourers earning a living wage and peasants and farmers who were compelled to spend months away from their families and fields for state building projects. They were also constructed by thousands of slaves and war captives. At first, Persia did not have an extensive slave economy and in the early Achaemenid era there was only a small number of slaves in Persia, certainly in relation to the number of free persons even in the most developed countries of the empire. Slave labour was in no position to supplant the labour of free workers, but as a result of the far-flung conquests of the Great Kings, a dramatic change took place within Persian society. Soon after the consolidation of imperial power under Cyrus and Cambyses, Achaemenid nobles became the owners of very large numbers of slaves. Information on privately owned slaves in Persia is scanty, but a substantial number of slaves performed domestic work for the Achaemenids and the Persian nobility as bakers, cooks, cup-bearers, entertainers, and perfumiers. The archaeological evidence also testifies to the mass presence of unskilled labourers in the Persian heartlands.

In the cuneiform sources an Elamite term *kurtash* (Old Persian, *māniya*) was used, very homogeneously, for agricultural labourers, artisans, and construction workers. The term offers little specificity as to the actual jobs undertaken. The Persepolis tablets tell of how *kurtash* received rations of food and drink at certain localities in and around Fārs. *Kurtash* were generically identified as 'workers of all trades' or 'workers at any task'. Some tablets recorded the transportation to Persepolis of grain, flour, and wine intended as rations for specialist master craftsmen such as sculptors in stone, goldsmiths, master woodworkers, metal workers, and skilled quarrymen. The *kurtash* found in the Persepolis tablets were foreigners – Ionians, Sardians, Egyptians, Carians, Bactrians, Elamites, Babylonians – who found themselves at the imperial core working on the building projects of the Great King.

What was it that brought foreigners to Persepolis in the first place? A small percentage of foreigners were master craftsmen, brought into Persia on work contracts. This policy might have been in operation since Cyrus' day, when craftsmen from Lydia and Ionia had been brought to Pasargadae to help build the pavilion-palaces. Cambyses too took craftsmen from Egypt and sent them to Persia. It is tempting to think that these master craftsmen and artisans might have come to Susa and Persepolis not because they were forced to but because they were requested by Persian officials. As such they participated in a kind of up-market corvée labour system. At the end of their term of employment they were free to return home or seek another contract. But this is merely a hypothesis, and even if it could be proved then it certainly would not have applied to the many thousands of unskilled workers repetitively carrying out mundane manual labour. It has been estimated that in 500 BCE some 10,000–15,000 individuals made up the workforce of Persepolis. Often divided up into subgroups of work gangs, classified by ethnicity, the Persepolis tablets show that, for instance, there were gangs of 300 Lycians, 150 Thracians, 547 Egyptians, and 980 Cappadocians. All in all twenty-seven ethnic groups of *kurtash* are attested at Persepolis.

It is doubtful that all of these people entered Persia as economic migrants seeking wages. The Persepolis Fortification tablets do not support that view. They clearly reveal that the food rations *kurtash* received from the administration were enough only for survival and nothing more and, in fact, the food doled out to the *kurtash* was only distributed at a subsistence level. For the workers, the risk of starvation was never far away. The *kurtash* of the Fortification tablets were not in Persia of their own free will to earn a wage. They had been brought there forcibly, in very large numbers, and were exploited by the Persians through direct coercion regardless of whether they were only temporarily located there or were settled in Persia for life. Usually *kurtash* were prisoners of war (the 'booty of the bow', as they were termed) recruited from those who had rebelled against Persian rule or had put up resistance to the Persian army. The Persepolis tablets make clear that, for the majority of the workers, their placement in Persia was permanent and that they had been uprooted from their homelands and deported there specifically to create an enslaved labour force. Babylonia alone was obliged to supply the Persian king for these purposes an annual tribute of 500 castrated boys. These lads were taken from their families and transported east to Pārs.

The policy of deportation of conquered populations was commonplace in the ancient Near East, and in the Assyrian and Neo-Babylonian periods the practice had flourished. During the nearly 300 years of Assyria's hegemony over the Near East, the state deported approximately 4.5 million people whose relocation in diverse areas of the Assyrian empire was carefully planned and organised. The Babylonians worked along the same guidelines, but on a more modest scale: some 4,600 persons in all were taken from Judah and led into captivity in Mesopotamia. The practice of uprooting whole communities and transplanting them in distant lands is equally well attested for the Persians too. Following the destruction of the city of Sidon by King Artaxerxes III in 351 BCE, for instance, men and women of the city were led captive into the Persian heartlands. The Milesians too were victims of Persian deportation, as were the Paeonians of Thrace, the Barcaeans, Eretrians, Boeotians, and the Carians. Deported populations often remained in Persia for many generations. A remarkable incident recorded by Diodorus Siculus occurred to Alexander of Macedon as he marched towards Persepolis during his invasion of Pārs:

At this point in his advance the king was confronted by a strange and dreadful sight, one to provoke indignation against the perpetrators and sympathetic pity for the unfortunate victims. He was met by Greeks bearing branches of supplication. They had been carried away from their homes by previous kings of Persia and were about 800 in number, most of them elderly. All had been mutilated, some lacking hands, some feet, and some ears and noses. They were persons who had acquired skills or crafts and had made good progress in their instruction; then their other extremities had been amputated and they were left only those which were vital to their profession. All the soldiers, seeing their venerable years and the losses which their bodies had suffered, pitied the lot of the wretches. Alexander most of all was affected by them and was unable to restrain his tears.

It is clear that these old Greeks, ripped from their homes many decades before, were *kurtash*. Even with some possible exaggeration about the rate of the mutilations they had been subject to, the story does provide a very grim perspective on Persia's labour system. The story's emotional pull stands in stark contrast with the Persepolis tablets' clinically cold administrative language. It would be too simple to dismiss Diodorus' narrative as anti-Persian propaganda. What we read here is an eye-opening account of the traumatic world of the *kurtash* and the fact that, for many enslaved war captives, brutality and cruelty were part of life.

The Fortification tablets reveal that there was an enormous bureaucratic push on the part of the Persians to micro-manage their huge foreign workforce. This was achieved through the careful rationing of a subsistence-only supply of food and drink. The rations were first given to various 'Heads of *Kurtash*' (Elamite, *Kurdabattish*) – overseers – who acted as distributors and doled out the rations to the work teams they supervised. Rations in kind – grain, barley, beer, oil, sometimes meat and vegetables – were distributed unequally according to gender and age. Men, boys, women, and girls were provided with different amounts of food.

There were many female workers at Persepolis. They were usually engaged in textile production and weaving as well as rope-making. One tablet records the make-up of a large textile workshop and notes that its staff comprises of 107 female textile-workers who received rations for a period of thirteen months. Some of these women had no doubt arrived in Persia alongside their husbands or fathers, and had been captured as a discreet family unit, but others were single women, war captives who lacked any familial ties. For those women who accompanied husbands or fathers into slavery, there was little hope that they could stay in family groups, since the Persian administration tended to break apart families and deploy individual workers wherever they were most needed. It was unlikely that any family newly brought to Persia would stay together for long. Nevertheless, unrelated male and female *kurtash* working on communal projects tended to group together to share food and, it is to be assumed, accommodation. Inevitably sexual (and perhaps emotional) bonds were made between workers. The Persians encouraged this. They even gave incentives to boost reproduction among the *kurtash* population. The Fortification texts tell a disconcertingly uncomfortable tale of a large-scale *kurtash* breeding programme throughout Pārs. The records kept a register of the number of pregnant women and show that their health was maintained through the provision of special rations. Post-partum women were also given 'feeding' rations, as one text specifies:

> 32 BAN of grain, supplied by Ashbashupish. Shedda, a priest at Persepolis . . . gave it as a bonus to Ionian women after giving birth at Persepolis, to the spinning-women, whose rations are set. Nine women who bore male children received two BAN and fourteen women who bore girls received one BAN.

These postnatal grain rations were provided over and above the normal subsistence rations. They were a reward, as it were, for successful reproduction. The food bonuses must have been welcomed by the new mothers though, since the extra calories allowed them to recuperate from the birth and gave them a rare opportunity to gain some weight. In this way they might produce healthy and nourishing breastmilk which would help an infant survive the perilous first months of life. The mother's food ration was doubled in the event of the birth of a boy, a detail that tells us much about the Persian perception of the hierarchies of gender. In the three-year period 500–497 BCE alone, the Fortification tablets record there were 449 live births at Persepolis – 247 of them were boys, who made up 55 per cent of all children born at that time. Oddly there are no examples of twins. A statistical analysis of the Persepolis tablets reveals that the fertility rate in *kurtash* communities was alarmingly low. Even allowing for the high infant mortality rate, which can be found in any ancient society, poor health and limited access to food took its toll on fertility. Moreover, many *kurtash* groups did not have equal numbers of men and women. The Persepolis tablets indicate that the administration assiduously tried to bring more women into the labour force so as to increase the working population, and it can be ascertained that between 502 and 499 BCE the number of *kurtash* children born in Pārs increased from sixteen to ninety-nine – a very successful outcome. However, it is important to note that in order to increase work productivity, the Persian administration actively broke apart family units or simply forbade their creation. It is doubtful that *kurtash* marriages were ever recognised by the Persians. 'Husbands' and 'wives' are never mentioned in the texts. The tablets also show that the bond between mother and child was not permanent either: mothers kept their children close at hand for the first few years of life, after which the children or youths were taken to different groups and started their working lives amid other *kurtash* communities.

The presence of enforced labour from captured peoples, an active breeding programme, the routine relocation of individuals, the breakdown of family bonds, and the control of bodies through the rationing of food – all indicate that the *kurtash* were slaves. It was slave labour that lay behind the hallmarks of the physical presence of Persia's empire. Achaemenid Persia was not a slave society in the way that the Roman empire was, given that Rome's expansion was based on a very simple formula: peasants became soldiers who captured enemies to enslave for the purpose of replacing the labour lost on the farm to the war. But it must be conceded that as Persia grew in power and status, it exponentially required and desired slaves to make the imperial system work. Enough information exists to convince us that Persia was a slave-owning society and that the Achaemenid empire benefited from slavery.

10

Crowns and Concubines

For most Westerners, 'harem' is a word which conjures up a heady image of some kind of closely guarded Oriental pleasure palace, filled with scantily clad nubile virgins, stretched out on pillows in languid preparation for nights of sexual adventure in a sultan's bed. It is a world of scatter cushions, jewels in the belly button, gyrating hips, and fluttering eyelashes set above gauzy *yashmaks* (face veils). These clichés find their most vivid expression in nineteenth-century Orientalist paintings and in popular movies. This vision of Eastern sensual excess has often led scholarship to dismiss the notion of the harem as a Western fabrication, an *open sesame* to an Arabian Nights fantasy world. If we want to utilise the word 'harem' in its correct context and use it to consolidate some legitimate facts about royal women in the Persian empire, we must dispense with the Orientalist clichés entirely and understand what, in historical terms, a 'harem' was all about.

From a historical perspective, a harem was a physical space in a palace or house which was used by family members: women, children, servants, and close-kin men. A harem could also simply refer to women and their blood kin when grouped together since the concept of 'harem' does not necessarily need a defining space. Walls are not that important. 'Harem' has at its core the meaning 'taboo', and by implication it means a group into which general access is prohibited or limited, and in which the presence of certain individuals or certain types of behaviour are forbidden. The fact that, historically, the private quarters in a domestic residence, and by extension its female occupants, were also referred to as a 'harem' comes from the practice of restricting access to these quarters, especially to males unrelated by blood kinship to the resident females. The word 'harem' is therefore a term of respect, evoking personal honour. In royal practice, 'harem' refers to a king's women and to all other individuals under his immediate protection – children, siblings, in-laws, and slaves. In other words, the people who made up his inner court, or the royal domestic sphere, were the 'harem'. This is the way to think about the royal harem in its ancient Persian context (although it is impossible to know how the ancient Persians referred to a harem, and so, pragmatically, 'harem' has been adopted here for expediency).

Separation is the key issue here. The modern Persian (Farsi) word *andarūnī* literally means 'the inside'. It is a term used by Iranians for the private family quarters of a home and for the people who inhabit it. It is used in opposition to *birun*, which refers to the public space and the part of a household used for welcoming and entertaining guests. In contemporary Iran, the *andarūnī* consists of all the males of a family and their respective wives, mothers, grandmothers, and a whole array of male and female offspring ranging from babies to adolescents.

It is important to get one thing straight: the royal women of Achaemenid Persia did not live in oppressive purdah, kept hidden away from all prying eyes. Nor did they inhabit a world of sultry sensuality. But they certainly did form a strict hierarchical structure which moved in close proximity to the king. Therefore they followed in the peripatetic lifestyle of the court. There can be little doubt that their honour and chastity were carefully guarded, but this does not mean that royal women were dislocated from interaction within the wider court society or that they lacked any autonomy. Women rode horses on royal hunting expeditions, they attended banquets, and they engaged in sports, including archery and the throwing of javelins. We must not imagine that the royal women of Persia were imprisoned behind walls.

However (and this is perhaps the most difficult point for a modern celebrity-obsessed audience to grasp), for women of the royal family, prestige and access to power lay in their separation *away from* the public gaze. There was no honour in being visible. In Persian antiquity, invisibility brought prestige. Yet the invisibility of Persia's elite women did not equate to a lack of freedom or a want of power. The mothers, consorts, and other women in the orbit of the Great King had real influence. Intimate proximity to the king imbued these privileged women with an opportunity to access genuine power. The royal harem was a vital component of Persian culture. It had profound political importance. The maintenance of dynastic power was directly passed through the harem as women gave birth to future heirs and vigilantly – sometimes ferociously – guarded their positions within the ever-changing structure of court hierarchy. We have noted how the Achaemenid dynasty was essentially a family-run business. At the heart of the operation was the harem.

Achaemenid kings were polygynous – that is to say, they had sexual access to many women: consorts, concubines, and even slaves. Women were gathered together within the Persian inner court to fulfil important social, cultural, and ritual roles and to undertake (it was hoped) important functions in dynastic continuity as mothers. The presence of so many women meant that the hierarchy of the Achaemenid harem was complex. In principle, it was headed by a chief queen, usually the king's mother or, in her absence, the most favoured (or influential) wife, who gathered about her the other royal and noble women – secondary wives, royal sisters, royal daughters, and other females. Some sort of hierarchical structure seems to be reflected in an all-female audience scene on a cylinder

Figure 11. Impression of a cylinder seal depicting a female audience scene. Possibly from Susa, *c.* 490 BCE.

seal (probably from Susa) in which a woman seated on a high-backed throne, wearing a crown and an enveloping veil, is offered a dove by a girl with a pigtail, in the presence of a standing woman wearing a crown and a short veil. Depicted here, perhaps, are three generations of royal females: the king's mother seated in the position of honour, a young princess (her granddaughter, maybe), and a crowned consort, showing her deference to the matriarch.

Beneath the favoured women who made up the immediate royal family ranked the concubines, the female administrative personnel and, at the lowest level, slaves. The harem hierarchy must have been in a state of continual flux, however, as, for instance, wives gave birth to sons rather than daughters and thereby gained some hierarchical cachet or a concubine suddenly became a favoured companion of the Great King and was propelled into a higher rank. According to the Persepolis tablets, high-ranking women of the royal house were honoured with the Old Persian title *duxthrī* (literally, 'daughter'), which has been preserved in Elamite transcription as *dukshish* (plural, *dukshishbe*), which can be generically translated as 'princess' or 'royal lady'. *Dukshishbe* was a collective term for Achaemenid royal women, but their individual status was determined by their relationship to the Great King.

Sex for an Achaemenid king, as for any absolute monarch in a hereditary dynasty, was never purely for pleasure. Sexual congress had significant political meaning and it had consequences – the production of offspring. Sex affected the succession to the throne, indeed, the very survival of the dynasty, and therefore sex was not a random activity for the Persian king. Sexual relations between the ruler and chosen women of the harem were embedded in a complex politics of dynastic reproduction. Any trivialisation of the Achaemenid royal harem as a brothel-like pleasure palace fails to do justice to its central role in the political milieu of the court or, indeed, of the empire at large. The king's sex drive was never the sole explanation of polygyny.

As a lion guards his pride of lionesses and cubs from the sexual advances of any other males, or sealion bulls savagely guard their cows and calves in large groups, so too the tendency towards reproductive control of females can be observed in human male behaviour too. Charles Darwin noted that in nature an aggressive male guardianship of females, often herded together in groups, was a common phenomenon. He named the instinctive herding of females 'defence polygyny'. In the animal kingdom, he noticed, females are clumped together by a male of a species because they can easily be monopolised by him, sexually. Much the same can be said of human sexual relations in a historical context. Indeed, a Darwinian perspective on the themes of reproduction and imperialism reveals that the human desire to amass females for reproductive purposes has been a feature of many societies throughout history. Absolute monarchies have profited from this sexual tendency exponentially. In fact, the capture, guardianship, and sexual monopoly of numerous women often lay behind royal male competitive aggression as demonstrated by wars, succession fights, and political display. As we have seen, for the Persians, military success translated into territorial and economic success and, by extension, the more power held by the Achaemenid kings invariably translated into bigger harems.

Imperialism clearly affected the scale of reproductive success, and royal Persian polygyny was very much in step with what occurred in other Near Eastern empires. In Mari (Syria) a king named Yasmah-Addu is recorded as having forty-four royal women (and their staff) in his palace, but his successor, Zimri-Lim, had a harem of 232 women. This was in no small part thanks to his military victories over his neighbour kings. The client kings of the much less powerful kingdom of Arrapha, therefore, had to make do with a few dozen women per palace. The most fertile Egyptian pharaoh, Ramses II, ruled at a time of almost unprecedented imperial expansion. He was said to have fathered around 99 sons and 120 daughters, taking in turn at least four daughters as Great Royal wives and fathering children on them too. The kings of Israel moved from the seven-plus wives under King David to 700 under Solomon at the height of his imperial glory and back down to eighteen after the division of the kingdom in the reign of his son,

Rehoboam. The following inventory of female captives brought to Nineveh, dated to the latter part of the reign of Esarhaddon of Assyria, constitutes a good observation point in that it articulates the nexus between military prowess and reproductive potential:

> 36 Aramean women; 15 Kushite women; 7 Assyrian women; 3 Tyrian women; Kassite women, female Corybantes; 3 Arpadite women; 1 replacement; 1 Ashdodite woman; 2 Hittite women: in all, 94 women and 36 maids of theirs. Grand total, of the father of the crown prince: in all, 140 women . . . Furthermore 8 female chief musicians; 3 Aramean women; 11 Hittite women; 13 Tyrian women; 13 female Corybantes; 4 women from Sahlu; 9 Kassite women: in all, 61 female musicians.

The Achaemenid Great King was Persia's alpha male. He was the sexually dominant man in multiple polygynous unions and cause of the production of numerous children. It was the presence of the royal harem which sanctioned and gave meaning to the king's image as the dynastic stud.

*

A Great King might have many wives and even more concubines, but he could only ever have one biological mother. The king's mother held the highest place of authority among all the women of the realm, a fact recognised even in court protocol: 'No one shared the table of the Persian king', Plutarch wrote, 'except his mother or his consort, the wife seated below him, the mother above him.' Of equal prestige to her position as the monarch's birth mother was her role in connecting two generations of rulers, father and son, king and heir. Although the king's mother was not expected to exercise official power, she might gain political clout through the close relationship she fostered with her son. In other words, a royal mother's power was indirect but effective and, if she was so inclined, she could influence her son in his policy-making. Nevertheless, the power that the king's mother could wield was limited by her sex and she acted only with the consent of the king. Within the domestic sphere of the palace, in the harem, her son probably gave her carte blanche to undertake decisions on his behalf. The Greek doctor Ctesias, who was a member of the Persian inner court for almost two decades, infers that the king's mother had absolute control over the harem, policing its mores and punishing the treasonous crimes of family, eunuchs, court doctors, servants, and other personnel.

There is bone fide Persian evidence for the high status of royal mothers contained in some seventy-five references found in the Persepolis Fortification and Treasury tablets to a very wealthy and influential female landowner with large, productive estates in the vicinity of Fārs. Her name was Irdabama. Recent scholarship suggests that, in all probability, she was the mother of Darius I and thus the most important and influential woman of the empire. Her name is Elamite and she descended from a family of local Elamite dynasts, centred at Susa, where Darius was probably born. Economically active, and with the authority to issue commands to the administrative hierarchy at Persepolis, Irdabama is well represented in the Persepolis texts. She is recorded overseeing her vast personal estates, receiving and distributing food supplies, commanding an entourage of *puhu* ('servants', 'pages') and some 480 *kurtash* (including groups of Lycians) at Tirazziš (near Shiraz) and elsewhere. Irdabama is attested at the ceremonial cities of Persepolis and Susa, and even as far away from the Persian heartland as Borsippa in Babylonia. She travelled widely around central Iran and Mesopotamia with her own courtly entourage, and she and her court are often attested in the sources travelling independently of the Great King. In this, the behaviour of the king's mother shadows that of her son, who, as we have seen, toured the country as an important element of his royal duty. As part of her personal progress Irdabama (and no doubt other important royal ladies too) could deputise for the king in his absence. European monarchies of the Middle Ages employed much the same tradition and European queens frequently travelled with their own households, setting up courts in places often far from the king, but always rejoining the monarch's court for religious festivals or state ceremonies.

Figure 12.
Impression from a seal
belonging to Rashda,
the chief steward of the
household of Irdabama,
the mother of Darius
the Great.

Irdabama was loyally served by a hardworking man named Rashda, the most important servant in her household. He is also well attested in the Persepolis texts. He was a significant royal commissioner, whose many jobs included taking care of Irdabama's vast workforce. He oversaw Irdabama's fruit plantation at Nupishtash, her many grain stores, the rations of workers at various *nutannuyash* ('livestock stations'), the transportation of her commodities, and the feeding of her horses. Rashda is immediately identifiable in the Persepolis tablets by his unique personal seal, an Elamite heirloom that represents an audience scene in which a man stands before an enthroned female protagonist. The choice of image is no coincidence, given the evident importance of Irdabama – and it is reasonable to envisage her holding audience ceremonies to mirror those of the Great King himself. Given its iconographic message of female authority, one wonders if Rashda selected this particular seal or if it was bestowed on him by Irdabama herself.

As the king's mother, Irdabama enjoyed the privilege of ruling over a court of her own, and she was responsible for its upkeep and maintenance, especially the feeding of her servants. The quantities of cereals, meat, wine, and beer consumed and poured 'before Irdabama', as the Persepolis tablets put it, are substantial and add up to roughly one tenth of the amount consumed at the king's own court. The Persepolis tablets and their seal images are of real significance in expanding the knowledge we have of the duties, privileges, and powers of Achaemenid royal women. They suggest that women of the very highest rank enjoyed exceptional autonomy within Persian society, although we should not postulate this high level of independence to all harem women. Spending power may have accrued political power too, but access to formidable levels of wealth, such as Irdabama enjoyed, was very limited. In spite of her ability to travel independently of the king, his mother was still a member of the royal harem, the hierarchical structure of which was maintained with or without her physical presence. Without any doubt, Irdabama was the wealthiest woman of her age, a significant presence at the royal court, and an economic powerhouse in her own right. It is therefore all the more extraordinary that Irdabama is entirely unknown to the Greek sources.

*

Achaemenid kings could be married to several wives at one time. As a rule, they took only Persian women as their consorts and refrained from marrying foreign women. Diplomatic marriages with non-Persian women are attested under Cyrus the Great, but the Achaemenid kings made more of a habit of making marriage alliances with great Persian noble families or married within the Achaemenid clan itself by taking cousins, nieces, sisters, and half-sisters as wives. It is difficult to know if the king picked out a 'chief' wife – on a par with the pharaonic Egyptian tradition of appointing a Great Royal Wife, who ranked higher than the other royal wives – or whether precedence in the harem's pecking order was negotiated on a more ad hoc basis. There does not seem to have been an official Persian title for a 'chief' or 'principal' wife, which suggests that it was not a recognised court position.

Knowledge of the names of Achaemenid royal consorts is chiefly derived from Greek sources and they usually provide the name for just one wife for each Great King. Reliance on the Greek sources would suggest that Persian monarchs were monogamists. This idiosyncrasy is probably the result of two factors: first, there was the Greeks' preoccupation with the 'norm' of monogamy and their inability to put themselves comfortably into a different cultural mindset. They preferred to think of the Persian king as a one-woman man (at least when it came to a wife; they were happy to imagine him with countless concubines). Second, the Greeks knew very little about the workings of the Great King's harem. They simply did not have access to details such as the names of the king's wives. The Greek representation of Persian royal monogamy is certainly wrong. Great Kings took multiple wives so that they could father many heirs.

Near Eastern sources emphasise the significance of multiple offspring – especially sons – to a king's success. It was his dynastic duty to take wives and beget children. An old Babylonian proverb stressed the point by calling down the blessings of the gods for healthy issue from a buxom consort:

> May Ishtar make you a hot-limbed wife to lie by you!
> May she bestow on you broad-armed sons!
> May she seek out for you a place of happiness.
> Marrying is human.
> Getting children is divine.

Kings were under enormous pressure to father many children, and the birth of healthy sons was tantamount to their success and reputation as mighty monarchs. Many heartfelt royal pleas to the gods are to be found in the cuneiform sources. In one addressed to the god Shamash, the childless Mesopotamian king Etana implores the god to 'Take away my shame and give me an heir!' Likewise, Kirta, the childless king of Ugarit, poured forth an anguished cry to his gods to grant him heirs. His *cri de cœur* is palpable in a prayer he composed to his gods:

> What to me is silver, or even yellow gold,
> Together with its land, and slaves forever mine?
> A triad of chariot horses
> From the stable of a slave woman's son?
> Let me procreate sons!
> Let me produce a brood!

The consorts of the Great Kings were expected to be fertile sexual partners. The wives were responsible for the promulgation of the Achaemenid dynasty because royal power was transmitted directly through the wombs of the royal wives. Darius the Great was married to at least six women (there may have been more), and we have seen how his marriage alliances were undertaken to endorse his legitimacy as Persia's monarch. His marriage to a daughter of Gobryas before becoming king tied together two important Persian houses; he had three sons with her. After his accession, he married Atossa, the daughter of Cyrus, who had previously been Cambyses' and Bardiya's wife and had four sons with her. He was also wed to Artystone, another daughter of Cyrus, who gave him at least one son. Next to be married was Parmys, daughter of Bardiya, and then Phaidymē, daughter of the tribal leader Otanes; earlier, she had been Bardiya's wife. Another spouse, Phratagoune, the *khān* Artanes' daughter, gave him two more sons. Darius therefore had six wives at the same time. Two of them stand out in the sources: Atossa and her sister Artystone.

According to Herodotus, it was the youngest of Cyrus' daughters, Artystone, who was the favourite of Darius' consorts; the king is even supposed to have commissioned a rare statue of her made from hammered gold. Beyond the Greek imaginings, her importance in the hierarchy of the court is confirmed by the Fortification texts of Persepolis, which show her to be a woman of great personal wealth and significant power. She appears over thirty times in the tablets, where she was known by her Persian name, Irtashtuna. She owned at least three estates managed by stewards and maintained by numerous *kurtash*. She too can be located travelling around the

Figure 13.
Impression of
a seal belonging
to Artystone.

empire's core, sometimes with her mother-in-law, Irdabama, and sometimes in the company of her son, Prince Arshama. Her elaborate personal heirloom seal was found on eight letter orders and nine documents listing foodstuffs which were delivered to feed her household. Some of the texts show the care which Darius lavished on his wife. One is an order sent by Darius directly to Parnakka, the chief administrator at Persepolis, to ensure that Irtashtuna had good wine to drink:

> Tell Yamakshedda the wine-bearer, Parnakka spoke as follows: 200 *marrish* [quarts] of wine are to be issued to the *dukshish* Irtashtuna. It was ordered by the king. First month, year 9. Ansukka wrote [the text]; Maraza communicated the contents (PF 0723).

Another reveals how the king ordered a hundred sheep to be taken from his personal flock and given to his wife for her own estate:

> Say to Harrena the overseer of livestock, Parnakka spoke thus: 'Darius the king ordered me, saying, "100 sheep from my estate are to be issued to the *dukshish* Irtashtuna."' And now Parnakka says: 'As the king ordered me, so I am ordering you. Now you are to issue 100 sheep to the *dukshish* Irtashtuna, as was commanded by the king.' First month, year 19. Ansukka wrote [the text]; Maraza communicated the contents (PF 6764).

More importantly, the Persepolis texts actually preserve for us the personal 'voice' of the queen, since several of the cuneiform tablets are commands issued directly from Artystone herself:

> Tell Datukka, Irtashtuna spoke as follows: '100 litres of wine to Ankanna; issue it from my estate at Mirandu. . . and from my estate at Kukake' (PF 1835).

The queen dictated her own letters to scribes, who diligently dashed them off in wet clay. She wrote frequently to one of her principal servants, a Semite named Shalamana, her chief Chamberlain. Her instructions to him were always curt and to the point:

Figure 14. Impression of a seal belonging to Shalamana, chief steward to Artystone.

Tell Shalamana, Irtashtuna spoke as follows: '200 litres of wine to Darizza. Issue it!'

Tell Shalamana, Irtashtuna spoke as follows: '500 litres of wine to Mitranka and his companions. Issue it!' (PF 1837).

Poor Shalamana's personal seal has now been identified – and its design says much about him: an enthroned woman holds an oversized pomegranate flower in one hand and raises a cup to her mouth. In front of her, on a small serving table, is an elegant vessel in the shape of a gazelle and an incense-burner, used to perfume the air. A bearded male servant enthusiastically extends his arm and proffers a wine jug and a ladle-cum-sieve – he has no doubt decanted the wine into the gazelle bowl and used the sieve to fill the woman's cup. Of course, this cannot be taken as a 'portrait' of Shalamana and his royal mistress, but it is certainly a representation of his office, which is why, no doubt, he chose that particular image for his personal seal. It demonstrates the social context of Shalamana's life and his place within Achaemenid society.

None of Darius' other wives are as conspicuous in the sources as is Artystone/Irtashtuna. In the period covered by the Fortification tablets, it is she and her son who are the most conspicuous of Darius' wives and children, suggesting, perhaps, that Herodotus was justified in his opinion that she was indeed Darius' favourite queen. In comparison with Artystone, her sister, Atossa, is rarely found in the Persepolis texts. She appears a maximum of six times. Two texts from Persepolis, dated to the 22nd regnal year of Darius

(500/499 BCE), refer to Udusana (Atossa's Old Persian name) receiving deposits of cereal from the central stores, while another tablet records her being given a ration of 11,368 quarts of wine. The amount of grain and wine implies that Atossa supported a very substantial entourage, easily on a par with that of her sister, and that she was on an economic footing more or less comparable with Artystone and Irdabama. Atossa also controlled property and *kurtash* near Persepolis, and drew on the Persepolis bureaucracy to support them and to provision her own household, which was a very large one. She was maintained by the state economy in a position which became her rank as Cyrus' daughter and a three-time royal bride.

*

For the sake of having many children, Persian rulers had a number of wives and a much greater number of concubines. Persian royal concubines were girls who had been sent to Persia as slaves, received by the Great King as tribute from satraps, or had been captured from rebellious subjects. In spite of the Orientalist harem sex myth and the lure of erotic exoticism that has been built up around them, concubines were not living sex toys. Like the king's consorts, concubines too were expected to act for the benefit of the ruling dynasty and provide healthy, and numerous, children. In their desire for multiple heirs, the kings of ancient Persia were not content to rely on the child-bearing capabilities of their consorts, but actively sought to procreate with concubines whom they could monopolise sexually.

Capturing women as war booty was a dominant way of replenishing Near Eastern harems. The childless king Kirta of Ugarit, who was encountered earlier, supposed that a brood of sons would follow once he had acquired, in the aftermath of battle, an aristocratic concubine as a breeding partner. With that goal in mind, he raised an army and marched on the kingdom of Udum, demanding of its king his eldest daughter:

> What is not in my house you must give me:
> You must give me Lady Huraya,

> The fair-one, your firstborn child
> Who is as fair as the goddess Anat,
> Who is as comely as the goddess Astarte.
> Who will bear a child for Kirta.

King Kirta set his cap high in his demand for princess Huraya of Udum, but it is doubtful that every concubine came from such illustrious stock, not even in Persia. As Ctesias of Cnidus recalled,

> when Cambyses learnt that Egyptian women were superior to others when it came to sexual intercourse, he sent to Amasis, the Egyptian king, asking for one of his daughters. But the king did not give him one of his own, since he suspected that she would have the status not of a wife but that of a concubine.

Most of the girls acquired for the Great Kings' harems were of humble stock. After Darius quelled the Ionian uprising, for instance, the most beautiful local girls were dragged from their homes and sent to his court. Not all captive women were bound for the privileges of the royal harem. Most of them would have disappeared into the huge regiment of domestic staff who worked throughout the palaces as *arad Shari* (Akkadian for 'royal slaves') and *arad ekalli* (Akkadian for 'palace slaves'). An Old Persian word for 'concubine' has thus far not been attested, but philologists reconstruct an Old Iranian term, *harči-* (derived from the Armenian *harč*), as 'secondary wife' or 'concubine'. It is unlikely that concubines were given the title *dukshish*, because in the highly formalised hierarchical structure of the court these foreign women were always on a lower rung of the social ladder from that of royal consorts.

Surprisingly, perhaps, it is the Old Testament that supplies us with some of the best information about the practice of concubinage in Achaemenid Iran. The Hebrew biblical book of Esther was created by an unknown Jewish author probably living in Susa (as part of a large population of Jews who settled in the area) in the fourth century BCE. Whoever he was, he understood the intimate workings of the Persian court very well and the use it made of royal wives, concubines, and palace slaves. Out of his knowledge, he crafted a perfect little novella which followed the rise of an orphaned Jewish girl to the position of queen. Esther is closer to a fairy tale than it is to history, of course, for we have already noticed that Achaemenid monarchs did not take foreign consorts. The prospect of a Jewish girl, no matter how beautiful, reaching the rank of a royal wife was negligible. Nevertheless, this charming story, which has provided much spiritual and cultural succour for Jewish peoples across the centuries, does tell much about the workings of Achaemenid royal concubinage. The story begins with a royal commission to restock the royal harem with young, attractive girls:

> The king's personal attendants proposed, 'Let a search be made for beautiful young virgins for the king. Let the king appoint commissioners in every province of his realm to bring all these beautiful young women into the harem at the citadel of Susa. Let them be placed under the care of Hegai, the king's eunuch, who is in charge of the women; and let beauty treatments be given to them' . . . When the king's order and edict had been proclaimed, many young women were brought to the citadel of Susa and put under the care of Hegai. Esther also was taken to the king's palace and entrusted to Hegai, who had charge of the harem.

Sounding very much like an opening to the *Tales of a Thousand and One Nights*, the book of Esther records a genuine royal practice, whereby scouts and spies were sent across the empire to bring back to court pretty girls who might be trained in the arts of music, poetry, and beauty to become royal concubines. Precisely the same practice operated under the Ottoman sultans, the Mughal emperors, and the Ming and Qing emperors of China. It was an effective way to restock a harem and bring new DNA into the imperial bloodline.

The book of Esther further notes that the more fortunate of the young women chosen for the harem were instructed for a year in courtly arts and etiquette before being considered eligible for congress with the monarch. According to the bible, Esther found favour with the eunuch in charge of the novices' harem and he provided her with beauty treatments and special food. He assigned to her seven female maids selected from the king's palace and moved her and her maids into the best sleeping quarters in the harem. From the details given by the author of Esther, upon the king's command, and only after she had completed her etiquette training, a novice was sent to the king's bedchamber. Anything she wanted was given to her as she departed from the harem and went to the king's quarters. She would go there in the evening, and if by morning she had managed to remain in the king's bedchamber, and had found his favour, then she graduated to a higher level of harem society and entered another part of the harem. This was under the supervision of Shaashgaz, the king's eunuch, who was in charge of the concubines. She would not return to the king unless he summoned her by name.

Concubinage was a difficult existence. Concubines tended to oscillate between pleasure-women and women of state. Many concubines were trained by eunuch overseers and senior women to be skilled musicians, cultured dancers, and brilliant storytellers, and were, like the geisha of Japan, highly prized for their services in the arts of entertainment. But concubines were not prostitutes. Certainly, the concubines of Persian kings, should not be classed even as reputable disreputable women, and in no way should these women be confused with courtesans or mistresses. Nonetheless, in legal terms it is doubtful that concubines were ever thought of as being 'married' to a king. There were, as far as we know, no vows or financial transfers of bride price or dowry and no ceremony or banquet of celebration. When a grey-haired monarch, as Darius surely was at the close of his reign, selected his fiftieth girl from among the novices of the harem (perhaps a woman of a conquered province, or one of his dancers) as his latest love interest, was this ever a marriage? No, it was not. Yet concubinage could lead to a stable relationship with the king. An established concubine would find prestige and honour within the harem-system when children she had borne the king were officially acknowledged as his heirs. Nevertheless, unlike a wife, a concubine did not have the same status socially or legally as her mate. Dinon, a Greek who lived in

Persia for several years, gives an interesting glimpse of how court etiquette was employed within the female household to carefully demarcate concubines from more superior royal ladies: 'Among the Persians', he noted, 'the queen tolerates an enormous number of concubines because . . . the queen is treated with deference by the them. In fact, they do obeisance in front of her.'

Concubines had an important part to play in the fortunes of the Achaemenid dynasty. They were expected to be fertile sexual partners and, as such, they were as much responsible for a dynasty's promulgation as any royal wife. The lives of these women were not for themselves, but for creating other lives. They were required to keep intact the dynasty, and secure future generations to come; they were supposed to be physically appealing since the arousal of desire in the ruler was essential. King Artaxerxes I fathered at least eighteen sons from his concubines and Artaxerxes II had no fewer than 150 sons by his. The birth of a son terminated the concubine's sexual relationship with the ruler, even if their relationship was one of passion. Court tradition dictated that she give him no more male children (there were no concubine-born Persian kings who had full-blood brothers). If the concubine gave the monarch a series of daughters, then the sexual relationship could continue, but once the couple were blessed with a son, sexual congress ceased and the ruler moved on to a new concubine. From there on, the singular purpose of the concubine mother was to work towards her son's political advancement. While the official take was that sons born to concubines were regarded as inferior to any child born to a royal wife, the history of the succession of the Achaemenids tells another story. Not infrequently the son of a concubine ascended his way to the throne. Darius II, the son of a Babylonian concubine, for instance, was crowned Great King on the death of his father, Artaxerxes I. Greek writings about the sons of Persian concubines consistently – but inaccurately – refer to them as 'bastards' (*nothoi*), but in Persia there was no stigma attached to being the offspring of a concubine, and in the harem status system, the child of a concubine always outranked its mother, since the child took its eminence (and the blood-royal) from its father.

Concubinage was not necessarily a dormant institution and some concubines gained access to high status, even becoming the mothers of kings. But the great majority of concubines must have passed their lives as nameless nonentities in a court full of competitive women. The reality of the harem was that circumstance or personal ambition could change the hierarchy, and with it the course of dynastic politics. Antagonism between concubines and between wives and concubines was common. Women who had sexual relations with the king would have had (even if only temporarily) greater status than those who had no access to his bed, and therefore we can speculate how competition to attract and keep the king's sexual attention could be intense. Concubinage was not a satisfying state of existence.

What of the number of concubines found at the Persian court? How many were there? Greek authors, captivated by their own erotic seraglio fantasies, claimed that there were around 360 concubines in the royal harem – one (almost) for each day of the year. Very few Greeks ever saw into the domestic quarters of the palace of a Persian Great King, and so the subject of his harem was ripe for titillating speculation. Diodorus Siculus was just one of many Greeks who fantasised about the Persian king's sex life, conjuring up the image of 'concubines, outstanding in beauty, selected from all the women of Asia'. He daydreamed how 'each night these women paraded about the couch of the king so that he might select the one with whom he would lie that night'. The Greeks envisaged the royal concubines as abandoned, licentious girls, and as beautiful off-limits Eastern erotica. The heated fantasy of a carousel of nubile concubines, there to be ogled and stripped, gladdened the heart of many a Hellene. But in their wonderment the Greeks did perceive something else besides: the fact that the Great King had the ability and resources to amass, house, support, and sexually exploit so many women. In truth, the ranks of the royal concubines were never fixed at 360. There was a continual traffic in concubines and female slaves entering into the harem, and although it is impossible to state with any authority the exact number of women who found themselves in concubinage throughout the Achaemenid era, we must suppose that the numbers ran from a few dozen to many hundreds, depending on the fortunes of conquest, the payment of tribute, and the sexual inclination of any Great King.

The accumulation of females on an imperial scale spoke for the monarch's virility as well as his wealth. Consorts and concubines were there to provide for his bodily comforts and for the needs of the dynasty. Their bodies were symbols of his dominance – not simply of man over women or of master over slaves, but of monarch over empire. Like the diverse food served at the royal table, the precious stones and timbers brought to the workshops at Susa, or the rare flora planted in the royal gardens, the women who lay in the king's bed were physical manifestations of the Persian empire itself. Through their fertility the monarch populated his court and prolonged his dynasty.

11

The Politics of Etiquette

The Achaemenid Great Kings relied upon formalised etiquette and court ceremony to create a special aura around the throne. Elaborate rituals were enacted as a means of distancing the king from his subjects. Even courtiers had only a very limited access to the royal personage and approached him only during a tightly controlled audience ceremony in which matters of security and etiquette were paramount. To enjoy the benefits of a royal audience, courtiers and visitors had to undergo tight security checks and had to be conversant with palace protocol procedures to ensure that they behaved with dignified decorum and observed preordained rules in the presence of the monarch.

We might think of the Great King, costumed in his finery, as an actor in a great royal drama and his courtiers as part-players and spectators. Thinking about the court in terms of theatre is, of course, not new. Historians and others writing about the court of Louis XIV at Versailles, for instance, have found the metaphor of theatre irresistible. The metaphor is perfectly apropos. No less a person than Elizabeth I of England declared that 'We princes are set on stages, in the sight of the world duly observed', implying that monarchs saw themselves as performers in the drama of court life. The close association between the performance of etiquette and the performance of ceremony must not be dismissed lightly as a mere frippery of a privileged aristocratic lifestyle, for in Persia etiquette had a major symbolic function in the structure of court society. In the hothouse world of the Achaemenid royal court every individual was hypersensitive to the slightest change in the mechanism of etiquette. 'Doing the right thing' was paramount. The laws of protocol, the knowledge of employing the correct formulae (spoken or non-verbal) for greeting, showing respect or deference, and the arts of obsequiousness had to be mastered by courtiers who were eager to maintain court positions or to climb the ladder of success. Conversely, failure to 'do the right thing' could be used as a weapon to bring about the fall of an enemy at court, and courtiers carefully observed the actions and speech of others to measure their knowledge of the correct courtly behaviour.

Perhaps the greatest test of court protocol for any aspiring courtier was the royal audience. Representations of this important ceremony come in the form of numerous seal and gemstone images, a small painted image on a sarcophagus, and from the sculptured monumental door jambs at Persepolis. The finest surviving examples of an audience scene come in the form of two big stone reliefs once located at the two staircases to the Persepolis *Apadana* (throne room) but later moved to the Treasury. The Great King is shown in audience in a 'frozen moment'. He wears a court robe and a crown and holds a pomegranate blossom and a sceptre (which he might stretch out to grant favours). In order to accentuate the notion of dynastic rule, he is accompanied by the crown prince, who is depicted wearing the same garb as the king, and who is also given the prerogative of holding an Iranian pomegranate blossom. Also in attendance are high-ranking members of the court and the military. Two incense-burners help to demarcate the royal

Figure 15.
Detail taken from the so-called 'Treasury Relief' at Persepolis; the Great King and crown prince are shown in royal audience.

space and accentuate its sacredness, as does the dais upon which the throne is placed and the baldachin, or textile awning, which covers the scene. The theatrical paraphernalia of the throne room and the awesome setting of the *Apadana* were intended to instil fear and wonder in suppliants, and the figure of the king himself, the protagonist of the courtly drama, must have been an impressive, almost overwhelming, sight. The anonymous author of the Greek version of the biblical book of Esther brilliantly captures the scene of the terrified queen approaching the enthroned king:

> Going through all the doors, Esther stood there before the king. And he was sitting upon his royal throne and he was clothed in a robe which manifested his status, gold all throughout and with expensive stones. And he was extremely awe-inspiring. And lifting his face which had been set afire in glory, he gazed directly at her – like a bull in the height of anger. And the queen was afraid, and her face changed over in faintness, and she leaned on the servant who was going in front of her ... But the king leaped down from his throne and he took her up in his arms.

The royal throne was a significant icon of kingship and in the Near East both monarchs and gods were frequently por-trayed enthroned. The Achaemenid throne was high-backed and rested upon leonine-feet – a rare example of sections of an actual Achaemenid-period throne (probably from a satrapal palace) was discovered near Samaria in Israel. The unmistakable message sent by this ornate piece of furniture was obvious: the one who sat on the throne had absolute authority. The Great King had a footstool as well, and this was also an important emblem of his kingship. Like the throne, it too was loaded with ritual and symbolism. At the Achaemenid court there was even an office associated with the footstool, and a footstool-bearer, a nobleman of important rank, is depicted on the north and east wings of the *Apadana* at Persepolis. According to the Roman historian Quintus Curtius Rufus, when Alexander of Macedon first conquered Persia and took over the

luxurious tent of Darius III, he clumsily bungled court etiquette by
misappropriating a low table as a royal footstool:

> Alexander now sat on the royal throne, but it was too high for
> him and so, because his feet could not touch the floor, one of
> his pages placed a small table under them. Noticing the dis-
> tress on the face of one of Darius' eunuchs, the king asked him
> why he was upset. The eunuch declared that the table was used
> by Darius to eat from, and he could not help his tears, seeing
> it consigned to such a disrespectful use. The king was struck
> with shame . . . and was ordering the table's removal when
> Philotas said, 'No, Your Majesty, don't do that! Take this as an
> omen: the table your enemy used for his feasts has become
> your footstool.'

The story only reconfirms the centrality of this seemingly
inconspicuous piece of furniture in royal display and ideology.
It was a given that the Great King's feet should never touch the
ground and must be protected by soft carpets, as the Greek Deinon
had observed for himself:

> Through their court the king would proceed on foot, walking
> upon Sardis carpets spread on the floor, which no one else
> would walk upon. And when he reached the final court, he
> would mount his chariot or, sometimes, his horse; but outside
> the palace he was never seen on foot.

At the centre of the Treasury Relief, a chiliarch, or vizier, dressed
in the traditional Iranian riding habit, performs a ritual gesture of
obeisance to the monarch. It was one of the principal roles of the
chiliarch to present individuals or delegations to the king, so his
presence in the scene makes sense. He stoops forward and raises his
hand to his mouth and makes a gesture that is closely associated
with the *sala'am*, or formal greeting, used in later Muslim courts.
A society that requires such codes of respectful behaviour is very
likely to have autocratic political organisation, characterised by the
coercive power of a king. Unspontaneous, semi-ritualised gestures
of this sort were a hallmark of Persian social communication, at

least according to Herodotus, who describes in some detail a series of greeting gestures used in daily life, noting that,

> when the Persians meet one another in the roads, you can see whether those who meet are of equal rank. For instead of greeting by words, they kiss each other on the mouth; but if one of them is inferior to the other, they kiss one another on the cheeks, and if one is of much less noble rank than the other, he falls down before him and worships him.

These gestures were even more ritualised at the Persian court. In a Near Eastern context, the Persian practice of bowing and kissing as a sign of submission and respect looks very much at home since kowtowing, prostration, kissing the ground, or even kissing the hem of a garment or the feet of the monarch were familiar gestures in Mesopotamian courtly settings.

Known to the Greeks as *proskynesis*, the exact nature of the ceremonial obeisance to a Persian monarch is much debated by scholars. Etymologically, the term *proskynesis* incorporates the idea of a kiss, being a compound of the Greek *pros*, meaning 'towards', and *kyneo*, 'to kiss'. Yet Herodotus implies that *proskynesis* was a prostrating of oneself or a bowing down. So perhaps the 'kiss' followed on from the prostration. The Treasury Relief depicts that moment: having arisen from his prostration, the chaliarch performs a sala'am by touching his fingers to his lips, and offering the kiss to the king from his hand. For the Greeks, prostration was a religious act and suitable only for performance before a god. For a Greek to humble himself in that fashion before any man undermined his concept of *eleutheria*, or 'freedom'. Greek visitors to the Persian court found the act of prostration repellent and struggled to perform it, even though it was a non-negotiable rule for being granted a royal audience. This is clearly what the chiliarch Artabanus intended to convey to the Athenian Themistocles when he briefed the Greek about the importance of the ritual:

> 'Among our many excellent customs, this we account the best, to honour the king and to kowtow to him [*proskynein*], as

the image of the god of all things. If then you approve of our practices, fall down before the king and revere him, you may both see him and speak to him; but if you think otherwise, you will need to use messengers to intercede for you, for it is not our national custom for the king to grant audience to any man who does not pay him obeisance' ... When Themistocles was led into the king's presence, he kissed the ground in front of him and waited silently.

As in all other aspects of his official life, the ideology of invisibility governed the king's dining habits too. The sovereign tended to dine alone, hidden from view in a chamber (or some other specified space) while his guests sat outside to eat, in full sight of anyone who wished to look on. Only the most highly honoured guests were served by the royal butlers in a hall close to the king's dining room. The two spaces were separated by a screen or hanging that permitted the king to view his guests but kept him obscured from their sight. As the dinner drew to a close, a few special guests were summoned by a eunuch to approach the king and to drink in his company. This was a mark of exceptional distinction because it was during these drinking bouts that important matters of state were discussed – and personal ambitions might be realised. The courtier honoured with a regular place at the king's table was known as a *homotrapezus* ('messmate'), a very rare and enviable title held by trusted nobles of the highest rank.

Great pleasure could be had in eating and drinking in the festive atmosphere of a royal banquet, such as an almost legendary one thrown by Xerxes in the third year of his reign when he gave a state feast for all his administrators, ministers, and satraps, and for all the women of the court. Xerxes' banquet lasted a full 180 days. It represented something more than the simple provision of daily bread, for a royal banquet gave eating and drinking their full meaning. A banquet broke with the ordinary, occasioned as it most often was by fortunate circumstances in life that were outside the daily routine. With surplus food, and the rule for the drinking being 'No restrictions!' (as the book of Esther recalls), dining at a royal banquet might be regarded as a form of extreme sport, and one on a par with another Achaemenid courtly passion: hunting.

In its own way, hunting was less of a sport per se than an art form. The royal hunt was never simply a matter of killing animals. It too was a ceremonial loaded with rules of etiquette. A successful hunt had to end in an animal's death, but it had to be a specific type of animal that was killed: gazelle, deer, ibex, wild ass, wild horses, bears, and lions were all considered to be proper sport. The victim needed to be dispatched in a particular way. The animal must have been free to run from its predator, or turn and attack the hunter, but it also must have been killed deliberately – and with violence (but there could be no use of traps, poisoned baits, or nets). But. more than anything else, the hunter's prey had to be a wild animal with every chance of being hostile to the hunter, and it could not be thought to have been tame or docile around humans. There was no sport in hunting dairy cows. Hunting was regarded as an armed confrontation between the human world and the untamed wilderness, between culture and nature. For the elite of Persia, the hunt became an elaborate ritual encrusted with jargon and stiff with ceremonial. The royal hunt served to validate the aristocratic credentials of the hunters, for the court hunt had nothing to do with providing for economic necessity – it was predominantly a political and ideological activity. The countless depictions of the hunt on Achaemenid seals demonstrate the centrality of the image in Persian thought.

The frequency and duration of royal hunts also demonstrates the nexus between hunting and governance. It is difficult to get precise data about the number of hours the Persian king spent in the saddle, but classical texts suggest that he was at least conceived of being *à la chasse* for considerable amounts of his time each day. Monarchs have always laid stress on their ability in the hunt, and it was in this display of chivalric bravery that the Great King was able to demonstrate his manhood, for hunting was set on a par with warfare. Essentially, the same skills were necessary for both, and thus monarchs had to be leaders in both war and hunting.

Hunts took place in *paridaida* and in the open field. Xenophon suggested that the best thrill could be had when hunting game in the wild because game-park hunting meant chasing prey which had been captured and brought into the locale specifically to be killed. An event of this kind in a game park may have lacked the frisson of danger of hunting in the open terrain but, nonetheless, it was the symbolic execution of the hunted creature that was the most important part of the hunt. In many cases this simply led to the time-saving method of pre-capturing animals to be slaughtered by the monarch later. Every royal hunt was meticulously planned and was under the charge of court officials who were responsible for procuring wild animals and training and caring for the huge mastiff dogs which accompanied the hunting party. Grooms and stable hands were needed for the horses, and bodyguards were ever-present – on a hunt the Great King's life was particularly vulnerable. Successful royal hunts also required military personnel to be involved as 'beaters' to flush out the prey. Persian monarchs tended to participate in the so-called 'ring hunt', a formation which involved a massive number of people and eliminated the problem of chasing the prey. Cornered by a diminishing circle of hunters, the animal tended to flounder so that the monarch could then enter the ring to kill it. A refinement of this was the idea of 'fencing', where large nets might be employed by a section of the military to literally fence off an area, such as an entire mountainside, to force the prey to confront the king and his courtiers. Whatever methods were involved, accompanied by a large escort of nobles, servants, and even concubines, the Great King must have been an impressive sight in the saddle, as the Greek author Chariton imagined:

> A magnificent hunt was announced. Horsemen rode out, splendidly attired – Persian courtiers and the elite of the army. Every one of them was a sight to behold, but the most impressive was the king himself; he was riding a powerful and striking Nisaean horse whose trappings – bit, cheekpieces, frontlet, breastplate – were all of gold; he was wearing a mantle of Tyrian purple made from Babylonian cloth and his tiara was

the colour of hyacinths; he had a sword at his waist and carried two spears, and slung over his shoulder were a bow and quiver of the finest Chinese craftsmanship. . . . Soon the mountains were full of people shouting and running, dogs barking, horses neighing, game fleeing.

The greatest kudos was to be had in hunting lions. This was royal sport indeed. From very ancient times, lion hunting was the strict preserve of royalty: 'To finish the lion with the weapon was my own privilege', affirms one Old Babylonian ruler. Persians hunted lions by throwing spears from horseback and with bows and slings, but protocol strictly governed this aspect of the royal lion hunt and prerogatives were given to the king so that it was his right alone to cast the first spear at the prey. Darius I is depicted shooting arrows at a rearing lion, while the carcass of another slayed feline lies beneath his chariot's wheels. The use of chariots in hunting seems to have developed in Egypt and Assyria where they were used extensively in both war and the hunt as indicators of prestige, so closely associated were they with kings and the nobility. In fact chariots were far from ideal hunting platforms as they were fragile and liable to break on unsuitable terrain. While one way round this was to change to horseback if the prey fled into a forest or marsh, teams of troops were also sometimes used to stop the animal from fleeing from the flat plains. Whatever the reality of the royal lion hunt, the motif of the king as slayer of lions is repeated on Persian coinage and in seals and reliefs, where the lion sometimes morphs into a mythical hybrid creature and is dispatched by the king in his guise as 'Persian hero'.

Achaemenid kings used the royal court as a political tool in order to consolidate and augment their absolutist rule. Through codified ceremonial, the Persian nobility were tamed and domesticated. Closely watched, stripped of effective power, and kept occupied with the minutiae of etiquette, the Persian elite became obsessed with their positions in the courtly orbit of the Great King, forgetting that they were ostensibly prisoners within a gilded cage.

12

Also Sprach Zarathustra

Knowledge of the religious world of the Achaemenids is steadily improving. This is chiefly due to the scholars working in the Oriental Insitute of Chicago and the National Museum in Tehran on the corpus of the Persepolis Fortification tablets. These dry little clay documents are overturning preconceptions of the religious landscape of ancient Persia and because of them we are seeing anew the way in which the Persians expressed and practised their religious faith. The tablets speak of the worship of the old Elamite gods alongside Iranian deities and they name various kinds of priests and the rituals they enacted. Whereas scholars were once completely dependent upon Greek sources for information about Persian religion, today we can access the genuine Persian experience and get much closer to the root of Achaemenid faith and its ritual practices.

Believing that Herodotus made salient and accurate observations on the nature of the Achaemenid world, scholars at one time put all their trust in what the 'Father of History' had to say about Persian religion. 'The customs which I know the Persians to practise are the following: they have no images of the gods, no temples nor altars, and consider the use of them a sign of foolishness', he stated dogmatically. Now that we can read and analyse the indigenous Persian texts for ourselves, we can categorically state that on each of his 'observations', Herodotus was simply wrong. The Persepolis tablets contain evidence to show that in their worship the Persians *did* use images, temples, and altars. In his *Histories*, as we have noted, Herodotus was trying to depict Persia as a topsy-turvy world, the antithesis of Greek civilisation. Because the Greeks routinely used temples, altars, and images in their worship, to craft the Persians as the ultimate 'Other', Herodotus created for them a religious world which operated without the fundamentals of a 'civilised' organised religion. But, at last, the Persepolis texts are correcting Herodotus' very persuasive images of Persia's alien religion.

In the Persepolis records we find an Elamite word of common usage: *ziyan*. It literally means 'a place of seeing' and it was used to refer to a 'temple', 'shrine', or 'cult building'. *Ziyan* refers to a place of divine epiphany, a locale where the gods are seen or experienced. It was the same word the Elamites had used for many centuries for a variety of religious architectural features and the term was later adopted by the Persian administrators. In the Persepolis tablets the word routinely appears – for instance, deliveries of wine are sent to a *ziyan* at a place called Harkurtush, and of vinegar to the *ziyan* at a town named Zarnamiya. But we can look beyond the Elamite language for references to cultic structures for they exist in Old Persian royal epigraphy too. In Darius' Bisitun Inscription, the king proudly proclaims that he has rebuilt the *āyadanā* (Old Persian, 'places of worship') which had been destroyed by the usurper Gaumâta. In the Akkadian and Elamite versions of the text, this word is translated as 'houses of gods', which affords us the image that when Darius thought of the *āyadanā*, he was envisioning some kind of physical man-made structure, a 'temple' or 'shrine'.

For thousands of years, the Elamites had built religious shrines throughout their territories. Consequently, the landscape of the imperial Persian homeland was covered with ancient Elamite sanctuaries. Mountain tops, rock surfaces, and hillsides served as sacred sites, as these had long been the Elamites' preferred locations for the construction of temples or shrines. In their turn, the Achaemenids gravitated to these same ancient cult centres and located their own religious practices there also. Herodotus wrote that it was the custom of the Persians 'to ascend the summits of the loftiest mountains, and there to offer sacrifice'. He conjures up an image of Tibetan-like monks performing their solitary rituals on high snow-covered precipices, but the reality is different and we now know that the Persians performed their religious duties within the enclosed spaces of small temples and shrines which dotted the mountains and hills.

Archaeology is very slowly revealing these temples. One of the most important shrine structures has been uncovered in Dahan-i Ghulaman ('Gateway of the Slaves'), the Achaemenid provincial capital of the satrapy of Drangiana in eastern Iran. Dating to the early decades of the fifth century BCE, it is built of mud bricks and its layout is almost square, consisting of four corner rooms and a central courtyard with four inward-facing porticoes, all of which are design elements which find parallels in the royal architecture of Persepolis. At the centre of the courtyard, three monumental stepped altars were erected (perhaps for the worship of a triad of gods), and the remains of ashes mixed with animal fat and burned bones were found on the altars and scattered throughout the sanctuary too.

The remains of another temple dated to 400 BCE were excavated at Tash-Kirman Tepe in Chorsamia. in western Central Asia (today Chorsamia straddles Uzbekistan and Turkmenistan), on the south side of the Aral Sea. The temple complex had a high podium, a small courtyard, and a labyrinthine series of rooms and adjoining corridors, some of which contained thick layers of burnt ash. Several altars were also found at the site. No exact parallels to the layout of this temple are known, but it is probable that some kind of Persian cult was practised there in the Achaemenid period. The excavators claimed that what they found was a fire temple, a place where the sacred flame was kindled and cared for by priests, but it is impossible to be certain.

The built-in flexibility of the word *ziyan* allows us great variation in our understanding of the shape and use of Persian religious structures. Small square temples, rock-carved shrines, and even cave sanctuaries can easily be accommodated in its meaning. If *ziyan* can refer to *any* cult-dedicated building or shrine, then it might refer to the stone architectural structures known as the Zendan-i Soleyman and Ka'ba-ye Zardosht, the great 'twin towers' of Pasargadae and Naqsh-i Rustam. These two sister buildings are square structures constructed of white limestone blocks. Each face is decorated with slightly recessed false windows of black limestone. Both buildings once contained an inner chamber which was accessed through a flight of steps. It has been suggested that the towers were fire temples, but with our new understanding of Persian religious practices and that both structures may qualify as *ziyan* in the wider sense, it is possible that they were shrines for other forms of worship, including a royal cult whereby the spirits of monarchs were venerated, ancestor worship, and sacrifice. Certainly, the Kaʻba-ye Zardosht at Naqsh-i Rustam was surrounded by many other buildings, as yet to be unearthed, and future archaeological work at the site might well expose evidence for them being religious structures too, built there to serve the funerary cults of the dead kings whose tombs form the impressive backdrop to the whole area.

*

On his tomb relief, the person of Darius lifts his hand in a gesture of salutation to a human-like figure who rises forth from a winged disc. As he hovers above Darius, this anthropomorphic entity offers the king a ring, representing 'kingship' itself. It is clear that just as Darius and the winged entity share close intimacy of space in the carved relief, so too they share a physical form. The Great King encodes in his appearance the best physical attributes of the anthropomorphic figure. The Great King is the god's doppelgänger. King and entity adopt the same hairstyle and beard shape, the same crown, and the same garment. On the walls of Persepolis, where he is depicted with some frequency, the figure in the winged circle is associated with other powerful symbols, such as flowering rosettes (a symbol of immortality), with snarling lions and angry bulls (symbols of cosmic might and conflict), and with date palms (representing wealth and fecundity).

Because of the associations with the figure of the king and the symbols of power, some scholars argue that the man emerging from the winged disc is Ahuramazda himself, the Wise Lord, and that his iconography derives from earlier foreign prototypes. In Egypt, the winged sun disc was a commonly used symbol of pharaonic divinity, and it had been appropriated and used by the Assyrians to help them visualise their supreme god, Ashur. He was represented rising out of a nimbus, fully armed and prepared for battle. It is possible that the pragmatic Persians adopted this iconographic trope as a way to represent Ahuramazda, who was, indeed, sometimes shown with a bow and arrows. More frequently though, he was depicted as an unarmed passive god. Darius' tomb iconography stresses the reciprocity between the king and the god and echoes an idea found in an inscription from Susa where Darius confidently stated that 'Ahuramazda is mine; I am Ahuramazda's' (DSk). It is clear that Darius thought he enjoyed an intimate relationship with the divine being. Xerxes too attributed his success in the succession struggle which followed the death of Darius to the divine favour and celestial support of Ahuramazda: 'by the grace of Ahuramazda I became king on my father's throne' (XPf).

However, there is no complete consensus that the figure in the winged disc is Ahuramazda at all. Some scholars see it as a representation of an ancient Avestan (early Iranian) concept of *khvarenah*, or 'brilliance', 'luminosity', or 'splendour'. Linked to the old Indo-European word for 'sun', *hvar*, the *khvarenah* was a kind of halo-like 'glory' which emanated from a charismatic king (the Greek word *charis*, from which is derived the English 'charisma', also denotes 'brilliance'). It was a way of expressing that divine grace was present with the ruler and rested in him and shone out of him. *Khvarenah* attached itself to the whole dynasty through the sacred power of royal blood. The *khvarenah* was therefore visualised as a spirit counterpart of the king. If the king failed to act in accordance with the Truth, *Arta*, then the *khvarenah* could easily disappear, leaving the monarch an empty shell, devoid of divine light.

What then does the figure in the winged disc represent? God or 'glory'? The answer is simple: he is both god and glory. There is no detriment to championing a simultaneous double reading of the iconography. The figure is Ahuramazda, the god who supports the king; the king receives the glory of the god through the gift of the divine *khvarenah*. As he looks into the face of the god, the king sees himself reflected there. There can be no doubt that when

Darius was depicted reverencing the *khvarenah* he was also thought to be worshipping his creator and protector, Ahuramazda, whom he evoked so frequently, and so enthusiastically, in his inscriptions.

The earliest reference to Ahuramazda is actually found in an eighth century BCE Assyrian text, in which *as-sa-ra ma-za-ash* is named as one deity in a list of many gods. The presence of this Iranian deity in a Mesopotamian god list suggests that a form of Ahuramazda had moved into the Iranian plateau at the time of the great migrations, but it is impossible to know if he was widely worshipped throughout Iran. Cyrus the Great made no mention of this god; nor did Cambyses II. There was no attempt to promote a cult of Ahuramazda among the subject peoples of the early empire either. In fact, as we have seen, both Cyrus and Cambyses promoted and supported divine cults at a local level in both Babylonia and Egypt.

Nevertheless, there are numerous references to Ahuramazda in the Achaemenid royal inscriptions, and especially those of Darius the Great who lauded the god as the ultimate creator deity: 'A great god is Ahuramazda, who created this earth, who created yonder sky, who created man, who created happiness for man' (DV). In other words, Darius envisaged the Wise Lord as a Creator only of what is good, and he expressed over and over again his faith in Ahuramazda and his belief that he served the god as a divine instrument for establishing order and justice on earth: 'When Ahuramazda saw this earth in disorder, then he gave it to me . . . Because of Ahuramazda I put things in order again . . . After Ahuramazda had created me king of this world, I did what was fitting by the will of Ahuramazda' (DNa). One gains the impression that these inscriptions were written for the king himself. The court scribes and poets created for Darius his own idiosyncratic image as a heroic and pious king. The texts represented Darius as he wanted to see himself. In the royal inscriptions, the relationship between Ahuramazda and the Achaemenid kings is portrayed as one of mutual indebtedness between god and his worshipper. Ahuramazda, in return for worship and sacrifice, assists the king in maintaining his land in peace and stability.

Ahuramazda was the father of all things, the holy one who established the course of the sun and the moon and the stars, and who upheld the earth. It was he who separated the earth from the heavens and created light and dark, man, woman, plants, and animals – all by the power of thought. He was often thought of in naturalistic terms. He wore a star-bespattered robe, and the 'swift-horsed sun' was said to be his eye. His throne was set in the highest heaven, bathed in celestial light. There Ahuramazda held court, and ministering angels carried out his commands. If all this sounds a little 'biblical', that is because it is. When Jewish scribes and priests, some working in Babylonia and Persia, came to edit and fix the sacred scriptures of the Hebrews, the vision of the Jewish God was very much influenced by Persia's invisible creator, Ahuramazda, and just as Ahuramazda was above all the manifestation of perfect goodness, so too the Hebrew God took on that magnanimous divine persona.

To protect his great Creation, through an act of divine will Ahuramazda created a group of six *Amesha Spentas*, or 'Bounteous Immortals' (we should note the appearance yet again of a Gang of Seven, when we include Ahuramazda himself). These six were: Vohu Manu (Good Thoughts), Asha Vahishta (Best Righteousness), Spenta Armaiti (Holy Devotion), Khsathra Vaiyra (Desirable Dominion), Haruvatat (Wholeness), and Amertat (Immortality). This somewhat abstract group of immortals banded together to protect Ahuramazda's Creation from the forces of evil that were led by the dark force known as Angra Mainyu, or Ahriman, the leader of the demonic hordes. The Persians put much emphasis on the concept of dualism and recognised that for every good there is a bad, and for each right there is a wrong. For every Truth there was a Lie. Ahuramazda met his counterpart in the form of Angra Mainyu, an evil spirit who is said to have created 'non-life', that is, a form of existence diametrically opposed to what is good in 'real' life. Angra Mainyu was aided by spirits too – Fury and Bad Intentions – with whom he dwelt in an abyss of endless darkness. As the ultimate evil, Angra Mainyu took no material form of his own. Instead, he resided, parasite-like, in the bodies of humans and

animals. In the Persian mind there was no greater sin than to associate Ahuramazda with evil. Good and evil, Truth and Lie, are as
contrary to creation as are darkness and light and life and death. To
emphasise this notion, the Persian afterlife was thought to include a
final judgement which took place on the mythical Chinvat Bridge
(which spanned the world of the living and the dead). The deceased
who had walked the path of Truth would find paradise in the
House of Song; he who had listened to Angra Mainyu would drop
down into the hell known as the House of Lies.

Which path was followed through life was open to choice. In
his inscriptions, Darius made his option very clear. The path he followed led to Ahuramazda and to the Truth. In the inscriptions, his
announcements are often introduced by the formula 'King Darius
says', or 'So speaks King Darius', employing the Old Persian verb
thātiy, 'to proclaim'. Darius' declarations always focused on the
praise of Ahuramazda and his Creation, and on the denunciation
of the Lie. His pronouncements therefore served to uphold the
order of the land. Darius stated which side he takes in the cosmic
battle and how he fights evil by praising and conferring fame on
Ahuramazda. In announcing his name and his ancestry and his
adherence to Ahuramazda, who bestowed the royal command upon
him, Darius showed himself to be combating the forces of the Lie
and to be matching Ahuramazda's efforts in the heavenly realm.
The happiness established for mankind by Ahuramazda was maintained by and through Darius and, by extension, his Achaemenid
successors.

*

Every god needed his prophet and Ahuramazda found his in the
figure of Zarathustra. The Greeks came to know him as Zoroaster;
in modern Persian he is Zardosht. Zarathustra was a camel-herder
from what is now Afghanistan or possibly Azerbaijan – the traditions vary. As a young man he served as a priest, worshipping a series
of 'lesser deities', until he heard the voice of the true god calling
him. Compared with Mohammed, Jesus, the Buddha, or even
Moses, Zarathustra is a remote figure, hard to pin down in time or

place. Yet as a key figure in the history of religious thought, he is as important as any of the other prophets. Today, in wall posters and illustrated prayer books, his Zoroastrian followers – for that is the name given to the gentle faith he developed – depict him so as to resemble Victorian Sunday school portraits of Jesus Christ, with a clean beard, flowing white robes, and dazzling halo, although this glossy image belies his rough mountainous origin. The details of his life are obscure and those that we have are more fable than fact. One story says that at the moment of his nativity Zarathustra did not cry, but rather laughed, delighting in his good fortune to be part of Ahuramazda's great Creation. Modern Zoroastrian tradition places the moment of that birth at 600 BCE, and it associates him too with a Persian princely patron called Hystaspes, the name, of course, of the father of Darius the Great. Scholars rightly tend to push back the date of Zarathustra's birth to 1000 or 1200 BCE, the era – or shortly after – of the great migrations.

The rationale for an earlier date is due to the language and imagery contained in a series of religious texts known as the *Gathas*, allegedly a cycle of hymns composed and sung by Zarathustra himself. They reflect the nomadic lifestyle of the early Iranians but lack any references to Medes or Persians, or to any rulers or other historical peoples. Annoyingly, Zarathustra's hymns and all other Zoroastrian sacred texts, most importantly the *Avesta*, were first written down over a thousand years after the prophet's death and mostly date to the sixth century CE. This makes it difficult to filter out the genuine early Zarathustran materials from later additions.

The *Gathas* contain fragmentary episodes from the life of Zarathustra and suggest that when he was around forty years of age, he received a call to prophesy from Ahuramazda. In the course of his early ministry in Central Asia, Zarathustra seems to have made powerful enemies, and the *Gathas* state that prominent among his detractors were the powerful *karpans* (priests) and *kawis* (princes) who conducted their religious rituals in ways antithetical to Zarathustra's vision of Ahuramazda's message. Zarathustra condemned them as impious pagans, but they stubbornly refused to accept his teachings. Hostilities grew to such a point that his position within his own society became so precarious that he was forced to flee. Remarkably a superb lyric hymn, *Yasht* 46, contains a fascinating résumé of his flight into exile:

> What land to flee to?
> Where should I go to flee?
> From my family
> and from my clan they banish me.
> The community to which
> I belong has not satisfied me,
> nor have the rulers of the country!
> How can I satisfy you, O Ahuramazda?
>
> I know the reason why
> I am powerless, O Ahuramazda:
> because of my lack of cattle
> and that I am few in men.
> I lament to Thee.
> Hear me, O Ahuramazda!
> Granting support,
> as a friend would give a friend,
> Look upon the power
> of Good Mind through Truth!

Away from his homeland, now on the fringes of eastern Iran, Zarathustra experienced a further seven encounters with Ahuramazda and other divine beings who orbited around the Wise Lord. As a result, 'he accepted the religion' as the *Yasht* puts it. This suggests that Zarathustra was called not so much to establish a new religion but to reform and refine an already existing faith which was being practised badly by the *karpans* and *kawis* of his homeland. Accepting that a prophet is never recognised in his own land, Zarathustra took his message deeper into the Iranian plateau, and through the development of a sophisticated theology in which justice and morality took precedence over all things, Zarathustra gave new form and new meaning to an ancient, faltering faith. He emphasised the dualistic nature of the Creation of Ahuramazda and asked the followers of the faith to play their part in the rejection of the Lie and the establishment of divine Truth, and to this day Zoroastrians maintain a personal commitment to three principal tenets: to have good thoughts, to speak good words, and to perform good deeds.

Like all religions, Zoroastrianism has evolved over time, and the faith as it is now practised is a far cry from its founder's original system and intentions. The faith has undergone many elaborations and has had to conform to the traditions of other, powerful, rival faiths in order to survive. However, the original words of Zarathustra still survive to enlighten the faithful, in spite of the fact that the sacred books of the *Avesta* are written in a long-dead language. The main components of the Avesta are the *Yashna* ('Worship'), a liturgical corpus in the divine service, the *Yashts*, or hymns of praise to the various divinities, and the *Videvdat*, a body of ritual prescriptions and purity laws which bear resemblance to the biblical book of Leviticus. At the centre of the *Yashna* is a series of very ancient texts known as the *Litany in Seven Chapters*, a magnificent prose composition dating back to the time of the prophet himself and in which are enclosed the five *Gathas*, which are actually made up of seventeen separate poems, all composed by Zarathustra himself. Ahuramazda lies at the heart of Zarathustra's hymns and the prophet constantly praises the god and exalts his munificence, as well as upholding the goodness of the other abstract deities which emanate from the supreme Wise Lord. Zarathustra called himself both a *zoatar* – minister – and a *rishi* – a poet-cum-prophet – and it is clear that he meant the *Gathas* to be heard by worshippers. The poems were never intended to be whispered in private adoration, but were composed for public worship, sung aloud and joyously. The texts speak of him proclaiming his gospel, 'facing the zealous in the house of song' with these words:

> Let the Creator of existence
> promote through Good Mind
> the making real what, according to His will,
> is most wonderful!

Holy, then, You
do I consider, O Ahuramazda
in that I see You
as the first in the birth of life,
in that You assign
deeds and also words which entail recompense,
the bad to the bad,
the good reward to the good,
through Your skill
at the final turning point of creation.

This I ask You,
speak to me truly, O Lord!
Who through his generative power
is the original father of Truth?
Who fixed
the paths of the sun and the stars?
Who is it through whom the moon
waxes, now wanes?
Even these answers, O Ahuramazda,
and others I wish to know.

It is unknown when Zarathustra died; that too is the stuff of Zoroastrian legend. According to one tradition, he expired of natural causes when he was seventy-seven, in bed at home surrounded by his three wives, three sons, and three daughters. Another tradition insists that he was assassinated by a *karpan* in retaliation for overturning the old religious order. In the West a fascination with Zarathustra was already apparent in antiquity in the works of Plato and Aristotle and during the age of European Enlightenment, he was a hero for Voltaire. Rameau composed an opera about him, very loosely based on ancient Greek accounts of his life. But it was when Friedrich Nietzsche published the four parts of his *Also sprach Zarathustra* (1883–5) that the ancient prophet became a superstar. Immediately following the publication of Nietzsche's masterwork, more than thirty books relating to Zoroastrian texts went to press in Germany in less than five years. For Nietzsche, the unique significance of the historical Zarathustra in the history of humanity consisted in his metaphysical interpretation of morality, especially his idea that the fight between good and evil was the real force in the order of the universe. Nietzsche believed that Zarathustra was 'more veracious than any other thinker', but he was also the first who had realised his error and came to believe that religion is doomed to fail; and hence Nietzsche used the figure of Zarathustra to articulate his core philosophy: 'God is dead.'

*

Ahuramazda had a priesthood whose members were known as Magi, and they formed a sort of elite caste of religious observers. The word 'Magus' (singular) is first attested in the Bisitun Inscription of Darius I, referring to 'Gaumâta', who, Darius insisted, claimed to be King Bardiya. Herodotus believed that the Magi were a Median tribe composed of hereditary priests who occupied an influential position at the Median court as dream-interpreters and soothsayers. No indigenous Persian evidence supports his understanding. The Magi were priests, it is true, but they did not have the monopoly on the religious life of Persia. In the Elamite regions of south-western Iran, priests of ancient local cults also performed their duties. References to the Magi (Elamite, *makush*; Old Persian, *magu-*) are frequently found in the Persepolis Fortification tablets, where they are listed among the recipients of barley and wine rations. Interestingly, in several of the texts, the title 'Magus' occurs as a proper name.

From the reign of Darius I, the Magi were the official priests of the Achaemenid monarchs and they performed important services at the royal court and came to enjoy great influence at the centre of power. They were entrusted with guarding tombs and performing the rituals for dead kings and they undertook rites in investiture ceremonies. They chanted the divine hymns of praise appropriate to the acts of sacrifice, and poured the libations of milk or wine or beer, standing before fire altars with their mouths covered, holding wands of barsum twigs to fan the sacred flames. As the rituals were performed, the priests prepared a sacred drink from the *haoma* plant by mashing its twigs with a mortar and pestle. The paste was mixed with mare's milk and was drunk by the priests, who quickly became intoxicated with its powerful hallucinogenic properties. In a drug-induced ecstasy the priests were able to communicate directly with the gods and hear their orders, desires, or complaints. Through communion with the gods, the priests were thought to help uphold cosmic order. Representations of Magi show them engaged in these ritual acts. For instance, on a relief from the fifth century BCE found in Daskyleion, the capital of Phrygia in Asia Minor, two Magi are shown attending at a

Figure 16. Two Magi, their mouths covered, conduct sacrificial rituals at an altar. They hold wands of balsam wood. From Dascylium, *c.* 450 BCE.

fire altar, having performed a sacrifice (the heads of a slaughtered sheep and ox are placed as offerings in front of them); they are dressed in tunics and trousers, and cover their noses and mouths with folds of their headgear so that their breath does not pollute the sacred flame.

Alongside their religious duties, which included the performance of cultic libations and sacrifices of livestock, the Magi participated in administrative and economic roles. The Persepolis tablets locate them not only in Persepolis itself, but throughout all of south-western Iran, where they received rations of grain, flour, livestock, wine, beer, and fruit from the royal warehouses. The names of several recipients of the goods are mentioned: there was Irdazana, who bore the title *pirramasda*, which might have meant something like 'outstanding memoriser' (it probably designated him as a priest who knew religious hymns by heart). There was the Magus Ukpish, who was known as a *haturmaksha*, responsible for issuing grain from a royal storehouse for various purposes. The title *haturmaksha* is probably the Elamite transcription of the Old Iranian word *atar-vahsha*, 'fire-watcher', a title bestowed on the priest who kindled the sacred fire, a very prestigious rank indeed. The Greek author Strabo offers some interesting observations on the use of fire in Persian cult, saying that:

> With fire . . . they offer sacrifice by adding dry wood without the bark and by placing fat on top of it. Then they pour oil upon it and light it below, not blowing with their breath, but fanning it; and those who blow the fire with their breath or put anything dead or filthy on it are put to death . . . And they continue their incantations for a long time, holding in their hands a bundle of slender myrtle wands.

As important as their cultic role was the Magi's deep knowledge of Persia's sacred lore and tribal past, for the Magi were the custodians of history and their learning made them valued royal advisers. They often occupied positions at the Persian court and their roles there might be compared with the famous scholar-priests who surrounded the Assyrian kings. The Magi interpreted celestial phenomena and dreams, they read omens, and instructed the king in all aspects of ritual, from what hymns should be sung and when, to selecting the war booty to be dedicated to the gods. The Magi were able to identify which local gods within the king's empire needed assuaging, and understood how to placate them. The Magi were, in all things, the indispensable wise men of the Persian empire.

*

Were the Achaemenids Zoroastrians? The absence of a clear set of criteria for *what* Zoroastrianism was in the Achaemenid period makes it hard to be certain that the Achaemenids were followers of that faith. The term 'Zoroastrian' is a relatively modern one. Before the nineteenth century, the adherents of the teaching of Zarathustra did not see themselves as 'Zoroastrians' per se. Until we have a coherent definition of what was required in order to be considered a 'Zoroastrian' in Achaemenid antiquity, we cannot demarcate the Achaemenids as Zoroastrians. *If*, for instance, a criterion for being Zoroastrian was to follow the teachings of Zarathustra, then Darius and the rest of the Achaemenids failed the test of faith, for there is not one mention of the prophet in any Achaemenid-period text. It does not appear that the Achaemenid kings knew of his existence. It also remains a great unknown as to whether the Achaemenid elements of 'Zoroastrianism' that we can identify in their rituals or pronouncements were inherited or adopted. It is clear that the supreme god of the Achaemenid kings, Ahuramazda, was conceived as being the royal god par excellence, given that the intimate relationship between the deity and the ruler is reiterated repeatedly in the royal inscriptions. But this still does not qualify the Achaemenid kings as 'Zoroastrians' in our understanding. Ahuramazda was certainly the champion of the Achaemenid clan, and the Great King was expected, under the auspices of the Magi, to carry out the prayers and rituals in Ahuramazda's honour. Each and every Great King was Ahuramazda's chosen one and functioned as mediator between heaven and earth, yet never made mention of his prophet, or his teachings.

In the early Achaemenid royal inscriptions Ahuramazda alone was named as the supreme deity, but occasionally he was mentioned alongside 'all the gods' or 'the other gods who are', or as simply the 'greatest of the gods'. In one of the tablets from Persepolis he appears with the *baga* ('gods'), proving that other deities were worshipped alongside him too. Of these the most important were undoubtedly Mithra (or Mithras) and Anahita. Mithra was described in the *Avesta* as 'the Lord of Wide Pastures, of the Thousand Ears, and of the Myriad Eyes, the Lofty, and the Everlasting Ruler', and he was conceived to be a deity connected to judicial matters and was the all-seeing protector of Truth. He also personified a fertility aspect of life too, as the guardian of cattle and of the harvest and, according to one of the *Yashts*, he was a much-loved creation of Ahuramazda:

Ahura Mazda spoke . . . saying: 'Hear me, when I created Mithra, the Lord of Wide Pastures, I created him as worthy of sacrifice, as worthy of prayer as myself, Ahuramazda. The ruffian who lies to Mithra brings death to the whole country, injuring as much the faithful world as a hundred evil-doers could do. Mithra, the Lord of Wide Pastures, gives swiftness to the horses of those who do not lie to Mithra.'

Mithra was a chariot-driving warrior too, holding in his hands a mace, although he also used arrows, spears, hatchets, and knives. However, any really bloody work required was done by his companion, Verethragna who in his manifestation as a wild boar killed the followers of the Lie by knocking the opponent down, smashing his vertebrae, and mangling their bones, hair and blood. To those who were faithful to the Truth, Mithra brought rain and made the crops grow. In other words, the welfare of an individual depended on his or her moral behaviour.

The goddess Anahita was a water-divinity, worshipped as a bringer of fertility, who purified the seed of all men, and the wombs of all women, and made the milk flow from their breasts to nourish their young children. Described in the *Yashts* as having 'beautiful white arms, thick as a horse's shoulder', she was always keen to bestow upon her worshippers desirable possessions such as chariots, weapons, and household goods, as well as victory in battle and the destruction of foes. For such gifts the goddess demanded sacrifice:

> Who will praise me? Who will offer me a sacrifice with libations cleanly prepared and well-strained, together with the *haoma* and meat? To whom shall I cleave, who cleaves to me, and thinks with me, and bestows gifts upon me, and is good to me?

The cult of Anahita united her divine aspects as water-goddess and mother-goddess, and became royally promoted in the reign of Artaxerxes II, who was an especial devotee of the goddess. Thanks to this royal support she became widely popular throughout Persia.

The Persepolis texts boldly testify to the presence of 'the other gods who are' and show how the royal administration supplied cultic necessities for the worship of numerous deities, both Iranian and Elamite. In addition to Ahuramazda, the Persepolis texts name other Iranian gods worthy of ritual offerings, including Zurvan (a weather god), Mizdushi (a fertility goddess), Narvasanga (a fire deity), Hvarita (Spirit of the Rising Sun), and Visai Baga (a collective entity of deities). It is important to realise, however, that the bulk of the Persepolis texts speak of Elamite gods who were being worshipped in and around the palace-city, including ancient deities such as Humban, Inshushinak, Naparisha, Adad, and Shimat. While Ahuramazda is omnipresent in the royal inscriptions, his name occurs only ten times in the Persepolis Fortification tablets, whereas the Elamite god Humban, unknown in the royal texts, makes his appearance in twenty-seven of the Persepolis tablets. Likewise, the popular god Mitra, who is found in the theophoric names of so many Persians in the Achaemenid period, is never attested in the Persepolis documents at all.

The Fortification tablets reveal an astonishingly varied religious landscape of Fārs during Darius' reign. For instance, blood sacrifices – known as *lan*-offerings – had long been part of the Elamite tradition, and they were enthusiastically accepted and practised under Persian rule. Daily sacrifices for the gods had a long history in Elam, and in a stele from Susa an Elamite king proclaims his institution of daily offerings for the god Inshushinak: one sheep at dawn and one sheep at dusk. These may have been consumed by cultic singers, performing at the temple gates twice daily, or by other temple personnel. This system was retained by the Persians and can be seen operating at Persepolis. Instead of suggesting any kind of Zoroastrian taboo on animal sacrifices, the Persepolis tablets reveal the administration's concern for keeping large flocks of sheep and goats which were used for, among other purposes, sacrifice. Moreover, the Persepolis tablets reveal that the Persian Magi did not have a monopoly over the religious life of the empire, for another priestly group bearing the Elamite title *shatîn* were just as present in Persia's religious world. What is most remarkable, however, is that the tablets clearly show that the *shatîn* offered service and sacrifice to both Elamite and Iranian gods, and that the Persian Magi followed the same practice too. In terms of ritual practice, there was no separation between Elamites and Persians. It is clear that the *lan*-sacrifice was taken beyond its original geographical and cultural spheres to be integrated into Achaemenid ritual activity in both the Persian heartland and the outlying regions of Pārs. The Achaemenids chose to sponsor the cults of a mixed group of gods, some Iranian and others Elamite. The mix of deities is best defined as a Persian pantheon, and the combination of blended Indo-European and Mesopotamian gods and goddesses supports the notion that the Achaemenids had a proclivity to merge ancient Iranian and ancient Elamite concepts of the divine and the rituals of their worship.

PART THREE

HIGH EMPIRE

In Book 3 of his *Laws*, written around 360 BCE, the Greek philosopher Plato reserves a place for a relatively long exposition on Persian society, dedicated by and large to a description of, and explanation for, its degeneracy. 'Since the time of Xerxes, whose career resembled that of the misfortunate Cambyses', he writes, 'hardly any king of the Persians had been truly "great" except in title and magnificence. I hold that the reason for this is the shocking life that they always lead.' Plato argues that the megalomaniac autocracy of Xerxes led Persia into an inevitable decline and that 'the Persians have failed to halt the downward slope towards decadence'. For the Greeks, and as for Western critics over many centuries, 'decadence' became the buzzword through which Persia was filtered. Persia's decline as a global superpower was perceived to have been the result of an abandonment of morals on the part of its rulers. This moralising but flippantly superficial judgement has been the chief rationale historians have used in their approach to the late Achaemenid period. It shoehorned the Persian empire into the standard 'Rise and Fall' scenario, so much beloved by European historians from Gibbon onwards. The familiar story goes that the Persian Great Kings (like the emperors of Rome) let slip their imperial duties, downed arms, and gave themselves over to the hedonism of good living. An orientalist gloss further castigated the Persian monarchs for, it was said, having been ruled from the harem by the machinations of castrati and courtesans.

But in actuality, the post-Darius era was not an age of deterioration. At the time of the Macedonian invasion of Persia in 334 BCE, which came as a surprise to the Persians, the empire was far from being in a state of decay. It was very much the vibrant, thriving, and forceful institution it had always been, displaying no signs of fracture. Here, in Part Three, we rejoin the historical narrative and show that while the empire received its fair share of problems, it overcame them with elan and experienced something of a power surge under two of its last warrior kings, Artaxerxes III and Darius III. For this reason alone, the period deserves the epithet 'high empire': it was an era when Persia reaped the benefits of imperialism. We will see, however, how family infighting did jeopardise the stability of the dynasty, although ultimately, the empire itself held together in the face of regicide and fratricide. Let us now explore Persia's history in the long century that followed the death of Darius the Great.

13

Exit Darius

Around 490 BCE, as Darius aged and his once energetic body grew tired, his thoughts turned to the succession. Which of his many sons should follow him on the throne? Primogeniture was not practised by the Achaemenids nor any of the great royal dynastic houses of the Near East. Rulers preferred to hedge their bets on destiny and wait to appoint any one of the (potentially) many sons born to the any number of women of the royal harem. Why did ancient rulers play dynastic Russian roulette and refuse to adopt the simple system of appointing the first-born son as the heir as a means of quelling any threats of murder and mayhem? The rationale for this choice could have had a practical basis. In an age of high infant mortality rates even among the aristocracy, it might be considered prudent for a father to hold off making decisions on appointing an heir until his sons began to reach maturity. Even then, there was no guarantee of long life. Warfare too could have a detrimental impact upon primogeniture.

Other reasons for rejecting primogeniture were more personal. A king waited to see which of his sons showed the most potential for rulership, or displayed characteristics which he himself recognised as desirable. In ancient Persia the law of succession was a 'free-for-all' in which the strongest of the sons (or those with more political support) inherited the throne. The relationship between a king and his women, the birth mothers of potential heirs, could also dictate a prince's future. Between the sheets, the throne lost its magic and no one could get closer to the royal ear than one of the king's women. Consorts and concubines were therefore influential king-makers. Darius' consort, Atossa, must have worked hard to secure her son's position as the next king because Xerxes was not the eldest of Darius' many sons.

In an inscription from Persepolis we find a text commissioned by Xerxes to commemorate the moment he was appointed as Darius' heir. In the inscription, Xerxes carefully allied himself to his father's memory and designated himself by the Old Persian word *mathishta* ('the greatest'):

> Darius had other sons, but thus was the god Ahuramazda's desire – my father Darius made me the greatest [*mathishta*] after him. When my father Darius went away from the throne, by the grace of Ahuramazda I became king on my father's throne (XPf).

Xerxes' statement is full of bravado. It derives from an important fact: Xerxes was the first of Darius' children to have the blood of Cyrus the Great flow though his veins. He was the vindication behind Darius' coup. It was Atossa's 'dynastic womb' that had united the Teispid and Achaemenid lines, and it was Xerxes whom Darius chose as his successor as a living symbol of the unity of the royal house.

*

The last document dated to the reign of Darius the Great comes in the form of a letter from Babylon written on 17 November 486 BCE. The first document of the reign of his son and heir Xerxes was written on 1 December that same year. Sometime in the fortnight between the composition of the two letters Darius had died, after thirty days of illness. He was around sixty-five years old. Darius had been a remarkable ruler. His vision of an empire linked together by bureaucracy, communication systems, and the law propelled Persia into an age of world domination. Even his Athenian enemies admitted that Darius had been an exemplary monarch. Darius the Great had reigned over Persia for thirty-six years. He had succeeded in strengthening the Achaemenid hold along the edges of the empire and had even attempted to conquer the Scythian lands beyond the

Danube. His ambitions for the empire had been bold, and if they did not always bear fruit, Darius had left it in a healthier state of being than when he first grabbed hold of it and made it his own.

At his death, Persia's sacred fires were extinguished and normal life throughout the empire was put on hold as a period of deep mourning was observed. Persian men shaved their heads and beards and they lamented their loss by cropping their horses' manes too. The piercing lamentations of Persia's women filled the air. This was a sensitive period, marked by official rites of mourning throughout the empire, although, sadly, our knowledge of the rituals and traditions surrounding the death of the Great King is sparse. But perhaps a recently found Neo-Assyrian text, composed in the Babylonian language, might offer some insight to both the feelings solicited by a monarch's death and the rituals his heir-designate enacted for the comfort of the king in the afterlife:

> The ditches wailed, the canals respond, all trees and fruit, their faces darkened. Birds wept [. . .] I slaughtered horses and mares to the gods and I gave them to be buried . . . Father, my begetter, I gently laid him in the midst of that tomb, a secret place, in royal oil. The stone coffin, his resting place – I sealed its opening with strong copper and secured the clay sealing. I displayed gold and silver objects, everything proper for a tomb, the emblems of his lordship, that he loved before gods and I placed them in the tomb with my begetter.

At Susa, Darius' corpse was prepared by specialist morticians (perhaps they were Egyptian embalmers) and was then transported from Elam to Pārs for burial in a rock-cut tomb chamber at Naqsh-i Rustam. As the royal hearse trundled across country in the company of a vast cortège, the Persian populace witnessed for a final time the spectacular display of King Darius' brilliance. The body had been placed in a large chariot drawn by sixty-four mules, beneath a canopied pavilion of gold with a fringe of net-work to which were fastened large bells, whose sound was heard at a great distance. A statue of the king was carried in the procession too. The chariot and the statue were followed by the royal guards, all in arms, and brilliantly costumed. A multitude of spectators were drawn together in veneration of the memory of Darius. The spectacle and magnificence of the funerary pomp were fitting tributes to this remarkable King of Kings.

The Persepolis texts make it clear that the Persians established royal cults for their dead monarchs, and for some high-ranking officials too. This was an old Elamite practice. The Persians also adopted the Elamite veneration of statues or relief-stelae that portrayed the dead individuals who were the subjects of funerary cults. A recently translated text from Babylon dating to the first year of the reign of Xerxes in 485 BCE, for instance, shows that a royal cult was quickly established for Darius the Great and that its focus was on a statue of the late king himself. The tablet tells of provisions of barley provided for the rituals around the monarch's likeness:

> Barley for making beer for the daily offerings to the statue of King Darius. Bunene-ibni, the slave, is the person in charge of the rations for the king . . . he has received the barley.

Hints of a flourishing royal funerary cult are preserved in one of the Persepolis tablets. It makes reference to a tomb of Hystaspes, the father of Darius, one of Persia's great *khāns*, and, as the revered elder of the Achaemenid line, Hystaspes deserved a funerary cult. It was managed and maintained by courtiers who saw to it that the deceased *khān* received regular food and drink offerings. For many centuries the Elamites had referred to these funerary gifts as *sumar*, and the same word is found in the Persepolis texts. It was Persepolis' deputy administrator, Zishshawish, who ordered the 600 quarts of grain due to the men who were the keepers of the *sumar* of Hystaspes.

Where exactly at Persepolis was Hystaspes buried? Where was his funerary shrine located? Archaeologists have long known about a rather dilapidated square tomb-like structure built near Persepolis at a place called Takht-i Gohar. Today it looks quite battered and weathered, but its platform base, composed of two courses of well-dressed, polished stone, once supported an elegant plastered brick chamber. At the time of its completion, it would have looked something like the tomb of Cyrus the Great and would have been a fitting burial chamber for a high officer of state. Architectural plans of the monument, before its modern restoration, show that there were originally two human-sized spaces between the stones and that interment pits had been dug deep into the earth in both. Ernst Herzfeld, the Chicago-based excavator of Persepolis, believed that the tomb had belonged to Cambyses II, but thanks to the Persepolis tablets we now know that he was interred elsewhere, so it is highly likely that Takht-i Gohar was indeed the burial site of the great Hystaspes, who died around 499 BCE. It is possible that Lady Irdabama, Darius' mother, was also interred here. It was at this spot too that the spirits of the august dead received sacrifices.

Evidence also survives for an official funerary cult for the dead King Cambyses II. It was equipped with its own monthly offerings of meat and grain and drink. He was honoured alongside his spouse, Phaidymē (Old Persian, Upandush) at a place called Narezzash (modern day Niriz in Fārs). One text records how Persepolis' administrative director, Parnakka, issued '24 head of small cattle for the *sumar* of Cambyses and the woman Upandush at Narezzash'. Today Niriz is a vast nature reserve, home to the bulk of Iran's ibex population and to herds of wild asses. We know that in antiquity it was the site of a large *paridaida* and was certainly a very fitting spot for a royal tomb. However, the Persepolis tablets offer up even more information about the functioning of the royal cult since they show that, at Niriz, Cambyses' queen received her very own sacrifices, separate from those performed for her husband. One text reveals that twenty-four litres of fine wine were offered at the 'sacrificial table of Upandush', confirming that Persian royal women could be recipients of funerary cults too. Their rank and prestige afforded them this ultimate mark of distinction.

Darius the Great obviously received the most flamboyant funerary cult of all. By virtue of his office, the Great King held a position both remote and mystical. If he was less than a god, he was still more than a man and he deserved the honour of a royal cult. Although no Persian ruler ever dared regard himself as a living god, the Greeks routinely insisted that the Achaemenid kings

thought themselves to be divine. This mistake is easy to understand. The ceremonial surrounding the cult of a dead ruler easily
persuaded the Greek outsiders that the Persians thought their king
was indeed divine. A text by Plutarch attempted to articulate what
was perceived to be a bone fide Persian belief: 'Among our many
excellent customs', a Persian noble explains to a visiting Greek,
'this we account the best: to honour the king and to worship him,
as the image of the preserver of all things.' Likewise, in his tragedy
Persians, Aeschylus called the dead king Darius *isotheos*, 'equal to the
gods'; *theion*, 'divine'; and *akakos*, 'knowing no wrong'. While the
Athenian playwright must not be taken literally on these points,
he was capable, nonetheless, of thinking of the kings of the Achaemenid dynasty in this way. Some Greeks went so far as to imagine
that the Great King had a divine daemon (Greek, *daimon*), or spirit.
Plutarch insisted that courtiers revered and worshipped the *daimon*
of the king, while the Greek historian Theopompus went so far as
to say that the Persians piled tables high with food for the pleasure
of the king's daimon. Here we clearly have a garbled Greek understanding of the Persian royal funerary cult. Nevertheless, the Greek
belief in the king's *daimon* is a reasonable interpretation of the
Persian belief in the *fravashi*, or 'soul' of the monarch. Herodotus
said that the Persians were duty-bound to pray for the king and his
sons during their private acts of worship, which demonstrates that
at least the Greeks understood how Persians intertwined notions of
god, king, and empire.

Tomb burials were very rare among the Iranians and only the
royal family seems to have enjoyed this privilege. It is possible that
the Achaemenids clung to an old Iranian belief that earth, water,
and fire were constantly in danger of being polluted by agents of
death, especially by decomposing corpses. To bury a corpse in the
ground, or to cremate it with fire, or to submerge it in a river or
lake, was to contaminate the world of the living. Pollution of the
earth and the elements was a constant worry for the Iranians, but
the pollution caused by the putrefaction of a corpse was particularly chilling. To avoid that most heinous miasma, it is possible
that, from early times, Iranian peoples had exposed the bodies of

the dead to the open elements, leaving them to be picked clean of flesh by birds and animals. Herodotus noted that the bodies of the dead were buried only after they had been torn by dogs or birds of prey, and that the priests covered the bodies (by which he must mean bones) with wax before burying them. For the wealthy, a container for bones (*astōdān*) might have been employed after they had been picked clean of bodily tissues. The container was carved from stone, and plaster was used to tightly pack it, in order to prevent any further miasmic seepage. The amazing rock-cut tombs of the Achaemenid kings at Naqsh-i Rustam and Persepolis suggest that some of these old Persian death traditions were upheld and practised by the Achaemenids. When all is said and done, the great rock-face sepulchres of the monarchs, hewed out of the living stone, and sealed by giant doors, acted as vast, monumental ossuaries.

Naqsh-i Rustam had long been a sacred area for the Elamites. Their presence was still to be found there in the form of religious wall reliefs when Darius the Great chose it as his burial place. He was the first Achaemenid king to locate his tomb in the ancient cliff, which is known locally as the *Huseyn Kuh*, and his successors slavishly imitated his idea of a rock-face tomb and attentively copied the layout of the whole structure. The cliff face itself measures some sixty-four metres in height. Reaching some fifteen metres above ground level is the façade of the tomb itself. The Persia-based Greek historian Ctesias recorded that Darius' favourite eunuch, Bagapates, had guarded Darius' tomb for seven years before the Great King died, suggesting that it was therefore finished by 493 BCE. The façade was constructed in the shape of a giant cross. A sculpted relief representation, once brightly painted, depicted a palace portico with bull capitals, and an Egyptian-style pediment placed over the entrance into the tomb chamber, which was cut deep into the rock. A long, narrow entrance corridor runs parallel to the rock face, and from this, three rectangular vaults extend back into the cliff. The floors of the vaults are over a metre higher than the entrance corridor. Inside, nine cists are hewn out of the rock, but none of them are differentiated in terms of size or quality, so it is impossible to know where Darius' body was placed. It is likely that metal or metal-covered coffins were placed within the cists and that these were once covered with monolithic slabs. Clearly the tomb was intended for more than one occupant and perhaps several of Darius' consorts or offspring were buried here too. It must have been well-furnished in antiquity, but the riches which Darius took with him in the afterlife have long disappeared, together with the heavy stone door which once blocked the entranceway.

Outside the tomb chamber, in the panel above the doorway, a carved relief depicts the king standing on a three-stepped pedestal in front of a fire altar; both king and altar are supported by throne-bearers representing the twenty-eight nations of the empire. On the side panels are the Great King's weapon-bearers and his bodyguards. The trilingual cuneiform inscriptions on three panels of the rock wall enumerated the twenty-eight nations upholding the throne and glorified the king and his rule, reminding all subjects to be loyal to their king and his god: 'Oh man, that which is the command of Ahuramazda, let this not seem repugnant to you; do not leave the right path; do not rise in rebellion!'

14

Ruling Over Heroes

Xerxes dominates the popular Western perception of ancient Persia. It was Xerxes who had the audacity to invade Greece in 480 BCE and to threaten the sacred birthplace of democracy itself. Thanks to the ongoing mythologisation of the Greco-Persian wars, Xerxes still lives large in the imagination of the West. The successful Warner Bros. movie franchise *300* and *300: Rise of an Empire* characterises Xerxes as (in the words of his actor-creator, Rodrigo Santoro) 'not human . . . a creature . . . an entity lacking nobility, piety, and probity'. In the film, he is represented as a menacing despot, a figure of perverse sexual ambiguity, an eastern malevolence, a golden god-king who commands the armies of the dead.

Much of the blame for this misconceived image of Xerxes has to be put at the feet of Herodotus because it was he who so painstakingly created this successful caricature of Xerxes as a narcissistic tyrant. In the *Histories*, Herodotus misrepresents and maligns the Persian king skilfully and deliberately. His Xerxes is crafted with great subtlety. When, for instance, Herodotus narrates Xerxes' march through Asia into Greece, he notes that as the king reaches the town of Kallatebos, not far from the crossing of the River Maeander in south-western Turkey, Xerxes saw by the roadside a magnificent plane tree. He was smitten with love for it. He mooned over it, praised it, adored it, and loaded it with lavish gifts, like those bestowed on a lover. Xerxes hung the tree's branches with golden ornaments – necklaces, earrings, and bracelets – until they groaned under the weight of his generosity. He arranged that a man should stay there as the tree's guardian for ever after. Then, bidding the tree a sad farewell, the king proceeded on to Sardis.

What a bizarre tale. It serves no purpose in the narrative of the Persian invasion other than to lampoon Xerxes. It was Herodotus' way to show that Xerxes was quite unhinged, unfocused, and unworthy of a victory over so fine a people as the Hellenes. The story became very famous. Later generations of Greeks and Romans thought it very funny, but they nonetheless believed it. The second century CE author Aelian went as far as declaring that Xerxes had made himself 'ridiculous' by falling in love with a plane tree and 'setting a guard over it, as he might command one of his eunuchs to keep an eye on the harem'.

In the same vein, the Xerxes in the Hebrew Bible's book of Esther is a carnivalesque creature. He closely resembles the Herodotean creation. In Esther, the Persian king is an emblem of both great power and great ineptitude – the biblical Xerxes is a somewhat pathetic character. It is little wonder that some commentators have thought of him as a comic, well-honed creation and that Rabbinic stories reworked him as both a capricious fool and a cruel villain.

The Western classical tradition, so enamoured of the crazy despot of Herodotus' tale, brought the story of Xerxes' foolish infatuation for a plant to the operatic stage in Georg Frederik Handel's only comic opera, *Serse*, produced in 1738. The musical comedy opens with the strange spectacle of Xerxes seated beneath the tree, which he woos in fine song – the celebrated *Largo*:

Ombra mai fu	Never was a shade
di vegetabile	of any plant
cara ed amabile	more beloved or lovely
soave piu	or more sweet

Herodotus' ambition to create a Xerxes both villainous and foolish worked very well. It is a triumph of character assassination. But sitting far behind Herodotus' weird story – and Handel's tuneful opera – is a genuine fact about the ancient Persians: they had a deep, religious reverence for trees. The Greek tale has enfolded within it an important form of ancient symbolism, for ancient Near

Figure 17. A seal impression
depicting Xerxes decorating a tree
with offerings of jewellery.

Eastern kings were traditionally identified with – or even *as* – trees.
The Sumerian monarch Shulgi, for instance, was at one and the
same time lauded as 'a date palm planted by a water ditch' and 'a
cedar planted by water'. Famously, the kings of ancient Israel and
Judah were depicted as both a 'shoot' and a 'branch' of the tree of
the House of David, and Assyrian kings were frequently represented
with and as the 'Tree of Life'. Trees were a common motif in Near
Eastern literature and imagery, where they were connected with fertility and with the power of divine sanction. They had a particular
potency and were regarded as sacred objects, where humans and
the gods come together and meet. This is why in a cylinder seal
image, Xerxes (whose name is boldly inscribed) is shown in the act
of adorning a tree with votive offerings of jewellery. He worships
at the tree because it is a holy conduit where he can encounter
god (one might think of the biblical Moses and his experience of
Yahweh in the burning bush in the same way). The seal is a neat
visual antidote to the poisonous Herodotean spin manufactured to
deride the king. The seal shows us the Persian Version of a long-
established Near Eastern tree cult.

*

Who was the real Xerxes, known to the Persians? His subjects did
not know him as 'Xerxes', of course. To them he was Xshayarashā,
a good Old Persian name meaning 'ruling over heroes' or 'hero
among rulers'. It is a fine royal name, potent and powerful and

packed with martial valour. It resonates with self-confidence. However, the bravado suggested in the name was not in evidence in actuality when, in 486 BCE, the 35-year-old Xerxes, the King of Kings, acceded to power. Darius was a hard act to follow, and, from inscriptions dating to the opening years of Xerxes' reign, one gains the impression that he found it difficult to come out from beneath his father's shadow. Several royal pronouncements demonstrate the diligence with which Xerxes connected himself to the legacy of his esteemed father. He constructed new buildings at Persepolis, true, but made the point of mentioning how he had merely completed the work of Darius:

> When I became king, much that is superior I built. What had been built by my father, that I took into my care and other work I added. But what I have done and what my father has done, all that we have done by the favour of Ahuramazda. King Xerxes proclaims: Me may Ahuramazda protect and my kingdom! And what has been built by me and what has been built by my father, that also may Ahuramazda protect (XPf).

Xerxes' admiration for his father was so pronounced that references to his own building activities are quite rare. It became customary for later Achaemenid kings to follow Xerxes' model and set themselves in line with the great Darius. In Xerxes' case, he never missed a chance to state that he was the son of Darius, and an Achaemenid.

In 486 BCE Xerxes was in the prime of health. He had a boundless nervous energy that worked well to his advantage. He appears to have been a man beloved by the gods, for he had been blessed with the good looks and the type of stature that naturally drew all eyes towards him. He had a skill for conversation which made all he said compelling to the listener. His face was arresting, with its almond-shaped dark eyes, a slight hook to the nose, a thick moustache which was twisted as it drooped elegantly at the ends, and a distinctive square-cut beard. Every perfumed curl was a masterpiece of the beautician's craft. The beard reached down to his breast bone, but Xerxes hoped that one day it would reach his midriff – as his father's had done. His clothing always announced his unique status and he tended to wear a voluminous court robe, draped and belted at the waist. He thought that it made a big impression on all who saw it, and he was right, it did. He opted for garments dyed in rich Tyrian purple or expensive saffron yellow. The woven patterns of his robe – chevrons and floral buds, stripes and rosettes – were augmented by golden appliquéd lion heads which shone and tinkled when he walked. Underneath the robe Xerxes wore trousers – never forgetting his nomadic ancestry – but these were made of fine white silk and had ankle bands of blue embroidery. His soft suede shoes were of a deep blue hue and were fastened with side-laces. To finish the look, he wore lion-headed torques and bracelets and intricate cloisonné earrings. His dress was worth a small fortune; some 12,000 talents, it was said. No man in the empire looked as splendid as Xerxes. Even Herodotus had to confess to that: 'in terms of handsomeness and physical stature, none was more worthy to hold power than Xerxes.'

We know the name of only one of Xerxes' consorts: Amestris. She was the daughter of the powerful *khān* Otanes, who was one of the seven conspirators who had plotted with Darius the Great against King Bardiya. In her early thirties when Xerxes became Great King, Amestris was to have an influential role in court politics for many decades to come. She certainly lived up to her name, which in Old Persian meant 'strength'. This beautiful woman, of pure Persian stock, dressed in a finery comparable to her husband's. Amestris bore Xerxes at least three sons, Dariaios, Hystaspes, and Artaxerxes, and two daughters, Amytis and Rhodogune. She carefully reared her boys in the harem until it was time for them to join the world of men, and she taught her daughters etiquette and prepared them for good marriages. There were, no doubt, more wives and concubines in Xerxes' harem, since we learn of other children who do not appear to be Amestris' – such as Princess Ratashah, who was just an infant in 486 BCE when she makes a fleeting appearance in the records. But no other woman gained the authority of Amestris.

Xerxes sat at the centre of an interconnected circle of obligation. In the mafioso-like atmosphere of the royal court, he interacted

with nobles and advisors and with the personal servants who were
his confidants. But who could really be trusted in such a hothouse
of potential troublemakers? Wasn't there always a risk for a king
when it came to making friends and intimates? Low-ranking servants could easily abuse the king's confidence, and high-ranking
nobles might attempt power grabs. Even consorts, concubines,
and offspring could turn against the ruler and become embroiled
in dynastic infighting. Nominally all-powerful and untouchable,
Xerxes recognised this fundamental tension within his family and
looked for unwavering loyalty. He found it in his mother, Atossa,
who was his chief support and aid, and he often turned to her for
advice. She remained the most influential figure at court until her
death around 475 BCE.

*

On ascending the throne Xerxes' chief task had been to choose a
group of able ministers who would offer him advice and, above
and beyond all else, loyalty. Ctesias of Cnidus, with his insider
knowledge of the court, lets us know who these select people were:
'Darius' son, Xerxes, became king', he recorded, 'and Artapanus,
son of Artasyras, was influential with him, just as his father had
been with Xerxes' father – and Mardonius the Elder was influential,
too.' So Xerxes, it seems, relied at first upon the old guard of court
ministers who had been attached to his father's government. This is
not in itself unusual, as many regime changes are softened through
the continuation of older, still-functioning institutions or personnel. The royal court was Xerxes 'household', his extended family.
Here thousands of people moved in close proximity to the king.
For the nobility, the attractions of court life were obvious – power,
prestige, and remuneration could all be obtained through service
and closeness to the Great King, and there was clearly a hierarchy of
rank, although trying to decode the precise function of every royal
office is difficult. We can be certain of one thing: the Persian Great
Kings were surrounded by a variety of courtiers ranging in status
from satraps to stable boys. The Greeks believed that because they
were too grand to bother themselves with the mundane tasks of

governing the empire themselves, Persian kings required legions of staff. An unknown author we know as Pseudo-Aristotle commented that 'It was beneath the dignity of Xerxes to administer his own empire and to carry out his own desires and superintend the government of his kingdom; such functions were not becoming for a god.' Other sources suggest that in the past Great Kings had learned the arts of the court the hard way, with hands-on experience. In his youth, Cyrus the Great had held several court positions – 'master of the wand-bearers', 'master of the squires', and 'cup-bearer'. Darius the Great had been 'quiver-bearer' to Cyrus II and was Cambyses' 'lance-bearer'. These titles are typical of similar designations found in the Persepolis texts, such as a 'chair-and footstool-carrier' and 'bow-and-arrow-case carrier'.

The entire court was under the watch of a powerful official known as the *hazārapatish* (literally, 'master of a thousand'), or *chiliarch*, who commanded the royal bodyguard and was responsible for all elements of court security. He enjoyed the complete confidence of the ruler, controlling access to his personage through the protocol of the royal audience. Other prominent inner-court dignitaries included the steward of the royal household, the royal charioteer, and the king's cup-bearer. Court titles did not necessarily have bearing on the duties expected of the courtier who held them, and nobles with courtly titles perhaps only 'acted' the prescribed roles at state ceremonies.

The Achaemenids created a complex pyramid-like court structure with the Great King at its narrow apex and slaves, the *kurtash*, at its broad base. A comparatively small group of Persian nobles occupied a high place in this pyramidal assemblage. These were the hereditary nobility, whom the Greeks called the 'People of the Gate' and who were obliged – because of blood and status – to serve at court and wait on the king. A multitude of middlemen operated in the administrative rungs of the social pyramid and communicated with other ranks above and below them. Any individual who had rendered important service to the king was a 'benefactor' and his name was recorded in the royal archives. These royal benefactors were rewarded by the king with gifts of clothing, jewellery, livestock, and land. Even foreigners could benefit from this gift-giving system. Xenophon records the way in which one Great King expressed his favour to a courtier 'with the customary royal gift, that is to say, a horse with a gold bit, a necklace of gold, a gold bracelet, and a gold scimitar, and a Persian robe'. This formalised gift-giving was an important tool for the Persian monarchy as it established a system of debt and dependency between the nobles and the crown.

Courtiers designated as 'friends of the king' were given the highest rights of all: the opportunity to eat at the royal table or assist the king as a body servant. These were highly prized and ferociously guarded privileges. Tiribazus, the powerful satrap of Armenia, was a particularly favoured 'friend of the king' (in this case, Artaxerxes II), and, when resident at court, away from his satrapy, 'he alone had the privilege of mounting the king upon his horse'. Menial tasks held big meaning within the royal circle. To be seen to be doing the king a personal service was a way of enhancing status and this is why it was important for hereditary nobles to make regular appearances at court. Satraps like Tiribazus were expected to leave their provinces in order to do their duties for the Great King. They held a parasol above his head, performed *punkah wallah* duties with a fan, or kept the flies away with a horsehair whisk. Masistes, Xerxes' brother, was a regular attendee at court even though he was satrap of far-away Bactria, and starting in 410 BCE, Arshama, the long-serving satrap of Egypt, took a two-year leave of absence from his official post in Memphis to visit the royal court back in Persia and make his presence known.

One significant group of courtiers fits less easily into the pyramidal hierarchical structure of the court. Eunuchs could, in theory, interweave themselves into multiple court strata so that positioning them securely in one place within the hierarchical structure is difficult. These castrated men and boys served at court as high-ranking officials, bureaucrats, and body attendants, as well as menials and drudges. As castrati, they were seen as a kind of 'third sex', and because of this they were able to negotiate and play with the permeable barriers of the court. Eunuchs were commonly attested at other Near Eastern courts and featured prominently in the Neo-Assyrian world where, besides serving at court, they also took positions in the military, even as high-ranking generals. According to Greek reports (and it must be made clear that the Greeks had great difficulties in coming to terms with this alien Eastern practice), the Persians valued eunuchs for their honesty and loyalty. The process of castration, it was thought, made men, like gelded horses and dogs, docile and more malleable. Xenophon unambiguously affirmed that it was Cyrus the Great who had first introduced eunuchs into his army for just this reason, although this cannot be qualified since castration was already a Mesopotamian practice long before Cyrus' time. Herodotus recounts an interesting tale of how a Greek-speaking youth, Hermotimus of Pedasa, was captured and sold to the slave-dealer Panionius, who specialised in trading beautiful boys to elite customers in Asia Minor, having first castrated them. Hermotimus subsequently found himself at the Persian court, where he quickly caught the eye and gained the favour of Xerxes, who charged him with the privileged and trusted task of tutoring the children of the royal harem. Herodotus further ascertains that Babylon was required to send the Great King an annual tribute of 500 boys, who were to be castrated and turned into eunuchs, and by implication it is possible that the five boys he mentions being sent every three years from Ethiopia and the 100 boys sent by the Colchians to court as tribute were turned into castrati too. Herodotus also pointed out that at the suppression of the Ionian revolt, the Persians emasculated the prettiest boys they captured and shipped them off to Persia. It is clear that Herodotus, like all Greeks, found the practice of castration abhorrent and the creation of eunuchs perverse. He nonetheless found stories of them utterly compelling. The Persian reliance on eunuchs gave Herodotus a neat opportunity to criticise Persian moral laxity.

We need not look for excuses to exonerate the Achaemenids of the practice of castrating boys and men. Eunuchism had always been commonplace in the Near East. It remained so in the Achaemenid period and for millennia afterwards. For those castrated men and boys in court service, the rewards could be great. Many eunuchs rose to positions of high influence, prestige, and wealth, and a smaller group knew the pleasures and pains of outright power. At the start of Xerxes' reign, a eunuch named Natacas held the greatest sway at court. So important was this royal castrato that Xerxes supposedly sent him to plunder the sanctuary of Apollo at Delphi during the campaign in Greece. Eunuchs had served in the courts of Cyrus, Cambyses, and Darius, but it was during the reign of Xerxes that they began to acquire more overt personal power. From the 480s BCE they appear in the sources entering into espionage, sometimes working for the king, sometimes against him. Plots and coups followed and eventually climaxed with regicide. Eunuch power was set to dominate the late Achaemenid court.

Above and beyond the royal eunuchs, perhaps the most influential courtiers to serve Xerxes were his many brothers and half-brothers (some of whom were more cooperative than others). The court was a locus of practical political decision-making and imperial power, and the hereditary nobility of Persia, like Xerxes' male siblings, had an important role to play in policy-making and the governance of the realm. The author of the biblical book of Esther noted that 'Since it was customary for the king to consult experts in matters of law and justice, he spoke with the wise men who understood the times and were closest to the king.' None were closer to Xerxes than his blood kin, and none could be more dangerous to his throne. Xerxes kept a tight rein on his brothers and kept them occupied. Xerxes' sisters had been given high-profile Persians as husbands and through these marriage alliances many noble families were brought into the orbit of Xerxes' throne; their presence (and offspring) further swelled the Achaemenid clan. The two brothers of Queen Amestris, the king's brothers-in-law, were also part of the extended family, as was Megabyzus II, the brilliant son of the satrap Zopyros, who married Xerxes' daughter, Amytis. These men were destined to play important roles in Xerxes' reign, as war and rebellion marked out its passage.

*

Shortly before Darius' death in 486 BCE, sensing that a succession crisis was at hand, the Egyptians had revolted against Achaemenid rule. Immediately upon his accession, Xerxes took personal command of the army and inaugurated his reign with a military expedition into Egypt. He successfully crushed the rebellion and restored order to the land, installing his brother Achaemenes as the satrap of Egypt and leaving him behind to keep the Egyptians in check. Under his brother's governance, Xerxes anticipated that the country would settle down and cease being bothersome. In many respects, the victory over the Egyptians set the tone for Xerxes' rule, because it galvanised his self-belief that he was worthy to be Darius' successor and proved to his nobility that, like Darius, he too was a warrior king.

Xerxes hardly had time to draw breath after the Egyptian victory before news reached him that Babylon too had erupted in revolt. Two short-lived rebellions were led by a man named Bel-shimanni, who took the titles 'King of Babylon, King of the Lands'. He was swiftly eliminated, but the revolts reflect the fact that Babylon was not a happy place; a troubled atmosphere had been felt in the city ever since Darius' death. While it is possible that Xerxes ordered the removal of a precious metal statue of one of Babylon's gods as a reprisal for one of the Babylonian revolts, it is certain that Xerxes did not destroy any Babylonian temples, as Greek historians later claimed. In the neighbouring province of Across-the-River, in Judah, there was discontent too, and the building of the Temple of Yahweh was delayed by a series of uprisings which were not really settled until the 440s BCE. It is impossible to understand the nuances which underpinned these brief but bothersome uprisings, but we can observe that the troubles in Egypt, Babylonia, and Judah suggest that Darius' imperialism had reached its natural limits. This, however, did not seem to have been apparent to Xerxes at the time. It had not even crossed his mind.

15

Let Slip the Dogs of War

There is no good evidence for why the Persians invaded Greece in 480 BCE. Herodotus insisted that the war was an act of retaliation against the Athenians, who had helped the insurgents in the Ionian Revolt, but there is no reason to take him at face value. A more likely explanation for the war was Xerxes' own territorial ambitions, which were very much in line with those of his father. Extension of power was, after all, the natural consequence of power, and like the Romans and the British after them, the Persians too aspired to *imperium sine fine*, an empire without end.

From the moment the Persians had come into military contact with the Greeks in 499 BCE, it was clear that, one day, Greece would face invasion. If Darius' ambition to integrate Greece into the empire had not collapsed at Marathon, then the fate of the Athenians would have been the same as for other conquered peoples: deportation into Mesopotamia or further east. Athens would have been the centre of operations for the invasion of the Peloponnese, and, who knows, it might have become a satrapal capital too. Darius' failure in Greece was behind Xerxes' ambition to conquer it, and his chief desire in the years after his accession was to incorporate mainland Greece into the Persian empire.

Persian sources say absolutely nothing of Xerxes' Greek war. It is as though the Greek campaign never happened. We are therefore entirely dependent on Greek accounts for the events of 480 BCE and the years that followed. We have seen how Herodotus pieced together the *Histories* with great precision, but this is especially true of his version of the war narrative. The closer Herodotus takes his audience to the events of 480 BCE, the more emphasis he puts on casting the Persians as menacing *barbaroi* – destructive, merciless, and cruel. Yet Books Seven, Eight, and Nine of the *Histories* do not, with any confidence, provide a reliable account of what *actually* happened in 480 and 479 BCE. Much of what Herodotus passes as history is, in fact, make-believe. For instance, Herodotus depicts a scene in Susa where Xerxes is surrounded by his chief councillors, including Mardonius, his cousin and brother-in-law, and his uncle, Artabanus. The king is harangued by some of his councillors to bring the arrogance of Athens to heel, while others plead for peace. Later, away from the council chamber, in his bed, the king suffers dreams and nightmares, ominous portents of disaster, in which even the gods drive Xerxes towards his inevitable fate. Finally, the decision is taken: War it is! These scenes make for great reading, but it goes without saying that Herodotus did not have knowledge of what was said in the Privy Council of the Great King, let alone know what Xerxes saw in his dreams. When it comes to what was said about strategic military decisions during the campaign itself, though, there *is* the possibility that Herodotus got second-hand accounts from Queen Artemisia, the ruler of his home city of Halicarnassus. However, reports of inner-circle discussions between Xerxes, Mardonius, and Artabanus in far-off Susa are entirely fictitious and must be expunged from any serious attempt to answer the question of why the Persians attacked Greece.

Reading Herodotus is a delightful experience, that must be conceded. The Father of History deserves his place in the canon of Great Literature, but as a 'history' of Xerxes' campaign into Greece, he offers us little more than a ragbag of stories of war exploits, strung together by the themes of Greek heroism and moral probity. It is not so much that his tales are questionable, as that they leave us in the dark. This puts us in something of a dilemma. We cannot believe much of what Herodotus said, and yet we cannot do without him. Some historical truths about the Persians may well lie hidden in Herodotus, but one needs to dig deep through the layers of fantasy and fiction to find them.

*

Xerxes' goal was to bring Greece into the Persian empire, and to do this, he knew that he would need a huge number of fighting men to overcome the Greeks, who had, back in Darius' day, proven to be such tough and intrepid fighters. To that end, Xerxes wrote off using the royal navy because he realised that, even with his wealth, he could not raise enough ships to transport so vast an army across the Aegean Sea. However, intelligence reports brought news that the Greeks had already built up a huge fleet of triremes, or warships. This made Xerxes anxious. Losing control of the seas would be disastrous, and so he pondered his plan of action. His army, he knew, needed to be big enough to defeat the enemy – the combined forces of the allied Greek city states – yet not be so big that it could not be fed and watered. The Persians had had their past successes in northern Greece in a series of campaigns led by Mardonius, and Xerxes recognised that a land campaign over the terrain of Greece would suit his men very well. His reconnaissance told him that the march south from Macedon into Attica would be clear of obstacles and pretty much unhampered, barring a narrow pass at a place that the Greeks called Thermopylae, the 'Hot Gates', a defensive position to which the Greeks would naturally be drawn. Xerxes was told that he could expect battle there. Pleased with the reports, Xerxes concocted a plan that would play to his strengths and he decided to use *both* land forces and the navy in a tight combination. The land army would march ahead and secure beaches, where they would be joined by ships carrying supplies; the navy would also protect the army from any attacks from the Greek fleet.

In 481 BCE, as a form of psychological pre-attack, Xerxes sent ambassadors around Greece demanding earth and water from the various city states. He deliberately omitted Athens and Sparta from the rounds since, back in 491 BCE, the men of those cities had killed the heralds Darius had sent in an act of shocking impiety which had only strengthened the Persian belief that the Greeks were the ultimate barbarian peoples and needed to be brought under control. In late October 481 BCE, Xerxes' army began to assemble at Sardis and the king himself, together with the vast entourage of his court, left Susa to join it. Throughout the winter of 481–480 BCE the army was drilled and prepared for action as Xerxes and his generals discussed tactics, planned routes, and drew up battle plans. They took advice from Demaratus of Sparta, a confirmed exiled ally, who told them that the mainland Greeks were quarrelsome and often disunited, and frequently fought between themselves. Good diplomacy, he said, could win over the majority of Greek *poleis* (independent city states) without the need for conflict. But Xerxes was unconvinced. He knew that there were many Greek diehards who would never surrender to him or acknowledge his sovereignty. Their conquest and their complete forced submission was the only option. Intelligence units informed Xerxes that the Greeks had the capacity to muster 40,000 hoplites, the best of whom would come from Sparta, under the leadership of the resolute King Leonidas and his co-ruler, King Leotychidas, who had many military allies in the Peloponnese. The Athenians would supply ships for the allied navy, some 400 lumbering triremes, heavier and more threatening than the Persian warships. It was difficult for Xerxes' scouts to keep pace with the political developments in Athens. Its radical democratic regime seemed to change leaders on a weekly basis, but Persian intelligence finally learned that a man named Themistocles, the son of a greengrocer, had become popular in the city and had played an important part in building the Greek fleet. He was currently much fêted by the Athenians. With characteristic insight, Xerxes knew that he needed to watch this Themistocles very closely.

In the spring of 480 BCE, as the bright sun shone down on the satrapal palace at Sardis and a myriad of flowers blossomed in the royal gardens, Xerxes, his army, and the assemblage of his entire court set off on the 800-mile journey to Athens. The mission was to bring Greece to its knees.

*

According to Herodotus, when Xerxes arrived at Doriskos in Thrace, he decided to marshal and count his army. Herodotus lists the ethnic contingents serving in the infantry, cavalry, and navy, describing their particular clothing and headgear and weapons.

'The total of the land army', Herodotus said, 'amounted to 170 myriads.' That equates to 1,700,000 men, to which must be added the totals of cavalry and navy, of non-combatants, and the contingents levied in Greece. All in all, Herodotus maintained that there were some 1,700,000 infantry, 517,610 different men of the fleet, 80,000 cavalry, and 20,000 camel-cavalry and charioteers, totalling 2,317,610 individuals. Adding the troops levied in Europe, Herodotus arrived at an astronomical figure: there were 5,283,220 fighting men serving in Xerxes' army. Unsurprisingly, military specialists have questioned Herodotus' figures and have concluded that even if reduced by 20, 50, or even 60 per cent, an army of that scale could not have executed the kind of manoeuvres Xerxes demanded of it. It was simply too cumbersome. Herodotus' catalogue of troops should not be read literally. He was intent on creating a vivid portrait of the immensity of power which he imagined the Great King had at his disposal. This was bolstered by the emphasis Herodotus placed on the ethnic diversity of Xerxes' troops: there were Kushites, Egyptians, Indians, Bactrians, Lycians . . . the list went on. The world, Herodotus implied, was set to take on Greece. Herodotus used the spectacle of Xerxes' racially diverse army to emphasise the effect of inequality between the overwhelming forces of Persia and the paucity of men who made up the Greek troops.

For Xerxes too, the principal function of the review parade at Doriskos was to stress the power and diversity of his empire. His soldiers formed a picturesque assemblage of clothes and weapons – a living variation on the theme of empire carved into the staircases of the *Apadana* at Persepolis. Babylonian evidence testifies to the fact that these parade reviews happened at other times and places as well, and that soldiers settled on military land allotments were also sometimes called up for impromptu royal reviews. For this they needed to bring the correct equipment: 'a horse with a harness and reins, a coat with neckpiece and hood, iron armour and hood, a quiver, 120 arrows, some with heads, some without, a sword with its scabbard, and two iron spears'. Xerxes' parade army, called up by the central authorities, was there to provide a spectacle at the outset of the campaign. But it is clear that it did not take part in the march on Greece, let alone in battle. That task was left to the real fighting force.

The campaign soldiers were drawn from Persia, Media, and the eastern satrapies, including India and Central Asia. Many of these men had already seen service in Egypt and Babylon, where they had crushed the rebellions and so entered the Greek campaign as a well-honed fighting force. Historians now estimate that Xerxes' forces for the Greek campaign numbered around 70,000 infantry and 9,000 horsemen.

In addition to the veteran troops, Xerxes also employed the most famous of the army units, the crack fighting team known as the Ten Thousand (or 'Immortals'), a division of the army which served as the royal bodyguard. The Immortals (Greek, *athánatoi*, literally, 'those without death') was the name of an elite corps of 10,000 Achaemenid Persian infantry soldiers. Herodotus called them a 'body of hand-picked Persian troops' and glossed the title 'Immortals' by ascertaining that 'if a man was killed or fell sick, the vacancy he left was at once filled, so that the strength [of the group] was never more or less than 10,000'. In Old Persian this exclusive unit might have been known as *anushiya*, literally meaning 'being behind' or 'follower'. However, the word is taken from the Avestan *aosha*, 'death' or 'destruction', and so it is possible that *anushiya* could be read as 'behind death' or 'deathless', which would make sense of Herodotus' understanding of the concept. The Immortals were regarded as a league apart from the common Persian soldiery. Bona fide Persian sources for the Immortals are elusive, however, although it is generally assumed that the bearded and richly liveried soldiers represented in the beautiful faience tiles from the Achaemenid palace at Susa represent this elite warrior group. And yet there are no references to a corps of Immortals in the Persian written sources, although it is likely that the Achaemenid monarch was accompanied at all times by a special defence force. All in all, there are more questions surrounding this special corps of the Persian army than there are answers. Their exact tasks, and even their genuine Persian name, remain unknown.

Xerxes' well-drilled and disciplined infantrymen – *kardakes*, as they were known – worked together to provide protection and support. They wore soft caps, multicoloured sleeved tunics, iron armour like fish scales, and trousers. They carried short spears, big wicker shields called *spara*, large bows, cane arrows, and daggers that hung from their belts beside their right thighs. In time-honoured Iranian tradition, the horse cavalry used lances and bows and arrows to slaughter their enemies from afar, charged their horses into the melee, and pursued adversaries as they fled. But there were other men in Xerxes' forces who came from a very different military background: many Ionian Greek hoplites augmented the Persian army and, primarily armed with spears and shields, they used the phalanx formation as their chief tactic. Later, as Xerxes marched through northern Greece, he was joined by other Greek hoplites who were also prepared to fight for the Persian cause.

The oligarchs of the *polis* of Thebes, the largest and most powerful city in Boeotia in northern Greece, had viewed the approach of the Persians with a certain ambivalence, but their deep hatred of the Athenians led them to side with the Persians. Even Argos in the Peloponnese sent troops north to aid Xerxes. Delphi too sided with Persia. This was something of a psychological victory for Xerxes, who was able to solicit support from the sanctuary of Apollo with its powerful oracular capabilities – a smart propaganda move on the part of the Persian king. The fact is, the Greeks were never completely united in a combined drive to repel the Persian advance from mainland Greece. Many Greek *poleis* believed that an alliance with Xerxes would mean preferential treatment for their citizens once his victory had been concluded and he had returned to Iran. This inconvenient truth is often overlooked in histories which perpetuate the myth of the clash of civilisations, for it does not play to the simple narratives of 'freedom' and 'slavery' or of 'democracy' over 'despotism'. In actuality, many Greeks, reckoning that a better life could be found within the empire, looked to Persia for leadership and for future rule.

The Greeks who took up arms against the Persians – the Greek resistance – designated the states and individuals who supported

Xerxes as collaborators. They employed the Greek verb *Medidzö*, 'to side with the Medes', or the noun *Medizmos*, 'leaning towards the Medes', as ways of maligning them. The expression implied that Greek collaborators rejected the 'free' lifestyle of the Hellenic world in favour of the corrupting behaviour of the slavish Orient. The Greeks who supported Xerxes were seen as low-life traitors.

*

Logistics ensured that Xerxes' troops were well-supplied with good food and plentiful fresh water. This was achieved through the construction and conscription of an impressive fleet of ships, some 1,200 triremes and 3,000 other vessels, according to Herodotus, who once again can be seen to have widely exaggerated his calculations. The actual number of triremes supplied by Ionia, Phoenicia, and Egypt was closer to 500, a long way off Herodotus' exaggeration. The ships were under the command of trusted and experienced Persian nobles, including twelve of Xerxes' own brothers. This was a strategic decision, for in committing his own kin to key posts in the invasion, the king sent out a strong message – the Greek war was not his alone, it was an Achaemenid war, a dynastic enterprise.

The real heroes of Xerxes' campaign have largely gone unmentioned, yet without their contribution to the war effort, the Persians would have had a slow and drawn-out experience of conflict in Greece. The names of the engineers who drew up plans for canals and bridges and roadways are lost to us. But their skills show them to have been bold and ambitious project managers. The natural landscape was no barrier to their commitment to provide Xerxes with a swift, trouble-free route into Europe, as they cut, dug, and wrought through rock or dragged the continents together by lassoing Asia to Europe with extraordinarily makeshift bridges. Already in 483 BCE the Persians had begun preparing for the invasion of Greece by cutting a canal through the Athos Peninsula in north-east Greece, the site of a Persian naval disaster in 492 BCE. The canal – which recent geophysics revealed to be one mile long, 100 feet wide, and ten feet deep – meant that Xerxes' ships could bypass a treacherous and potentially lethal stretch of water which surrounded the peninsula. Herodotus claimed that Xerxes ordered the construction of the canal out of hubris, but the king simply recognised the importance of ensuring that his army had a swift and safe passage into Greece. More importantly, in building the canal Xerxes was looking to the future when Greece, securely incorporated into the empire, could be routinely accessed via this great man-made structure. It would give the Persians safe, year-round sea contact with mainland Greece.

Xerxes oversaw the construction of two pontoon bridges at the Hellespont, connecting Asia to Europe. Each bridge was formed of a row of boats anchored parallel to the current and lashed together with papyrus and flax cables. These stretched across the wide channel. Xerxes' men laid down a mile-long wooden roadway over the row of ships and erected linen screens on each side of the walkway so that horses could cross the water without panicking. Darius had bridged the Bosporus and possibly the Danube in a campaign against Scythia in 513 BCE, but Xerxes' structures well surpassed those of his father, both in scale and in ambition. The powerful currents of the Hellespont, together with ferocious winds, meant that the first set of bridges constructed had to be rebuilt, stronger and more durable than before. Herodotus' description of Xerxes' anger in the face of the storm is infamous:

> Xerxes flew into a rage and he commanded that the Hellespont be struck with three hundred strokes of the whip and that a pair of foot-chains be thrown into the sea . . . He also commanded the scourgers to speak outlandish and arrogant words: 'You hateful waters, our master lays his judgement on you thus, for you have unjustly punished him even though he's done you no wrong! Xerxes the king will pass over you, whether you wish it or not! It is fitting that no man offer you sacrifices, for you're a muddy and salty river!'

As ever, hiding behind Herodotus' account there is a Persian Version. In his role as the King of Nature, Xerxes propitiated the Hellespont with prayers and hymns (and not the wild raging of the Herodotean report), and offered gifts to its majesty – gold necklaces and torques (and not the iron chains of Herodotus' story). The construction of the Hellespont bridges was a triumph of engineering and a masterstroke of propaganda, for as Xerxes' army strode into Europe, reports of the crossing of the Hellespont reached Athens. 'How', the Athenians questioned, 'how can we hope to rout a people who can trek across the seas?'

*

Marching at a pace of some ten miles a day and divided into three vast columns, each a mile apart so as not to clog the roads, Xerxes' army trooped north from Sardis to the Hellespont, crossed the pontoon bridges, and entered into Thrace. From there, they marched west into Macedon. For any new recruits, this was uncharted territory and they were marching into a brave new world, but for Xerxes' veterans, those who had enjoyed taking the rich spoils of Egypt and Babylon, the Greek campaign was a bit of a trudge. Greece offered very little possibility of acquiring wealth. Everybody knew that the Greeks pecked out a living from a hostile environment, so what booty lay ahead in the gnarled rocky landscape of Greece? Sitting, as it did, on the edge of the world, what plunder could it possibly afford? Stones? Olives? Radishes?

The northern Greeks who watched the spectacle of Xerxes' army march through the landscape were left with the impression that the Persians were unstoppable. Well-drilled, motivated, and loyal, the Persian army pushed on and on, mile upon mile. The Thracians were so in awe of the invading troops that years later, in Herodotus' time, they could still point out the roadway taken by Xerxes and wonder at the splendour of his army, for the presence of so many foreign armed men was both exciting and unnerving. Communities quickly came forward offering food and supplies to the army as it passed through their lands, although they also hid valuables from marauding Persian eyes and made sure that their loved ones – especially pretty girls and boys – were kept out of sight.

The Persians entered Macedon and Xerxes met with his ally, the client king Alexander I (the great-great-great-grandfather of the man who would one day bring the Achaemenid dynasty crashing down). He then marched south into Thessaly, where many thousands of Thessalonians joined the Persian troops. From a Persian perspective, so far the land campaign was an unqualified success: Xerxes had already taken half of mainland Greece without a single battle. His fleet of ships advanced down the coast, and although the armada had been weathered by storms and some ships had run aground, by and large it was in a good state and it kept the ever-growing army supplied. As news of Xerxes' unhindered progress reached Attica, the Athenians, Spartans, and other defiant Greeks – about thirty city states in all – formed a defensive league. Their single aim was to blockade the Persian advance and they would use the landscape of Greece to their advantage to draw the Persian invaders into narrow passes and straits so as to forcibly filter down the number of their troops. Some Greeks wanted to lure the Persians into the Peloponnese for an open fight, but it was decided to mount a forward offence in central Greece on land at the pass of Thermopylae, about 200 kilometres north-west of Athens, and on the sea at the straits of Artemisium.

Because of sediment formation and the slow build-up of silt deposits, the landscape around the thermal springs at Thermopylae has changed considerably since 480 BCE, when it was a very narrow pass indeed, with ragged mountains on one side and the sea directly opposite, on the other. The thin gorge was around twenty metres wide, or one wagon's width, as Herodotus qualified it. To the east of Thermopylae lay the closed-in straits of Artemisium, formed by the long coastline of the island of Euboea, which stretched down the eastern coast of mainland Greece. In order to move south and be parallel with the coast of the eastern mainland, the Persian navy needed to squeeze its way through the tricky channel with its choppy waters and perilous strong currents. The rocky sea cliffs of Euboea meant that the ships had no room for manoeuvre and no alternative but to steer ahead and pass through the strait. Xerxes' scouts had warned him of these natural treacherous barriers, and the army and navy were well prepared when, in August 480 BCE, the Great King arrived at Thermopylae. Some 700 Greeks were waiting ready to repel him, including 300 Spartan warriors under the leadership of King Leonidas. The full force of the Greek alliance had not yet assembled because August was Greece's leisure time, the period of the Olympic Games, and most Greeks were glued to their favourite sports, never imagining that Xerxes would move his army through central Greece so quickly. But the Athenian Themistocles was ahead of the game. Always on the alert, ever vigilant, he and his ships had assembled off the east coast, where they waited patiently for the Persian ships to come into view.

Notwithstanding the Western fixation with the story of the 300 Spartans, the Battle of Thermopylae can only be interpreted as a great Persian victory. It was a resounding success for Xerxes' kingship. For the first few days of fighting, the Great King bombarded the Greeks with frontal attacks, wearing them down and overwhelming them with Persia's vast resources. Xerxes' scouts soon found a pathway through the mountains inland and he sent his Immortals to outflank the Greek position. When Leonidas discovered that the Persians were inching closer, he ordered the other Greek forces to withdraw, allowing his Spartans to set themselves up as a rearguard. It was a suicide mission, for certain. Herodotus presents Leonidas' decision to stay and die as a combination of concern for his allies and a heroic desire for *kleos* – an immortal glory, like that enjoyed by the Homeric heroes of old. But the main reason he stayed was more practical: the Persians had archers and cavalry, and if all the Greeks retreated and left the pass unguarded, they would be overtaken and butchered. A rearguard was needed to block the path and hold back the enemy while their comrades retreated. The Spartans stayed in place to give the other Greeks some escape time, but the Persians quickly surrounded the Spartan soldiers and slaughtered them to a man. In less than seven days, Xerxes had broken the last barrier that lay between his troops and Athens. He had also killed the Spartan king, a Liar-King who had dared to oppose Xerxes' aim of incorporating Greece into his god-given realm. Ahuramazda was with Xerxes. Ahuramazda had granted Xerxes a great victory.

The Battle of Artemisium was more evenly matched though, and both sides suffered equal losses. The naval battle took place simultaneously with the events at Thermopylae, and Xerxes received a rally of missives, keeping him up to speed with the development of the action at sea. During the first two days of the encounter, the Greeks captured thirty Persian ships and destroyed the flotilla of the Cilicians, who served Xerxes. However, on the third day, the Persians came out at full strength and roundly beat the Greeks. Sensing that defeat was imminent, Themistocles had no choice but to quickly take his fleet out of the channel and head back to Athens. Herodotus presented Artemisium as a significant Greek victory, but even he could not hide the fact that the Greeks suffered heavy losses. It was the Persians who won out at Artemisium, and, unchallenged, their army marched south through the friendly territory of Boeotia, past Thebes, and on into Attica.

Late in August 480 BCE, Xerxes entered Athens. By the time he got there, it was practically a ghost town. Having gathered together what possessions they most needed, many of its citizens had fled to the island of Salamis, where they set up a makeshift shanty town and settled down, well out of harm's way. Only a few diehard Athenians remained in their claustrophobic little city, determined to tough it out on the Acropolis, the ancient and revered sanctuary of their divine patroness, Athene Polias (her statue had been moved for safekeeping to Salamis too). High on the sacred hill, they had erected wooden barricades for protection, but after only a few days' stand-off, the Persians broke through the blockade and stormed the holy Acropolis. 'They did not respect the images of the gods, they burned temples, levelled holy altars, uprooted sacred precincts, and reduced everything to debris', Aeschylus later lamented. Archaeological investigations on the Acropolis confirm the great tragedian's lamentation, for Xerxes' soldiers vented their fury on the elegant marble statues which had once graced the shrines and courtyards of the sanctuary. Discovered in the early 1900s in carefully made pits which had been dug by the Athenians after the war, a 'graveyard' of statues of handsome young men (kouroi) and elegant young women (korai), has been labelled by archaeologists as the Perserschutt, a German word meaning 'Persian rubble'.

Having slaughtered every Athenian who had held out in the Acropolis, Xerxes' troops set fire to the city. The small houses made of wood and mud-brick were packed tightly together in narrow streets, and they burned like dry tinder. The city was quickly ablaze. The Athenians hiding out on Salamis could see the great conflagration and they despaired. For Xerxes, though, this was the moment he had longed for. Twenty years after the Athenians had set fire to Sardis, now their own city was burned to ashes. Looking at the charred rubble and scorched wreckage of that arrogant, upstart little *polis*, Xerxes knew that Ahuramazda was working with him and through him. Like his father, he too had crushed the Lie. Xerxes could now brag that the Truth had been brought to bear on Greece.

And yet the war dragged on. In the hidden bays and coves of Salamis, Themistocles saw to it that the Greek fleet had regrouped and was prepared once again for battle. Xerxes was brought news of this and decided to send his remaining ships against the Greek triremes. The final battle would be at sea. Then Greece would be his.

Hindsight is a glorious thing. We now recognise that if Xerxes had only pressed ahead and attacked the Greeks on land, as he had been doing with such spectacular success, then the ultimate victory almost certainly would have been his. If he had ignored the presence of the Greek fleet at Salamis and marched his troops directly into the Peloponnese, he could easily have split and destroyed the Greek alliance. The Spartans would soon have returned home to defend their territory against a marauding Persian army, leaving the Athenians friendless and defenceless. After accepting the submission of Themistocles, Xerxes' massive army would have outnumbered the Spartans, and even if the fighting had been fierce, a Spartan defeat was guaranteed. But it was not to be. In sending his fleet against Themistocles' ships, Xerxes made a devastating mistake.

Herodotus ascertained that Xerxes' defeat occurred because of a trick. Themistocles, Herodotus advocated, lied to Xerxes, saying that he was now Persia's loyal ally, and he sent an embassy to the Great King to negotiate peace terms. He stated that the Athenian ships planned to abandon their position at sea and that, if the Persians would enter the strait between Salamis and the mainland, they would easily defeat the remaining Greeks on the water. The story of Themistocles' lie was already known to Aeschylus, a contemporary of the battle, and what Herodotus wrote later may well have been true. We know that Xerxes ignored the advice of his officers, his brothers, and even of Artemisia of Halicarnassus, in whom he placed his complete trust. It is possible that it was people close to Artemisia who informed Herodotus of the events which occurred early in the morning of 29 September 480 BCE.

When it was still very dark, the Persians started to enter the narrow strait. Xerxes watched what happened from a nearby hill, and saw how, at dawn's first light, his ships were attacked on their flank. The Greek fleet had the home advantage since it knew how the currents and the winds affected navigation in the narrow strait, whereas the Persians were in uncharted water. Rowing hard at breakneck speed, the heavy Greek triremes rammed into the lighter Persian ships, smashing their hulls and throwing the Persian oarsmen into the sea. By nightfall, after repeated attacks, at least a third of the Persian ships were reduced to floating debris. The corpses of drowned Persians clogged the passageway of the triumphant Greek fleet. Among the dead were several of Xerxes' brothers and many more of Persia's nobility.

The Battle of Salamis entered into Greek legend. It was replayed on the Athenian stage in Aeschylus' great tragedy, *Persians*, and it was relived in the songs of Timotheus of Miletus too. His *Persians*, a flamboyant Mozartian-like concert aria for a virtuoso solo voice, sung to his own harp accompaniment, saw the performer imitate a host of Persians, a cross-section of the barbarians the Athenians encountered in battle. He performed a pidgin-Greek-speaking soldier, slowly drowning in the waters of Salamis, and then switched character and sang the loftily ornate lamentations of Xerxes himself:

'Woe for the razing of homes! and alas for you, you desolating Greek ships that have destroyed a populous generation of young men, and have so done that our ships that should have carried them back home shall burn in the flaming might of furious fire, and the pains of lamentation be upon the land of

Persia! O ill fate that led me to Greece! But ho! Come quickly, yoke me my chariot and four and you bring out my countless wealth to the wagons, and burn my pavilions that they profit them not of my riches.'

The backbone of Xerxes' navy was broken at Salamis. It would have been difficult for him to build a new fleet quickly. Moreover, the infantry and cavalry could no longer depend on supplies coming from the ships. And so, exhausted and demoralised, the Persians were forced to retreat from Attica. Xerxes spent the winter in Thebes, ruminating on his mistakes and castigating the mistakes of others. But the push to conquer the Greeks was not yet over. Xerxes left his gifted brother-in-law, Mardonius, in Greece with a squad of excellent soldiers, as he, and the remainder of the troops, marched back to Sardis. It must have been an overwhelmingly difficult return journey for all concerned, but for Xerxes, it was especially painful. He had broken with the military examples of his forebears – Cyrus, Cambyses, and Darius – whose victories in war had seen the empire grow in size and strength. Now that he had left Greece, Xerxes knew that he had stirred up a hornets' nest and was leaving behind him a rebellious and troublesome people whose resistance to the Persian empire would continue to grow. And the most troublesome of all were the Athenians, who, many decades later, sitting in their open-air theatre carved into the rock of the Acropolis which Xerxes had so maliciously defiled, laughed at Aristophanes' latest political comedy, *The Wasps*. The chorus of grouchy old insects buzz with scorn at Athens' political class and remember the olden days when, as young wasps, they had driven the Persians from their city:

We charged at them with spear and shield right away and we fought them, clashed with them, with hardened hearts, each wasp standing next to another in tight lines, biting our lips while the enemy's arrows filled the sky. But with the help of the gods we pushed the bastards back and we saw Athene's loving bird the owl flying over our men. And then we chased them away, digging our sharp stingers into their baggy trousers and as they were fleeing, we stung them on the jaws and on their eyebrows. That's why to this day all barbarians everywhere say that there's nowhere a more valiant wasp than that of Athens.

On the plain north of Plataea in Boeotia in August 479 BCE, a series of decisive battles took place between the allied Greeks and the forces of Mardonius, which included his Theban allies. The Greek army, under the Spartan Pausanias, assembled on hills near the Persians' camp to confront them. At first, neither side wanted to make a full-scale attack but it was the Persian cavalry which eventually made the first move, successfully raiding the Greeks' supply waggons and blocking the springs that supplied their fresh water. Pausanias counterattacked with a night move to a new position, but when dawn broke the Greeks found themselves strung out, disorganised, and vulnerable, an opportunity Mardonius saw as too good to be true. He attacked. This offensive gave the Greek hoplites the opportunity they needed and in close-quarter fighting they gradually gained the upper hand. This was the moment when the ancient arms race changed. Bow and arrow gave way to spear and sword. Brave Mardonius was killed in action and the leaderless Persians lost heart, broke ranks, and fled, only to be cut down by the Athenians as they ran. As always in an ancient battle, the casualties of a routed army were horrific and thousands of Persians were slaughtered on the retreat or in their camp. What was left of the Persian army withdrew north into Thessaly and finally made its way back to Sardis. As it marched, it heard the latest news from the Aegean – the Greek fleet had made an amphibious landing at Mycale in Ionia and had defeated a Persian troop based there. It was the first Greek victory in Asia, and although the Athenians and Spartans overcame a demoralised opponent, it was an important event. From now on, the Greeks were taking the offensive. Fighting between Greeks and Persians would continue for many decades, but the Persians never invaded Greece again.

*

Many scholars still insist that Plataea was the beginning of the end for the Persian empire and that its slide into decadence, corruption, and inertia started with Xerxes' defeat. This approach makes no sense. The Persian empire still had another 150 years to run and was still strong and vigorous, showing no signs of weakening. Indeed, in Xerxes' inscriptions erected after 479 BCE, we have claims of new territorial expansions which outdo the boarders of his father's realm:

> Xerxes the king proclaims: By the favour of Ahuramazda, these are the countries of which I was King outside Persia; I ruled them; they bore me tribute. What was said to them by me, that they did. The law that was mine, that held them firm: Media, Elam, Arachosia, Armenia, Drangiana, Parthia, Areia, Bactria, Sogdiana, Chorasmia, Babylonia, Assyria, Sattagydia, Lydia, Egypt, Ionians who dwell by the Sea and those who dwell beyond the Sea, the Maka people, Arabia, Gandara, Indus, Cappadocia, Dahae, Scythians (Saka) who drink *haoma*, Scythians (Saka) who wear pointed hats, Thrace, the Akaufaka people, Libyans, Carians, Nubians (XPh).

Although it is probable that this inscription dates to after the Greek campaign, the royal rhetoric pays no attention to territorial losses on the north-western front of the empire. In fact, Xerxes expanded the standard lists of the royal inscriptions and claimed victories over the Saka people and the Dahae, who lived east of the Caspian Sea, as well as the conquest of the land of Akaufaka, a mountainous area in the far north-east of the empire in modern-day Pakistan.

The Persians (at least in their official presentation) did not consider themselves defeated by the Greeks. Even though the real aim of the war had been the complete subjugation of Greece, the Persians were able to brazen it out by claiming that actually their chief objective had been met – Athens had been taken and had been soundly humiliated. An oblique reference to the Greek campaign may be found on one of Xerxes' inscriptions at Persepolis in which he states that 'when I became King, there was among

Figure 18. A seal impression of a Great King killing a Greek hoplite. This was probably produced in Asia Minor and is carved in a 'Greek' style.

the countries . . . one [Greece?] which was in disorder . . . By the favour of Ahuramazda, I overwhelmed that country and put it in its proper place' (XPh). Persian iconography showed images of the war with the Greek enemies, who are always armed with spears and shields, but collapsed on the ground, or fallen to their knees in front of triumphant Persians, often the figure of the Great King himself. There is no Persian war narrative to compare them to, but it is certain that the Greeks widely exaggerated the significance of their victories. Timotheus' *Persians*, the ulti-mate jingoistic, triumphalist, popular classic abounds with imagery drawn from the long-standing Greek creation of the barbarian 'other'. It rejoices in Xerxes' humiliation and depicts Persia's fall with glee. But for the Achaemenid empire, with its vast reserve of resources, Xerxes' Greek campaign, like that of Darius in 490 BCE, was just another attempt at territorial expansion in a far-flung area of the western periphery of the realm. Truth in war is an illusion, a deception made to bolster one side and denigrate the other. The Greeks wrote the history of the war in their favour – and auda-ciously acted it out on stage and in song too – but the Persians had their own history of the conflict in which they justified themselves by claiming they had no weaknesses in the war because, as Xerxes put it, his rule was a god-gift: 'Ahuramazda made me king, one king over many kings, one commander of many commanders . . . Ahuramazda and the gods protect me and my kingdom' (XPf).

16

Les Liaisons dangereuses

Following the war in Greece something changed in Xerxes. From 479 BCE, his inscriptions began to put increasing emphasis on the paramount importance of loyalty and they began to stress the consequences of insurrection against the throne, warning subjects to know their place and remain faithful to their king. It was as if a feeling of generalised restlessness in the empire threatened to disturb the imperial tranquillity. Xerxes' disquiet reached a peak in a lengthy text he issued in multiple copies, castigating the worship of what he referred to as '*daivas*'.

This Old Iranian word was related to an Indo-European term meaning 'shine' or 'be bright'. It was a compound of the name Dyḗus, an ancient 'daylight'-sky-god, and was the root of many Indo-European words for 'god' or 'goddess' (Sanskrit and Hindi: *dev(i)*; Latin: *deus*; Welsh: *duw*; French: *dieu*). In the Achaemenid era *daiva* (singular) had a different, more sinister meaning. In the holy *Gathas*, the sacred scriptures of the Zoroastrians, the *daivas* were specifically categorised as 'gods that are to be rejected' and, in keeping with this notion, it would appear that when Xerxes referred to *daivas* he too seems to have designated some kind of undesirable phenomena, perhaps demonic beings, false gods, or wicked spirits. In foreign lands, these abhorrent creatures of the dark, the vassals of the Lie, were the recipients of holy rituals, as Xerxes made clear:

> Among those countries of the empire there were some where formerly the *daivas* had been worshipped. Afterwards, by the favour of Ahuramazda, I destroyed that place of the *daivas*, and

I gave orders: 'The *daivas* shall not be worshipped any longer!'
Wherever formerly the *daivas* have been worshipped, there
I worshipped Ahuramazda, at the proper time and with the
proper ceremony (XPh).

This extraordinary text, labelled by scholars the 'Daivâ Inscription', was discovered by archaeologists carved into seven stone slabs
in the Garrison Quarters (a group of structures near the south-east
corner) of Persepolis. Another copy of the Daivâ Inscription was
discovered by the British Institute of Persian Studies during excavations at Pasargadae. The text of the inscriptions seems to have
been an attempt by Xerxes to galvanise the empire's central authority through a series of religious reforms in which the worship of
Ahuramazda was promoted as the preferred (or perhaps official)
cult of the empire. This was an unusual, draconian manoeuvre
and was entirely out of touch with the mechanisms and theologies
of ancient polytheism, and with the standard Persian laissez-faire
approach to the religious life of the empire. Curiously, the Daivâ
Inscription insists that priority must be given to the correct rites
and rituals of Ahuramazda's worship, which strongly suggests that
Xerxes was concerned to dictate points of doctrine, observance
and, indeed, morality to his subjects. The focus of his ire ('some
[countries] where formerly the *daivas* had been worshipped') is
opaque. Was he referring to the gods of Egypt, Babylon, or Athens,
all of whom had 'suffered' in his campaigns? Or were the *daivas*
closer to home? Were they actually the 'other gods who are', the
ancient Elamite deities who were still worshipped in the Persian
heartlands? Was Xerxes purging the old Mesopotamian beliefs
and replacing them with a more ostensibly Iranian belief system?
Infuriatingly, it is impossible to answer any of these questions with
complete conviction, but it is possible to read the Daivâ Inscription
as more of an ideological manifesto than a proselytiser's pamphlet.
The Daivâ Inscription seems to have been Xerxes' attempt to
promote worldwide allegiance to Ahuramazda and, by extension,
to Xerxes himself as the Achaemenid King of Kings. It was a declaration on the highest level of the benefits and virtues of the *Pax*

Persica because the Daivâ Inscription promoted a *Pax Achaemenica* through the supremacy of Xerxes' supreme god.

*

If Xerxes' chief concern was the promotion and longevity of his dynasty, then he failed spectacularly in the direct maintenance of it. His domestic life was a shambles. The Greek war had cost him the lives of several brothers as well as that of a gifted and loyal brother-in-law. Mardonius' body disappeared from the field of Plataea, never to be seen again, and his widow, Xerxes' sister, Artazostre, mourned his death profoundly, while his son, Artontes, campaigned in vain to have his father's corpse brought to Persia. Xerxes' sons, Dariaios, Hystaspes, and Artaxerxes, Amestris' three boys, had grown to be energetic and able young men, and each of them harboured a desire for power and all thought themselves worthy to be Xerxes' successor. But the king had named Dariaios, the eldest, as his heir, and Hystaspes and Artaxerxes burned with jealousy and ambition.

Sometime around 478 BCE Xerxes arranged for Dariaios to take a wife – a clear-cut sign that the prince was being groomed for kingship. Xerxes chose for his son's bride a niece, Artayntē, the daughter of his brother, Masistes, one of the chief marshals of the Greek campaign, the satrap of Bactria, and a renowned hero of the recent wars. Nothing could have been more straightforward in the Achaemenid family than the endogamous union of the offspring of two brothers. The wedding of Dariaios and Artayntē was intended to bind Xerxes and Masistes, loving brothers, close together in dynastic harmony. Nothing was less certain, for in the months leading up to the wedding, Xerxes had secretly made Artayntē, the pretty young bride-to-be, his mistress. She enthusiastically accepted the role and played her part with gusto. After she was married to his son, Xerxes was guaranteed easy access to the girl, since as the king's daughter-in-law and niece, Artayntē could legitimately reside among the women of the royal harem. The affair was set to continue.

The relationship between Xerxes and Artayntē had a particularly sordid background, however, for before Xerxes had ever met the girl, his desire was for her mother, Masistes' wife (sadly unnamed in our sources). While Masistes was fighting the Greeks at Mycale, Xerxes had developed an overwhelming crush on his sister-in-law, whom he saw every day while the court and the army were set up in Sardis. When he returned to Susa, he pressed his suit, but Masistes' wife adamantly refused to give herself to him, or even favour him with as much as a winning smile; her honour was at stake, as was her marriage. Xerxes' lust proved to be farcically fickle. We do not know when Xerxes first laid eyes on his niece, but it was probably while she was in her mother's presence. Overnight, Xerxes decided that he wanted the daughter rather than the mother, and Artaynte became his lover. His obsessive nature fixated on her. He could not get enough of her, and would spend many hours each day in her company. Xerxes could have his choice of any woman in the empire; his harem was packed with concubines whose only duty was sex. So his decision to sleep with his son's wife is mindboggling. Unless, of course, it was Artaynte herself who had the upper hand. Perhaps it was she who played Xerxes for a fool. The king's obsession had led to the dishonouring of her mother and, by implication, her father too; maybe Artaynte could do something to put Xerxes in his place. The events which followed suggest that was the case.

Amestris, Xerxes' queen, was oblivious to her husband's affair. There were so many women in his world that she was quite desensitised to his sex life. So long as the other wives and concubines gave her the respect her office as the mother of the heir-designate deserved, she was content. She passed much of her time, as most elite women across the ancient world did, weaving and sewing, and, one day, she gave Xerxes a gift of a beautiful long-sleeved *gaunaka*, the old Iranian-style coat so prized by the Persians. It was well-woven in many coloured threads and was sumptuously decorated with intricate patterns. More importantly, it was the work of her own hands, the product of endless hours of careful labour. Amestris' gift was an important expression of the courtly code of elite obligation. In giving Xerxes so valuable a gift Amestris brought her husband into a nexus of obligation. Very pleased with the coat, Xerxes put it on. At that moment, as all Persians would have recognised, the garment itself became imbued with the essence of majesty – that special, sacred charisma known as *farr* or *khavaneh* which oozed in and out of the body of the king. Any *gaunaka* worn by the king became saturated with the profound religious aura of the royal *farr*, but a garment made on the loom of a queen was particularly special. The most costly version of this special garment was made in purple, white, and gold threads and was decorated with the motif of gilded hawks. It was this ensemble which, Ctesias noted, struck the Persians with an almost religious awe. The Great King's *gaunaka* was a magical talisman and the Persians believed that it possessed the supernatural powers of monarchy.

It was while wearing his new robe that Xerxes went to visit Artayntē. In a happy and giving mood, Xerxes told the girl to ask for anything she might desire as a reward for her many favours, and he promised to grant it. Artayntē doubted the king's word and so Xerxes pledged his oath to give her what she most desired. Artayntē demanded the robe. Xerxes was stunned. Backtracking, he tried offering her other gifts – cities, unlimited gold, an army of her own – but to no effect. Nothing would do for Artayntē but the robe. Browbeaten and dizzy with the incomprehension at what had just occurred, Xerxes gave it to her. Delighted, she put it on, and gloried in wearing it.

There was more to Artaynte's acquisition of the royal garment than first meets the eye. In demanding this symbolic vestment, Artaynte surreptitiously laid claim to the sovereignty of Persia, not for herself of course, for it was impossible in the Persian tradition for a woman to reign in her own right, but for her already powerful family. Artaynte took the robe in order to hand it on to her father. The royal robe was a powerful symbol of legitimate Achaemenid kingship and Artaynte intended it not for her husband, Dariaios, Xerxes' heir-designate, but for Masistes, her father. Xerxes' brother, a man of ambition, considered that he deserved much better than an eastern satrapy. In fact, his name derives from an Old Persian word, *mathishta* – 'the greatest' – and it provides an added dimension to his character. *Mathishta* may have been his nickname or soubriquet;

if so, it was a bold statement. If Xerxes recognised that Artaynte's ploy was to inch her father closer to the throne, then, lovesick as he was, he did nothing about it.

Soon afterwards, however, Amestris discovered that Artaynte had taken possession of the robe, and she saw very clearly the motives behind her daughter-in-law's actions. Rather than lash out in anger or warn her husband of the high treason that was at hand, Amestris decided to play the long game and waited for the right time to act. That day came when her husband gave a particularly grand banquet. It was a once-a-year occasion, a feast held to celebrate the king's birthday. According to tradition, this was the one time of the year when the king anointed his head with the finest perfumed oil and bestowed extravagant gifts on his family and courtiers; it was a time for a lavish display of royal largess. It was at Xerxes' birthday feast that Amestris asked for her present, knowing that etiquette required that Xerxes give her what she wanted. Amestris demanded that Masistes' wife be brought to her in chains, as a prisoner. Dumbfounded, but suddenly all too aware that his wife – and now the whole court – knew of his affair with his daughter-in-law, Xerxes was horrified. Nothing good could come of this. Amestris repeated her request and cited the long-held belief in the 'law' of the royal supper which stated that on that auspicious day no one should be refused a request. So, much against his will, Xerxes was forced to consent. Having told his wife to do with the woman as she pleased, he withdrew from the party. Immediately, Xerxes wrote to his brother (hoping to save his honour and divert further trouble), begging him to repudiate his wife at once and to dismiss her from the family. In return, Xerxes promised, he would give Masistes one of his own daughters as a replacement bride and thereby tighten their bond even more. Masistes, completely nonplussed by Xerxes' outrageous request, refused to renounce his consort. His wife, he said, was an honourable woman from a good family and she was an exemplary mother to his many sons; she would remain his spouse.

Meanwhile, Amestris acted swiftly and with a bloody and chilling determination. The queen was intent on securing the succession of her son Dariaios and she understood Artaynte's request for the robe to be the treasonous act it was, even if her husband remained as yet deluded. Amestris' wrath did not focus on Artaynté herself, however, because as Prince Dariaios' wife she might yet prove to be the possible mother of a future Achaemenid heir. Instead, Amestris' fury fell on Artaynté's (unnamed) mother, who was, in dynastic terms, Amestris' equal. The imperial matriarch Amestris turned on a rival dynastic matron in order to put a halt to any ambitions which Masistes and his family harboured towards the crown. Artaynté's acquisition of the royal *gaunaka* was proof that the family saw themselves as Persia's future rulers.

Amestris sent for soldiers from the royal bodyguard and had Masistes' wife dragged to the royal palace. There she was beaten. Her nose, ears, and lips were cut off, and her tongue was torn out. The type of punishment imposed on the woman was consistent with that doled out to traitors. Impaling, burning, whipping, strangling, stoning, blinding, cutting off nose, ears, lips, hands, arms, snipping out the tongue, branding, flaying, crucifixion, and skinning alive were all part of the Persian system of torture, and the sex of the victim did not act as an excuse for lighter chastisement. However, the violence against Masistes' wife was not the result of the consequences of the brutalities of war or insurrection, but was perpetrated on the order of the vengeful Amestris. It was one matriarch against another. To finish off the punishment, Amestris ordered that the woman's breasts – symbols of motherhood and fecundity – were cut off and thrown to the dogs who sat around in the palace courtyard. Since dogs were thought of as dirty scavengers and eaters of refuse, their presence in the torture is particularly telling. The image of scavenger dogs feeding on corpses or mutilated body parts was a common feature of ancient Near Eastern curses. Thus, an Assyrian anti-witchcraft ritual envisaged the following torment for a deceased individual: 'May eagle and vulture prey on your corpse, may silence and shivering fall upon you, may dog and bitch tear you apart, may a dog and a bitch tear apart your flesh'. In feeding the flesh of Masistes' wife to the dogs, Amestris was annihilating her very existence. Nevertheless, the bodyguards had their instructions to keep the woman alive long enough for her husband to see her. In that dire state, she was sent home. We do not know if she lived or died, but we do know that when Masistes saw his wife's inhuman mutilations, he took immediate counsel with his sons and they all, with their private troops, set off for Bactria with the aim of stirring up rebellion against the king who had allowed this horror to occur. Nothing came to pass and the eastern satrapies did not rise in revolt. Ambitious Masistes, his poor wife, and his anguished sons disappear from the sources. Artayntē also vanishes from the scene. She certainly never became Persia's queen. It is probable that she and all her family were put to death.

As horrific as Amestris' vendetta against Masistes' wife was, we must be careful not to judge it too harshly but to see it in its ancient dynastic context. In routing out the insurrection brewing in Masistes' household, Amestris served the welfare of the state and ultimately secured the continuity of Xerxes' reign and the succession of Prince Dariaios. Amestris did not act because she suffered any personal wrong at the hands of either Masistes' wife or his daughter. Artayntē's sexual liaison with Xerxes did not affect Amestris on a personal level. But, on a higher playing ground, Amestris was exceedingly cognisant that her honour and her high standing at court had been slighted and challenged by Artayntē's naked ambition. Amestris acted in order to maintain her supremacy at court, as Persia's First Lady, as it were. She acted also for the security of the crown itself. That is why her revenge knew no limits.

*

Xerxes' final years as king were spent on building projects. He enlarged Persepolis by erecting his own palace-harem and completed the beautiful and impressive Gate of All Nations, with its fine cuneiform inscriptions which reiterated his name and titles: 'Xerxes, the Great King, King of Kings, son of Darius the King, an Achaemenid' (XPa). His enormous Hall of a Hundred Columns was growing fast too, but was still some way off completion. His busy construction activities are to be seen in the Treasury tablets dating to 484–482 BCE which show that workers from Caria, Syria, Ionia, Egypt, and Babylonia were regularly moved around Persepolis' construction sites. The place must have been a hive of industry. Excavations at Susa in the early 1970s proved that Xerxes' building efforts were not restricted to Persepolis either. Two short inscriptions attest to his construction of a palace on the Susa acropolis, and he also completed the huge Darius Gate, bringing the two over-life-size statues of his father from Egypt and planting them in the soil of Susa.

In an odd twist of fate, towards the very end of his life, Xerxes won a new Greek friend and supporter in the person of his old nemesis from the 480s BCE. Themistocles, the victor of Salamis, had been banished from his home city by the strangely volatile 'democratic' Athenians, and had sought asylum in Argos, Macedon, Thassos, and Aeolis, and had eventually found himself in Aegae, a backwater town in Aeolis. Here he made contact with people who worked at the satrapal court of Dascylium, ruled over by Artabazus, who had commanded the Parthians and the Chorasmians in Xerxes' Greek war. The satrap authorised Themistocles to write to the Great King, and to Themistocles' astonishment, Xerxes invited the Athenian to join him in Persia. Themistocles was welcomed with great joy by Xerxes, who saw in his arrival a new adviser on Greek affairs and (according to Thucydides) 'awoke in the king the hope of seeing ... the Greek world enslaved'. Themistocles became a Persian courtier and a minister of state, learned to speak Persian to fluency and was made a very wealthy man when Xerxes bestowed on him the revenues of several towns in Asia Minor, including Magnesia and Myus. Themistocles went on to be much favoured by Xerxes' successor too.

Inscriptions dating to the close of Xerxes' reign reflected the times. They were full of earnest prayers: 'Me may Ahuramazda protect from evil, and my royal house and this land! This I pray of Ahuramazda; this may Ahuramazda grant me' (XPg). Xerxes needed all the help he could get as his family life continued its descent into turmoil. Inevitably the family's dysfunction played out in the empire too and it was reported that Sataspes, an Achaemenid princeling, and a nephew of Darius I (through his mother), had raped the virgin daughter of Zopyrus and had brought great dishonour and shame to the powerful *khān*'s household. In Persia, as in many ancient societies, familial honour was generally thought of as residing in the bodies of women, and women who transgressed traditional norms – including those who through no fault of their own were raped and abused – brought shame to the men of their family. Accordingly, Zopyrus demanded the prince's life, as was his prerogative. But Sataspes' mother, Xerxes' aunt, solicited the king for her son's life. He was pardoned by Xerxes but was exiled and sent far away from court. Some years later, after Xerxes' aunt had died, Sataspes fool-ishly returned to Persia where he was executed by impalement. The king had not forgotten Sataspes' crimes.

The next family crisis arose in the household of Xerxes' daugh-ter, Amytis. Her husband, Megabyzus, who had long suffered the princess's many infidelities, began to make public accusations against his wife's immorality and instigated ways to renounce her. Xerxes was mortified. He could not afford any more family scandals, nor did he wish to break with Megabyzus, who had always been a loyal and hardworking servant. Xerxes admonished Amytis in no uncertain terms, and she promised to behave with the requisite decorum of an Achaemenid princess in future, but Megabyzus was left embittered by the whole embarrassing affair.

According to Ctesias' court sources, towards the end of his reign, around 470 BCE, Xerxes was under the influence of the com-mander of the royal guard, named Artabanus, a powerful eunuch from Hyrcania, south-east of the Caspian Sea in modern-day Turk-menistan, and another eunuch named Aspamitres. It was a bad time for Persia. The country (according to tablets from Persepolis) was suffering a severe famine – food was in short supply, the royal storehouses were running empty, and the price of grain had risen to a level many times higher than normal. Discontent and threats of revolt engulfed Persia, and Xerxes' means of coping with the menace was to discharge over a hundred government officials from their posts in the hope of assuaging public anger over the mismanagement of food supplies. Increasingly, Xerxes backed away from taking responsibility, leaving the government in the hands of Artabanus and Aspamitres. This was not a solution.

In the fifth month of the Babylonian calendar, Xerxes' twenty-first regnal year, an astrologer was recording lunar eclipses on clay tablets. It was standard work. But sometime between 4 and 8 August 465 BCE (the cuneiform tablet is damaged and we cannot be certain of the exact date), he recorded an extraordinary event:

Abu 14, day [?] – Xerxes' son killed him.

This remarkable little cuneiform document, fragmentary though it is, is the only Near Eastern evidence we have for Xerxes' murder. All other references come from three classical authors – the Greek historians Ctesias and Diodorus Siculus, and the Roman historian Justin – who recount various stories of Xerxes' assassination with little agreement on the 'how' and 'wherefore'. That said, all three authors *do* follow an essential scenario: the powerful Artabanus was the initiator of the plot. He convinced Xerxes' youngest son, Artaxerxes, that his eldest brother, and the next in line to the throne, Dariaios, had killed their father. Diodorus noted that the middle son, Hystaspes, was away in his satrapy in Bactria and therefore was absolved of guilt. Dariaios protested his innocence (so said Ctesias). According to Diodorus, Xerxes was killed while in bed, asleep – an image which some scholars have seen as suspect, suggesting a repetitive Greek literary motif was being used. But incredulity is unwarranted. Diodorus' account is logical and wide-ranging, and ancient kings were frequently murdered in their beds, as Xenophon noted: 'nowhere are men more obvious prey to harm than when at dinner, or when drinking wine, in the bath, or asleep in bed'. There is no reason to doubt that the elimination of Xerxes took place as he slept.

Diodorus goes on to state that Artabanus was aided and abetted by a eunuch called Mithradates, who had access to the royal bedchamber, and that afterwards Artabanus set out to murder Xerxes' three sons. Ctesias adds that Artaxerxes had his brother Dariaios swiftly executed on the double charge of regicide and patricide. When Artabanus subsequently swore loyalty to the middle brother, Hystaspes (who was still in far-off Bactria, but who was now next in succession), the ambitious commander was also killed on the oders of Artaxerxes.

Intrigue, plotting, and murder were realities of court life in Persia. Conspiracies could quickly escalate into rebellion and even to regicide. The Achaemenid court was a brutal place and the violence which erupted there often dictated dynastic politics. Persia was controlled by an absolute ruler – that is not an Orientalist cliché, it is a fact – and absolute monarchies were open to a particular form of political tension which usually focused on the royal family itself and could lead to the direct use of personal violence. At least seven of the twelve Achaemenid Great Kings met their deaths at the hands of an assassin of some sort (only three monarchs had the luxury of a peaceful death), and to this we can add the murder (or execution) of at least two crown princes.

But who killed Xerxes? Given his prominence in each of the bewilderingly confusing classical sources, there can be little doubt of Artabanus' implication in the regicide in some way, but what to make of the Babylonian evidence that Xerxes was murdered by his son? Which of his three sons did the deed? The Greek stories smack of an elaborate cover-up by Prince Artaxerxes. It is highly likely that he, perhaps with Artabanus and several other eunuchs, banded together to rebel against Xerxes. In the coup, the prince availed himself of the opportunity to dispose of both his father *and* his elder brother in an audacious, ambitious (and successful) bid for the throne. The Babylonian evidence stated that the perpetrator of Xerxes' murder was clearly his son – and no other. Perhaps Artaxerxes was the sole operator of the deadly deed. Certainly, his scheming ambition paid off nicely. By January 464 BCE Artaxerxes I was recognised as the new Great King. As far away as Elephantine in southern Egypt, a papyrus document read:

> On the 18th day of Kislev, that is the seventh day of Thoth, in the year 21 of Xerxes, the beginning of the reign when king Artaxerxes sat on his throne.

17

The Times They are a-Changin'

Artaxerxes I dutifully buried his father at the royal cemetery of Naqsh-i Rustam and then proceeded to remove from public sight each copy of his father's troublesome Daivâ Inscription, the document that had promoted religious reform. The archaeologists working at Persepolis in the 1930s found the elegantly carved inscriptions relocated to out-of-the-way places: three slabs were used as part of a bench in the Garrison Quarter, a fourth formed part of a door sill and another was part of a drainage system. So much for Xerxes' reformation.

Artaxerxes' court was ripe with intrigue and it was for this reason that the new ruler ordered two huge relief sculptures to be removed from their highly visible location at the centre of the north and east stairways of the *Apadana*, or throne hall, at Persepolis. These two striking painted stone carvings showed an Achaemenid king and his crown prince in royal audience. Although we cannot be certain of the identity of the royal pair (King Darius I and Crown Prince Xerxes or King Xerxes and Crown Prince Dariaios), the new ruler, clearly sensitive to the unexpected vicissitudes of royal succession, decided that what they depicted – the orderly line of inheritance – was now very inappropriate and had the offending images removed. They were placed out of sight in the privacy of a courtyard in the Treasury, far away from public view.

Straightaway, Artaxerxes I undertook a series of show trials and tortured and executed those who had had a part in the murder of his father, although courtiers knew that most of the victims were mere scapegoats, not connected to the regicide that Artaxerxes himself had perpetrated. Next came a series of pogroms aimed at his father's ministers and advisors as Artaxerxes began to reorganise the affairs of the empire in his own interests. He dismissed the satraps who were hostile to him and chose replacements from among his friends and supporters – those that seemed most able and most loyal. The removal of existing ministers and the appointment of new ones is only attested in relation to Artaxerxes I, for no other Achaemenid monarch attempted to do so radical an act. It strongly suggests that the new king was determined to break with Xerxes' reign.

However, not to short-change his father, Artaxerxes did complete the building of the Hall of a Hundred Columns at Persepolis, and acknowledged himself as Xerxes' son – and, perhaps more importantly, as Darius' grandson – in the inscriptions he placed in the newly finished structure:

> I am Artaxerxes, Great King, King of Kings, King of Countries, King on this Great Earth Far and Wide, son of King Xerxes, son of Darius, the Achaemenid. Artaxerxes, the Great King, proclaims: With the protection of Ahuramazda, this palace which my father, King Xerxes, made, I completed it. Me may Ahuramazda protect, together with the gods, as well as my kingship and what I have made (A¹Pa).

A similar inscription has been found punched in Old Persian cuneiform in a single line around the inner rim of an elegant silver *phiale* (bowl) showing a stylised lotus-flower design on the interior. It reads: 'Artaxerxes, the Great King, King of Kings, King of Lands, son of Xerxes the king, Xerxes son of Darius the king, the Achaemenid: in his house this silver bowl was made' (A¹VSa).

Needless to say, the new monarch's inscriptions, big or small, did not breathe a word of the bloody carnage that had secured his place on the throne. Instead, court propaganda (which we find reflected in Greek sources too) bestowed on Artaxerxes all of the standard royal virtues. The king was praised for his imposing and handsome figure, his gentleness, and noble spirit. He was nicknamed Long Arm, a curious moniker, which we can interpret in two ways: either Artaxerxes had a physical abnormality, with one arm longer than the other, or (more likely) that by means of the scale of his empire, his 'reach' extended to the ends of the earth – a notion that is in keeping with royal Persian propaganda, where a similar idea was expressed in the inscriptions of Darius and Xerxes.

We know the name of only one consort in Artaxerxes' harem, Damaspia. She was a Persian noblewoman for sure, although it is not certain if she was from the Achaemenid family itself. She bore the king one (known) son, Prince Xerxes. There were probably other wives too; there were certainly many concubines. The names of three of them (all Babylonians) were preserved by Ctesias: there was Alogyne, the mother of Prince Sogdianus; Cosmartidene, mother to the princes Ochus and Aristes; and Andia, the mother of Prince Bagapaeus and Princess Parysatis. Artaxerxes had at least another thirteen more sons born to him by his consorts and concubines, or so Ctesias has it, and there must have been other daughters too. The harem was under the leadership of Amestris, Xerxes' domineering widow, who was now in the exulted position of being the king's mother. There are no records which testify that she had any involvement in her husband's murder, nor can we ascertain how she felt about the killing of Dariaios, her eldest boy. If she did grieve his death, she did not let it interfere in her relationship with Artaxerxes and she enthusiastically threw herself into the role of Queen Mother. In all probability, Amestris was fully conscious of the plans for the coup d'état and supported the ambitions of Artaxerxes. Her relationship with Dariaios had no doubt plummeted because of the Artaynté affair; guessing that his future would be uncertain, she had backed her youngest son in his bid for power. But it was perhaps rumours of her involvement in the assassination of Xerxes that led Herodotus to describe Amestris as a cruel woman, who, to lengthen her own life, took the lives of innocent children: 'I am informed', Herodotus wrote, 'that Amestris, the wife of Xerxes, when she had grown old, made a bargain for her own life to the god of the underworld by burying alive seven Persian boys, the offspring of noblemen.' There is nothing in the Persian sources that supports this gruesome picture of human sacrifice, and it is certainly little more than another grisly Herodotean fantasy. Yet the story does highlight the fact that the name of Amestris was known in the Greek-speaking world and that her power was almost proverbial.

*

Shortly after the coup that took Xerxes' life, Artaxerxes was forced into conflict with his brother, Hystaspes, the satrap of Bactria, who, cheated of the kingship, revolted against the usurpation of his father's throne. There were a series of evenly matched battles fought in Bactria which resulted in no advancement for either side, but eventually Hystaspes was forced to withdraw his troops from conflict. By default Artaxerxes was victorious and all of Bactria surrendered to him. A series of seal images depicting Persians fighting men wearing the clothing of Central Asians were perhaps crafted at that time as miniature mementoes of a foiled rebellion. It would not be unusual if some high-ranking military men, or possibly also their family members, commissioned such keepsakes to commemorate these celebratory events, and as a by-product these artefacts became tokens of a Persian Version of history as defined and remembered by the Achaemenid elite. The seals, which represent a Persian perspective on warfare, are an important visual documentation of the political conflicts between the central power of the empire and its opponents and they can be used as evidence for the reconstruction of the political history of the Achaemenids. Texts, after all, do not tell the full story.

Figure 19. Seal impression depicting a Persian soldier killing nomadic warriors. Ahuramazda hovers above the scene.

Because of a heavy tax burden and mismanagement of food reserves, in 460 BCE a major revolt broke out in Egypt, led by a Libyan named Inarus, the son of Psammetichus (a name which leads us to believe he was descended from the pharaonic Saite royal house). In a demotic inscription from the Kharga Oasis, this Inarus was audaciously referred to as the 'Prince of Rebels', because, under his rule, the Nile Delta erupted in anger. The Egyptians drove the Persian tax-collectors out of the Delta and the Nile valley quickly followed suit. Only Upper Egypt and the satrapal capital of Memphis in the north stayed in Persian hands. Evidence found in the Wadi Hammamat proves that Inarus was not accepted everywhere in Egypt though: dated to the fifth regnal year of Artaxerxes I, a papyrus document gives the Persian ruler his customary titles, 'King of Upper and Lower Egypt'.

The satrap of Egypt was Achaemenes, Artaxerxes' uncle. He had been given command of the country by his brother, Xerxes, when Egypt had rebelled at his accession. Now, Achaemenes assembled an army and attacked the insurgents in the north, fighting a decisive battle at Papremis (modern-day Sakha), where the Persian army was completely overpowered. The Achaemenid troops suffered a tremendous loss of life. Herodotus visited the site of the battle some twenty years later and reported that everywhere the place was covered with the skulls of the Persian dead. Achaemenes was numbered among the slaughtered, and his corpse was sent back to Persia on the order of Inarus as a means of goading Artaxerxes. The death of the king's uncle and the dishonourable maltreatment of his corpse sent shockwaves throughout the court. Amestris in particular grieved for her much-admired brother-in-law and swore to avenge his death and disgrace.

Ambitious to bring the whole of Egypt under his rule, Inarus appealed to the Greeks for support and before long the Athenians, keen to see Persian hegemony in Egypt ended once and for all, offered help and sent 200 ships to assist the rebellious Egyptians. The Athenians sailed to Persian-friendly Cyprus and plundered the island before moving into the Egyptian Delta and navigating their way up the Nile, where they quickly thrashed the Persian navy. They moved on to Memphis, where the Persian garrison was stationed. They overpowered the city and the Persian troops were forced to take refuge in the city's citadel, called by the Egyptians the White Wall, but known to the Greeks as the White Castle.

The siege of Memphis' inner fortress lasted for over a year and the Athenians, the rebel Egyptians, the Persians, and their Egyptian loyalists all suffered from hunger and disease and the inevitability of death. In 456 BCE, Artaxerxes dispatched his uncle, Megabyzus, the satrap in Syria, to Egypt at the head of an army and a fleet of Phoenician ships. He used his forces to smash through the rebel lines and retake Memphis as Inarus and his followers, together with the Athenians, fled to the island of Prosopitis in the Delta. They were held there, surrounded by Megabyzus' troops, for a year and a half. The Persians constructed a dam which bridged Prosopitis to the mainland and stormed the island, slaughtering thousands of rebels and Athenians. Inarus was wounded in the hip in a frantic hand-to-hand combat with Megabyzus, but agreed to surrender to the satrap on condition that his life would be spared. Megabyzus petitioned Artaxerxes, who consented to the plea, and Inarus was taken captive alive.

The Egyptian revolt came to an end in 454 BCE, after six long, bloody years of conflict. A new satrap was installed in Memphis – Arshama, a grandson of Darius the Great, who was referred to as a 'son of the house' (Aramaic, *bar bayta*) – conventionally glossed to

Figure 20.
Seal impression of Artaxerxes I shown as the master of Egypt.

mean royal prince. He would hold the position of Egyptian satrap for forty-seven years (454–407 BCE). A cylinder seal discovered in the region of the Black Sea, but now in Moscow, captures the mood of the time: it shows Artaxerxes I, crowned and armed with a spear, a bow, and a quiver full of arrows, leading four fettered captives behind him, each wearing Greek-style wrap-around garments. Inarus is on his knees. This tiny seal made a large imperial announcement: Egypt was once again subsumed back into the Persian empire.

*

In the province of Yehud (Judah), there was much disquiet too. The effect the Egyptian revolt had on the tiny remnant of people that inhabited Jerusalem and its surrounding countryside was profoundly disturbing as a plethora of rumours reached the vulnerable towns and villages via the soldiers and the merchants who passed through the city. Apprehension led the Jews to believe that the portentous day of judgement was at hand, a theme which is central to the biblical prophecy of Malachi, whose sayings date to this era:

> Surely the day is coming; it will burn like a furnace. All the arrogant and every evildoer will be stubble, and the day that is coming will set them on fire . . . Not a root or a branch will be left to them . . . they will be ashes under the soles of your feet on the day when I do these things, says the Lord Almighty.

It was into this world of fear that Ezra stepped. He was a Jewish scribe and priest who had been born and educated in Persia. He had been commissioned by Artaxerxes I to return to his homeland with the royal authority to enforce the local Jewish law and to ensure that Persian laws were being honoured. Before departing Mesopotamia, Ezra started a campaign to return all the Jews to their homeland, travelling from town to town throughout Babylonia, informing them of the impending return to the Promised Land and the rebuilding of the Temple of Solomon. His words went mostly unheeded. The majority of the Jews remained in Babylonia. Ezra, who took along with him to Jerusalem much gold and silver for the temple's construction, seems to have been granted some measure of civil authority by Artaxerxes. He began to rebuild the walls of Jerusalem as a move to strengthen the city and ensure the safety of its inhabitants, but a group of powerful Samaritans, a break-away community of Jews who claimed to be the true successors of the early Hebrew tribes who had escaped bondage in Egypt, vehemently opposed the restoration of the walls. They wrote to Artaxerxes (in Aramaic) with their grievances. When Cyrus the Great had decreed the Jews might return home, they complained, he had permitted them to rebuild the temple, but not the city. The rebuilding of Jerusalem's walls, they stated, was a clear sign that the Jews threatened to rebel. The king duly replied and sent a response:

> The letter you sent us has been read and translated in my presence. I issued an order and a search was made, and it was found that this city has a long history of revolt against kings and has been a place of rebellion and sedition. Jerusalem has had powerful kings ruling over the whole of Trans-Euphrates, and taxes, tribute, and duty were paid to them. Now issue an order to these men to stop work, so that this city will not be rebuilt until I so order. Be careful not to neglect this matter. Why let this threat grow, to the detriment of the royal interests?

As soon as the copy of the letter was read to the elders of the Samaritans, they went immediately to Ezra and the Jerusalem Jews and compelled them to stop all construction work, both on the city walls and on the temple. It was some years later that a high-ranking Jewish courtier, who had once served as a cup-bearer to Artaxerxes, managed to persuade the king to allow him to go to Jerusalem and to continue the building work on the fortifications which had been so dramatically brought to a halt. Artaxerxes granted Nehemiah's request, and by August 445 BCE the latter had commenced the rebuilding of the city walls. Jerusalem's derelict defences had left its people exposed to great trouble and to an even greater shame, for the Jews had long felt that the collapsed wall was a sign that they had been abandoned by God. Rebuilding the wall revealed that their God was still present in Judah and it served as a sign to their enemies that God was still with His people. The walls provided protection and dignity to a people who had suffered the judgement of God and through the actions of Ezra and Nehemiah, Jerusalem was restored and returned to His favour. According to the Hebrew Bible, the temple was completed in the sixth regnal year of Darius II, which would place the event around 418 BCE, although it is impossible to be absolutely certain about that, since the dating of biblical texts and events in the Persian period is notoriously difficult.

Meanwhile, in Persia, there was no such harmony. Amestris was exasperated at the fact that Inarus and his Greek supporters were enjoying the privilege of a royal pardon and had not been brought to justice, especially as they had been responsible for the death of the distinguished Achaemenid prince, Achaemenes. She petitioned her son to hand Inarus over to her control so that she herself might see justice delivered, but Artaxerxes refused to break with the protocol of the royal pardon. Amestris next tried to persuade Megabyzus, the king's uncle, to give her the prisoners, but he sent her away with short shrift, telling her in no uncertain terms that he had vowed, with the king's blessing, that the prisoners would not be harmed and that he staked his honour on that pledge. But Amestris refused to listen. She barraged Artaxerxes with ongoing demands for the prisoners and she kept on hounding her son until, after five long years, she finally got her way. Inarus and the Greeks were delivered into her hands. She beheaded as many Greeks as she was able to get hold of – fifty in all – but she was determined to provide Inarus with a lingering and public death. She settled on impalement, a fitting punishment for rebels and traitors against the empire, as Darius I had proved. Stripped naked, the rebel Inarus was positioned on top of a long, sharpened, wooden stake and after many days of lingering agony, he expired.

Megabyzus was horrified at the death of the rebels and especially the way in which Inarus had been treated. He was even angrier with Artaxerxes for the weakness he had shown in allowing his mother to behave with such forceful determination and, more importantly, for breaking his oath of protection. Megabyzus asked for Artaxerxes' permission to return to his own satrapy in Syria, and once there he amassed a powerful force and rose up in rebellion against the king. Two battles were fought against Artaxerxes' troops. Megabyzus was victorious in both.

He had proved his capabilities and had let Artaxerxes know that his control over the empire was weak and might easily be taken from him. Megabyzus made it clear that he wanted to make a peace treaty, but he did not want to go to the king. He would make peace on condition that he could stay in Syria, where he was safe. Artaxerxes took counsel from his most persuasive court eunuch, the Paphlagonian-born Artoxares, himself the influential satrap of Armenia, as well as from Megabyzus' estranged wife, Amytis. Both urged Artaxerxes to sue for peace. The king reluctantly agreed, although he demanded that Megabyzus come to court and make his presence known in a formal audience before the throne. Artoxares and Amytis travelled to Syria to petition Megabyzus to return with them to Persia, and although he saw nothing but danger lying ahead, the satrap acquiesced and returned with them to court, where he was affectionately welcomed and forgiven by the king.

Some months later, while out hunting, Artaxerxes was attacked by a ferocious young lion, but thanks to Megabyzus, who speared the animal with a javelin as it leapt through the air, the king's life was saved. Instead of expressing his gratitude to Megabyzus, Artaxerxes exploded with anger: Megabyzus had killed the lion before he himself had had the chance to do it; Megabyzus had caused the king to lose face. Using the faux pas of the hunting episode as a pretext, Artaxerxes ordered Megabyzus' decapitation. Amestris, Amytis, and the eunuch Artoxares immediately flew into action and, falling on their knees before the king, begged, cajoled, and entreated Artaxerxes to spare Megabyzus' life. For the sake of the many brave actions Megabyzus had undertaken in the Greek campaigns of his father's day, Artaxerxes relented. The punishment was converted from execution to exile and Megabyzus was forced to emigrate to a city by the Red Sea called Cyrta, under the watch of an armed escort. The eunuch Artoxares was also banished from court, back to his satrapy of Armenia, because he had too often spoken to the king on Megabyzus' behalf. Artaxerxes was determined to hear no more of his tiresome nemesis.

Ctesias makes much of the story of Megabyzus in his *Persika*. He seems to have acquired information about Megabyzus directly from the satrap's family, and perhaps at their behest he wrote him up as a tragic hero, a sad protagonist of King Lear-like dimensions. Megabyzus spent five years in lonely exile in Cyrta, craving for home and longing for his family. Thereafter, Ctesias wrote, Megabyzus escaped Cyrta disguised as a leper and made his long, lonely way home to Persia, where Amytis barely recognised him, so ravaged was he by the years of exile. She persuaded Megabyzus to petition the king for forgiveness, and, thanks again to the loyal interventions of Amestris and Amytis, Artaxerxes was joyfully reconciled with his uncle and made him a *bandaka* (friend), just as he had been before. As a coda, Ctesias notes that the noble Megabyzus died at the age of seventy-six, beloved of the king, who grieved for him deeply and genuinely.

*

The Persepolis texts show that many of the servants at the Achaemenid court were recruited from the peoples of the empire. Foreigners certainly made up a significant portion of the court, but none of the court's foreign personnel were as important as the Greek physicians who were brought to Persia to serve the medical needs of the royal family. The Great Kings had long esteemed the skills of Greek doctors, even more so than Egyptian physicians, who are also attested as medical practitioners at the Persian court – we hear of individuals such as Udjahorresnet (whom we encountered in Egypt serving under Cambyses II and Darius I), Semtutefnakht and Wenen-Nefer. But the Persian monarchs actively sought out Greek doctors from around the empire. During the reign of Darius, the celebrated physician Democedes of Conon had been captured as a prisoner of war and coerced into serving as a doctor within the inner court. He had reset Darius' sprained ankle (the result of a fall during a royal hunt) when the Egyptian court physicians proved useless and, later, he cured Atossa, Darius' wife and Xerxes' mother, of an abscess in her breast. Darius rewarded Democedes richly for his skills: he lived in a fine house in Susa, took his meals at the king's table, and allegedly had great influence over Darius' decision-making.

To what extent the office of royal physician was a voluntary one is debatable though. We know that Udjahorresnet returned to his native country with the blessing of the Great King (and perhaps a handsome pension) after serving many years at the court of Persia, but Democedes always considered himself a prisoner. He later escaped the court and fled to Croton, where he was protected by the citizens of the city from being taken back to Persia.

Whatever their level of personal freedom might have been, foreign doctors served an important function at the royal court. A particularly fêted Greek doctor was Apollonides of Cos, who came to prominence as a court physician during the reign of Artaxerxes I. He cured Megabyzus of a dangerous wound he had received during the fighting which had broken out at the death of Xerxes, and his star rose quickly. But his glory turned to infamy when, after Megabyzus' death, Apollonides began an affair with his widow, Amytis, Artaxerxes' sister. She was already notorious for her sexual liaisons with courtiers, and although Artaxerxes had tried to conceal the extent of her philandering, her behaviour was still the scandal of the court. According to Ctesias, Apollonides, well aware of Amytis' man-hunting reputation, used his profession and reputation to gain access to her living quarters. She was by far his social superior, but as soon as he set eyes on her, Apollonides developed an infatuation for the princess.

The opportunity for Apollonides to get close to Amytis occurred when the princess got ill. At first, her sickness was mild and not (apparently) serious; she was having irregular pains and cramps in her pelvis. These were the first stages of what turned out to be (as we would identify it) cervical cancer. Apollonides was commanded by Artaxerxes to help his sister. The doctor began to speak with Amytis, privately – a very privileged position, even for a doctor in the enclosed world of the inner palace. He made plays at diagnosing her illness and opportunistically told her that she would recover her health if she continued to have regular sex with men because, he insisted, she had a disease of the womb. Vigorous intercourse, he reasserted, would cure her of her many pains. The treatment suggested by Apollonides was in fact a state-of-the-art diagnosis which many Greek doctors, especially those of the Hippocratic school, would have enthused over. All good medical practitioners (male, inevitably) knew that the female womb, unanchored and almost having a life of its own, was apt to wander around the body, putting pressure on other organs and so causing serious illness and even death. While in a state of flux, the wandering womb resulted in women having fainting spells, menstrual pain, and a loss of verbal coherence. To stop this, the womb needed to be coaxed back into its correct place in the body. One treatment prescribed by Hippocratic physicians was to place sweet-smelling herbs or spices at the entrance to the vagina and foul-smelling potions (animal and human excrement mixed with beer froth was popular) by the nose in order to lure the uterus back to the woman's lower groin and fix the womb in place. Regular coitus was thought to be another way in which the womb could be encouraged to stay in its place too, and therefore, in Greek medical thought, a sexually active woman (available only to her husband, of course) was a well woman.

Having bamboozled Amytis with the latest Western medical theories, Apollonides prescribed the princess the medicine she most required. He started having regular sex with her. Her affection for the doctor grew with every visit, although he himself did not reciprocate with any emotional commitment. And he did nothing to help the spread of the vicious disease that was gradually eating away her body. There can be little doubt that Apollonides recognised the signs of Amytis' real illness, since the Greek doctors of the Hippocratic school had already identified several kinds of cancer (calling them *karkinos*, the Greek word for 'crab'), although since ancient Greek practice prohibited autopsy, doctors only described and made drawings of visible tumours on the skin, face, and breasts. Physicians also knew that cancerous tumours were palpable and rather hard, cool, or cold to the touch and irregularly shaped, and that sometimes sores would build up in the surrounding area of the body. Tumours were observed to cause swelling, sometimes bleeding, and were recorded to be acutely painful. As for treatment, since all Hippocratic diagnostics were based on humoral theory, cancer was considered to be the result of a build-up of cold black bile in the body. It was essential that the bile be evacuated, otherwise the patient's cancer would continue to grow. To remove the malignant black bile, doctors might have performed a phlebotomy or, if that proved unresponsive, they removed the tumour through cutting and bleeding. For the patient, this was agonising, traumatic, and unlikely to work.

Amytis began to waste away. She was unable to stomach much food, and the disease rendered her so weak and pathetic that Apollonides found himself repulsed by her appearance and put an end to their sexual relations. Jilted, scorned, in agony, and aware of her impending end, Amytis simply stopped eating altogether. As she lay on her death bed, perhaps in a fit of conscience, Amytis confessed all to her mother, Amestris, and begged her to take revenge on Apollonides. The Queen Mother told Artaxerxes everything she had heard, scandalised that her daughter had polluted the royal blood through sexual contact with a barbarian Greek, yet heartbroken to see her child so sick. The king, shocked and shaken, asked his mother to deal with the embarrassing situation. Amestris saw to it that Apollonides was punished. For two months, until the day Amytis died, she had him tortured, and on the day of Amytis' death, he was buried alive.

In addition to pain and sorrow, the story of Apollonides and Amytis is full of lies, deceit, secrets, and misinformation. The doctor not only betrayed his office and his ethics, but also flagrantly abused his royal master and shattered the norms of court protocol. Emotionally and physically, he destroyed the princess. If we choose to believe Ctesias' account of the scandal (and there is no obvious reason not to), Apollonides' punishment for unethical behaviour served as a warning that, no matter how valuable a service they might perform, doctors were nonetheless merely servants of the Great King. Their lives were at his command.

*

Beyond the complexities of court life and family dramas, there was an international dimension to Artaxerxes reign too. What of the Greeks, for instance? In what ways did their presence impact

10: The eastern staircase of the *Apadana* at Persepolis is richly carved with human, animal, and plant figures. They were once painted in vivid colours.

11: An over-life-size, now headless statue of Darius the Great was once part of a pair. Made in Egypt, but moved to Susa by Xerxes, the statue was unearthed at the royal gateway into the Susa palace in 1972.

12: A small turquoise head found at Persepolis depicts a royal woman, or perhaps a young man, or maybe a eunuch. It is impossible to be certain.

13: Carved into a door jamb at the palace of Darius in Persepolis is this elegant figure of a young eunuch. He carries a perfume flask and a towel.

14: Beautifully rendered human-headed sphinx from Persepolis

15: A delegation of Lydians brings gifts of tableware, jewellery, and horses to the Great King. Persepolis, eastern staircase of the *Apadana*.

16: Syrians offer gifts of textiles and shaggy-fleeced rams. Persepolis, eastern staircase of the *Apadana*.

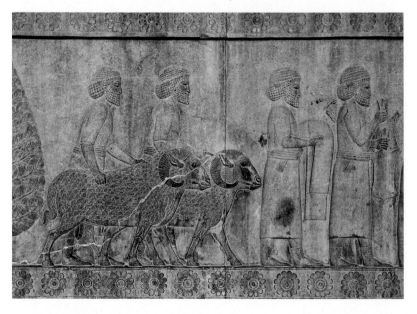

17: A Persian courtier leads an Armenian diplomat by the hand. The gift he brings the king is a stocky Nisaean horse. Persepolis, eastern staircase of the *Apadana*.

18: A Bactrian leads a grumpy camel by a rope. Persepolis, eastern staircase of the *Apadana*.

19: A silver dish belonging to Artaxerxes I. A cuneiform inscription
in Old Persian runs around the interior of the rim and reads: 'Artaxerxes, the
Great King, King of Kings, King of Lands, son of Xerxes the king, Xerxes son of
Darius the king, the Achaemenid: in his house this silver bowl was made'.

20: A silver rhyton (a drinking vessel with a spout at the bottom),
in the shape of a kneeling ram ibex

21: A colourful glazed-brick wall panel from Susa depicting royal bodyguards, or 'Immortals'

22: The Sasanian monarchs associated themselves with the Achaemenids by carving huge reliefs close to the tombs of their illustrious predecessors at Naqsh-i Rustam.

Artaxerxes' reign? Ever since the Persian defeats in Greece at Plataea and Mycale in 479 BCE, the Athenians had been pursuing aggressive empire-building ambitions of their own. When the Aegean islands of Lesbos, Chios, and Samos managed to wriggle free of Persia prior to Xerxes' assassination, Athens decided to offer them protection, but by 479 BCE that protection had morphed into defensive ownership with the establishment of the Delian League, an alliance of Greek *poleis* determined to rebut any further Persian interference in the Aegean. The Delian League was intended to be an association of equal partners, but Athens quickly dominated it and turned its own substantial naval power on the member states, making them provinces of a fast-expanding Athenian empire. In many respects, although on a smaller scale, the rise of the Athenian empire resembled that of Persia itself. The Athenians systematically grabbed territories and demanded tribute of the people whom they made dependants and subjects. The profits of their empire-building resulted, of course, in the glorification of the city of Athens itself. It gleamed with white marble.

Meanwhile, the Athenian army and navy kept growing. The Delian League was never an existential threat to Artaxerxes' empire, however, and no matter how much it nibbled at the edges of the Achaemenid realm, there was no danger of the League swallowing it up. In fact, the Greeks were never able to project their power very far inland along the Ionian coast or elsewhere. In the 470s, the Delian League failed to take Sardis from the Persians, for instance, even though it was situated less than 100 miles from the coast.

Nevertheless, the creation of the Delian League and the rise of Athens as a wealthy naval power played badly with the Spartans, who were rightly threatened by the aggressive power-grabbing protection racket that the Athenians were successfully operating. Sensing the tension between these two Greek powers, Artaxerxes I sent an embassy to Sparta, offering the Spartans money and troops if they would agree to attack Athens and put an end to the threat which the Athenians posed to the Persian-held cities of Ionia. Although Sparta refused the Persian bribe, Artaxerxes' overture to the powerful Peloponnesian *polis* introduced a new trend in

Achaemenid foreign policy – it meant that the Persians became increasingly interested in using diplomacy (and money) as the preferred way of interfering in Aegean affairs. In 450 BCE, the Persians and the Greeks drew up the Peace of Callias (named for the Athenian-born Callias, a statesman, soldier, and diplomat who negotiated it), which was designed to end the hostilities between Persia and Athens and define the new political map of the Aegean. The Athenians promised to desist from attacking Persian territories and in return the Persians agreed to give the Ionian coastal cities their autonomy. Territorial lines were drawn up and both sides swore to remain within their areas of sovereignty.

Persia's chance to re-establish its control along its north-western frontier arrived with the outbreak of the Peloponnesian War in 431 BCE, some thirty years after the Peace of Callias. For twenty-six years the Peloponnesian War plunged Athens and Sparta into a life-and-death struggle for the military supremacy of Greece. The Spartans realised that seeking Persian aid was the most obvious way to counter Athens' naval and financial superiority and although Artaxerxes had no intention of replacing an Athenian empire with a Spartan protectorate, he nevertheless supported the Spartan commitment to a Greece free from corrupting Athenian influence, and agreed to make a deal with Sparta. In 425 BCE, the Great King sent an embassy to Sparta to negotiate plans.

18

(Un)Happy Families

The Queen Mother, Amestris, died early in 424 BCE. She was close to the age of ninety. Babylonian documents provide evidence that her son Artaxerxes I, in his sixties, expired soon afterwards, sometime between 24 December 424 BCE and 10 January 423 BCE, when a new king was recognised as ruler. Artaxerxes had ruled for forty-one successful years and was succeeded, peacefully, by his son Xerxes II, named for his grandfather. The new ruler was the only son born to Artaxerxes I's consort, Damaspia (there may have been others who died young), and there is no sign of a succession struggle. It is probable that Artaxerxes had named Xerxes II as his heir in the decade leading up to his death, although several of Artaxerxes' other boys, the sons of concubines, saw the old king's passing as an opportunity to grab the throne. One of them, Sogdianus ('the Sogdian' – a name given to commemorate his father's victories in the east at the commencement of his reign), fomented a conspiracy against his half-brother in which he was aided and abetted by two important courtiers, Menostanes (a military man of some standing) and the eunuch Phranacyas, and just forty-five days into his reign, Xerxes II was murdered while sleeping off a hangover in his bed. Sogdianus seized the throne, but even with the support of Menostanes, he failed to win over the army, which reviled him for killing his brother and disrupting the succession process.

Another of Artaxerxes' sons, Ochus, had been serving as the satrap of Hycarnia (modern Turkmenistan), but when he learned of Sogdianus' grab for power, he hastened back to Persia to make his own move on the throne and quickly gathered the support

of a coterie of nobles, including Sogdianus' former cavalry commander, Arbarios, the eunuch Artoxares, who returned from exile in
Armenia, and Arshama, the influential and wealthy satrap of Egypt.
Ochus was hailed by the Persians as king and took a throne name
(the first clear attestation of such a practice in Achaemenid dynastic history): Darius II. It was a powerful statement. In choosing the
name Darius, the young monarch linked himself to one of Persia's
most important rulers. In effect, Darius II claimed to be inaugurat-
ing a new golden age for the empire. But first he needed to get rid
of Sogdianus, the rival half-brother-king.

In the period when he had served the crown as the Hycarnian
satrap, Darius had taken as wife his half-sister, Parysatis, a woman
destined to play an unprecedentedly decisive role in Achaemenid
dynastic politics. Like Darius, she too was the child of a Babylonian concubine, and although we do not know if their marriage
was arranged or was a love match, it is clear that they developed
a very close and successful interdependent relationship. A woman
of great intelligence and driving ambition, Parysatis crafted for
herself an important role at her husband's side as his confidante
and advisor, and, in his turn, Darius made it known that he would
always take special account of his wife's guidance. It would be so
easy to paint Parysatis as an interfering scold, more motivated by
petty insults than political strategy, or, worse, she might be interpreted as a Lady Macbeth-like villainess, hellbent on power and
ruthless in her bloody ambition. But this would do her a terrible
disservice, because Parysatis was one of the greatest politicians
the Achaemenid dynasty ever encountered. With great care and
control, she surreptitiously policed the family's fortunes, attacking
and destroying its enemies, and defending and supporting its loyal
followers. She had performed her dynastic duty in the early years
of her marriage by bearing two children before Darius had become
Great King: a daughter, Amestris (II), and a son, Arsicas (or Arsës as
the name appears in some sources). When she was queen, she bore
him another son, whom she named Cyrus, and then gave birth to
another boy, Otanes. Nine more children appeared, all of whom
died young. A final son, Oxendras, lived long enough to finish

off the family group. It was love (and loathing) for her children that drove Parysatis to attain a power which neither Atossa under Darius I nor Amestris under Xerxes could ever have acquired. The continuance of the dynasty meant everything to Parysatis, but the methods she employed to maintain and sustain it would have catastrophic consequences.

It was Parysatis who gave Darius II the method to deal with his half-brother, Sogdianus, and get him off the throne. She advised Darius to use persuasion instead of force against the usurper king, and to coax Sogdianus to surrender his claim to kingship, acquired as it was (she stressed) by murder. On Parysatis' advice, Darius told Sogdianus some hard facts – that he lacked the support of both the army, which despised him, and the court, which rejected him – but softened his criticisms by promising that should he peacefully renounce all claims to the kingship, then all would be forgiven and all would be forgotten; no retributions would follow. Naïvely perhaps, Sogdianus took Darius at his word. He was quickly taken captive and condemned to death. The method of execution was particular to Persia: suffocation in cold ashes. It was a rarefied, horrifying punishment, reserved for the worst criminals, especially those guilty of high treason. For this strange form of execution, the Persians used a tall, hollow brick tower and filled it with nothing but ashes – the burnt remnants of anything combustible – and into this tower the condemned Sogdianus was placed. He stood there, for hours on end, waist-high in burnt cinders, breathing in minuscule particles of ash until, eventually, he collapsed from fatigue. He fell headlong into the ashes, breathing them deep into his lungs. Even if Sogdianus had managed to pick himself up at that point, his lungs would have filled up with the grey flakes which resulted, sooner or later, in his slow suffocation. Sogdianus' reign had lasted a mere six months and fifteen days. It was never recognised in Babylon, where the cuneiform tablets ignore it completely.

Darius II now ruled as king. Three eunuchs, Artoxares, Artibarzanes, and Athöus, provided him with customary council, although even they – gifted as they were in matters of state – kowtowed to Parysatis when she offered the king guidance. Her acumen and foresight were much needed when yet another succession crisis erupted to challenge Darius' unsteady rule. This time the threat came from Aristes, Darius' full brother, who revolted from the king, saying that as Artaxerxes' son, he had as much right to the throne as Darius ever had. The events of this new uprising are poorly understood due to the fragmentary nature of the sources, but it appears that Aristes was supported by Artyphius, Megabyzus' son, and that two battles were fought before Aristes surrendered himself to the king. Parysatis advised the king to throw Artyphius and Aristes into the ashes, even though the king did not want to kill his brother, but partly by persuasion, partly through anger tantrums, Parysatis saw to it that Aristes and his sidekick were dispatched.

*

On 16 February 423 BCE, in the first regnal year of Darius II, an influential businessman from Nippur in Babylonia named Enlil-nadin-shum, a banker by trade, signed a contract to rent a house in Babylon for the egregiously high price of a pound and a half of silver. The lease would last, the contract stated, 'until the going forth of the king'. The rental lease was signed to coincide with Darius II's visit to Babylonia. Having murdered two troublesome brothers, Darius now felt secure enough to tour his new realm and visit Babylon. He wanted to consolidate his reign there, and to take in the sights. Enlil-nadin-shum was there to see him, fawning over Darius' entourage, desperate to secure an audience with the king and to pay respects to the gracious Lady Parysatis. Much depended on Enlil-nadin-shum talking with the king. He was the head of an old and illustrious establishment, Murashu and Sons, Bankers, and he was very much hoping to win the support of King Darius. After all, old King Artaxerxes had been a friendly royal ally to the firm, and so why shouldn't the royal patronage continue?

Murashu and Sons of Nippur were notorious for their high interest rates. More loan sharks than bankers, they set their rates of interest at as much as 40 per cent per annum, approximately double the rate recorded in any earlier time in Babylonian history. It was customary for the Murashu boys to hold a borrower's land as collateral, which they then worked for a profit until the borrower paid back the loan – if he ever did. Abuses like this had operated for decades without royal censure or intervention, which suggests that Murashu and Sons kept the Persian authorities sweet by making regular and extravagant donations to the imperial treasury in return for royal protection, or at least royal indifference. No wonder that Enlil-nadin-shum was so anxious to have an audience with the Great King, even at the outrageous cost of a pound and a half of silver in rent payments. But Babylon was crowded with people, all hoping to kiss the king's feet and petition him for some favour or other, and Enlil-nadin-shum never got the audience he so desired. Darius II left for Susa and eleven days after signing the housing contract, a frustrated Enlil-nadin-shum was back home in Nippur, making up for his lost expenses by charging two women the usual rate of 40 per cent on a loan.

Enlil-nadin-shum's Babylonian expedition is just one detail we get from a huge archive of cuneiform documents archaeologists discovered in the ruins of Nippur. The Murashu archive consists of almost 900 cuneiform tablets documenting the business activities of one Murashu, son of Hatin, including three sons, three grand-sons, and their respective agents. They lived and worked in and around Nippur during the second half of the fifth century BCE. The archive illustrates the firm's management of agricultural lands and water rights which were leased by the firm from local owners of fiefs and were held on condition of military service and payment of taxes. Most of these lands were then sublet, along with animals and other necessary equipment, to tenants of the Murashu. In addition, the firm issued mortgages to landowners who received high-interest loans against pledges of their property. It was a lucra-tive affair but the archive shows how and why the empire was beginning to stagger under its tax burden.

Persia itself paid no taxes, but every other province of the empire was required to pay high annual portions. Media was assessed at 450 talents of silver and the tribute of 100,000 sheep; Susa paid 300 talents, Armenia 400 and 20,000 prized Nissean horses. Libya and Egypt both provided 700 talents, the products of their fisheries, and 120,000 measures of grain; Arabia gave 1,000 talents' worth of frankincense, and Ethiopia provided gold, ebony, and ivory every two years. Babylonia paid the highest silver tax levy – 1,000 talents – and was expected to use the products of its fertile land to feed the court three times a year. The combined annual amount of silver, gold, and precious goods amounted to some 14,560 talents, with a purchasing power many times higher than the sum suggests. We know that silver and gold were often melted down and poured into amphorae to harden and use as bullion; some was made into coins. Although businesses continued to use credit, many, like Murashu and Sons, demanded repayment in actual silver. The payment of taxes in silver became increasingly expected, and within a short time, loan sharks and satraps held the bulk of the coinage, which led to an increase in inflation as prices for all sorts of goods soared, and across the empire non-Persians suffered.

Economic pressures meant that Darius II's reign was conspicuous for frequent revolts, led partly by satraps and courtiers who had acquired a power base in regions where their families had ruled for generations. Close to home, at the royal court, one plot to overthrow Darius emerged in the person of the Paphlagonian eunuch Artoxares, who had once helped Darius to become king. The date of the attempted coup is uncertain, but it probably occurred around 419 BCE. Its details were briefly recounted by Ctesias and they make for bizarre reading:

> Artoxares the eunuch, who was very influential with the king, plotted against the king because he wished to rule himself. As he was a eunuch, he ordered a woman to procure a moustache and beard for him so he could look like a man. She informed against him and he was arrested and handed over to Parysatis. And he was killed.

This *Monty Python*-esque scenario of false beards and crafty castrati seems laughable, but at a time when beards were *de rigueur* for men, eunuchs (who, if castrated before puberty, could never sprout facial hair) must have appeared very incongruous – at best 'half-men', at worst, subhuman. Ctesias' point was to confirm that to rule as a king, one had to look the part. The vital accoutrement for the job was the luxuriant royal beard and since Artoxares was incapable of growing his own, he seized on the fashion for false hair and wore a counterfeit one. Preserved in Ctesias' tale is a genuine Persian belief that the monarch was the first among men and that his ability to rule and to preserve cosmic order was signified through his masculine appearance.

As ever, there was trouble in Egypt. Arshama, the aged satrap, kept up a regular correspondence with Darius II (several of the missives are still preserved on leather documents). The communications spoke of dangerous times, of widespread banditry, kidnapping, and theft, and there were some allusions to disturbances or revolts in the public sphere. In Aswan tensions between Egyptians and Jews had erupted into violence. There had been Jews living on the Nilotic island of Elephantine ever since the Babylonian invasion of Jerusalem in 597 BCE, and having seen Solomon's Temple destroyed, the Elephantine Jews had built a new temple on the island. Here they burned incense, performed animal sacrifice, and worshipped the God of Abraham. They also observed the Sabbath and the Feast of Matzah (Passover). However, the regular sacrifices of sheep and goats were anathema to the priests of the Egyptian ram-headed deity, Khnum, who also had a temple on the island. After centuries of harmonious coexistence, the Jewish temple was destroyed by a group of Egyptian priests in league with the local Persian administrator. Arshama duly punished the culprits, but felt himself obliged to avoid any future unrest by outlawing the ritual slaughter of goats.

Between 420 and 415 BCE the satrap of Lydia, Pissoúthnēs, began a revolt at Sardis and recruited Greek mercenaries under the generalship of Lycon to fight for him. Darius sent Tissaphernes, grandson of the eminent nobleman Hydarnes, to suppress the revolt. His skills went well beyond the battlefield when he managed to bribe Lycon's mercenaries to desert Pissoúthnēs, who was then lured to Susa with promises of clemency. He was executed and Tissaphernes was appointed satrap of Lydia in his place. His sojourn in Asia Minor signalled the start of intensified Persian intrusion in Greek affairs during the Peloponnesian War (431–404 BCE). The Athenians were familiar with Darius II from the outset of his reign, and they appear to have begun negotiations with the king almost immediately upon his accession to the throne, for rich evidence survives for Athenian embassies to the Persian court early in the reign of Darius, and it appears that many Athenians of upper rank visited his court. This might well help explain a vogue in Athens for red-figure pottery showing (invented) scenes of the Great King enjoying the pleasures of the court: his female fan-bearers, his gorgeously attired courtiers, and his dancers and musicians – a *topos* scene of Oriental hedonism similarly expounded on the stage by Euripides in his comi-tragical drama *Orestes* of 408 BCE, which is redolent with 'Arabian Nights'-style motifs.

Athenian–Persian relations soured quickly when in 413 BCE the Athenians interfered in Persian affairs by supporting the rebel Amorges, Pissoúthnēs' son, against the throne. Darius commanded Tissaphernes to crush the uprising and to ensure that the outstanding tribute from the Greek cities of Asia Minor was duly collected and sent to Persia. But Tissaphernes had plans of his own. He allied himself with the Spartans against Athens and in 412 BCE led his troops to take back for Persia the greater part of Ionia. Alcibiades, the Athenian playboy general renowned for his dark and unscrupulous politicking, persuaded Tissaphernes that Persia's best interest lay in maintaining a steady balance between Athens and Sparta and not privileging the one over the other. Tissaphernes was happy to leave the Greeks in peace and turn his attention to curbing the territorial ambitions of Pharnabazus II, the satrap of Hellespontine Phrygia – Tissaphernes' greatest nemesis. Pharnabazus too had attempted to get involved in the Peloponnesian War, favouring the Spartans. Thucydides explained why:

> The king had lately called upon him for the tribute from his government, for which he was in arrears, being unable to raise it from the Hellenic towns by reason of the Athenians; and he therefore calculated that by weakening the Athenians he should get the tribute better paid, and should also draw the Spartans into alliance with the king.

It was Pharnabazus who in all probability arranged the murder of Alcibiades at the request of Sparta. In 408 BCE Darius II decided to give Sparta his formal support and gifted money to build a fleet of war ships to use against Athens. In return the Spartans gave the Persians carte blanche to retake the Greek cities of Asia Minor as they saw fit. This was a great success for Darius.

The situation in Asia Minor changed when, around 407 BCE, Darius dismissed Tissaphernes from office, removing him to the lesser satrapy of Caria. In his place Darius handed the governance of Lydia, Cappadocia, and Phrygia (in other words, all of western Anatolia) to his son, Cyrus – named for the illustrious Cyrus the Great and known to history as Cyrus the Younger. It was Parysatis who persuaded Darius to give Cyrus this important imperial commission, for she doted on the boy, idolised and cherished him; she pampered and petted him, and even though he was just sixteen years old, she easily convinced Darius that her over-indulged darling had the requisite skills and temperament for this most prestigious posting. In many ways Parysatis was right. Young Cyrus was a brilliant individual, a naturally gifted leader, quick-minded, intelligent, and brave. But years of adoration and unnaturally demonstrative mother-love meant that he was also self-centred, cruel, vindictive, and brutal; he had violent mood swings and would turn on friends and enemies alike, thinking nothing of torturing them or of ordering for them the most agonising mutilations (hands, arms, or feet cut off) or excruciating executions (such as flaying alive). There was, it must be conceded, something sociopathic about Prince Cyrus. Tissaphernes hated him.

19

Blood Brothers

'Darius and Parysatis had two sons born to them . . . Cyrus had the support of Parysatis, his mother, for she loved him better than the other.' So wrote Xenophon, in the famous introduction to his *Anabasis*, his memoir of serving Cyrus the Younger as a mercenary soldier in Persia. By the time Xenophon wrote those words around 370 BCE, it was already common knowledge that from the moment of his birth the queen had fawned on her second son and privileged him over the eldest of her brood, Prince Arsicas. Yet Darius saw the good in Arsicas and found him intelligent, patient, thoughtful, and systematic, all qualities which made him the logical candidate to be the heir to the throne. His younger brother Cyrus was way too hotheaded for that role and so, much to Parysatis' chagrin, Darius named Arsicas as crown prince and heir to the Achaemenid empire. Cantankerously, Parysatis went out of her way to encourage strife between her sons, and even set Cyrus in opposition to his father. Her blind love for Cyrus overwhelmed Parysatis' dynastic circumspection and she worked peevishly and without ceasing for his advancement. As a result, Cyrus grew up prone to sociopathic behaviour, and tended to be blindly egocentric. He was ill-prepared for the trials of real life.

Cyrus understood all too well that his future depended on his mother's support, and although he found her grip on him overwhelmingly stifling, he recognised that without her he would be nothing; he would need to dance to her tune if he was ever to be king. It is little surprise though that in his years as satrap of Lydia, far away from the royal court and, happily, with many miles between Parysatis and himself, Cyrus sought some independence, politically and privately. By the time he was nineteen or twenty, the prince had established his own harem in the palace of Sardis and he had taken a consort, or more, although we have no details of his marriages. We do know though that he fell deeply in love with a Greek girl, a Phocian lass of very humble family. Her name was Aspasia.

Aspasia of Phocis was renowned for her breathtaking, god-given beauty: 'of hair yellow, locks a little curling', her admirers lyricised, 'she had glorious eyes, delicate skin, and a complexion like roses . . . Her lips were red, teeth whiter than snow . . . Her voice was sweet and smooth, that whosoever heard her might justly say he heard the voice of a Siren.' She was also known to be pure-minded, modest, and determinedly, resolutely, categorically, chaste. She had been delivered to Cyrus as a war captive, one of many virgins who were gifted to him from the campaigns in Ionia. He desired ornaments for his harem, and accepted the young women as concubines. Aspasia was presented to Cyrus one evening, after he had enjoyed a good supper. He went off to drink with his companions, as was usual in Persian high society (drink was enjoyed only after a meal had been consumed), and during the drinking bout four of the Greek girls were brought to him. Aspasia was among them. They were dressed in finery, the best clothes and jewels the harem had to offer – robes of fine, chiffon-like linen, gauzy cotton, and shimmering silk. Their eyes were lined with kohl, their lips had been painted red, and henna had been applied to their hands and feet in fanciful patterns. Their hair had been dressed with golden fillets and diaphanous multicoloured veils. They had been instructed by the eunuchs on how to behave and deport themselves before Cyrus, and were given tips to best gain his favour; not to turn away when he approached them, not to be coy when he touched them, and to permit him to kiss them. Each girl contended to outvie the others in willingness, but Aspasia was silent and sullen and refused to cooperate. It had taken several blows with a cane before a eunuch finally forced her to wear the expensive clothes and jewellery required to meet the prince.

When they came into Cyrus' presence, three of the girls smiled and giggled and blushed appropriately. Aspasia kept her gaze on the ground, her eyes full of tears. When Cyrus commanded them to sit down by him, the rest instantly obeyed, but Aspasia refused, until a eunuch pushed her down by force. When Cyrus touched their cheeks and fingers and breasts, the three girls responded willingly to his touch. But when he approached Aspasia, she wept, saying that her gods would punish him for his actions. As he reached across to grasp her waist, she rose up, and would have run away had not the eunuch stopped her and forced her back into her seat. Cyrus was hooked, totally smitten by her modesty and her astonishing beauty. On the spot he declared her to be his chief favourite and made her a concubine of the highest rank. She was escorted into the harem and provided with a private chamber of superlative quality, such as might be given to a royal consort.

Cyrus loved Aspasia more than any other woman – consort, concubine, or mother. Over many months, there developed between them a bond of trust and admiration that soon developed into passion. They became famous throughout the Persian empire and across the Greek world, as word of his affection for Aspasia spread first to Ionia and Asia Minor and then to Greece. Even the Great King came to know of it. As did Parysatis, who experienced that particular twang of jealousy that mothers know when their sons give their hearts to other women. Suppliants and clients of Cyrus began to petition Aspasia with requests, sweetening her with gifts in the hope she might put in a good word with the prince, for he was increasingly reliant on Aspasia's counsel and it was said that he made no decision without first consulting her. A tale is told of how the Greek master sculptor Scopas once sent Aspasia a necklace of extraordinary workmanship; it was a gift of astonishing exquisiteness, made up of tiny golden pomegranates and minuscule lotus buds in lapis lazuli, strung together on a chain of delicate filigree work. It was a masterpiece. On seeing it, she promptly declared it to be 'worthy either of the daughter or of the mother of a king', and quickly dispatched it to Parysatis, who received the present gratefully. It was a prudent move on Aspasia's part, for the gift of that extraordinary necklace played to

Parysatis' vanity and put her at her ease. Aspasia's gift demonstrated the girl's subservience to the queen.

Crown Prince Arsicas fell in love too. But the woman to whom he gave his heart was of impeccable Persian pedigree. She would prove to be far more problematic for Parysatis than any Greek concubine. Stateira was the daughter of the influential *khān* Hydarnes III, of the family that had helped put Darius the Great on the throne. She was one of the highest-ranking women of the empire and she guarded her status with a determined vigilance. In terms of family and line, she easily outranked Parysatis, who, even though the daughter of a king, still had a foreign concubine for a mother – and such things mattered among the women of the court. Stateira was a beauty too, but did not have the pale skin and fair hair of Aspasia; Stateira's beauty was classically Persian. She was dark-eyed, with sleek black hair, and an aquiline nose. Her face, the court poets eulogised, was fairer than the sun, her cheeks resembled pomegranate blossoms, her eyes were twin narcissi in a garden, adorned with long black lashes, and her black hair was so long that it fell in two musky ringlets over her silver neck down to her waist. In short, 'from head to feet, she was as Paradise'. Her body was round and fulsome and fleshy, a physicality that Persian men found irresistible. When Xenophon travelled into the Achaemenid empire, he was quick to notice the beauty of the Persian women he encountered. He described them as 'beautiful and big' (*kalai kai megalai*), by which he meant that they were plump and curvaceous.

Stateira's father, Hydarnes, had several offspring by his principal consort. His sons included Tissaphernes, the infamous satrap of Asia Minor, and Terituchmes, a pushy hothead of a youth. We know that Stateira had a sister, Rhoxane, although Ctesias says that Hydarnes had a further two girls, but their names are lost to us. Hard-working Hydarnes had served Darius II faithfully as the satrap of Armenia. During that time, he had carefully manoeuvred his children into the royal family, hoping to secure a royal future for his grandchildren. Therefore, quarrelsome Terituchmes was married off to Princess Amestris (II), the eldest daughter of Darius and Parysatis, and Stateira was wedded to Crown Prince Arsicas.

On the death of his father, Hydarnes, Terituchmes inherited the Armenian satrapy, and it was hoped that he would retire to Armenia and keep out of court circles. But just at the moment he was due to leave for his satrapy, his marriage fell into crisis. It transpired that he held a burning desire for his own sister, the enchanting Rhoxane, a woman described by Ctesias as 'beautiful to look at and an extremely experienced archer and javelin-thrower'. They had begun a physical affair and had, allegedly, fallen in love. Repudiating the daughter of the king was not easily done though, and as Terituchmes looked for ways to rid himself of Amestris he decided that the best option was to get rid of the main obstacle to their separation: King Darius would have to die. Terituchmes had Amestris taken captive. His intent (according to Ctesias) was to throw Amestris into a sack and to have her pierced through with spears. Some 300 men supported the revolt, it was claimed. The numbers were no doubt exaggerated, but it is certain that Amestris' life was in dire peril. Darius petitioned Terituchmes for his daughter's immediate release. His pleas fell on deaf ears. Realising that Terituchmes meant to rebel against the throne, and kill him, the king decided to move against his son-in-law. Darius' bodyguards attacked and killed Terituchmes, and many of his followers were executed in the aftermath. Not content with this, Parysatis gave orders for Terituchmes' mother, brothers, and two of his sisters – Stateira was not included – to be buried alive. Rhoxane, the focus of the trouble, was hacked to pieces while still living. Parysatis also had Terituchmes' young son poisoned for good measure.

The extermination of the house of Hydarnes looked set to continue when the king ordered the execution of Stateira too. Prince Arsicas, 'with tearful lamentations' (Ctesias says), begged his mother to intervene and save the life of his wife. Moved to an unusual level of compassion, Parysatis agreed to speak with Darius. Her intervention somehow worked, and the king agreed to reprieve Stateira from death, but with a sharp prophetic foresight, he warned Parysatis that she would one day come to regret keeping Stateira alive. The last surviving daughter of the house of Hydarnes, Darius warned, would become the cause of unending strife within the royal household.

Yet the woman was spared and Arsicas was thankful and jubilant at his father's beneficence and demonstrated his gratitude by being a hard-working and obedient son, careful to learn the lessons of state from his father and always eager to please him.

Saved from the jaws of death, Stateira never learned to be grateful. She refused to forget that Darius and his meddling wife were responsible for the elimination of much of her blood clan and she held them in complete contempt. Only her brother, Tissapherenes, remained alive because, thankfully, he was clever, industrious, and indispensable to the king. He would be Stateira's only guardian. But Stateira's anger burned against Parysatis. The princess went out of her way to offend, disparage, and denigrate the queen, using every weapon in her armoury to provoke Parysatis into a fury. When, for instance, Stateira became determined to make herself popular with the Persian people, her future subjects, she did so principally to aggravate Parysatis. Stateira made a habit of travelling through Persia in her covered carriage with the window blinds pulled open so that the people could see her. She often paused her journey, stopping the carriage to speak to local women who pressed against the wheels of the *harmamaxa* in order to see her and even to loyally kiss her hands. Parysatis found this far too outré. The touchy-feely approach to the job radically undermined the office of queenship. A queen, Parysatis professed, should be dignified, aloof, and invisible to the common herd. Pressing the flesh was not Parysatis' forte, and she would sooner avoid it. When Parysatis travelled, as she often did, the shutters of her carriage were firmly closed.

For almost two decades, the two determined, resourceful women fought out a prolonged bitter Cold War of manners. Etiquette became the weapon of choice and the royal court became a theatre of war. As with any major conflict, the war of the women was to claim numerous casualties and account for many unforeseen deaths.

*

Late in the autumn of 405 BCE, Darius II fell gravely ill and took to his bed. It was obvious to all who saw him that his life was quickly drawing to its end. Darius recognised this too and he sent instructions for his children to join him at Susa. Arsicas and his brother and sister, Oxendras and Amestris, got there quickly, but it took Cyrus the Younger until early 404 BCE to make the long journey from Sardis. Fervent greetings gushed forth from Parysatis as she embraced her best boy, safely back in her arms again after so many long months. Holding him close to her, she whispered instructions into Cyrus' ear, 'Follow my moves, do nothing without my consent.' Cyrus had made his journey inland, back to Susa, in the full hope that his mother would be motivated enough to have him designated heir to the throne, and now, with Darius' death so close, he realised that this was the last chance to get the king to change his mind about the succession. We can imagine the scene as Parysatis prostrated herself before King Darius, who, appearing so shrivelled on his sickbed, was propped up on many soft pillows, and supported by the arms of several nursing concubines. Touching her forehead to the ground, again and again, in extravagant subservience, she would have pleaded with him: 'My lord, you yourself know that Cyrus should be king, for he was born when you had ascended the throne; your elder son was born to us while we were still common people.' In another attempt, kissing the many rings of the king's bejewelled hand, Parysatis, implored, 'My lord, as soon as my lord the king is laid to rest, I and my son Cyrus will be treated as criminals. We will be killed by Arsicas and his wife, the daughter of Hydarnes.' She tried every tactic with her husband – pleasing, pleading, scolding, weeping – but to no avail. Darius remained resolute: Arsicas was his heir, the prince had been expertly trained, by himself, in the affairs of royal governance. So it was that when Darius II died early in 404 BCE, after a reign of thirty-five years, he was succeeded by Arsicas, his eldest son. He took the throne name Artaxerxes II, in homage to his illustrious grandfather.

Following the funeral of Darius II, the court moved to Pasargadae, where preparations had been made, in the usual custom, to have Artaxerxes II invested as the next Achaemenid ruler. As the investiture was playing out, the king's brother-in-law, Tissaphernes, newly arrived in Persia from Asia Minor for the sacred ceremony, approached Artaxerxes to tell him that he had uncovered a plot:

Cyrus was already attempting to oust him from the throne in a coup d'état. He was supported by some of the Magi who were actually officiating at the ceremonies. The plan, Tissaphernes testified, was for Cyrus to lie in wait in the holy sanctuary of the goddess Anahita, so as to attack and kill the king when he was removing his clothing in order to prepare for the ceremony. It is difficult to know the veracity of the story because even Ctesias, our primary source for the episode, was undecided about it, noting that 'some say that this false charge resulted in Cyrus' arrest, others that Cyrus entered the sanctuary and was handed over by a priest when he was found hiding'.

Whatever the reality of the situation, Artaxerxes clearly believed that there was enough evidence against Cyrus to accuse him of plotting treason and to order his execution. As the Immortal guards began to drag the prince away, Parysatis let out a wail and threw herself at Cyrus, tearing off her veil and entwining her locks of hair around him, and pressing her head against his. With howls and cries of entreaty, in what was a fist-bitingly histrionic performance, she pleaded with the king to pardon Cyrus and send him back to Sardis in Lydia. Once back in Asia Minor, she pleaded, he could prove himself to be a loyal subject and a beloved brother once more. Tissaphernes and Stateira warned Artaxerxes against relenting in the face of Parysatis' melodrama and to remember that Cyrus' burning ambition to rule would never be assuaged. The new Great King was by nature gentle and personable (in the Greek accounts of his reign, his amiability was his chief characteristic; they called him *Memnon*, 'the thoughtful one'), and he pardoned his brother. As Parysatis requested, Cyrus was sent back to Lydia to continue his job. But as Ctesias recognised, 'Cyrus was not content with his position and, since it was not his release that he remembered but his arrest, his anger made him crave the kingship even more than before.'

Back home in Sardis, and in the loving, supportive embrace of Aspasia, Cyrus began to plot in earnest. It is difficult to understand what objectives he had set himself, beyond seizing the throne which he genuinely believed should be his. Perhaps he hoped to diminish the influence of the Persian nobility, like the troublesome Hydarnes clan with its disruptive star players, Tissaphernes and Stateira. Maybe he wanted to create a more centralised government. He was now *karanos* (from the Old Persian *kāra* 'army'), or Supreme Commander, of Asia Minor. He held one of the greatest army commands of the empire. He certainly had the clout needed to grab the throne. He was, after all, both the civilian governor and the supreme military commander of the whole of Asia Minor. Cyrus began to build an army of infantry and cavalry, some 20,000 troops, and hired the service of 12,000 mercenaries, 10,000 of whom were Greek hoplites. Greeks had served in the armies of the Near East for centuries, and in more recent times they had aided the western satraps to repel Athenian attacks, although their presence in such numbers – Cyrus' mercenary force was the largest ever assembled – did not go unnoticed by Tissaphernes. Cyrus put on the appearance of a loyal subject, however, and continued to send Artaxerxes the tribute of the provinces that were under his authority. He aroused no undue attention from the central administration in Persia.

The Greek hoplite mercenaries were among the best fighters of the ancient world, hardy war veterans with many years of battle experience, willing to undertake anything for the right price. They were split into numerous brigades, each under the command of a general, the most distinguished of whom was Clearchus of Sparta, who had, during the Peloponnesian War, commanded a Spartan naval operation in the Hellespont, during which the city of Byzantium was successfully taken. Ferociously short-tempered and alarmingly over-confident, he began a reign of terror in the city that raised the ire of the authorities in distant Sparta, who soon removed him from his post. Clearchus was sentenced to death for failing to keep the peace, but he avoided execution and, at the beginning of 402 BCE, he entered the service of Cyrus the Younger, who, recognising Clearchus' obvious skills, supplied him with funds and instructed him to lick the mercenaries into shape. Clearchus eventually became commander-in-chief of the entire Greek force and served Cyrus with unswerving loyalty.

Another Greek drawn to Cyrus' service was the 28-year-old anti-democratic Athenian aristocrat Xenophon, who joined the

Persian prince more as a gentleman adventurer than a bone fide soldier. Apart from Socratic links and presumed service in the Athenian cavalry, little is known of him until he joined Cyrus in 401 BCE, although he was destined to become one of the superstars of ancient historiography. His *Cyropaedia*, or 'The Education of Cyrus', is one of the most remarkable works of literature to survive from antiquity. Ostensibly a study of Cyrus the Great, it is in fact a paean of praise, a panygyric, to Cyrus the Younger, who, as far as Xenophon was concerned, was a born leader of men.

In the spring of 402 BCE, Cyrus, his army, and the entourage of camp-followers, including his cooks, stewards, eunuchs, and concubines – Aspasia among them – started out from Sardis on their journey towards Persia. The soldiers knew they were marching east, but to where and for what purpose they were ignorant. Cyrus withheld the true intention of the march inland, fearing that the army would refuse to fight against the Great King. Only Clearchus and a few privileged Persians knew the truth of the manoeuvres. The army advanced east by way of Colossae, Peltae, Tyrtaeum, Iconium (modern Konya), and Tarsus, where there was almost a mutiny and Clearchus had to intervene to restore order. Marching over the Tauris mountains and through the Cilician Gates, Cyrus and his troops passed through northern Syria and into the heartland of Mesopotamia. By mid-summer Cyrus' army had reached the Euphrates river, at a place called Thapsacus. Only at that point did Cyrus disclose to his men that he was in fact rebelling against his brother, the king. As he had anticipated, the Greek hoplites were reluctant to march on, and he was only able to overcome their hesitance with promises of a substantial increase in pay. Finally, the troops agreed to carry on. They crossed the river and marched south along the east bank of the Euphrates without meeting any opposition, until, in August, they reached Babylonia.

The Great King Artaxerxes had been forewarned by Tissaphernes that Cyrus was marching east at the head of a huge force of soldiers, and he had been busy preparing his own forces – some 40,000 fighting men. With Tissaphernes at his side, Artaxerxes advanced into Babylonia, arriving at the tiny village of Cunaxa, some fifty miles north of Babylon. It was the king's plan to draw Cyrus to him, and so he camped his men there, making certain that they were well-fed and rested.

Exactly 180 days after their departure from Sardis (84 marching days and 96 days of rest, according to the detailed report in Xenophon's *Anabasis*), on 3 September 401 BCE, Cyrus' troops approached Cunaxa, having marched throughout the heat of the day and feeling completely disorientated. As Cyrus' men advanced over the horizon, Artaxerxes' troops began to prepare for battle, although it took a further two hours for both armies to ready themselves in battle formation. By mid-afternoon the armies were ready – their lines spread across the desert towards the Euphrates for over a mile.

Remarkably, we have two eyewitness accounts of the battle that followed. The events at Cunaxa were recorded by Xenophon, observing the action from Cyrus' side, and Ctesias of Cnidus, billeted close to Artaxerxes II. The exact time and reason for Ctesias' arrival in Persia is unknown. Diodorus Siculus suggested that he arrived there as a prisoner of war, although the validity of this report is uncertain, and some scholars have rejected the idea, preferring instead to see Ctesias invited and received graciously at court by Artaxerxes II because of his medical skills sometime around 405 BCE. There is no doubt that Ctesias was at Cunaxa at the heart of the fighting, for he cared for Artaxerxes and dressed and healed the wounds he received, which strongly suggests that Ctesias was Artaxerxes' physician before the revolt of Cyrus. Certainly, after the battle, Ctesias received numerous honours from the king. But exactly what took Ctesias to Persia remains a mystery.

Both witnesses agree that Cyrus attacked first. He ordered Clearchus, whose Greek mercenaries constituted his right wing, to attack the enemy head on at the centre, but Clearchus refused to abandon his position on the riverbank, which offered cover from the right and ensured that he could not be surrounded. Cyrus, riding a thoroughbred horse which was unruly – it was named Pasacas, according to Ctesias – plunged into the centre of Artaxerxes' army. When he saw his brother directly ahead, Cyrus threw caution to the wind and rushed at him ferociously, launched his spear at the king and wounded him in the chest, through his breastplate. The spear entered to a depth of two fingers. Under the force of the blow, Artaxerxes fell off his horse, but he managed to get back up on his feet and along with a few others – Ctesias among them – occupied a nearby hill and laid low. Cyrus was carried off by his horse into the midst of the enemy. It was already getting dark, and Cyrus went unrecognised by his enemies and cantered into the fray, shouting at soldiers and cavalrymen to clear a pathway and generally making himself conspicuous with his shouting. Realising who was addressing them, the soldiers got out of his way and prostrated themselves on the ground. Just then, a young Persian named Mithridates ran up and threw a spear. It struck Cyrus in the face, close to his eye. Stunned and bleeding profusely from the wound, Cyrus became dizzy and collapsed to the ground and lay there until some nearby eunuchs in his service got him back on his feet. He wanted to walk by himself, but he was so dazed that his servants had to support his weight as they dragged him along. He staggered and tottered as if drunk. It was just then that a soldier from Caria in the king's service – unaware of who Cyrus was – struck him from behind with a lance. The vein in the back of his leg ruptured and Cyrus fell to the ground once again, striking his wounded and bleeding temple on a rock. He died instantly. He was twenty-two years old.

The eunuchs immediately let out their ritual wails of lamentation and attracted the attention of Artasyras, the King's Eye, who was riding past. Ctesias recorded their conversation: 'when he discovered the eunuchs in mourning, he asked the most trustworthy of them, "Who is this man beside whom you sit mourning?" And they said, "Can't you see, Artasyras, that Cyrus is dead?"' Cyrus' horse, which had run off, was found wandering around the battlefield; its felt saddlecloth was saturated with the prince's blood. Artasyras dutifully reported to King Artaxerxes (who was in a poor state and suffering badly from his chest wound) that he had seen Cyrus' body and that the prince was most certainly dead. A reconnaissance mission to look for Cyrus' corpse was ordered, and thirty men were dispatched with torches, under the leadership of Masabates, the king's most trusted eunuch. He had instructions to bring Artaxerxes proof that Cyrus was dead. Standing over the corpse, and in accordance with Persian custom, Masabates saw to it that the right hand and head were cut off the body and sent straight back to Artaxerxes. The Great King was dumbstruck yet jubilant, shocked, yet relieved. Silently, and with great determination, he seized the head by its long, shaggy hair and held it up high for all to see. This was the ultimate trophy of his victory, proof that his throne was safe, that his rulership could continue and his greatest enemy was dead.

The Battle of Cunaxa was a resounding victory for Artaxerxes II, but after Cyrus' death, the Greek mercenaries who had served him, having forced their way so far into hostile territory, found themselves in a difficult situation. Clearchus managed to hold the Greek troops together, and while parlaying with the Persians began to retreat up the Tigris until he was taken captive by Tissaphernes, leaving the mercenaries leaderless. The much-reduced troops, about 5,000 men of the original 12,000, eventually succeeded in reaching the Black Sea and Ionia two years after Cunaxa in 399 BCE after suffering a difficult and dangerous retreat through Syria and Anatolia, an eyewitness account of which was provided by Xenophon in his brilliant *Anabasis* – 'The Expedition' – the world's first surviving soldier's memoir.

*

When the sun rose on the morning after the Battle of Cunaxa and shed its light on the corpse-strewn battlefield, Artaxerxes gave thanks to Ahuramazda for giving him so decisive a victory and for returning *Arta* – 'Truth' – to his kingdom. Ctesias stated that 9,000 corpses were brought to Artaxerxes, although it seemed to Ctesias that the dead numbered at least 20,000. Care was taken to root out defectors and to punish them according to their crimes. A Mede named Arbaces, for instance, who had defected to Cyrus during the battle, but who had come back to the king's side after Cyrus' death, was charged with cowardice and weakness and was given the extraordinary punishment of having to carry a naked prostitute around for an entire day. Another man, who, in addition to defecting, had falsely claimed to have killed two of the enemy, was punished in a much more conventional way: his tongue was cut out. Those who had fought well for Artaxerxes – like Ctesias – were duly rewarded. He sent gifts to Mithridates, who had struck Cyrus in the face with his lance, and made the Carian who had hit the hollow of Cyrus' knee a very wealthy man. The remainder of Cyrus' army who remained behind at Cunaxa were taken as prisoners and handed over to Artaxerxes together with other spoils of war – Cyrus' fine tents, horses, hunting dogs, clothes and jewellery, camp-followers, and concubines who had made up part of the expedition. Aspasia was diligently sought for among Cyrus' women, because Artaxerxes had heard of her fame and needed to see for himself the concubine who had so bewitched his brother. When the royal guards brought her to him, bound and gagged, he was angry and threw her captors into prison, commanding that a rich robe should be given to her. He instructed his eunuchs to care for her every need. Aspasia mourned for Cyrus, but Artaxerxes nevertheless incorporated her into his own harem (as was his right by conquest) and endeavoured to ingratiate himself into her favour, hoping to make her forget Cyrus and to love him as she had done his brother. But it would be a long time before Artaxerxes would accomplish his aim; the love Aspasia had had for Cyrus was deep and real and could not easily be rooted out.

The royal court, which was assembled in Babylon, was on tenterhooks waiting for news of the outcome of the battle. Who was king? Artaxerxes or Cyrus? Artaxerxes dispatched a messenger to ride swiftly to Babylon to break the news and tell Parysatis that her beloved son had fallen in combat and was dead. When the messenger arrived in the palace, he was straight away ushered into Parysatis' apartment, where he threw himself at the queen's feet, kissing her sandals in a display of abject servitude. According to Ctesias, who claimed to have heard what next passed from Parysatis herself, the messenger announced that Cyrus fought bravely and brilliantly, which both pleased and worried the queen and she asked, 'How did Artaxerxes fare?' The messenger answered that he had been wounded and that he had taken flight from the battlefield.

'Yes', the queen retorted, 'it is Tissaphernes who is responsible for what has happened to him.' Then she asked, 'Where is Cyrus now?' And the messenger replied, 'In the place where brave men have to camp.' He continued with great difficulty to break the news to Parysatis, and only gradually, bit by bit, did he edge towards the climax of his missive. The queen grew frustrated and angry with him. She scolded him until he finally blurted it out: 'My Lord Cyrus is dead!' Parysatis fell into a state of shock, Ctesias says, as she slowly began her soft lamentation for her boy, and remembering him as a youth, she spoke about his horses, dogs, and armaments and how much she had loved him. And then she wept. She wept for many days.

When Artaxerxes returned to Babylon there was no victory parade and no rejoicing, and he kept a respectable silence in front of his mother. For her part, dressed in mourning clothes, she made the required prostrations in front of her son, now universally recognised as the only king of Persia, and he dutifully raised her up on her feet and placed her on a seat at his right-hand side, the position of honour. To her son, nothing more was said of Cyrus, and no word was spoken of the battle, although every time she looked upon Stateira and Tissaphernes, the gall rose to her throat. Slowly, quietly, without the king's knowledge, she acquired information about the events at Cunaxa, finding out who did what to whom and how. In this she was aided by Ctesias, whom she trusted. Slowly a picture emerged of Cyrus' movements in the battle and the events surrounding his death. Finally, Parysatis had a list of names of persons she held accountable for her son's demise. Their persecution could begin.

The first victims of Parysatis' vendetta were easily tracked down. The Carian who had struck Cyrus with his spear had become drunk on good fortune and began to boast that it was he himself who had killed Cyrus and that he was now unjustly deprived of his fame by the king, who was jealous of his success on the battlefield. Artaxerxes' ire was aroused and he ordered the man to be beheaded. His mother, who, Ctesias says, was present when Artaxerxes issued the order, intervened and said, 'Don't you let this wretched Carian off like this, my king! He shall receive his reward for what he has dared to say from me instead.' The king turned him over to Parysatis and she ordered the guards to seize the terrified man. Her only purpose was to cause him the maximum pain, until death relieved him of agony. Accordingly, the Carian was put on the rack for ten days as his body was stretched and broken to the point of death; his eyes were gouged out and, finally, molten bronze was poured into his mouth and ears until he died in agonised convulsions.

Next in line was Mithridates, who had pierced Cyrus below the eye with a lance. He also came to a bad end through his own stupidity, for having been invited to a dinner which was hosted by some of Parysatis' eunuchs, he arrived adorned in gold jewellery and clothing which Artaxerxes had given him as part of his reward. As the night wore on, and the drink flowed freely, Sparamizes, the most powerful of the queen's eunuchs, said to him, 'What beautiful clothing this is, Mithridates, that the king has given you – and what beautiful neck-chains and bracelets! And what an expensive sword! He has made you a truly blessed man, admired by all.' Mithridates, who was already very drunk, retorted, 'What about these things, Sparamizes? I showed myself worthy of bigger and more beautiful things from the king for my actions that day.' Smiling beneficently, Sparamizes replied, 'No one grudges you them, Mithridates.' Vanity and good wine continued to embolden Mithridates, however, and made him talkative. He began to let his guard down until, finally, he declared, 'You lot can say what you like but I tell you, Cyrus was killed by *this* hand. For I did not throw my spear idly: I struck and pierced his cheek, only just missing his eye, and brought the man down. And it was from that wound that he died.' A sudden hush filled the room as the other guests, already sensing Mithradtes' fate, bent their heads to the ground, but Sparamizes merely said, 'Mithradtes, my friend, for now let us eat and drink to the king's good fortune and leave to one side subjects that are too big for us.' After the dinner the eunuch repaired to Parysatis' apartment and told her about the events of the night. In turn, she told the king, who ordered that Mithridates be put to death.

Mithridates was escorted to a barren place outside the city walls, to an exposed area which had been prepared for his execution. He saw there that a hole had been dug into the earth, into which had been placed the hull of a little rowing boat or skiff, the kind that plied the River Euphrates, day in and day out, providing the city with its supply of freshwater fish. With his arms and legs bound, Mithridates was placed into the boat on his back, his head propped up at, and out of, the prow. Three guards approached, carrying another small boat, roughly the same size as the one that contained Mithridates, but held upside down. They placed it over the skiff in the ground and made it to fit on top of the other and fastened both together with ropes. Then they covered the whole structure in mud. When the mud dried, it took on the form of a curiously large cocoon. Earth was piled on top of the structure and the hole was refilled, but Mithridates' head was left projecting outside, the rest of his body concealed inside the hollow buried chamber.

Over the next days, Mithridates was force-fed with all sorts of food, and plenty of it. Each time he was uncooperative and refused to eat, the guards forced him to swallow by pricking his eyes with splinters of wood. Once he had eaten, they gave him a mixture of milk and honey to drink and they liberally poured the mixture into his mouth and all over his face until it ran wet with the syrupy mixture. Day after day the milk and honey came, and Mithridates' head and face started to bake in the blazing sun. Soon swarms of flies, wasps, and bees covered his face, entered into his mouth and crawled up his nostrils and filled his ears. His enforced milk-and-honey diet caused severe diarrhoea that left Mithridates feeling feeble and dehydrated, and the more he was fed the mixture, the more he would defecate. Mithridates' ordeal went on for days. Slowly his living body began to decay and putrefy within the cocoon, as maggots and worms swarmed out of the excrement and began to consume him from the inside. More days passed. When it became clear that Mithridates had finally died, the guards removed the upper boat and saw for themselves that the flesh had been completely eaten away and that around the entrails swarms of insects were feeding and clinging fast; rats and other vermin had burrowed into the hull too and were gnawing on the flesh. The stench was rank. It had taken Mithridates seventeen days to die.

The 'Ordeal of the Boats', as it was known, was one of several institutionalised forms of the death penalty in the Achaemenid era, and it is sometimes hard to reconcile this image of a cruel Persia with that of peaceful Persians on, say, the walls of the *Apadana* staircases at Persepolis, where all is imperial harmony. The punishment of 'The Boats' can too easily be seen as a spectacular theatre of cruelty, and an Orientalist reading of the execution process is easy: the Persians can be seen as cruel despots concocting sublime, elaborate punishments to thrill and delight their tyrant kings. But the Persian Version of the punishment is far more complex and must relate to the Persian views of religious purity. The thought of slowly rotting away in one's own excrement, gnawed on by vermin and infested with worms, must have ranked as a hellish nightmare among the Persians, who valued the religious connotations of cleanliness and purity so very highly. It was an ending to life deserved by those who had willingly followed the Lie – traitors, rebels, and other perverters of *Arta*. Death through scaphism, with its flies, faeces, milk, and honey, effectively brought about a hell on earth.

The one individual who remained in Parysatis' sights was the eunuch who had cut off Cyrus' head and hand, Masabates, Artaxerxes' most important and influential servant. Since he gave her no way of getting a hold on him, Parysatis had to think carefully about how to bring about Masabates' death without attracting her son's attention or seeming to be too interested in the eunuch. She would need to play the long game, and wait until the moment was right.

*

After the war of the brothers, Parysatis slowly became reconciled with Artaxerxes again and he was pleased to be back in her affections. When they were young, Parysatis had frequently played boardgames with her children and she was known to be a formidable dice-player; indeed, she had often played dice with the king before the war and now she began playing with him again. All in all, she left Artaxerxes little opportunity to spend time with Stateira, since Parysatis' hatred for her daughter-in-law grew more intense with each day. Besides which, she wanted to exercise the most influence over the king herself.

After months of slowly drawing Artaxerxes closer to her, one day Parysatis challenged him to a game of dice, with a high stake of 1,000 golden darics. He accepted the bet and she saw to it that he won the game. She handed over the gold to him, but pretending that she was annoyed, and keen to get her own back, she suggested another game, the stake this time being not coinage, but a eunuch, who would become part of the winner's household staff. Artaxerxes consented. This time there was to be no charade of being a bad player and Parysatis applied herself properly to the game, playing with steely determination. The dice fell in her favour and she won. For her prize, she claimed Masabates and he was duly transferred to the queen's service. Before the king's suspicions were aroused, she ordered Masabates to go to her apartment and wait for her there. Having bid the king good night, she handed the eunuch over to the executioners and gave them the order to flay him alive, impale his body sideways on three stakes, and separately peg out his stretched-out skin.

The king found his mother's behaviour insufferable. He had been conned by her conniving, fooled by her smarming, and made a dupe by her cold-bloodedness. Masabates had done nothing but carry out royal commands to the letter, yet he had died cruelly and needlessly because of the Queen Mother's inability to face the reality of Cyrus' death. Even dead and decapitated, Cyrus was loved by Parysatis in a way Artaxerxes would never experience; the Great King recognised this and lamented it. Even though he was angry with Parysatis, he yet yearned for her affection, for a mother's touch. When Artaxerxes finally plucked up enough courage to rebuke his mother and protest against Masabates' execution, she feigned ignorance and with a smile (so Ctesias puts it) said cheerfully, 'How sweet you are! Good for you that you get angry on account of a useless old eunuch! On the other hand, I lost 1,000 gold darics at dice, and have just accepted my loss without saying a word.' Artaxerxes was a broken man.

Time passed, and although the king regretted ever having trusted Parysatis, and even though he continued to be hurt by her vindictiveness and bullying, he nevertheless held his tongue and tried his utmost to live in concord with his mother. For the sake of the empire, an appearance of harmony within the royal family was important. But Stateira's loathing of Parysatis festered like an open wound that would not heal. She deplored the brutality and lawlessness of Parysatis' vendettas and the way that she belittled the king, so cruelly using him in her plots and machinations. Stateira began to openly oppose Parysatis in day-to-day matters at court, asserting her role as the chief consort of the Great King and the mother of his heirs. She started pushing her own dynastic agenda, sidetracking Parysatis' influence and undermining her authority. Stateira swore to herself that she would not allow Parysatis any more power.

20

Women Beware Women

By the early winter of 401 BCE Parysatis had ceased her pogrom against Artaxerxes' collaborators in the Battle of Cunaxa. Her revered son Cyrus had been dead for two months and the remains of his body, united again with its bloodied decapitated head and right hand, had been laid out in the open air, stripped clean of flesh, muscle, and sinews by the vultures and jackals of the desert. The Queen Mother's pain was still raw, but at least her blood lust seemed assuaged. It was just then that General Clearchus, Cyrus' esteemed Spartan general, arrived in Babylon.

Manacled and beaten, Clearchus had been taken captive by the satrap Tissaphernes after the Battle of Cunaxa as he and his Greek troops had begun to retreat up the Tigris, taking an alternative route to the one that had brought them into Babylonia. The cunning satrap had invited him to a banquet, softened him with wine and promises of a swift journey home to Sparta, and then had seized him and his companions and transported them to Babylon, yoked together, chained at the neck – their arms tied agonisingly tight behind their backs – and driven like pack animals through Mesopotamia. When Parysatis learned of Clearchus' arrival in the city, her wounds opened up afresh. She had heard the reports of his bravery on the battlefield of Cunaxa – in fact she had relished the telling of them, for she savoured any stories of Cyrus and she had come to love knowing of how Clearchus had worked away to support her son's noble quest. He was the most honourable of the Greeks. He deserved better than to suffer the disgrace of being a bound prisoner-of-war.

Artaxerxes regarded Clearchus very differently. For him the Spartan was a troublemaker, a low-born, no-good Greek with ideas well above his station. More than that, he was a traitor to the crown, a foreign meddler in the empire's internal affairs; he had knowingly upset the delicate balance of *Arta* and he had sided with the Lie, and had, by championing Cyrus so assiduously, scorned Ahuramazda's wisdom. He deserved his humiliation. His execution should not be ruled out either, the king declared to his ministers as he witnessed Clearchus led in chains through the palace courtyards. In this ambition Artaxerxes was supported by his wife. Ever watchful and always perceptive, Stateira recognised how deeply the trauma of Cunaxa and its gruesome aftermath had affected Artaxerxes' health and demeanour. For the two months since Cyrus' death he had been restless, distracted, and, given the hair's breadth by which he had escaped the battle with both his life and the throne, she knew that he was feeling decidedly insecure, twitchy even. For his own sanity he needed to put the past behind him and to retake the reins of government. Today we would say that Artaxerxes needed closure.

Stateira urged, entreated, and begged Artaxerxes to act with definitive authority and put the unwanted Greek to death; Parysatis must not have her way in this. Tissaphernes, working alongside his sister, also solicited the king to show some backbone and execute Clearchus and his followers there and then. But Artaxerxes opted to throw them into jail. Even so, Parysatis was flabbergasted to know that the hero of Cunaxa had been treated with such disdain and had been incarcerated in a prison cell like a common criminal or a wild animal, and she sent earnest entreaty after entreaty to her son, begging for the general's freedom. She knew that every day which passed drew him closer to the executioner's sword and she determined to secure his release from prison and the freedom to return home to Sparta. To each of her ever-desperate pleas though, Artaxerxes turned a deaf ear; he was tired of her incessant, exasperating meddling and, besides, he could still smell the sickening stench of the blood of her victims all around the palace. His nostrils were filled with it. Enough was enough. The Greek would remain locked away, awaiting the king's pleasure.

Clearchus' imprisonment occupied Parysatis' every waking hour and she could find no rest while he was in that cell, suffering such unwarranted dishonour. While Clearchus lived, she still had something left of her son, a vague tangential connection to her martyred boy, and it was with this fragile relationship in mind that she remembered that her doctor had attended Artaxerxes at Cunaxa and had treated the king's wounds. He spoke Greek. He could communicate with Clearchus.

We do not know if Ctesias of Cnidus agreed to work as a go-between for Parysatis out of dread of the queen's power, out of pity for a fellow Hellene imprisoned and far from home, or out of personal ambition – perhaps it was a mixture of all three. We do know though that his service to the queen drew him close into her circle and that, for the next seventeen years of his life in the gilded cage that was the Persian court, he served Parysatis and her family loyally and wholeheartedly, and he was rewarded with the queen's trust and praise (he was, in later years, gifted two finely crafted swords by Parysatis and Artaxerxes). Ctesias became Parysatis' unlikely confidant, and it is thanks to this relationship that we have so much detail preserved about life at the heart of the Persian empire during Artaxerxes' reign.

When Ctesias first visited Clearchus in the large cell he shared with his soldiers, he was surprised to see the general looking so gaunt and thin – the food rations that were sent to Clearchus were being taken and consumed by the shackled soldiers who gave little of them to their disgraced leader. Ctesias righted this situation by arranging (with the approval and understanding of Parysatis) for more provisions to be sent to Clearchus and for further supplies to be given separately to the soldiers. He also obtained for Clearchus what he most desired – a hair comb. The Spartans set much store by the careful grooming of their long, oiled hair, and the act, which was more ritualistic than cosmetic, served as a form of social therapy for them, a curious group activity whereby camaraderie and loyalty were established through mutual grooming. Clearchus' comb was therefore a kind of comfort blanket, and he was grateful to Ctesias for procuring it, rewarding him with a finger ring with a seal on it which showed dancing caryatids. When, however, a leg of ham was sent to Clearchus as part of his daily ration, he appealed to Ctesias to send him a small knife by hiding it inside the meat, so that he could use it to take his life and thereby not to allow his fate to depend on the king's cruelty. But Ctesias was unwilling to comply through fear of Artaxerxes finding out, and backed off from future meddling.

Somehow, but inevitably, Stateira got to hear of the preferential treatment Clearchus was receiving through the intervention of the Queen Mother, and these special privileges made her angry. She understood Parysatis' motivation towards the Greek, of course, and Stateira saw how the Queen Mother was being driven by an over-whelming desire to somehow keep the flame of Cyrus alive. Stateira recognised too that while this was the case, Artaxerxes would know no peace of mind. Stateira also perceived that the current – fortuitous – situation around Clearchus afforded her a uniquely serendipitous opportunity to make Parysatis suffer; she came to the conclusion that, at this moment, with Clearchus' fate hanging in the balance, she had a single golden opportunity to twist the knife of her mother-in-law's pain and plunge it even deeper into her despair. With calm rationality, Stateira easily convinced Artaxerxes that Clearchus must die. For the good of the empire, she said, for the security of the throne, and for the health of his mother, who was clinging on to the ghosts of the past through the very presence of this dangerous barbarian, Clearchus must die.

The Spartan and his soldiers were executed en masse outside the walls of Babylon, their bodies left exposed to nature, although, miraculously (and improbably) a whirlwind blew up and brought with it a large pile of earth and heaped it in a mound, covering Clearchus' body. Several date stones were scattered there by the wind and after a short time, so the story goes, an amazing date grove grew up out of the mound and shaded the place. It is probable that this miracle tale originated in the circle of Parysatis, who once again was trying to enhance the memory of Cyrus by dramatising a faithful general's extraordinary destiny. When Artaxerxes saw the luxuriant grove that graced Clearchus' improvised 'tomb', he 'declared his sorrow, concluding that in Clearchus he put to death a man beloved of the gods' – or so says Ctesias. In other words, the propaganda released by Parysatis' supporters claimed for Clearchus a royal ideological trope: a privileged relationship with the deities who guaranteed prosperity. Clearchus was honoured by vegetation that thrived without human intervention, for it was the gods themselves who had created a paradise in the form of a sacred grove whose foliage overshadowed a tumulus located in an arid region beyond the walls of Babylon. Through Clearchus, therefore, as Ctesias wrote, 'a sign was sent by the gods' that posthumously confirmed the royal attributes which Cyrus the Younger liked to claim.

*

The months – and then the years – which followed Clearchus' execution saw an unnatural quiet settle over the court. The routine of the palace went into operation again as the rituals of royalty started up and the Great King travelled through his lands, oversaw his dominions, and received the empire's diplomats as in the past.

Like his forefathers, Artaxerxes saw himself as something of a master builder and concentrated much of his time and money on royal building projects. He had an *Apadana* throne-hall built at Ecbatana, ordered the construction of a new Achaemenid summer palace in Babylon (it stood there until the end of the second century BCE), and, as excavations and inscriptions prove, he built a new palace below the royal terrace at Susa. It was here too that he lovingly rebuilt Darius I's beautiful *Apadana* which had perished in a fire early in the reign of Artaxerxes I. The restorations were marked out with fresh new cuneiform inscriptions carved into the drum bases of the huge fluted columns which supported the vast cedar-wood roof, in which Artaxerxes stressed his royal pedigree and his devotion to his great ancestor, Darius I:

> Artaxerxes, the Great King, the King of Kings, the King of all Nations, the King of this World, the son of King Darius [II], Darius the son of King Artaxerxes [I], Artaxerxes the son of King Xerxes, Xerxes the son of King Darius, Darius the son

of Hystaspes, the Achaemenid, says: My ancestor Darius [the Great] made this audience hall, but during the reign of my grandfather Artaxerxes, it was burnt down; but, by the grace of Ahuramazda, Anahita, and Mithras, I reconstructed this audience hall (A²Sa).

The main task of Artaxerxes' entire reign, however, was the maintenance of the empire's frontiers. At his accession to his father's throne, Egypt had rebelled and a local dynasty ruled in virtual independence. For two decades Achaemenid campaigns, often with the aid of expensive Greek mercenaries, had attempted to bring Egypt back under the Great King's control, but it was not to be. Artaxerxes II was still recognised as pharaoh in some parts of Egypt as late as 401 BCE, although his inactive response to the rebellion, especially following the Battle of Cunaxa, allowed Egypt to solidify its independence. While Egypt's loss did challenge Artaxerxes' sense of pride, successful undertakings against King Evagoras of Salamis in Cyprus in 381 BCE and the repression of rebels in Ionia, Paphlagonia, and elsewhere in the west gave him a boost of morale. There was trouble in Asia Minor, as usual, for the area was a battlefield upon which the forces of good administration contended with the forces of maladministration, and Artaxerxes dispatched satrap upon satrap there in the hope of finding someone whose competence as a soldier-bureaucrat might bring the area into line. The trouble was that satrapies had by then become in part hereditary. Satraps felt cut off from the imperial core of government and thought that they could rule independently of the Great King. Over the course of a decade from 368 BCE some of the western satraps, from Egypt to Bithynia and from Caria to Syria, formed a coalition against the central government and even minted their own coins. The entire revolt, if it deserves so dramatic a title, was suppressed when Artaxerxes sent his troops into Anatolia; some of the satraps were pardoned and allowed to return to their satrapies and others paid with their lives – more as exemplars to others than as victims of the king's fury. Artaxerxes was not threatened by the insurrection. The inner vigour of the empire's administration was, perhaps, weakened by Artaxerxes' inefficiency, and if many of his troubles came to a favourable end, it was due to such able people around him as Tissaphernes and, not least, his mother, Parysatis.

At the close of Cyrus' rebellion, Tissaphernes had been honoured for his loyalty to the crown, allowed to marry the king's daughter, and reappointed as satrap of Lydia. But he could not escape the fate that hounded him: a courtier named Tithraustes invited Tissaphernes to a dinner in his honour, to be held at Colossae, one of the most celebrated cities of southern Anatolia. Upon arrival, Tissaphernes was met by Ariaeus, who had fought alongside Cyrus at Cunaxa, and was murdered. The Greek historian Polyaenus provided the details:

> Tissaphernes did not suspect that anything was being plotted against him, so he left his camp at Sardis and, accompanied by a regiment of three hundred Arcadians and Milesians, he went immediately to Ariaeus. On arrival, he took off his sword to have a bath. Ariaeus with his servants seized him. They bound him in a covered wagon to transport him and handed him over to Tithraustes. He conveyed him secretly to Celaenae, where he cut off his head and sent it to the king. The king sent it to his mother, Parysatis, who was especially keen to punish Tissaphernes for Cyrus' death.

The order to have Tissaphernes killed undoubtedly came from Parysatis, whose hatred of the man who had destroyed her Cyrus never abated, and whose reach was long. Tissaphernes had been the most loyal of Artaxerxes' servants, a nobleman of great honour and renown who, sadly, through his long service to the crown, made a deadly enemy of Parysatis. Artaxerxes made no move to protect the man who had saved his throne, and the great Tissaphernes died as one more victim of Parysatis' vendetta on the house of Hydarnes.

*

Over the years, as the banquets, hunts, and royal audiences carried on in a timeless circle, a few unexpected and surprising events occurred. One such was when Teridates the eunuch died quite unexpectedly, but naturally. As Artaxerxes' favourite eunuch, Teridates had been lavishly praised as the most beautiful youth in Asia and was reckoned to be the prettiest of all the young castrati at court. The king was said to have loved him passionately – and although our sources are remarkably silent about sexual practices in ancient Persia (quite prudishly so, in fact), it is highly likely that male-to-male sex was a feature of life. Pretty castrated boys were probably taken as catamites by elite men.

Artaxerxes was truly grieved at Teridates' death, and he declared a period of mourning throughout the court, which everyone sought to obey. None of the courtiers dared to approach him and comfort him, for they believed his grief was too painful, but after three days of hesitation the concubine Aspasia, wearing dark mourning garments, approached the king and stood weeping in his presence, her eyes cast on the ground. 'I come, O King', she whispered, 'to comfort your grief and affliction, if you so please; otherwise, I shall go back to my chamber.' The king was happy to know of the attention she showed him and commanded that Aspasia should retire to her room and wait his coming. A short time later he arrived at Aspasia's chamber carrying in his arms the clothes which had once belonged to Teridates. He instructed her to put them on. Dressed in the eunuch's garments, Aspasia aroused his desire and he had sex with her as she was, still dressed in the boy's clothes. Afterwards the king demanded that she always wear those clothes in his presence, at least until his grief had lifted. And so, more than all his other women, even Stateira, it was Aspasia of Phocis, his brother's great love, who comforted Artaxerxes and relieved his sorrow. The Teridates–Aspasia story must rank among the earliest examples of what Sigmund Freud called *Übertragung* – 'transference' – known to history.

*

As the years passed, Parysatis and Stateira had operated a strange *Entente Cordiale* – mainly by avoiding one another. When they did meet, at official functions, the rival queens demonstrated civility and respect, with Stateira always offering a low *proskynesis* to her mother-in-law, as was demanded by court protocol. For her part, Parysatis always raised her daughter-in-law from her knees and kissed her on the cheeks, as too was expected from the observance of etiquette. The Cold War seemed to thaw and Artaxerxes was pleased, and more than a little relieved, to see his mother and his chief wife begin to engage in civilities – pleasantries, even. After their former suspicion, and given their differences, they nonetheless began to frequent the same places again and to dine together. Their mutual fear and caution nevertheless led them to eat the same food as each other, always served on the same dishes, for both women were aware of the threat of being poisoned.

It must be conceded that poisonings were a familiar hazard at the Persian court, so regular were they in fact as to be common-place. No one doubted the efficacy of a well-conceived, elegant poisoning, and foreign visitors to Persia openly noted, almost with a frisson of wonder, how troublesome courtiers died at the hands of skilled poisoners: 'nowhere are so many men killed or ruined because of poisonous drugs than at the court', Xenophon was keen to stress. For the Persians, the use of poison was akin to the composition of fine poetry; it was a court art of the highest sophistication. So it is significant that we know that the office of royal food-taster functioned prominently at the Persian court; his was a privileged if perilous job, requiring him to enter the royal kitchen as food was being prepared, to chew and swallow a mouthful of it from every dish, to wait for any effects to take their toll, and to (hopefully) give his consent and have the dish set before the king. Working in conjunction with the royal food-taster was the royal cup-bearer, another prestigious office held only by the monarch's most trusted courtiers, such as the Hebrew eunuch Nehemiah, who performed that duty for Artaxerxes I (it was Nehemiah's routine proximity to the king as his cup-bearer which later saw him rise to power as a governor of Judah). The royal cup-bearer was charged with managing all of the court's wine-pourers and tasters, although he alone poured the king's wine into the royal cup and tasted the monarch's drink, drawn off in a silver ladle to check that it was poison-free.

The threat of poison might be a reason why the Great King drank a wine unique to him – a fine Chalybonian vintage, imported from Syria – as well as chilled water expressly drawn from the crystal-clear Choaspes River in Elam, which was stored within the king's household in special bronze pots.

But for every courtier who worked at preventing a death by poison, another plotted its use. Professional poisoners were known and their lucrative skills as pharmacists and herbalists could be bought and paid for; they could whip up a batch of something to cause a quick and painless end, or a vial of something longer-lasting, painful yet limb-numbing. There was even a specific death sentence reserved for individuals convicted of poisoning: 'there is a broad stone on which they place the poisoners' heads and with another stone they pound and crush until their face and head are mashed to a pulp.' The existence of this messy death torture implies that the threat of poison was taken very seriously.

Of course, untouchable by any law, Parysatis had a reputation for being a crafty exponent of this most deadly of courtly arts; she had, after all, killed Terituchmes' son with poison. There were probably many more victims like him. After all, Ctesias also reports that the Queen Mother and the king were the only two people in the empire to have access to an exclusive and rare Indian poison kept within the palace for the purpose of causing a swift death. Its chief ingredient, it seems, was bird dung:

> There is a species of very small Indian birds which build their nests both within the high rocks and also the so-called 'soft cliffs'. The little bird is the size of a partridge egg and its colour is orange. If someone should swallow a speck of its dung placed in a drink, he would die by the evening. The death is like sleep – very agreeable and free of pain – the sort the poets like to call 'limb-relaxing' and 'easy'. The Indians go to enormous lengths to get it and include this substance among their most precious tribute for the Persian king, who receives it as a gift revered above all others. No one else in Persia owns this substance except the king himself and his mother.

As all practised poisoners knew, the same draft mixed with different ingredients could also act as a remedy to poisoning, and could even serve as a medicine or healing balm. Thus, notes Ctesias, the king and Queen Mother 'hoard the Indian poison as a remedy and antidote for incurable illness – should they contract one'. To be on the safe side, they stockpiled precious antidotes against all known poisons.

And so it was with a skilled use of poison that Parysatis enacted her revenge on Stateira. The reports we have of how the murder was brought to pass look like a plot from a fairy tale – the Snow White motif of the wicked old queen and the loveable ingénue – but the amount of detail which has been preserved in their retelling by Ctesias and others convinces that Parysatis' plot against Stateira resulted in cold-blooded murder, having been expertly planned and executed with genuine panache.

It was in the Queen Mother's finely furnished apartment at the heart of the harem at Susa (the court having resettled at Artaxerxes' new riverside palace for the winter) that the denouement of the queens' long and intertwined story was played out. Parysatis invited Stateira to an informal dinner to confirm their new-found harmony. Stateira, who always took extreme care to avoid confrontational situations, approached the apartment with caution, but she knew too that propriety demanded that she respond favourably to an invitation from the Queen Mother and that, if she pulled off a successful visit to those hallowed inner chambers, then she would earn the gratitude of her husband, the king. It was a risk worth taking.

What was on the menu that night? We know something of Persian elite eating habits. Herodotus noted that the Persians 'eat only a few main dishes, but they frequently consume an assortment of nibbles – but these are not served together at one time but are distributed randomly throughout the course of the meal', and Xenophon confirms the Persian fondness for 'fancy side dishes and all sorts of sauces and meats'. These mezze dishes were rounded off with syrupy and milky desserts, which were particular favourites of the sweet-toothed Persians. There is no doubt that specialist cuisiniers produced such *amuse-bouches* to satisfy the two queens as they reclined together on their couches to dine. We know little of the recipes concocted by the royal chefs. One text is useful in providing us with knowledge about the ingredients which were used: the *Stratagems of Polyaenus* record an inscribed inventory, purportedly found by Alexander of Macedon, of the foodstuffs required for feeding the Great King and his household on a daily basis. There was cardamom, mustard seed, garlic, parsley, cumin, anise flowers, coriander, melon seed; pickled capers; sesame oil, sweet almond oil, vinegar; mutton and lamb, gazelle meat, horse meat, geese, turtle doves; fresh milk, sour milk sweetened with whey; sweet wine; cream with cinnamon; palm wine and grape wine, honey, and saffron rice. Occasionally the royal chefs outdid themselves with some particularly rich haute cuisine, such as a delicately roasted rare pigeon-sized bird which the Persians loved and called a *rhyntaces*. Since every part of it could be eaten (because it was entirely full of fat inside), they claimed that the bird fed only on air and dew.

It was this demi-magical *plat-unique* that was set before Stateira on that fateful evening in Susa. Queen Parysatis ordered her handmaid, Gigis, to cut the precious roast bird in two with a small knife. This had been smeared with poison on one side, and Gigis wiped the poison off on just one part of the bird, then handed the undefiled, clean part to Parysatis who put it in her mouth and swallowed it. The poisoned half was given to Stateira, who, unsuspectingly, ate the delicate meat.

It was later that night, back in her own bedchamber, that Stateira died, writhing in convulsions of pain. Parysatis had bided her time, carefully and purposefully choosing a poison that would cause Stateira a leisurely and wretched death so that she would be fully conscious of the fate that had befallen her. As she lay dying, almost paralysed from the poison's toxins, Stateira managed to make her suspicions about his mother known to the king, who was already all too aware of Parysatis' implacability.

Artaxerxes immediately set out in search of his mother's servants and attendants at table, arrested them and tortured them. Gigis was quickly given sanctuary by Parysatis, who would not surrender her when the king asked, but after several weeks sequestered in the royal harem, Gigis begged leave to go home so that she might attend her family. The king got wind of this, set an ambush, seized her, and condemned her to death. Like all others executed for poisoning, Gigis' face and skull were crushed to a jelly.

Artaxerxes took the unprecedented step of dismissing his mother from court and sent her into exile in Babylonia, vowing that while she resided there, he would not see Babylon again. Parysatis' shame, played out in front of all the court, was overwhelming: what mother had ever been turned out of doors by her own son? Why was she being victimised and treated with such ignominy? What had she done to deserve such dishonour? Parysatis' Babylonian exile is the only account we have of a queen being ostracised from court. Not that the Queen Mother's exile would be particularly arduous, for Parysatis had family lands in Babylonia (her concubine mother, after all, was from Babylon) and Darius II had loaded her with estates and lands throughout that province. At Nippur in Babylonia we know there were fields and gardens belonging to Parysatis. Recently it was shown that she owned other land near Babylon, and we can follow her fortunes through the archives of the Murashu Brothers for about thirty years. The Murashu Brothers were in charge of the daily administration of the queen's lands and settled the accounts with her representative, a Jew named Mattanya, 'the servant of Ea-bullissu, the employee of Parysatis'. On his journey home after Cunaxa in 401 BCE, Xenophon travelled through 'the villages of Parysatis, the mother of Cyrus the Younger and of the king'. These lands were on the Tigris near Ashur in northern Iraq, so she had estates there also. Parysatis' affluence became proverbial throughout the empire, evidence of this powerful woman's economic independence and acumen.

The king's anger after the murder of Stateira did not last; after he exiled Parysatis to Babylon, Ctesias notes that he 'was reconciled to her, and sent for her, being assured that she had wisdom and courage fit for royal power'. In fact, after the elimination of her daughter-in-law, Parysatis' political influence, which had been far from negligible, grew considerably: 'She obtained great power with Artaxerxes, and was gratified in all her requests', Ctesias

noted, and she was quick to use her influence to grant prerogatives to those who showed their loyalty to the king. And this is
the key to understanding Parysatis' nature: happily accepting the
lurid anecdotes spun around her, historians have portrayed her as
a baleful figure who corrupted the royal blood and hastened the
degeneration of the royal house and the failure of its empire, but
they misunderstand her purpose, because, like other Achaemenid
matriarchs, Parysatis' drive was for the security of the dynasty.
When her husband, Darius II, was battling his way to the throne,
the marriage alliances he made between their son Arsicas (Artaxerxes II) and Stateira of the powerful Hydarnes clan and between
her brother, Terituchmes, and Amestris II were a pragmatic way for
him to increase his power and prestige. But once he was securely
established as Great King, Darius II had less incentive to seek out
(or even maintain) inter-dynastic marriages. After all, both he and
Parysatis, as half-sibling spouses, carried the blood of Artaxerxes I
in their veins, which gave them all the authority they required
in the familial hierarchy; to expand the pool of successors too
much through marriage into other noble clans could ultimately
weaken the Achaemenid hold on the empire. This is why, in the
final decades of his life, Artaxerxes II married two of his daughters,
Atossa II and Amestris III (both named, appropriately, after dynastic
greats). Endogamous marriage of this kind was not an atrocious
perversion, as most Greeks saw it, but a dynastically driven precau-
tion against imperial blood dilution.

With her brother Tissaphernes already slain, Stateira's death
meant that the entire clan of Hydarnes had been eliminated once
and for all, and with her poison blade Parysatis had ensured that
the control of the empire was in no danger of being sidetracked to
a rival family. The powerful Achaemenid women – Atossa, Amestris,
and Parysatis – played the part of dynastic guard dogs, and although
they did indeed maim, hurt, or destroy those who crossed them, it
was because they were protecting the household of the monarch
whose bloodline they vigilantly sought to keep pure.

We do not know when Parysatis died, but she disappears from
the records shortly after having engineered her son's marriage to

her granddaughters. She must have been around ninety years old. She was one of the great women of ancient history who achieved prominence while living in the shadow of men, yet excelled in controlling them all. She served the empire as a symbol of the loyal wife and devoted mother, yet behind the scenes at the imperial court she spent much of her adult life plotting Cyrus' future as heir to Darius II's throne whether he wanted it or not, and, following his death at Cunaxa, she thereafter worked assiduously at being Artaxerxes' minister-in-chief. Parysatis' tragedy lay in the fact that the Persian imperial system afforded no official space to women of her ability, as her ancestresses had known. Her frustration at the limits of her power was palpable. She dominated court life for more than sixty years, and if no tears were wept openly at her passing, the empire must have acknowledged that with the death of such a formidably great lady, an era had come to its end.

21

Violent Delights Have Violent Ends

Artaxerxes II's final years were strewn with problems, as the royal family began to buckle under its own weight. Competition, rivalry, and feuding marked the finale of his forty-six-year reign. Stateira had given Artaxerxes three sons, Dareius (the eldest), Ariaspes, and Ochus (the youngest), but he had at least another 150 sons by other consorts and concubines. Many daughters were born to him also, two of whom he had married – these were symbolic marital unions which stressed the 'exclusivity' of the dynasty.

Complications had started for Artaxerxes shortly before Parysatis' death around 385 BCE when he decided to reward several of his nobles for loyal service to the crown by drawing them closer into the royal house through marriage alliances. Princess Apame was given in marriage to the nobleman Pharnabazus; Princess Rhodogyne to the courtier Orontes; and Princess Amestris III was due to be wed to the great satrap Tiribazus (ruler of western Armenia and, later, Lydia), a man who stood higher than any other in the royal favour. However, shortly before the wedding, Artaxerxes reneged on the pledge and married Amestris himself. Tiribazus was humiliated and angered at the snub, and so Artaxerxes arranged that a younger daughter, Atossa II, should marry the satrap instead. Tiribazus was satisfied until, once again, the king broke his promise and married that girl too. The second humiliation, more stinging than the first, made Tiribazus an implacable enemy to Artaxerxes. He often spoke out against the king and openly criticised his character. When he fell from favour, he was neither humble nor quiet, but ferociously and incessantly attacked Artaxerxes' rulership.

Of his three sons by Stateira, Artaxerxes chose the fifty-year-old Dareius – his firstborn – as his heir. His youngest son, Ochus, who was known for his violent temper and impatience, was not content with the role of a royal also-ran and, having many adherents at court, hoped to win over his father and get himself appointed as crown prince. He was aided and abetted by his sister-cum-step-mother, Atossa II, after promising to make her his consort following the death of their father (in fact, a rumour circulated around the court that even while Artaxerxes lived, Ochus was Atossa's lover). She used her influence with Artaxerxes to poison the king's ear against Dareius and to promote the interests of Ochus.

According to royal custom, the individual appointed to the royal succession might ask a request of the king, who was constrained to grant it, if it was within his power. Accordingly, Dareius requested Aspasia, the former concubine of Cyrus the Younger and, latterly, of Artaxerxes II himself, as a concubine. No longer in the first flush of youth, Aspasia, although still beautiful, was beyond the age of childbearing but that did not perturb Dareius. Begetting more children was not his aim (he already had adult sons and daughters by his wives and concubines). Aspasia personified the transference of power; her body had long been an effective symbol of the conveyance of imperial authority, passed as she had been from one Achaemenid prince to another, and the woman herself had become a powerful totem of rulership – whoever owned Aspasia had the power of rulership too. By incorporating Aspasia into his own harem, Dareius would demonstrate that he was, without doubt, Persia's next king. His request for Aspasia was a clear message to his ambitious brother, telling him that he should back off.

At first, albeit reluctantly, Artaxerxes agreed to hand over the concubine to his heir, but afterwards – typically – he changed his mind and would not let her go. Not much later, Artaxerxes appointed Aspasia a priestess of Anahita in Ecbatana, effectively taking her away from Dareius once and for all. The prince's resentment towards the king knew no bounds and Dareius began to take counsel from Tiribazus, who encouraged him to stand up to Artaxerxes and to assert his authority as crown prince, especially now that his brother Ochus was insinuating himself into affairs of state by way of the harem. Besides, Artaxerxes was proving to be fickle and insincere. Dareius had already been declared the next king, Tiribazus reiterated, and therefore it was his right to mount the throne unhindered. Together they conspired to kill Artaxerxes, expecting that many courtiers would be ready to follow them, including at least fifty of Artaxerxes' many sons.

Witnessing the schism between the king and the crown prince, Ochus was sanguine in the hopes he held for the future, although Atossa inspired him to act quickly and decisively. Ochus alerted his father to the plot being hatched between Dareius and Tiribazus, although he used a eunuch as a go-between. Dareius, together with his sons, was led before Artaxerxes. The king instructed the royal judges to try Dareius and to bring the final verdict to him. None of the courtiers nor any of Artaxerxes' sons stepped in to help the prince when, unanimous in their decision, the judges pronounced Dareius guilty of high treason and ordered his execution. On hearing the verdict, Artaxerxes had Dareius brought to him. The prince fell prostrate before his father, humbly begging his pardon, but instead of granting clemency, Artaxerxes grabbed Dareius by the hair and, bringing his face to the ground with one hand, cut through his neck with a knife and killed him. Walking out into the sunshine of one of the palace courtyards, the Great King lifted his bloodstained hands in worship, saying, 'Depart in peace, you Persians, and declare to your fellow subjects how the mighty Ahuramazda has dealt out vengeance to the contrivers of the Lie over the Truth.' All of Dareius' sons, except for one infant, were executed too. Once again, the Achaemenid dynasty had experienced a failure of its procedures. Artaxerxes II had been careful in designating an heir – and in this he had followed the model of his predecessors – but ultimately, as had happened before, the status and institution of crown prince were not robust enough to battle and withstand opposition. The great failing of the Achaemenids was their terminal inability to deal with royal succession and to prepare for the orderly transfer of power from one ruler to another.

Ochus had scored a silent victory over Dareius, but he was still fearful of his older brother Ariaspes' influence on the king. Ariaspes was quiet, unassuming, and nervous, and yet he was popular with the Persians, many of whom thought him worthy to be their king. Artaxerxes thought highly of him too, and in all probability Ariaspes was the favourite of his many children. Another of the king's sons, Arsames, born of a concubine mother, was thought to be wise and just, and was also very close to his father, who valued his intellect – a fact that had not passed Ochus by. Accordingly, he plotted against both men. Ochus, together with a cohort of eunuchs, began a campaign to terrorise poor, paranoid Ariaspes, implying that Artaxerxes suspected him of being an accomplice in Dareius' plot and that it was only a matter of time before the king would have him arrested, tortured, and killed. Despairing of his future, the edgy and neurotic Ariaspes committed suicide. But instead of switching his affections to Ochus, the last surviving son of Stateira, Artaxerxes II declared his intention to make Arsames the crown prince. Arsames was as good as dead. Within months, Ochus had overseen the prince's murder. Finally, after years of plotting, and by eventually eliminating all his key rivals, Ochus was appointed as Artaxerxes' heir, very shortly before the old king died at the age of eighty-six. It was December 359 BCE. He had been renowned for being a gentle ruler, 'a friend to his subjects', as Plutarch put it, plaintively.

Ochus took the throne name Artaxerxes III, thereby expressing his filial piety. During his investiture at Pasargadae, the Magi prophesised that his reign would see bounteous harvests but much bloodshed. Barely had they spoken their omens when part of the prophecy was fulfilled – the new Artaxerxes commanded the execution of all of his nearest kin in order to prevent any further conspiracies. In one day alone, eighty of his brothers were killed. On another day, more than a hundred Achaemenid princes – young and old – were herded into an empty courtyard and massacred in a hail of arrows. Atossa, the calculating sister who had worked so hard at putting Ochus into favour with the late king, was not made queen. She was buried alive on the instructions of her brother-lover. Sadly, we know little of Artaxerxes III's private life besides the facts that he was married to a niece, a daughter of one of his sisters (possibly of the murdered Atossa II), and to a daughter of Oxathres, son of Arsames, the satrap of Susa (Oxathres was brother to the future Darius III). Both of Artaxerxes' consorts remain nameless.

*

Artaxerxes III 'outstripped all in cruelty and bloodlust', said Plutarch. For twenty-one years (359–338 BCE), this man of immovable iron will ruled the Persian empire with brute force. He held the reins of government firmly in his fists and he put his full energy into restoring the empire, consolidating a centralised government, and returning Persia to its former glory. Upon his accession, immediately, the new king crushed rebellions which blew up in Syria and Asia Minor, and he annihilated the tribe of the Cadusians, who had been carrying out smash-and-grab raids in north-western Iran. It was a man named Artashiyāta (Old Persian, 'happy in truth'; known to the Greeks as Codomannus) who had distinguished himself in suppressing the Cadusians, for which Artaxerxes granted him the governance of the satrapy of Armenia.

To quash the power of the trouble-making satraps of Asia Minor, Artaxerxes ordered the disbanding of mercenary troops and outlawed the governors from raising military forces thereafter. By and large the satraps kowtowed to the imperial edict, although Artabazus, who oversaw Phrygia and commanded all of the Persian troops in Asia Minor, refused to comply and rose in revolt against Artaxerxes, aided in this enterprise by Orontes, governor of Mysia. In 352 BCE they were soundly beaten and punished. However, a bigger threat to Artaxerxes appeared in 349 BCE, when the Phoenician cities, supported by the Egyptians, broke out in revolt against Persia. In Sidon, the centre of the mutiny, rebels attacked and destroyed the satrapal palace and the beautiful garden that was so loved by the governor; they cut down trees, burned stocks of fodder intended for the Persian cavalry, and destroyed walls and gateways. In 346 BCE, Egypt's pharaoh, Nectanebo II, sent 4,000 Greek mercenaries to Sidon to assist with the revolt, and they successfully defeated two Persian attacks led by Belesys, the satrap of Across-the-River, and the

Cilician satrap, Mazaeus. The insurgency quickly spread into Judah and Syria and on to the island of Cyprus, where nine Cypriot kings united with Phoenicia to end the Persian occupation.

Enough was enough. In 345 BCE, Artaxerxes III took matters into his own hands, seized command of the Persian forces (some 30,000 infantry, 30,000 cavalry, and 300 triremes), and marched on Sidon. The Sidonians put up a brave fight but they were ultimately betrayed by their own leader, Tennes, who allowed the Persians to enter the city without opposition. Artaxerxes decided to chastise Sidon in the most brutal way and to make an example of the city for other people who thought to slough off Persian rule. Some 40,000 men, women, and children were killed as the city was burned to the ground and its treasuries were plundered. The surviving part of the population was sold into slavery and transported into Babylonia and Elam.

Unsurprisingly, the other Phoenician cities capitulated to Artaxerxes and ended their resistance and the city states of Phoenicia were incorporated into the satrapy of Cilicia and were put under the control of Mazaeus, who was commanded to be brutal in his governance of the rebellious Phoenicians. As for the Jews who had risen against the king in Judah, they were deported to Hycarnia on the Caspian Sea, where they were still found to be dwelling in the fifth century CE. As for Cyprus, its quest for independence was dealt a death blow when Artaxerxes commissioned Idrieus, prince of Caria, to reduce the island to dust; the Cypriot rulers paid a heavy price for their moment in the sun.

In the winter of 343 BCE an angry but resolute Artaxerxes marched off from Persia to Egypt, determined to bring it back under Persian control. Pharaoh Nectanebo, who had assembled an army of 60,000 Egyptians and 20,000 Greek mercenaries, marched to meet the Persians at the border city of Pelusium, in the far east of the Nile Delta. As Artaxerxes approached Egypt, he split his army of 330,000 Persians and 14,000 Greeks into separate branches, each under the command of a Persian and a Greek who, arriving at Pelusium, quickly out-manoeuvred the Egyptian forces, forcing Nectanebo to flee to Memphis, where he took cover. The Persians advanced rapidly into the Delta and stormed and destroyed numerous towns and villages across Lower Egypt as they advanced towards Memphis. After Nectanebo fled the country and sought refuge in Ethiopia, Artaxerxes' troops completely routed the Egyptians and occupied the whole of Lower Egypt. The Upper Egyptians quickly submitted to Artaxerxes, but neither they nor their Lower Egyptian neighbours were spared Artaxerxes' implacable wrath, as towns and temples were looted and wrecked, fortresses were reduced to rubble, and crops were slashed and burned. The Demotic Chronicle recorded the lamentations of the Egyptian people:

> Our ponds and islands are filled with weeping; the houses of the Egyptians will be bereft of people to dwell in them; one will say of this time, 'the Persians will bring them to ruination; they will take away their houses and dwell therein'.

One Egyptian nobleman left a short but dynamic account of Artaxerxes' invasion on a stele dedicated to the god Herishef, the principal deity of Heracleopolis, whom the author credits with saving his life at the time when the Persian troops and Greek mercenaries stormed Egypt: 'They slew a million at my side', he declared, adding with incredulity, 'yet no one raised his arm against me.' As for Egypt's Jewish colonies, they were largely disbanded and the populations were sent either to Babylon or to the Caspian Sea, the same location to which the Jews of Phoenicia had earlier been sent.

Artaxerxes is said to have continued his reign of terror in Egypt with acts of sacrilege. He is said to have slaughtered the Apis Bull and feasted on its roasted flesh, executed Egyptian priests, and contaminated temples. Such anecdotes are typical of anti-Persian spin, of course, and Cambyses II had been framed in a similar context by Egyptian propagandists. Yet while it is unlikely that the Apis Bull was killed by Artaxerxes III (let alone eaten), we must concede that the reinvasion of Egypt, and its subsequent re-Persianisation, was carried out with a harsher brutality than had been witnessed under Cambyses. After sixty years of independence, Egypt was back in the Persian empire, and the year 342 BCE therefore marks the 'Second

Persian Period' in Egypt and the founding of the Thirty-First Dynasty. The submission of renegade Egypt was Artaxerxes' greatest achievement, for the rich resources of the land of the Nile were once again in Persian possession and the trade routes of the Red Sea could function again.

Before he left Egypt, Artaxerxes III saw the old statue of Udjahorresnet, the Egyptian official who had served Cambyses and Darius I so loyally. It was somewhat dusty and battered, and Artaxerxes ordered its restoration. He left an inscription on the statue, proclaiming that 'All you dignitaries, all you scholars, I have caused the name of the chief physician Udjahorresnet to live, who has completed 177 years after his time, because I found his statue while it was in a state of decay.' Why Artaxerxes undertook the statue's restoration is uncertain, but it suggests that he wanted to revive the honours bestowed on old Udjahorresnet, an important supporter of the Persians in Egypt, an efficacious and energetic collaborator.

In 344 BCE, Artaxerxes departed from a submissive Egypt stunned by its forced reintegration into the Persian empire and forlorn at its loss of self-rule, and returned to Persia. He inaugurated Pherendates as the new Egyptian satrap and commissioned Mentor of Rhodes, who had distinguished himself at the Battle of Pelusium, as the commander-in-chief of the Persian forces in Egypt and western Asia Minor. But Egypt was not a happy place and Pherendates was unable to completely quell the growing unrest in the country. Around 340 BCE, an Egyptian bureaucrat named Petosiris, a priest of Thoth at Hermopolis, and in the service of the gods Sakhmet, Khnum, Amen-Re, and Hathor, recorded his autobiography in his own tomb in the necropolis at Tuna el-Gebel. He prided himself on having restored the fortunes of the temples in which he served, but lamented the overall state of Egypt, which he saw as lawless and chaotic:

> I spent seven years as a steward of the temple of Thoth although a foreign king [i.e. Artaxerxes III] was in full control of the land. Battles were fought in the centre of Egypt. The

south was in uproar; the north in revolt. The people travelled in fear . . . In the temples no work was done because the foreigners had come and invaded Egypt.

Artaxerxes III had fulfilled his ambition of restoring Persia's old borders and reuniting the empire under strong military leadership. Indeed, it seemed that the old days had returned and that the empire was being taken back to the glorious time of Darius the Great. In fact, Artaxerxes pushed this concept forward in a series of propagandistic inscriptions at Persepolis which – mainly through an archaising use of vocabulary and syntax – demonstrated his conscientious use of the imperial past. An inscription he had placed on a staircase at Persepolis, for instance, used the same phraseology Darius I had used on the façade of his tomb at Naqsh-i Rustam, although Artaxerxes' text incorporated the name of the god Mithra, who had grown in status and visibility since the reign of Artaxerxes I:

A great god is Ahuramazda, who created this earth, who created yonder heaven, who created happiness for man, who made Artaxerxes king. One king for many, one leader of many.

The Great King Artaxerxes, the King of Kings, the King of Countries, the King of this Earth, says: I am the son of King Artaxerxes [II]. Artaxerxes was the son of King Darius [II]. Darius was the son of King Artaxerxes [I]. Artaxerxes was the son of King Xerxes. Xerxes was the son of King Darius [the Great]. Darius was the son of a man named Hystaspes. Hystaspes was a son of a man named Arsames, the Achaemenid.

King Artaxerxes says: This stone staircase was built by me in my reign. King Artaxerxes says: May Ahuramazda and the god Mithra preserve me, my country, and what has been built by me (A^3Pa).

Most importantly, the inscription shows how Artaxerxes confidently placed himself in the line of the Achaemenid kings, beginning with Darius I, and it is worth noting that some 170 years after Darius seized the throne, the dynasty's (bogus) relationship to the Teispids, the house of Cyrus the Great, had completely ceased to matter.

*

Not even a strongman like Artaxerxes III could avoid the snares and traps of the court. As he grew older and appeared to weaken in body and mind, the monarch was gradually regarded as a suitable target for elimination by those with a taste for power; it was only a matter of time before he was dispatched. A Babylonian solar eclipse tablet dated to August/September 338 BCE is the most secure attestation we have of Artaxerxes' death, recording that in the 'Month [of] Ululu, Umakush [i.e. Artaxerxes III] went to his fate; Arshu, his son, sat on the throne.' Yet this simple statement of fact belies yet another episode of catastrophic dynastic rupture, for Artaxerxes was the victim of a bold plot hatched by a high-ranking court eunuch named Bagoas, a veritable creature of the court, born to corruption, whose ambitions were for the very highest office of state. He murdered the king.

Bagoas had made a name for himself with the king during the reconquest of Egypt when, alongside Mentor of Rhodes, he commanded the main body of the Persian army and Greek mercenaries at the Battle of Pelusium. Later, at the sack of the Egyptian city of Bubastis, Bagoas was taken prisoner, but was rescued by Mentor, and was later sent by Artaxerxes to put the 'upper satrapies' (as they were known) of the eastern part of the Persian empire in order, giving him supreme power over those lands. His friendship with Artaxerxes helped make Bagoas fabulously wealthy, and it is known that he owned famous gardens near Babylon and a palace of his own in Susa. And yet in spite of the authority and affluence he enjoyed through Artaxerxes' kindness, Bagoas yearned for more. He wanted to rule. He resolved that Artaxerxes should die. The eunuch's chosen weapon was poison, which was applied liberally in one deadly draught to the king's wine. The old man perished slowly and agonisingly. His throat contracted, then closed, and within minutes the Conqueror of Egypt asphyxiated and died.

Recognising that, as a castrato, he himself could never be king, Bagoas installed one of Artaxerxes' sons on the throne, and began to rule through him. Aged around thirty, and with children of his own, Prince Arshu was perfectly malleable and gave no trouble to Bagoas, who took on the role of the empire's chief administrator, holding royal audiences, granting petitions, and generally masterminding the governance of the empire. Arshu played out the ceremonial side of kingship, taking the throne name Artaxerxes IV, but was kept isolated from any genuine power. Two years into his reign, however, Arshu began to itch for more substantial royal duties, having ascertained that the role of king had the potential to afford him genuine authority, and he started to marginalise Bagoas from power by limiting his control over the royal council and reining in the tasks under his jurisdiction. Late in the second year of his reign, in the summer of 336 BCE, Arshu was assassinated at the hand of the very disgruntled Bagoas. For good measure, Arshu's wives, sons, and daughters were slain too. The Babylonian Dynastic Prophecy, a scrappy Akkadian cuneiform text, full of lacunae, which purports to be an oracle foretelling the future (although it was written after the events it describes), is the sole surviving Near Eastern evidence for the murder of Artaxerxes IV. It records:

> [. . .] kings [. . .] which his father . . . [. . .]. For three years he will exercise the kingship. That king will be murdered by a eunuch.

The prejudiced Greek authors (such as the historians Aelian and Plutarch), who told of the overthrow and murder of Arshu and other Achaemenid kings, employed the *topos* of the wicked eunuch to demonstrate the weaknesses of the last Achaemenids. But the fact that we have in the Babylonian cuneiform tablets unbiased and direct acknowledgement of the murder of kings, forces us to take the matter seriously. Rather than continuing to indulge the Orientalist fantasy of eunuch 'puppet-masters', it is time to acknowledge that the courts of absolute monarchs operated under strains and pressures which often led to rebellion and, sometimes, to murder. After all, physical proximity to the Achaemenid kings gave eunuchs an unrivalled opportunity to act as assassins. Rivalry was endemic at the Achaemenid court and, for all their beauty, royal palaces, as we have seen, were dangerous places. A 'lion pit' is how one Assyrian cuneiform text labelled the court with its antagonistic (sometimes vicious) inhabitants, and a set of old Sumerian proverbs dating to at least 2,900 BCE demonstrates how ancient that notion was:

> A palace is a huge river; its interior is a goring ox . . . A palace is a slippery place where one slithers. If you say, 'Let me go home!', just watch your step for a palace . . . is a wasteland. As a freeborn man cannot avoid corvée work, a princess cannot avoid this whorehouse.

The hub of dynastic and political life, the Achaemenid court was a stage on which the games of intrigue, faction, and revenge were played out with astonishing regularity. The tension of court politicking permeated every aspect of the royal household, and few individuals were untouched by some form of intrigue. Court nobility was highly susceptible to political machinations and personal rivalries, and the book of Esther demonstrates this clearly, based as it is on a story of destructive intrigue. Of course, none of this was unique to Persia, for court societies of all periods and all places have suffered from the strain of imposing and then maintaining power. We should be disposed to take seriously stories of the irrational caprice and malicious cruelty of Persian kings, queens, and courtiers. Nothing is reported of Xerxes, Artaxerxes III, Bagoas, or Parysatis which does not find ready parallels in well-attested information about Henry VIII, Ivan IV (the Terrible), or Wu Zetian, the only ruling female 'emperor' of China, and, allowing for some differences of institutions, the Persian court was subject to the same kind of pressures which have afflicted the courts of absolute monarchs down to the time of Stalin or Putin.

Having noted the murder of Artaxerxes IV, the Babylonian Dynastic Prophecy went on to record that:

> A rebel prince [...] will attack and [seize] the throne. For five years he will exercise kingship.

Who was this 'rebel prince'? There can only be one contender –
Artashiyāta, the champion warrior who had been rewarded for his
valour with the satrapy of Armenia after winning victory in Artaxerxes III's wars against the Cadusians. Later he was made governor
of Pārs. A grandson of Darius II, Artashiyāta was an Achaemenid
prince by blood – although from a collateral branch of the imperial family – and his father, Arsames, had served the throne in his
role as satrap of Susa, taking as one of his wives a high-ranking
noblewoman named Sisygambis, herself of the Achaemenid clan,
perhaps a cousin of Artaxerxes III. After his Cadusian victory, which
made him famous throughout the empire for his heroism and his
willingness to fight in single combat, Artashiyāta had been put in
charge of the administration of Persepolis and Pārs, perhaps the
same job that was ascribed to the great Parnakka in the Persepolis
Fortification tablets back in Darius the Great's day. About 340 BCE,
he married the royal princess Stateira II, his cousin, who gave him
one son, Ochus; he also fathered three daughters on other wives or
concubines.

Following the death of Artaxerxes IV, Bagoas, who had already
murdered two kings, now welcomed prince Artashiyāta to the
throne, installing him as Great King. Bagoas did this, no doubt,
because (Greek sources note) Artashiyāta's reputation for courage
in battle made him acceptable to the Persian *khāns* and nobles,
and his blood connection to the royal family and the memory of
Artaxerxes III's goodwill towards him must also have contributed
to their acceptance. Bagoas must have reckoned that as an outsider
to the intricacies of royal society, Artashiyāta would have no option
but to rely on him for advice and support, although it must be said
that there seems to have been no great empathy on the prince's part
towards the eunuch. When, as was bound to happen, Artashiyāta
started to assume full control of his new-found royal status, Bagoas
panicked and audaciously attempted to take Artashiyāta's life; his
method was the tried-and-tested ruse of secretly poisoning the royal
cup. Having been warned of Bagoas' plot, the new Great King magnanimously offered the eunuch the 'honour' of drinking from the
royal goblet first. As Diodorus puts it, 'the king called upon Bagoas

to drink a toast to him, and handing him his own cup the king compelled him to take his own medicine'.

It is clear from the fragmentary, late, and suspect sources we have used to patch together the events surrounding the regicides of Artaxerxes III and his son that solid and reliable evidence for the period is missing and what we have available is confused, confusing, and frustrating. What can be said with certainty though is that once more the Achaemenid royal house was a victim of its own inability to control the succession. Artaxerxes III had been a robust ruler, but as he aged, his power slipped away and he did not adequately quell the court factions which swiftly emerged. We do not know why he showed so little interest in his succession, but he does not seem, at any point in his reign, to have named a crown prince and to have taken, at the very least, the first steps towards a peaceful transfer of power. And yet to read these stories of court conspiracies and assassinations as evidence for the decay of the Persian empire, as has long been done by scholars, is not only fruitless, but completely wrong. Persia on the eve of the investiture of Artashiyāta as Persia's Great King was a powerful world force; it had lost none of its authority on the world stage, and while the violent history of the Achaemenid dynasty played out with its plots and assassinations, the family never lost its grip on the empire. In fact, Artaxerxes III had vigorously re-established and revitalised Persia's position as the dominant world superpower, and, thanks to him, Artashiyāta inherited a realm which was rich, stable, and not simply functioning, but thriving. Taking as his throne name Darius III, the new Great King allied himself to the deeds and memory of the first great Darius, and as a warrior of great renown his link to the old king was well-justified. Determined and single-minded, Darius III had the ambition and the ability to increase Persia's dominions and enrich his realm. His reign was set to be glorious.

*

Ever since the Macedonian King Amyntas I surrendered his country to Darius the Great about 512–511 BCE, Macedonians and Persians had been in close contact. The subjugation of Macedonia had occurred during Darius' Scythian campaign, when the gigantic Achaemenid army invaded the Balkans. On their way there, the Persians conquered gold-rich Thrace and the Greek cities of the Black Sea coastline, as well as Perinthus on the Sea of Marmara, and they sent envoys to Amyntas I demanding earth and water for Darius. The Macedonian king accepted Persian rule and his successors became vassals of the Great King. Indeed, the rulers of Macedon gained much with Persian aid and began to expand their territories, taking land from Balkan tribes and from Greeks. The Roman historian Justin noted that Alexander I of Macedon expanded his lands 'as much through his own valour as through Persian generosity' and that the Macedonians were 'willing and useful Persian allies'. In 480 BCE, Xerxes was given hospitality by Alexander I as he set out to conquer Athens and Sparta, and Macedonian soldiers fought in Xerxes' army in the campaign which followed.

Macedon was a land rich in natural resources: its mountains were dense with forests and timber was plentiful. The Athenians purchased Macedonian oak, fir, and pine in bulk in order to build their triremes, and gold flowed steadily and regularly into Macedon's coffers and its kings became very rich. Happy to trade with the Macedonians, the Athenians and other mainland Greeks considered Macedon to be a dangerous, lawless place; in effect, bandit country. The Greeks saw the Macedonians as foreigners, non-Greeks, and barbarians, and while there is some truth in this, it is also certain that the Macedonians saw themselves as belonging to the Hellenic world. The Argead dynasty, the ruling house of ancient Macedonia from about 700 BCE, traced its origins to Argos in the Peloponnese. Argaed spin mythologised the origins of the dynasty by proclaiming that the kings were descended from the family of Hercules, the ultimate demi-god-hero of the Greek world, and that they were integrally interconnected with the Hellenic universe.

In spite of the Hellenic character of Macedonian royalty, over the decades Macedonia became increasingly Persianised, particularly so the royal court, which closely modelled itself on Persian prototypes. When King Philip II, Macedon's most illustrious ruler, built up his power base following his accession to the throne in 359 BCE, he conscientiously copied many Achaemenid institutions and imitated Persian imperial practices, establishing a royal secretary and archive, and instituting royal pages and Companions (*hetairoi*) modelled on Achaemenid 'Kinsmen' (*syngeneis*). Philip sat upon a throne crafted on a Persian model and he drank from silver Achaemenid-style cups; his horses were fitted with Persian trappings. His polygynous household followed the royal Persian model, and his seven consorts were housed in apartments in the inner court of his palaces at Aegae and Pella; each wife had brought to the marriage bed lucrative economic and political ties with neighbouring chiefs and nobles. All in all, a Persian visiting Macedonia would have felt very much at home at Philip's court; to all intents and purposes it was a Persian court in miniature, with a Greek twist.

Philip's appropriation of Achaemenid-style court trappings and institutions did not go unnoticed by the Persians; nor did his ever-expanding territorial gains. It was also noticed that, with increasing regularity, Philip's court was becoming a safe haven for disgruntled Persians who had turned their backs on the Great King. During the reign of Artaxerxes III, two brothers, Mentor and Memnon of Rhodes, had supported the Persian Artabazus II in his campaign to succeed his father Pharnabazus as satrap of Hellespontine Phrygia. To cement an alliance with the brothers, Artabazus married their sister, and in turn he handed over his daughter, Barsine, in marriage to Mentor (following his death, Barsine would marry the other brother, Memnon, too). Artabazus rose up in rebellion against Artaxerxes III but the insurgence was short-lived and in 356 BCE his army was crushed and he and Memnon absconded to Macedonia, while Mentor fled to Egypt and eventually worked his way back into favour with Artaxerxes. Artabazus, however, was given sanctuary by Philip II, who also welcomed his family and harem to court; Barsine was certainly among the new arrivals. Other émigrés included Sisines and Amminapes, two important Persian courtiers who escaped the oppression of Artaxerxes' rule for the more welcoming atmosphere of Pella. They, and others like them, brought to Philip's court knowledge of Persian traditions, ideas, and rules; importantly, they brought with them the Persian language too. As a result, the world of Philip II was a rich hybrid of Macedonian, Greek, and Persian values, customs, and lifestyles.

Philip's overriding ambition was to improve the military and political strength of Macedonia. He reassembled the Macedonian army from its core, refining its method of training, armaments, and tactics, and replacing the outdated phalanx formation with hoplites armed with *sarissas* (a spear or pike about 4–6 metres in length) and *xiphos* (double-edged, one-handed short swords). Once he dealt with the inner turmoil of his country, the next step was expansion. With this formidable new fighting force, Philip added to his kingdom the lands of Thrace, from Chalkidiki to the Aegean Sea, and methodically eradicated coastal cities in the Balkans, winning battle after battle and increasing his international prestige.

Philip's military progress through Thrace and then mainland Greece was followed very carefully by Artaxerxes III, especially when, in the early 330s BCE, Philip actively tried to win over local rulers of Asia Minor by supporting them against the Great King or provoking them to rebellion. The first clash between Macedon and Persia flared up in 341–340 BCE when Philip attempted to overpower Persian-held Perinthus and Byzantium, Thracian cities which stood on the peninsula that looked out to, and almost touched, Asia. Both cities quickly received aid from the Phrygian and Carian satraps, ordered by an anxious Artaxerxes to provide full support to the victims of Philip's aggression, and it was because the Great King took an active interest in Philip's ambitions that he was able to neutralise them before they damaged Persian territories irrevocably. Philip decided that a complete withdrawal was necessary and he and his troops returned to Pella.

It was in the summer of 338 BCE that Philip scored his great victory over Athens and Thebes at the Battle of Chaeronea, and the balance of power in Greece and the Balkans changed overnight. Having broken Greece to his will, Philip made it known that he was preparing for an invasion of Persia and to that end he established what scholarship has referred to as the 'League of Corinth', the unification of many Greek *poleis* under the hegemony of Macedon, with the ultimate purpose of making war on the Persian empire. The timing was right: Artaxerxes III was murdered around the same time that Philip fought at Chaeronea and brought Greece to heel. Chaos reigned in the Persian royal court as Bagoas the eunuch, the regicide, set up his puppet king, Artaxerxes IV. The Persians, completely focused on court events, seem to have ignored the presence of some 10,000 Macedonian soldiers which Philip had sent into Asia Minor in the summer of 336 BCE, under the command of two of his most able generals, Parmenion and Attalos. It was only through the efforts of a Persian commander named Memnon that the Macedonian forces were pushed back off Persian territory, although it is possible that a few military bases were retained by Philip's soldiers during the melee; these would prove to be invaluable over the coming months. Unperturbed by the defeats he had experienced in Thrace and Asia Minor, Philip planned for a full-scale invasion of Persia.

Artaxerxes III was apprehensive about the rise of Macedon as a power; his actions against Philip show that he was far more fearful of Philip than he was of weak Greek city states. But what of his successor? How did Darius III view the Macedonian ruler and his empire-building ambitions? His intelligence agents brought him regular news and alerted him to the fact that the Macedonians and their allies were arming for war; week on week the news arrived that Philip was ready to fight. Then, in October 336 BCE, Darius received a communication telling him that Philip II was dead, murdered by one of his bodyguards as he walked into the theatre at Aegae. On the spot, the nobles and the army had proclaimed his twenty-year-old son king: Alexander III, Alexander of Macedon. Darius' mind must have raced.

22

Some Talk of Alexander

Alexander III ascended to the throne of Macedon in 336 BCE, within just months of the accession of Darius III in Persia. Fortune ensured that the two kings were brought together through a curious mixture of shared experiences. Both monarchs came to power after extended periods of bloody upheaval which resulted in the shame and trauma of regicide; both men were experienced soldiers and exceptional leaders on the battlefield, readily commanding the respect and loyalty of their troops; and both kings were ambitious and charismatic and self-confident. For five short yet pivotal years, an angst-ridden world held its breath and waited for Fate to declare who would emerge victorious as the King of Kings, Alexander or Darius. Their lives were irrefutably intertwined, but while Darius had everything to lose, Alexander had everything to gain. Destiny ensured that their names would be linked together for eternity as the story of Darius and Alexander became a mythology of its own making.

Indeed, the frustration encountered by many historians trying to write a life of Alexander of Macedon lies with the fact that it is almost impossible to separate the man from the legend. The myth-making process began early, during Alexander's lifetime, and climaxed in the work of the five great 'Alexander historians', all crafting their accounts some 200 years and more after Alexander's death: Diodorus Siculus' universal history of the late first century BCE; Arrian, who wrote the *Anabasis of Alexander*; Quintus Curtius Rufus' *History of Alexander*; Justin's second century CE Latin epitome of the lost account of Alexander's life by Pompeius Trogus; and Plutarch's

Life of Alexander, one of his *Parallel Lives* (where he is matched with Julius Caesar). These late texts are often contradictory; Arrian and Diodorus in particular seem to disagree on every detail, while their overall portraits of Alexander are starkly contrasted. Unfortunately, sources written during Alexander's lifetime, such as works by Callisthenes, Aristoboulus, and Cleitarchus (all of whom knew Alexander or his veterans), are long lost, meaning that we approach the life of Alexander only through the elaborately doctored later conceptions of his life and campaigns, each with its own bias, and each encoding its own agenda. Innocent and reliable they are not.

By means of contrast, given that the Persians had no taste for written histories, we have no great sweeping narrative for Darius III and no epic accounts of his campaigns. Sadly, even within his own realm, the sources cite his name but rarely. Where it is found, it is merely as part of a date on administrative documents – formulaic and somewhat disappointing. The material evidence provided by archaeology and numismatics is no better, for it offers nothing substantial about Darius the man or his policies as a ruler. When it comes down to it, the best we can do with the paltry knowledge gleaned of Darius from the Achaemenid sources is to insert it into the body of evidence provided by the much later classical sources. Persian documents do not shine any light on Darius' reign, they just amplify Alexander's story as told by Greek and Roman authors.

Thus, we meet with some very serious source problems. On the one hand, there are the lavishly mythologised Greek and Latin adventure stories of the Great Alexander – compelling, exciting, intriguing panegyrics– and on the other, there is a fragmented group of sources which are meant to testify to the life and deeds of Darius III. Naturally, the temptation is to flesh out what we know about Darius through the rich narratives of the classical writers, and, indeed, historians have determinedly followed that approach for centuries. They have been cavalier in glossing passages from the classical authors which allow them to downplay Darius' abilities as a warrior and to promote the idea of his ineptitude and gutlessness. But we must resist this approach. This book has attempted to forward the Persian Version over the Greek and Latin texts, and even though that endeavour becomes excruciatingly difficult when thinking about Darius III, it is not impossible to put him into focus more directly, with a new clarity of vision and understanding. The classical perception of Darius as a coward and a weakling cannot be substantiated. Nevertheless, given the woeful state of the Persian sources, any attempt to bring new evidence to the fore will be futile. What we can do, however, is to try and look at Alexander's campaign through Persian eyes, and privilege, wherever it is feasible, an Achaemenid understanding of the events as they unfolded.

*

In the bright, warm spring of 334 BCE, Alexander, with an army of around 30,000 infantry, and cavalry forces numbering about 5,000, crossed the Hellespont and stood in Asia. Persian spies carried the news to Darius: Alexander was now on Persian territory. 'On reaching the mainland, Alexander first hurled his spear into the soil', an intelligence scout reported to Darius, going on to explain that the young Macedonian king had come into Persian lands as 'a second Achilles', to bring war to Asia, and to avenge the Greeks who had lost lives and livelihoods when Xerxes marched on Greece. 'Achilles'? The name meant nothing to Darius. Xerxes in Greece? Darius remembered something of that incident from the tales he was told as a child. The Great King Xerxes had killed a Greek king, he recalled, and had enjoyed a fine victory over the liars and dissemblers who had ruled those far-off, chaotic shores. Darius was not overtly perturbed at the news of Alexander's landing. He must have felt some confidence in the fact that his Persian cavalry was 20,000 strong and that he had an infantry force of 20,000 paid mercenaries, somewhat lesser than Alexander's infantry, but of no great concern since the Persian cavalry easily outmatched that of the Macedonians. Besides, the financial resources at Darius' command were limitless. He had at his disposal the treasuries of Babylon, Persepolis, Ecbatana, and Susa, as well as the treasuries of all the satrapies, including the fabulous wealth of Sardis and, of course, the mints of the western provinces. All in all, the balance of power easily fell in Darius' favour.

Maybe it was this self-confidence that stopped Darius from acting with any kind of clear-sighted rationality, for, in hindsight, the sensible move would have been to hit the Hellespont hard with the full force of the Achaemenid navy and infantry, blockading the Macedonian's access to Asia, and pushing Alexander back into the sea, crippling the invasion before it had ever begun. After all, Darius had not been ignorant of the fact that the Macedonians had marshalled troops and ships. But no, Darius' forces remained completely inactive. In his defence, there was very little tradition among the Achaemenids to fully mobilise the troops, and it is probable that in the spring of 334 BCE Darius and his councillors regarded the Macedonian landings as just one more attempt at stirring up a petty rebellion in Asia Minor – and that it was certain to fail. They were wrong. For the first time in its history, the Persian empire found itself confronting an opponent who was determined to pursue total war to the bitter end. This was to be a war of conquest.

Darius followed the standard Persian practice when faced with conflict and ordered the local satraps to counter the Macedonian threat. It was Aristes of Phrygia who received Darius' order to face Alexander in battle, and he quickly formed a war council comprised of local satraps. Memnon of Rhodes, the Greek mercenary loyal to Darius, was welcomed as part of the team and he argued for taking a scorched-earth approach to the situation by destroying crops, farms, and any other outlet Alexander might use to feed and water his soldiers; depriving the Macedonians of provisions would be a costly but effective way to end the advance into Asia. Horrified at the thought of destroying their lucrative lands, the satraps rejected the idea. Confident in the superiority of their troops and tactics, the war council elected to put the arriving Macedonians on the defensive by gathering their combined forces at Zeleia, a village near the River Granicus in north-western Asia Minor, not far from the site of Troy. There they would wait for Alexander and engage him in battle, defeat him, and send the Macedonians packing.

When it came to it, the Battle of Granicus was a relatively small-scale but chaotic encounter, a tangled mass of horse clashing against horse and man against man, as each side struggled to achieve victory. Alexander and his cavalry, equipped with strong spears that were far more effective than the Persian lances, gained the upper hand in the fight. His light infantry moved among the horses and created panic in the Persian ranks. Two Persian satraps, Rhoesaces and Spitamenes, spotted Alexander fighting in the thick of the action and charged in on him. Rhoesaces smashed Alexander on the head with his sword, but Alexander's helmet bore the brunt of the blow and he countered by jabbing his lance through Rhoesaces' ribcage. Unexpectedly, Spitamenes appeared behind Alexander and raised his spear, but Cleitus, one of Alexander's senior generals, galloped in and sliced off Spitamenes' raised arm, lance and all.

The Macedonian cavalry finally delivered the hammer blow to the Persian forces and the victory easily went to Alexander. Those Persians who still could, took flight. A message was dispatched to Darius in which he learned he had lost over a thousand of his cavalry, and that many of his satraps had been killed too. The flower of the Achaemenid elite lay scattered and strewn over the battlefield. Darius was told how Alexander had captured many of Persia's Greek mercenaries, whom he labelled traitors, and had had them massacred. Darius also heard how Alexander had marched south through Asia Minor 'liberating' the Greek cities, punishing any who resisted, and removing local dynasts who were loyal to the Persian throne. The city of Sardis, Darius soon understood, had opened its gates to Alexander and welcomed him in – but then, Sardis had always spelled trouble.

The bulk of the Great King's army that had fled Granicus found itself stationed in Miletus, where Memnon of Rhodes took the command. He marched the army on to Halicarnassus, where it camped down to defend the city. The determination of the Persian troops meant that they put up a fearsome fight, and, in the winter of 334 BCE, Alexander left for Lycia, not having wholly captured or pacified Halicarnassus at all. Darius next heard how Alexander had taken the Lycian and Pamphylian coast and how he had marched on to inland Anatolia, where, in Greater Phrygia, he had installed his general, Demetrius-the-Beseiger, in the satrapal capital, Kelainai. The spring of 333 BCE saw Alexander at Gordion, receiving reinforcements from Greece and Macedon, a fact that prompted Darius to order Memnon to quickly reconquer the coast. But although he mounted an effective counterattack, Memnon died in July 333 BCE outside the walls of Mytilene on Lesbos. Alexander marched on, unimpeded, towards Cilicia, and skirted Cappadocia, which, on his own authority, he turned into a satrapy. Darius was dumbfounded to learn that Alexander had the audacity to try to reconfigure the Persian empire, but it was only when he found out that Alexander was minting his own coinage at Tarsus (on the modern southern Turkish sea border with Syria), that Darius proclaimed that he himself would lead his troops to battle, march into Syria, and put an end to the wearisome Macedonian incursion once and for all.

Darius departed from Babylon at the head of his army. His family followed along in the royal entourage. The great ladies of the court travelled with him in their luxury covered wagons: Sisygambis, Darius' honoured mother, was there, and so was his beautiful wife, Stateira II, his daughter, Stateira III, and her younger sister, Drypetis. The five-year-old heir to the throne, Ochus, voyaged with the women too. Three of Artaxerxes III's daughters, as well as one of his widows, were among Darius' train, as was Barsine, the widow of Memnon of Rhodes. The royal procession included a multitude of Darius' male relatives too, including the Achaemenid princes: Bisthanes, the sole surviving son of Artaxerxes III, who seems to have held a special position in Darius' esteem; Arbupales, a grandson of Artaxerxes II; Prince Bessus, the satrap of Bactria; Madates, governor of Uxiana; and Prince Hystaspes. Each prince was given important roles in the army, and they rode beside Darius III as his kinsmen. Arbupales, who had already encountered Alexander at the River Granicus, was present, as was his son-in-law, Mithradates, and Oxathres, the king's much-loved brother. When the gigantic entourage reached Damascus, the harem and the baggage train were left in the city for safety's sake as the army marched on towards the front.

On 5 November 333 BCE, a cold, damp day, at a place called Issus, close to a plain on the Gulf of Iskanderum in modern-day south-eastern Turkey, the two armies met. Wary estimates suggest that Darius had 108,000 men at his command and that Alexander had no more than 40,000 men fighting for him. The banks of the River Penarus set the boundaries of the fighting. The exact details of the Battle of Issus are unknown, for the 'Alexander historians' offer wildly divergent accounts. We are certain, though, that it did not go well for Darius. For Alexander, however, the battle ran to plan: a phalangite thrust, a break in the enemy line, and a quick cavalry charge into the enemy centre (a pretty routine manouvre for Alexander) won the day. Although both commanders had solid plans, Alexander had had more recent expertise in the field and so did his troops, meaning that they were able to execute their manoeuvres more efficiently and effectively than the Persians, and once the battle got going, Alexander was able to seize on all the opportunities he needed, quickly adapting to Darius' moves, and countering each one. The fighting soon became hand to hand, ferocious and bloody. Swords cut into flesh, arrows pierced chests and legs and necks, and spears were thrust home. Soon the screams of the wounded were mixed with the shouts of battle and the clang of metal. Again, Alexander led his cavalry and charged at full speed into the Persian flank. Amid a tremendous hullabaloo, forcing their way through the bodies of the dead and dying horses and men, Alexander pushed forward towards the Persians.

As he stood in his chariot, Darius saw that the Macedonian forces, with an infantry phalanx in the centre and cavalry on the sides, had begun to move rapidly towards his army, which was drawn up opposite Alexander, on the bank of the Pinarus River. He gawped as Alexander led a headlong charge across the river, shattering the Persian left flank before turning on the Greek mercenaries at the Persian centre. Suddenly, Darius locked eyes with Alexander as the Macedonian, cheeks flushed red and eyes flashing with determination, made a gallop towards him, raising a sword. Darius was surrounded by his royal household cavalry, led by his brother Oxathres, and although they fought bravely, they were no match for the Macedonians. Darius' chariot horses, peppered with arrows and mad with pain, began to panic, almost dragging the unwilling

Darius straight into the Greek line. The Great King fought to control the steeds as Alexander continued hacking his way headfirst into the melee, brandishing his sword, ignoring all danger, even when someone slashed open his thigh with a dagger. Darius, having lost his bow, shield, and spear, witnessed his bodyguards dying all around him. He abandoned his state chariot for horseback and galloped off to safety. This move sounds like cowardice – the majority of the classical historians certainly presented it that way – but it was not. Darius' only thought was for the future of his empire, which was, of course, embodied in his person. For the Achaemenid cause to triumph, it was essential that the occupant of the throne not be captured or killed. Darius rode away to Thapsacus, a small city on the Euphrates, and took refuge.

The Persian army were quick to follow their king, but in their panicked retreat, Alexander's cavalry slaughtered them in their thousands. Some of the escaping Persian infantry were even mowed down by their own cavalry. The battle was a resounding victory for Alexander. He had lost only 7,000 men to Darius' 20,000. The surviving Persian cavalrymen dragged themselves north, along the Royal Road, and camped in Cappadocia and Paphlagonia, where their commanders soon began conscripting substantial new forces with the intent of reconquering the whole of Asia Minor.

Meanwhile, some of Alexander's men found Darius' base camp, just beyond the battlefield. It was rich in plunder. Looting the Persian tents, the Macedonians took well-crafted armour, inlaid furniture, rich tapestries, and garments of linen and silk, as well as countless vessels of gold and silver. But Darius' own belongings were left alone, as they now belonged to Alexander himself. When a weary and blood-soaked Alexander turned up in Darius' tent, he decided that he would bathe, and ordered that a bathtub (found among the Great King's possessions) be brought to him, saying (as Plutarch recorded), 'Let us now cleanse ourselves from the toils of war in the bath of Darius.' 'Not so', replied one of his followers, 'but in "Alexander's bath" rather; for the property of the conquered is now the conqueror's.' Sinking into the warm, perfumed water and smelling the fragrant odours which hung in the air, Alexander turned to those about him and gestured with his hand, saying, 'This, it seems, is royalty.'

As the final weeks of 333 BCE approached, Darius learned that Alexander had entered Damascus and had captured the Persian baggage train. He had taken possession of the royal harem. Darius was stunned. His mother, wife, and children, including his young heir, were now in the hands of his enemy. Several of Persia's noble-women were taken too, including Barsine, whom Alexander might have remembered from his youth in Pella, where she had been given refuge by Philip II; she became his lover shortly after her capture. Alexander had seized the royal household. This was not a normal post-battle hostage situation, but a political scoring point, for it is important not to overlook the symbolic value of Alexander's acquisition of Darius III's harem en masse, and certainly the blow that the appropriation of the royal ladies meant to Darius. The possession of a predecessor's harem, and in particular the women of the royal house, ensured the successor's hold on the throne. The control of the harem gave the new ruler the potential to legitimise his reign through the physical possession of a former monarch's women – we will recall how Darius I had capitalised on this when in his bid for power he had married all the available royal women of the line of Cyrus the Great. Similarly, for Darius III, the Mace-donian king's seizure of the women of the royal harem prophesied the end of Achaemenid rule, since Alexander's appropriation of the reproductive capabilities of the women of the harem immediately jeopardised the legitimacy of Darius' reign.

The weeks and months following the Battle of Issus found Darius in anguish at the seizure of his family. In an attempt to secure their freedom, he made diplomatic overtures to Alexander no fewer than three times. He allegedly promised Alexander the hand of one of his daughters, and, as a dowry – according to the classical sources – even offered to cede him part of the Persian empire, as far as the Euphrates (in other words, half of his kingdom). Did Darius really plan to relinquish half of his empire? It is very doubtful. It might be expected that he was prepared to pay a very high ransom price to secure the return of his family, who were, in effect, living as privileged prisoners-of-war, but the idea that he would simply gift Alexander Persian territories does not chime with Darius' military tactics or his style of governance. To his dying moment, Darius was determined to fight for and hold together his empire no matter the cost, so it is impossible that he would ever have countenanced renouncing any of his territories by putting them directly into enemy hands. When Darius forsook his troops on the battlefield of Issus, and took horse and fled the combat, he was fully cognisant of the risk he was taking. In his escape from the battlefield, he took the active decision to abandon his family and he recognised that the likelihood of seeing them again depended on his strength as a warrior and a ruler. If he could defeat Alexander in a future conflict, his family would be safe, but until then they needed to remain in Macedonian hands. The survival of the whole Persian empire was at stake, and for Darius that meant that he had to maintain the Achaemenid dynasty's grip on power; that was more important than protecting any of the individuals who made up the family. There could be new wives and more children in the future. It was dynastic survival that was imperative.

*

When the dust had finally settled on Issus, Darius made his way back to Babylon and, for the next two years, he followed the usual peripatetic rhythms of the court, all the while replenishing his troops, drafting and training new recruits and instructing them in the use of the latest weaponry – including Macedonian-style spears. The Persians were quick to pick up the new fighting techniques and were keen to put them into practice at the earliest opportunity. Messengers delivered regular reports of Alexander's movements: he had taken the Phoenician city states; he had captured Joppa and Gaza, and he had entered Egypt, where he had been hailed as a liberator and as a living god-king. In the spring of 331 BCE, after reorganising Egypt's administration, Alexander was back on the move, putting down a revolt in Samaria, marching north to Tyre, and swinging east towards the River Euphrates, via Damascus and

Aleppo. Anticipating the Macedonian approach, Darius marched his immense army (between 53,000 and 100,000 men) north-west, into Babylonia, not far from the ancient Assyrian city of Nineveh (modern Mosul). There he set up his camp and waited for the Macedonians to arrive. Darius chose for the place of battle an open plain situated beneath a hill in the shape of a camel's hump; the silhouette had given it its name, derived from the Semitic word for 'camel', *Gammalu*. The Macedonians called it Gaugamela.

On the night of 20 September, immediately after the sun had set, Darius and his men observed that the moon had turned blood red and then went black. The Babylonian Astronomical Diaries captured the sensational moment and recorded an omen that it foretold:

> On the thirteenth day of the month of Ululu in the fifth year of Darius there was an eclipse of the moon, which was entirely darkened as Jupiter set. Saturn was four fingers distant. As the eclipse became total, a westerly wind was blowing; as the moon became visible again, an easterly wind arose. During the eclipse there were deaths and plagues.

The Magi and astrologers saw in the darkened, moonless sky nothing but doom. Morale in the royal camp was low. It declined further when a new omen was spotted in the heavens in the small hours of 23 September as a meteor flashed across the night sky. What could it mean? The diviners and priests were clueless, but the following morning Darius heard the news that his wife, Stateira, had died in childbirth. Darius' mind must have raced with doubts and anguish and loss.

The classical sources recall Alexander's courtly treatment of the royal women, and of how he referred to Darius' mother, Sisygambis, as his own mother, and how she was pleased to call him 'son'. Perhaps such a story was true. Alexander certainly had every cause to keep the Queen Mother in good health and comfort: he could ransom her for a very fine profit. His relationship with Stateira II, Darius' consort, is more a matter of concern though. She had been taken prisoner, probably in the summer of 332 BCE, when Alexander took possession of the royal entourage which Darius had stationed in Damascus. She died in childbirth around 21 September 331 BCE, in which case it is probable that the baby she bore in the last hours of her life was not Darius' child, but the offspring of Alexander. Arrian, in his account of the Persian campaign, tried to convince his readers that a chivalric Alexander never touched Darius' queen, but there is every reason to believe that she had perished giving birth to Alexander's child.

What was the background to this event? Had Stateira been raped by Alexander? Seduced? Had she fallen in love with him? It is impossible to say, although Alexander's motive is very clear: regardless of the way in which he had physically known Stateira, he had staked his claim on the Persian empire through the body of Darius' wife. If she had borne him a living son, then Alexander could have presented him as a ready-made heir, a child blessed with the intermingled blood of Argead and Achaemenid royalty. But it was not to be.

News of Stateira's death came as a dreadful blow for Darius. But things quickly got worse. On the morning of 1 October 331 BCE, Alexander and his troops (some 47,000 men) were assembled, ready to fight. The battle positions had been dictated by Darius who had commanded his men to flatten all vegetation across the plain in order to create a clear passage so that his chariots might wreak havoc on the Macedonian forces. As was the usual Persian practice, Darius placed himself in the centre of his army while Alexander split his troops into two units – a replication of the stance both sides took at the Battle of Issus. The Macedonians were the first to engage, as they marched forward towards the Persian centre. Suddenly, in a surprise manoeuvre, Alexander gathered his cavalry and rode them to the right, drawing the Persian cavalry over to its left to attack him. Consequently, a gap opened up in the Persian centre line. Exposed and vulnerable, Darius attacked Alexander's troops and launched his chariots at full speed, but the Macedonians used their *sarissas* to attack and kill the horses and the charioteers as they charged past. Somehow the Persians managed to filter into the Greek lines, but it was at this point that Alexander launched a massive strategic attack: cutting off the rear of the Persian line, he was able to storm the Persian centre. As at Issus, once again Darius realised that Alexander had an opportunity to strike at him, so, skilfully turning his chariot, he drove off the battlefield. Alexander could easily have followed and killed Darius on the spot, but he chose to stay in the battle to support his General Parmenion, whose left flank had taken the brunt of Persian attacks and needed aid badly. Nevertheless, the battle ended with a redoubtable victory for Alexander.

On his departure from Gaugamela, Darius fled to Arbela and from there he crossed the Zagros Mountains and arrived on the Iranian plateau. He straightaway made for Ecbatana, where he immediately began to raise more troops – as far as he was concerned, the fight was not yet over. Alexander meanwhile went south to Babylon and soon took control of the city, which welcomed him with enthusiasm. In fact, the city leaders, including Achaemenid commanders and aristocracy, came out of the city gates to lead him inside the walls. Like Cyrus the Great before him, Alexander took pains to work with the local priesthood and to show himself a loyal worshipper of Babylon's gods. He offered protection to the Babylonians against looting and pillage and paid his respects to the great temple of Marduk. The support of the city and its officials made it possible for Alexander to impose his rule over Babylonia. He employed the ancient traditions of Babylonian monarchy, even adopting its titles such as 'King of All Lands', just as the Persian Great Kings had done.

The loss of Babylon was a truly devastating moment for the Achaemenid state and Darius felt the shame of its loss acutely, and personally. But the news that followed made the situation worse: Alexander had marched on Susa, which fell without any resistance, and had fought against the Uxians, a tribe of hardy nomads who controlled the single route between Fahliyn and the Persian Gates in south-western Iran, and had now settled his troops in and around Persepolis, the jewel of the Persian empire. It was now in the hands of the barbarians. Its capture was unimaginable, calamitous, dishonourable. Darius must have wept.

Alexander had moved at full speed through the Zagros Mountains, determined to reach Persepolis before the Persians had time to deploy troops to defend the palace-city. By mid-January 330 BCE he had reached the walls of Persepolis, where the treasurer, Tiridates, opened the gates to the Macedonian troops. There were no crowds to welcome them, no open-hearted cries of 'Sikander! Sikander!', and there was no Babylon-style triumphant entry. The population of the area took refuge in their homes, terrified that the barbarians from across the Bitter Sea would kill them and devour their corpses. The Macedonian soldiers were restless but, up to now, had remained disciplined, even though they maintained that it was their right to pillage any place they passed through. Persepolis, surely, promised to offer great rewards, and hadn't Alexander promised them the riches of Persepolis, calling it the most hated city in Asia? By the time the army reached the city's gates, the troops had worked themselves into a frenzy of greed; they wanted to take everything they could – treasures, wine, food, women – and enjoy seeing the rest burn.

Alexander took possession of the royal terrace itself, settled down in its palaces, and gave the troops free rein to plunder the surrounding area. For over twenty-four hours the Macedonian soldiers ran amok through the environs of Persepolis, ransacking every dwelling, stealing goods, raping, torturing, and killing men, women, and children and rounding up captives as slaves. Houses and workshops were burned, farm animals were put to the sword in their thousands, horses were stolen, and crops were set alight. The violence unleashed upon Persepolis was vicious, prolonged, indiscriminate, and completely abandoned. Recently discovered archaeological evidence has proved that in spite of Alexander's dictum that the royal terrace was out of bounds, the palace complex was certainly attacked by his troops. The remains of over a dozen humans and animals have been unearthed in the water canals that ran beneath the terrace. Local people had clearly taken shelter in the dark tunnels to avoid death, but they had been tracked down and killed by Macedonian soldiers in an orgy of slaughter. The harrowing evidence speaks for itself and tells us that Alexander's men went on a killing spree for profit, certainly, but also for pleasure.

Pillaging occurred on the royal terrace too, and the Macedonians left visible archaeological traces of the looting. The archaeologists' excavation report of 1939 noted that Alexander's men were 'thorough in clearing out the treasure house at Persepolis', taking everything of value: 'They do not seem to have left a single vessel of precious metal; but the royal tableware of stone would have burdened their baggage train without bringing much gain. We have no doubt that they smashed hundreds of vessels which they did not care to take along.' The Macedonian soldiers smashed over 600 vessels made of alabaster, marble, lapis lazuli, and turquoise; they broke and scattered cylinder seals, jewellery, and precious stones; they tore and burned carpets, garments, and textile hangings; ritual objects too – altars and incense-burners – were stolen or damaged. And it was not only Achaemenid artefacts that were attacked. One famous Greek marble sculpture, known as the 'Penelope of Persepolis' (an image of the clever wife of Odysseus of Homeric mythology), had probably been brought to Persepolis by Xerxes after the sacking of Athens and had been carefully stored in the royal treasury. Archaeologists found it there, in situ still, but smashed and scattered about in the ruins, another victim of the undiscerning rampage. In an act of sheer vandalism, Penelope had been decapitated with a single blow of a heavy Macedonian sword. Her delicate arms had been hacked off too, so that only the torso and seated legs of the statue remained, too heavy to cart away easily. The marble arms and head were taken away as loot and have never been found.

Finally, after a full day and night of unimaginable terror for the Persian locals, Alexander ordered his men to cease the looting and stop the killing. There was little more to steal and few lives left to take. Persepolis was a ghost town, filled only with corpses. It was a scene of unutterable horror, a place of widows and orphans, of jackals and foxes; a site for lamentation.

*

For four months, Alexander was unable to decide on his next course of action. He knew that Darius was in the north, building up an army, but he seemed unwilling to leave Persepolis. True, Alexander had visited the tomb of Cyrus the Great at Pasargadae and had offered his respects to the legendary king, but he was not made welcome in Pārs. The Persians of the empire's south-western heartlands bristled under his control and threatened rebellion and open warfare. And so, in a month of campaigning across the Iranian plateau in the spring of 330 BCE, the Macedonians punished the locals by destroying fields and reducing settlements to ashes. In a telling assessment, Diodorus noted that Alexander simply 'did not trust the inhabitants and felt bitter enmity toward them'. It was to counter the growing wave of Persian patriotism and anti-Macedonian feeling that, in May of 330 BCE, Alexander set a torch to Persepolis and burned down the many palaces. This was no noble act of retaliation for Xerxes' burning of the Athenian Acropolis, as some classical authors later claimed – after all, Alexander had absolutely no affinity with Athens. No, it was a pragmatic attempt at curbing Persian military resistance in the countryside of Pārs and the strongholds of central Persia. The destruction of Persepolis sent a clear, unambiguous message to the Persians: their time in the sun was over, their days of imperial glory were through, and they were now the subjects of Alexander. Still, the destruction of Persepolis was a heavy price to pay. Parmenion, one of Alexander's advisors, had forewarned Alexander that its loss would be catastrophic, and Alexander himself later lamented that the arson had deprived him of a seat of power in the Achaemenid ancestral heartland. But in the short term the obliteration of Persepolis served him well: it was a statement of the Macedonian king's intent. He would be the sole master of Asia. To reinforce the fact, Alexander set out to hunt down and defeat King Darius, the last remaining symbol of Achaemenid power and the final obstacle to his conquest of Persia. The game was on.

Darius had spent the winter of 331 to 330 BCE at Ecbatana in Media, some 400 miles north of Persepolis, where he had gathered an impressive army of around 10,000 men, including, once more, his dependable Greek mercenaries. He was well aware, though, that he did not have the numbers of men required to face the Macedonians in open battle. His plan was to move east with his army, towards the mountains of Bactria, burning the fields and farms as he went, in the hope that the devastation would reduce Alexander's army, hot on his heels, to a pack of starving wraiths. Once securely inside Bactria, and supported by its powerful satrap, Bessus, Darius would turn his army around, head west, and retake his empire. The plan was good. Once he was ensconced beyond Bactria's borders in the mountains and valleys of the Hindu Kush, Darius could then hold off the Macedonians for years, wearing down Alexander, diverting his attention, and lowering his resources, with attacks from elsewhere in his kingdom.

Keenly aware of Darius' scorched-earth strategy (regular intelligence reports had made certain of that) and fearing its success, Alexander determined that Darius must die. The future of the Persian empire depended on stopping Darius from ever reaching Bactria. In his heart of hearts, Alexander knew that, in the eyes of the Persian nobles and the Persian army, he would never be regarded as the Great King until Darius lay dead. And so, as soon as the snow-covered passes between Persepolis and Ecbatana had thawed enough for travel, Alexander raced north, up the spine of the Zagros, leaving Persepolis in the hands of a strong Macedonian garrison.

What followed was an epic game of cat and mouse. Alexander pushed his men to cover over twenty miles each day in order to reach Darius at Ecbatana, and after almost three weeks at a blistering pace, having covered some 270 kilometers, Alexander learned that Darius had received reinforcements from Scythia and the Caspian Sea and had decided to meet the Macedonians outside Ecbatana. Alexander was delighted; he had hoped for such an outcome, and after he had instructed his baggage train to lag behind, he moved the army at breakneck pace towards Media. But within days he received a report that the reinforcements had failed to show and that Darius had sent his baggage train south towards the Caspian Gates while he himself rode on to the mountains east of Rhagae, a small backwater town that was destined to become Tehran. From there he had taken the road to Bactria. The news of Darius' flight had been brought to Alexander by the now turncoat Prince Bisthanes, who had earlier fought beside the king at Issus. He considered Darius to be an upstart with no right to the throne and had decided, with an eye to the future, to help Alexander. Bisthanes explained the route Darius had taken and alerted Alexander to the important fact that the king's baggage train held enough gold to pay his army and hire mercenaries for many years to come.

Panicked at this prospect, Alexander immediately departed from Ecbatana with a fast-moving cavalry and infantry, resolute on his mission to catch up with Darius. Many of his infantry fell behind exhausted, and the horses were driven so hard that some died in their tracks, but nevertheless they arrived at Rhagae – some 400 kilometres from Ecbatana – in just eleven days. Darius, they were told, was well ahead of them and had already passed through the Caspian Gates. It was while he camped overnight at Rhagae that Alexander received an unexpected embassy. Made up of two high-ranking Persians, Bagisthanes and Antibelus, who had absconded from Darius' retinue, they brought key intelligence to Alexander: instead of coming to the aid of the Great King, Bessus, the powerful satrap of Bactria, had taken Darius prisoner, although he had made no move to depose him from the throne.

Bessus, an Achaemenid prince in his own right, and one who had fought alongside Darius at Gaugamela, had conspired with the royal vizier, Nabarzanes, and with Barsaentes, the satrap of Arachosia-Drangiana, to end Darius' reign. The once mighty warrior, they asserted, had proven to be a failure; his constant losses to the Macedonian invaders meant that he had to be removed, for the good of (what remained of) the empire. Consequently, Bessus was named hegemon of all Achaemenid forces. Bactrian soldiers (whose obedience to Bessus was total) seized the king and, roughly manhandling him, put him in chains. All respect for his god-given office vanished when Bessus, Nabarzanes, and Barsaentes brusquely told Darius that his reign was over and he was now little more than a bargaining chip in the ongoing war with Macedon. Pushing him into a *harmamaxa*, one of those closed carriages used by women of the harem (presumably to keep him hidden), they transported him further eastward.

Alexander immediately set off from the Caspian Gates, without even waiting for fresh supplies to be packed. With a skeleton team of swift infantry and fleet-footed cavalry, he travelled throughout the night and into the following day, covering an astonishing eighty kilometres in just eighteen hours. When he arrived at the camp where Darius had been taken captive, he learned that Bessus, with the backing of the fierce Bactrian cavalry, had now assumed the name Artaxerxes V and was claiming to be the new Great King. Now Alexander needed to transform his efforts to kill Darius into a mission to capture him alive, for if anyone was going to end Darius' reign and life, it was he. But now this upstart Bessus needed to be dealt with too. Alexander and his team ploughed on in pursuit of Darius, taking an alternative route from that of Bessus through an old, dried-up wadi. It took the Macedonians almost fifty miles out of their way, but it saved them a hard trek across the desert, and with fast horses they covered the miles easily, riding into the night at full gallop. And sure enough, by dawn, Alexander was able see Bessus' troops in the near distance.

The Bactrian cavalry far outnumbered Alexander's small band, but many of them disappeared in a cloud of panic at seeing Alexander approach so quickly; his name and reputation had certainly preceded him. A small skirmish ensued, as Bessus attempted to haul Darius' wagon away from the throng of horses, chariots, and soldiers, all in alarm, but it was heavy and cumbersome and moved very slowly. Alexander thundered forward. Quickly, Bessus entered the covered carriage, a spear in his hand. Darius was sat on the floor, propped up by cushions. His eyes were tearful and his face was smeared with lines of kohl, dry now after much weeping. His lips were cracked and sore, his cheeks sunken, and his wrists were cut and bloodied by the chains which bound him too tight. Bessus approached Darius and thrust a blade into his stomach, running the point in deep. As Darius bled out, Bessus left him for dead. He killed the two attendants who accompanied the king as well as the wagon-driver, and slashed the necks of the two horses that had pulled the cart. Then, with his cavalry in tow, Bessus escaped into the eastern mountains.

Mistakenly, Alexander believed that Darius was with Bessus' troops and straightaway he commissioned a search party to venture into the mountains, locate Darius, and bring him back, unharmed. Meanwhile a few of Alexander's men came across the battered *harmamaxa*, with its wide-eyed horses dead on the ground. One young Macedonian soldier, a lad named Polystratus, completely exhausted and gasping for a drink, came by to collect water in his helmet, for, close to the abandoned carriage, there was a small, muddy waterhole. He heard the sound of soft moaning emanating from the carriage and, opening the curtains, he found lying in front of him the King of Kings himself, covered in blood, barely alive, but still breathing. We might suspect that the truth of Darius' death, in as much as it can ever be pieced together, was far less dramatic although, in a way, quietly tragic. When Polystratus entered the covered carriage and knelt alongside him, Darius, unable to speak, gestured for water. The young soldier helped him to sip a few drops from his helmet as he cradled the king's head in his arm. His parched lips moistened, Darius III, the Great King, King of Kings, King of Many Lands, an Achaemenid, shut his eyes and quietly died. It was June or July 330 BCE; Darius was about fifty years of age.

The Greek and Latin authors made much of Darius' death scene, as might be expected, each adding his own spin to the various traditions which had grown around the historical event over the centuries. There were stories which placed Alexander next to the dying Darius, affording the Macedonian king a chance to weep Homeric-type tears at the passing of so noble an adversary. Other variations had Darius speak to Polystratus (in pidgin Greek, it must be supposed), through whom he implored Alexander to care for his mother and the rest of his family, before passing the empire over to Alexander's care. Those legends were crafted, of course, to show that Alexander was the rightful king of Persia and that he had received nothing less than the blessing of the last of the Achaemenid monarchs, for it was Alexander himself who had turned the murder of Darius to his advantage. In later months, to tie himself into the Achaemenid clan, Alexander went on to marry Stateira III, Darius' eldest daughter, and also took as a consort Parysatis II, a daughter of

Artaxerxes III, one of the last *grandes dames* of the empire. Once he could claim a family union with the murdered Darius, Alexander vowed to exact retribution for the king's death. When Bessus was captured, tortured, and executed shortly afterwards in the spring of 329 BCE, Alexander was able to present himself as both Darius' avenger and his rightful successor. In a public demonstration of his grief, a state funeral for Darius was organised and the royal corpse was sent back to Persia in a lavish funerary cortège for its interment (Darius III's unfinished tomb has recently been located 482 metres south of the fortified walls of the Persepolis terrace). As the body departed on its long, slow, and stately journey through the Iranian plateau, surely Alexander wept silent, yet noble, tears. And then he must have smiled.

Epilogue

Persian Past; Iranian Present

How was the Achaemenid empire, the brightest and most brilliant moment in Iran's past, received and remembered in later eras of Persia's history? Did it fade in the collective memory? Or was it kept alive in the imagination as a beacon of civilisation? Does it play a role in Iran's contemporary national consciousness? Happily, there is much to be said on the subject, since Iran's conception of its pre-Islamic past and the use Iranians have made of the Achaemenid era has its own rich history. From the early Middle Ages through to the Islamic Republic, generations of Iranians have looked back to the era of Cyrus the Great, Darius, and Xerxes for sources of inspiration and the means to comment on contemporary politics, religion, and society. Another volume would be needed to discuss the richness, variety, and impact of Iran's conception of the Achaemenid empire, which has been approached through political tracts, propaganda, prose, poetry, song, painting, sculpture, drama, architecture, photography, fashion, and cinema (and, who knows, that book may yet see the light of day). Here, however, we look at three moments, snapshots as it were, in the long history of Iran's reception of its first great empire: the use made of the Achaemenids by their Sasanian successors, the last pre-Islamic dynasty of Iranian kings; the poetic mythology which grew up around the ancient Persian kings in Iranian epic storytelling; and the use of the Achaemenid period in the politics of twentieth-century Iran and the Islamic Revolution which brought an end to its long tradition of monarchy.

Since the time of the Greeks, the tendency of mainstream Western historians has been to accept history as an interpretative process that can achieve truth through objectivism. In other words, the historical imperative has always been this: getting the story straight. Yet at the beginning of this book we saw that in Iran a different conception of the past had emerged in antiquity and that Iran's idea of 'history' has always been, and remains, somewhat nebulous. Iranians have traditionally approached their past in a different way to the method adopted in the West. In Persian antiquity, the past was approached via oral transmission through song, poetry, and narrated epic, and the Iranians never acquired the need to formulate their conception of history on the lines of Western forensic study, the Greek-style of *historiē*, or 'enquiry'. Later, in the Islamic Middle Ages, Iranian historians such as Al-Tabari, Bal'amē, Gardēzē, and Beihaqē did compose many precise and authentic 'histories' in their pursuit of an earlier pre-Islamic Persian past, and each left an impressive mark on the establishment of innovative methods of historical research, but these men of learning rubbed shoulders with scholar-poets and learned priests, individuals who also preserved their own version of the past, often in verses or hymns. Rather than battle for the 'authenticity' of the past, the historians, poets, and priests allowed a synchronous flow of ideas to interweave themselves as a new, amalgamated form of poetic historiography developed. Out of this arose the Iranians' open and unrestricted concept of 'the past'. The Western form of history-writing was eventually adopted in Iran, but it took a long time to get recognised and it was not until the Iranian Constitutional Revolution (1905–11) that the Iranians began to know more about European historical research methodologies.

Customarily, though, in Iran, prose histories and verse histories, written or orally transmitted, were often based on the same historical materials (best not call them 'facts') and were crafted into diverse versions or readings of 'the past'; one version did not have supremacy over another since all shared a place in the Iranians' transmission of their 'history'. What actually happened in the past, or what was *said* to have happened in the past, or, indeed, what *might* have happened in the past or *never* happened at all, was permitted a space in the Persian understanding of the pre-Islamic era.

*

It is difficult for us to conceive just what a permanent fixture the Persian empire once appeared to be. For its subjects, living and toiling in the reign of Darius III, the empire was the whole world, older than anybody could recall, imperishable, abiding, mighty. The empire had been around for so long, had weathered so many storms, had reinvigorated itself with such energy, and had imprinted itself so completely into the landscape of the world, that no one dreamed that it would end. Yet end it did.

One hundred and fifty years after the death of Darius III, the Greek historian Polybius addressed his readers with a question: 'I ask you', he wrote, 'do you think that either the Persians and the Persian ruler or the Macedonians and their king . . . could ever have believed that at the time when we live the very name of "the Persians" would have perished utterly – those who were once the masters of the whole world?' Polybius was referring, naturally, to the Achaemenids and their empire. The fall of that remarkable, long-lived superpower marked a seismic shift in the history of antiquity. More specifically, for the Iranians, it heralded a period of – if not exactly decline – redundancy, at least as far as international politics went. The direct successors of Alexander of Macedon, the Seleucids (named for Alexander's brilliant general, Seleucus), turned their backs on the Iranian plateau, and during the centuries of their rule their kings were drawn increasingly westwards to the Mediterranean. The old imperial cities of the Iranian plateau, Susa and Ecbatana, became backwaters, politically defunct, and all but forgotten. Persepolis was largely in ruins, abandoned of life and systematically stripped of its stonework by local dynasts, the Frata-rakas, who used it to build their own small palaces nearby. Inertia set in. The heartlands of imperial Pārs declined.

Just when Persia seemed to be suffering its own form of devolution and began to fragment back into tribal units, from the eastern steppe of the desert came the next 'strong men' of Iranian history, the Parthians (also known as the Arsacids). They had lived to the east of the Caspian Sea for centuries, and were now set to revitalise Persian power. Slowly they infiltrated their way into the Iranian Plateau, surreptitiously colonising the Greek cities and settlements of the Seleucids by blending Hellenic culture with a more traditional Iranian feel and by the 140s BCE, the Parthians had moved into south-western Iran, the old Achaemenid stomping ground, and much of Mesopotamia too. They began edging their way towards the borders of the Hellenistic east in Syria and into the Levant. In 53 BCE, Rome, the new cocksure power in the West, was shaken to the core by the utter defeat of its legions – some 40,000 troops – at the hands of the little-known Parthians. At the Battle of Carrhae, in northern Mesopotamia, the bow-wielding Parthians, trained in horsemanship on the Eurasian Steppes, annihilated the Roman forces as the presence of a new Eastern superpower sent shockwaves throughout Europe. And yet the Parthians had no wish to become empire-builders in the manner of the Achaemenids. In fact, they showed no interest in the Achaemenid past and displayed no affinity with the old dynasty. The Parthians were a different 'type' of Iranian and their focus lay in northern Mesopotamia (in order to control the trade routes), eastern Iran, and Central Asia. Moreover, they depended on the loyalty of the old Iranian nobility and their hereditary system of governance, although the loyalty of the Iranian *khāns* was never guaranteed. In the old Persian heartland, the Parthians were not much liked. In 226 CE, a Persian from south-western Iran by the name of Ardashir defeated the last Parthian ruler in battle and established the Sasanian dynasty, taking its name from a Persian priest named Sasan, the revered ancestor of the family.

The Sasanians went on to rule the Iranian Plateau, parts of Central Asia, the Caucasus, Mesopotamia, and (at times) pieces of Syria and Anatolia for some 400 years and when its rulers looked back to the past for inspiration about the present, it was to the glory days of the Achaemenid empire that they were drawn. Like the Achaemenids, the new dynasty originated from Pārs and, to augment their right to rule, the Sasanians proudly exploited the fact that they shared a homeland with the most ancient and honoured of Iranian dynasties, the Elamites and the Achaemenids. Conscientiously and extremely dexterously, the Sasanian monarchs (224 CE–650 CE) promoted their connection to the Achaemenid empire and projected themselves as the heirs of the Great Kings of the past. When the influential Iranian scholar, historian, and theologian Al-Tabari (839–923 CE) wrote his famous *History of Prophets and Kings*, which covers the Sasanians and their Arab contemporaries, the account began with the careful tracing of the genealogy of Ardashir, whose ancestry, it was confirmed, put him close to the ancient King Dara – that is to say, Darius III:

> Ardashir rose up in Persis pretending to seek revenge for the blood of Dara . . . whom Iskander [Alexander] fought and whom two of his own chamberlains murdered. Ardashir wanted to restore the kingship to the legitimate family, and put it back exactly as it had been during the time of his forefathers who had lived before the Petty Kings [i.e. the Parthians], and to bring the empire back under one head and one king again.

The so-called 'Letter of Tansar', a piece of Sasanian propaganda originally composed in the time of Ardashir himself, portrayed the Parthians as heretical upstarts and used the memory of the Achaemenids to justify the Sasanian takeover of Iran, promoting too the ambition of re-establishing the superiority of the Persian empire:

> Today the King of Kings [Ardashir] has cast the shadow of his majesty over all who have acknowledged his pre-eminence and have sent him tribute ... Thereafter he shall devote all his thoughts to waging war on the Romans and pursue his quarrel against the people; and he will not rest till he has avenged Dara from the Alexandrites ['Westerners'] and has replenished his coffers and the treasury of state, and has restored by the capture of descendants of his soldiers the cities which Alexander laid waste in Iran. And he will impose on them tribute such as they have ever paid our kings for the land of Egypt and Syria.

For more than 300 years, the Sasanian rulers of Iran were at loggerheads with the emperors of Rome and war plagued East and West as decade after decade power struggles over imperial borders erupted into full-scale fighting. The memory of the Achaemenids was still lingering on in the mind of Shapur II (309–79 CE), the longest reigning Sasanian monarch and perhaps the greatest too. This warlike leader was inspired by the territorial supremacy of his Achaemenid ancestors and when he wrote a letter to the Roman emperor Constantius, he used the victories of the Achaemenid Great Kings to justify his own territorial ambitions. Half the world had once belonged to his ancestors, he stressed, and the time had come for him to take it back:

> I, Shapur, King of Kings, partner with the Stars, brother of the Sun and Moon, to my brother Constantius Caesar offer most ample greeting ... I shall state my proposal in brief terms, recalling that what I am about to say I have often repeated. That my forefathers' empire reached as far as the River Strymon and the boundaries of Macedonia even your own ancient records bear witness; these lands it is fitting that I should demand, since (and may what I say not seem arrogant) I surpass the kings of old in magnificence and array of conspicuous virtues.

The physical environment of Iran, and especially that of Pārs, was also exploited by the Sasanians to project their attachment to the Achaemenid past. Images of Ardashir, his brother, and father have been discovered engraved on a wall of the harem at Persepolis, indicating the close connection they felt with that monumental site, and Persepolitan-style sculptural and architectural elements were incorporated into the palaces of Ardashir at Firuzabad and those of his son Shapir I in Bishapur. In a Pahlavi (or Middle Persian) inscription belonging to Shapur Shakanshah, a brother of Shapur II, found on the north wall of the south portico of Darius I's palace at Persepolis, the Sasanian prince prayed for the souls of the departed ancestors who had built 'this palace'; it further ratifies the notion that the Sasanians evoked the memory of their illustrious Achaemenid forebears. But by far the clearest, and most impressive, Sasanian monument to interact with the memory of the Achaemenids was the huge relief sculptures which they erected in the shadows of the rock-cut tombs of old Great Kings at Naqsh-i Rustam. This site, so intimately linked to Persia's ancient Elamite and Achaemenid past, became a kind of historical theme park for the Sasanians, a place where they could happily intermingle their own imperial ambitions with the exploits and the successes of former, greater, empires.

In *War and Peace*, Leo Tolstoy observed that 'kings are the slaves of history', by which he meant, we can assume, that monarchs, perhaps more than any other humans, tend to become subject to the vagaries of memory; their lives, deeds, and legacies are more open to abuse, gloss, spin, mythologisation, heroisation, and villainisation than other historical persons. Their fame makes them vulnerable to memory. We have encountered this concept already when we explored the legends that grew up around the birth and death of Cyrus the Great and we saw how political expediency moulded the stories for propagandistic purposes. Throughout the Achaemenid era the name of Cyrus was utilised as a shorthand for 'empire', 'glory', and 'Persianness', and the boost provided by the Jewish and Greek accounts of his magnanimity and brilliance merely added to his reputation as the most powerful, just, and wise ruler under the heavens. Who would ever forget the name of Cyrus? Yet, forgotten it was. By the Sasanian period his name had been lost and the specifics of his reign were long forgotten; his legend was diluted, misremembered, or simply gone. No Sasanian text speaks of a 'Cyrus' or of a 'Xerxes'. Only the name 'Darius' lived on in the Sasanian memory, and even then it was not the Great Darius who was recalled, but the last Darius, the Persian king who had fought the monstrous Alexander and tragically had given up his life and empire.

As the long era of Sasanian rule drew to its close, the shadows of the Achaemenid kings grew ever more ghostly, until historical distance finally extinguished the shade of their remembrance altogether. In 651 CE the Sasanian empire fell to the Arabs of the south, and Iran became an Islamic state. The new Muslim administration overturned millennia's worth of Iranian political, social, and cultural institutions and traditions, as access to power meant that Iranians needed to adopt Arabism and Islam. The old Sasanian elite gradually espoused the new dogma and gained positions of authority by doing so. They promoted the exclusive use of Arabic, the language of the holy Koran, so that written Persian began to decline; its eradication steadily continued and, by the early ninth century CE, even the spoken Persian language was threatened with extinction, with only a pidgin form of the vernacular in circulation. It took 200 years for the population of the former Sasanian empire to become Muslim and 200 more for another form of the Persian language to develop in the east of Iran, far away from the Muslim heartland: New Persian, essentially the language we now recognise as modern Farsi.

It was Abul-Qâsem Ferdowsi, a man from Tus, in north-east Iran's province of Khorasan, who took the fresh form of the Persian language and made it a triumph of cultural revival. It was thanks to him that a new class of literati developed in Iran and it was through his writing that New Persian reached the peak of sophistication. His *Shahnameh* ('Book of Kings') is one of the greatest works of world literature and the national epic of Iran, still much loved (and often quoted) by millions of people throughout the Persian-speaking world. It is the longest poem ever written by a single named author.

After centuries of Arab domination, Ferdowsi was determined to restore the language and culture of Persia by composing a chronicle of its kings. *Shahnameh* covers the reigns of around fifty monarchs, from the first legendary rulers, the Kiyumars, down to the death of Yazdegerd III, the last ill-fated Sasanian, murdered as he ran from the marauding Arabs. Ferdowsi's kings and heroes – Sam, Rustam, Siyavash – are constantly involved in battles, hunts, and court festivities – *bazm va razm* ('feasting and fighting') – which were so central to the warrior code and the pastimes of the nobility. The epic is commonly divided into three sections: myths, legends, and history. The historical part of the poem begins with the fall of the Achaemenid dynasty and the conquest of Iran by Alexander and ends with the collapse of the Sasanian empire. This means that, prima facie, the Achaemenid kings were not regarded as real by Ferdowsi and his audience, but were mythical figures conjured up from Iran's deep past. They ruled from a place called *Takht-e Jamshid*, the 'Throne of Jamshid', a magnificent palace constructed from stone and precious stones and brought down from heaven by the great Jamshid, a Solomonic figure who governed the world for a thousand years. In Ferdowsi's day, the ancient ruins of Persepolis, which projected up and out from the desert sands that had swallowed them, were interpreted as that great heavenly monument, and today Iranians still know the archaeological site of Persepolis as *Takht-e Jamshid*.

For Ferdowsi, conceptualising the Achaemenids meant that myth and history had to be blurred; his Great Kings hovered indistinctly somewhere between the recorded past and the make-believe of legend. Yet they are there, in the thousands of verses of the *Shahnameh*, hidden, as it were, behind the names and exploits of Ferdowsi's kings. Kai Khosrow, for instance, was so brave and wise that he did not die a mortal's death, but was occulated to heaven, there to find eternal fame. Sitting behind this figure was Cyrus the Great himself, the ultimate King of Kings, who did not so much die as transcend time. Behind Ferdowsi's Gushtap was old Hystaspes; Esfandiyar was an avatar of Xerxes; Bahman was Artaxerxes I; Darab was Darius II; and Dara was, of course, Darius III.

Dara's story comes at the point in Ferdowsi's narrative where myth morphs into history, the intersection where he overwrites the 'what happened' with the 'what is better'. According to Ferdowsi, Darab (Darius II) was married to Nahid, a daughter of Filqis (Philip II), king of Rom (Rome, or the West), but shortly after their wedding he rejected her (the poor girl had the most dreadful halitosis), and sent her home to her father. Unknown to Darab, she was pregnant with his child, and when she gave birth, Filqis raised the baby boy as his own son and named him Iskandar (Alexander). Meanwhile Darab took a Persian wife and she gave him a son, Dara. After Filqis' death, when Iskandar came of age, Dara, who had become king of Persia, demanded tribute from Rom, but Iskandar decided to withhold it. War erupted between the two kingdoms and Iskandar defeated Dara in three battles and captured Istakhr (the area around Persepolis). In a fourth battle, Dara was killed by two of his own men, whom Ferdowsi named as Mahyar and Janusayar. Iskandar finds the king as he lies dying, and weeps with him for his misfortune. Dara gives Iskandar his daughter Rhoshanak

(Rhoxane) in marriage, hands the Persian empire over to Iskandar's hands, and then dies. Ferdowsi pictures the scene thus:

> He kissed Iskandar's palm and said, 'I pray
> That God will keep and guide you on your way.
> I give my flesh to dust, to God my spirit,
> My sovereignty is yours now to inherit.'

This is a key moment in the epic's narrative and in the conceptualisation of Iran's history: Iskandar is awarded the Persian empire thanks to his military prowess and his charismatic leadership; but, as Ferdowsi has made his readers aware, the empire was his by birthright and through blood. As the firstborn son of Darab, Iskandar was always destined to sit on the Persian throne, and through his death Dara, Iskandar's half-brother, rights the dynastic wrong and allows destiny to triumph. Iskandar, the Persian prince, takes his rightful place among the Great Kings of the past.

Why did Ferdowsi feel the need to rewrite the history of the Macedonian invasion, a truly bloody and catastrophic moment in Iran's long history? And why did he need to rehabilitate Alexander III by turning him into an Achaemenid prince, heir, and king? The answer must lie with the Arab invasion of Iran because, for Ferdowsi, the Arab conquest was an apocalyptic event, the nadir of Persia's long, celebrated past. In order to utterly villainise the Arabs and their vicious and total occupation of Persia, he needed to write out the bloody invasion of Iran by the Macedonians and turn it into a positive. The *Shahnameh* had room for only one villain – the Arab invaders.

*

On 12 October 1971 Muhammed Reza Shah Pahlavi, *Shahanshah* (King of Kings) of Iran and *Aryamehr* (Light of the Aryans), prepared to give the most important state broadcast of his twenty-seven-year reign. The world's media had assembled to record the event as he stood, stiffly, behind a deep bank of microphones and fidgeted uncomfortably in front of dozens of television cameras. Journalists had travelled many thousands of miles to Pasargadae, the city of Cyrus, in order to capture a historical moment as the Shah launched the Year of Cyrus the Great, a celebration of the 2,500th anniversary of the establishment of the Persian empire.

Muhammed Reza Shah was the second (and as it turned out the final) monarch of the short-lived Pahlavi dynasty (1925–79). He harboured a fascination for the grandeur of ancient Persia, which he exploited to an obsessive level: he wrote extensively, for instance, about dreams and visions in which he saw and talked with great figures from Iran's past – including Cyrus and Darius the Great – and in which, he claimed, they guided his hand and set his agenda for the governance of his kingdom. Such bafflingly honest pronouncements supported the Shah's vision for the monarchy as the single unifying force of the Iranian people. In a 1971 interview, he said it all: 'No foreigner can really understand what the monarchy means to Iran. It is our way of life. We could not be a nation without it.'

It was for this reason that the journalists had set up their recording equipment opposite the ancient tomb of Cyrus at the archaeological site of Pasargadae. The aim of the anniversary festival was to identify the Shah not only with Cyrus the Great himself but to associate him with the great historical monuments of Iran's pre-Islamic past and to celebrate all that was glorious in Iran's ancient heritage, before the shameful Arab conquest and the Muslim takeover of Persia. The Year of Cyrus the Great was to be marked in Iran by special programmes on television and radio, and articles in the press. Schools, universities, factories, trade unions, women's groups, and youth organisations were all encouraged to play a part in the festivities at a local level, while at the national level the Shah and his ministers promised to create a spectacle of history that would be remembered for a lifetime.

On the day of his speech, the 51-year-old King of Kings was rigged out in the full panoply of military splendour. His perfectly tailored uniform dripped with medals and shone with imperial insignia, blue taffeta sashes, gold frogging, and thick golden needlework embroidery; padded epaulettes accentuated his square shoulders, and a peaked cap, set firmly on his head, gave him the look of a serious military leader. It was a 'look' shared by other autocrats of the era: Argentina's Juan Perón, Uganda's Idi Amin, Spain's General Francisco Franco, and the Ethiopian emperor Haile Selassie, who happened to be the Shah's guest of honour at Pasargadae (he paid homage to his host by wearing an equally splendid uniform of dazzling white). Grey-haired, handsome, and distinguished, yet stern and short-tempered, the Shah certainly looked the part of a man in control of his country and its destiny. By his side stood the Shahbanou, his beautiful young wife, Farah, who shimmered in a white satin court dress embroidered in blue silk in traditional Persian motifs, her perfectly arranged coiffure sparkling with a heavy mass of Cartier diamonds. To complete the imperial triad, little Prince Reza, the nine-year-old heir to the wealthiest monarchy on earth, stood close to his father, dressed in a pocket-sized replica of his father's outlandish uniform – a mini-shah, the pint-sized hope of Iran.

The area around and about the tomb of Cyrus was usually a quiet place, visited only by keen foreign tourists or determined academics and archaeologists, but on that October day the place buzzed with life. Iranian flags carrying the Pahlavi dynasty's coat of arms – a sunburst rising from behind a sword-wielding lion – fluttered everywhere against the blue cloudless sky, and a huge open-air grandstand had been erected behind the Shah's podium so that invited guests might witness how the Iranian King of Kings would address the nation's great founder, Cyrus of Persia, and thereby bridge the centuries that separated them. Invited guests had been flown in (no expense spared) from every part of the world and the grandstand was packed with princes and princesses, heads of state, presidents, prime ministers, and other sundry VIPs (Imelda Marcos, the First Lady of the Philippines, was the Shahbanou's personal guest). Arriving at Shiraz, the fabled city of roses and nightingales, the bigwigs and dignitaries had been unceremoniously bussed to Pasargadae (a drive of one and a half hours) and were placed in staggered rows of cramped seating facing the tomb and looking directly into the sun. They sat there, squinting, for over an hour before the Shah and his entourage arrived.

When he finally spoke to deliver his eulogy, and in spite of the façade of confidence the uniform afforded, the Shah was visibly nervous. Muhammed Reza Shah had been born with a dazzling lack of charisma; most journalists who spoke to him remarked on it. Never one to court the media or to feel at home before the cameras anyway, he was now intently, terrifyingly, aware that the eyes of the world were on him. In halted speech, cold and unfeeling, his words, empty of emotions he simply did not understand, went forth into the dark, empty chamber of the tomb, as he addressed the ghost of his great forefather:

Cyrus, Great King, *Shahanshah*, Achaemenid king, king of the land of Iran, from me, *Shahanshah* of Iran and from my nation, I send greetings to you. To you the eternal hero of Iranian history, the founder of the oldest monarchy in the world, the great freedom-giver of the world, the worthy son of mankind, we send greetings! Cyrus, we have gathered here today at your eternal tomb to tell you: sleep in peace because we are awake and we will always be awake to look after our proud inheritance.

The Pasargadae ceremony concluded with a specially commissioned choral anthem entitled *Our Everlasting Happiness and Prosperity Derive from Your Kingly Glory, Oh Shah*. It was meant to be a stirring song of national unity, yet although the ceremony was intended to invoke pride in their past and inspire the Iranian people to look towards a glorious future, they were completely omitted from the patriotic pageant itself. The general Iranian population were not allowed to see the exclusive ceremony live and were instructed to watch it on television. The Shah's government boasted that the ceremony at Pasargadae was televised and transmitted throughout the world by Telstar satellite to allow millions all over the world to see it. Later it was to be claimed that some 2.4 billion people joined Iran in the celebrations, but the Shah's inner court of ministers and their families were the only Iranians who got close to the live action.

Once the Shah had left Pasargadae, the VIPs were driven to the archaeological site of Persepolis, the most magnificent and romantic of Iran's ancient ruins. There they were lodged alongside the Shah and his family within the 'Golden City', as it was called, a garden oasis planted with trees in full bloom – brought in directly from France – and with flower beds flown into Shiraz from Holland. Fifty yellow and blue tents (actually prefabricated apartments) were built on five streets forming a star representing the five continents, in the middle of which was an enormous fountain and the vast Tent of Honour where the official receptions took place and from where it was possible to reach the huge Banqueting Hall.

French caterers from Chez Maxim's in Paris (where the Shah and the Shahbanou were popular clients) created the menu for the state banquet, and the French couturier Lanvin designed new gala uniforms for the members of the Imperial Household. Drapes and curtains of Lyons silk, chandeliers of Bohemian crystal, Limoges china with the arms of the Pahlavis emblazoned in the centre, Baccarat glass services, two hairdressers from Paris with all their staff, thousands of bottles of wine, champagne, and sparkling water arrived in Shiraz from Paris and went straight to Persepolis. The festival's organising committee, under the leadership of the Empress Farah (herself an avowed Francophile), failed to see that the Shah's great spectacle was ultimately overwhelmed by the trappings and tastes of the West, to such an extent that the Persian flavour of the host culture was lost. In their tented, air-conditioned apartments, the Shah's VIP guests slept on Porthaut bedlinen, washed with commemorative soaps by Guerlain, and treated their hangovers with Alka-Seltzer individually boxed by Fauchon de Paris. Only the Persian carpets they stood on were made in Iran; even the caviar was flown in from Russia.

The centrepiece of the anniversary celebration was a march-past of 6,000 soldiers dressed in the uniforms of every Persian dynasty, from the Achaemenids to the Pahlavis. The parade, one journalist noted, 'surpassed in sheer spectacle the most florid celluloid imaginations of Hollywood epics'. The cavalcade took place at the base of the Persepolis terrace and had necessitated the building of a road on top of the delicate archaeology of the site. The Shah and his guests endured a three-hour-long spectacle of Persian military history which left visitors in no doubt about the imperial ambitions of their host. Finally, the Shah uttered a prayer which confirmed that God had appointed him to be the undisputed 'Light of the Aryans and the Custodian of the Land of Iran'. The Western media was impressed by both the spectacle and the rhetoric. *The Times* went as far as to comment that 'To the people of Iran, the institution of the Monarchy has run like a connecting thread, even like a lifeline, through twenty-five centuries of eventful history. Since the founding of the Persian Empire, the Monarchy has stood for nationhood, independence and unity.'

From his self-imposed exile in Najaf in Iraq, the Ayatollah Ruhollah Khomeini, the very vocal religious leader who opposed the increased Westernisation which Iran had experienced under the Shah, shook with wrath. 'Anyone who organises or participates in these festivals', he thundered (via the BBC Persian Service), 'is a traitor to Islam and the Iranian nation.' He went on to declare that Islam was fundamentally opposed to the Shah's obsession with the ancient pagan past and denounced the title King of Kings as 'the most hated of all titles in the sight of God'. As a result of Khomeini's condemnation of the Persepolis celebrations, Shia mullahs within Iran gathered in clandestine organisations to plot the destruction of the monarchy and, simultaneously, within their elegant homes in the northern suburbs of Tehran, Iran's left-wing intellectuals, many of whom were courtiers of the Shah, worked to the same purpose of toppling the Shah from off his throne – if not for the same aim of installing an Islamic government. Together, the two groups asked the same questions: Did Muhammad Reza Shah Pahlavi possess the charisma and authority of the ancient King of Kings? How could he compare his regime to the glories of the reigns of Cyrus, Darius, and Xerxes? When in 1976 the Shah replaced the Islamic calendar with a 'Persian Imperial' calendar, which began with the foundation of the Persian empire under Cyrus more than 2,500 years earlier, his actions were viewed as anti-Islamic and anti-democratic and resulted in a flowering of religious and secular hostility.

Did the Persepolis celebrations bring about the Iranian Islamic Revolution of 1979? No, that was (among other factors) more the result of a conservative backlash opposing the Westernisation, modernisation and secularisation of the Shah's regime, but, without doubt, the Year of Cyrus the Great made a contribution to the downfall of the Shah by exposing his inability to communicate effectively with his own people. In the end, the extravaganza at Pasargadae and Persepolis only separated the king further from his subjects.

Persia's monarchy effectively died on 16 January 1979 when the Shah, riddled with a terminal cancer, boarded a plane to take him out of Iran for the last time and into an uncertain exile which was mainly to be spent in hospital wards. By the time the sixty-year-old Muhammed Reza Shah Pahlavi took his last breath in a sickbed in a Cairo hospital on 27 July 1980, the mullahs in Iran were already at work expunging the memory of Persia's ancient – pagan – heritage from the history books.

The formation of the Islamic Republic of Iran under the leadership of the Ayatollah Khomeini and the Muslim clergy set in motion a systematic butchering of Persia's ancient past. By shutting down archaeological digs throughout Iran, closing university history programmes, and cordoning off all historical monuments, the theocratic regime began a bloodless crusade against Iran's own past, making the Muslim conquest of Persia by the Arabs the genesis of a new national chronology. The names Cyrus, Darius, and Xerxes were anathema and were expunged from school textbooks. Anticipating a cultural catastrophe, UNESCO named Persepolis a World Heritage Site in 1979 just at the point when Khomeini's Revolutionary Guards encircled the great archaeological site with bulldozers, ready to raze the place to the ground. Its close association with the Shah made Persepolis a potent symbol of the regime's hatred of the old order, and the site's safety tottered in the balance until 1988, when Khomeini made his one and only visit to the ruins. His pronouncement on what he saw and experienced that day revealed that the leader was torn between acknowledging that Persepolis 'still remains a marvel to mankind', but one built on 'lies, exploitation, and brute force'. The greatest monument of Achaemenid Persia's rich heritage was saved when the Ayatollah declared that 'We must recognise these monuments as a valuable treasury in which we can see history and humanity, Iran and the Iranians, together with their legacy. We must preserve them.'

Therein lies the struggle between Iranianism and Islamism which has continued to plague Iran for over four decades. The 1979 revolution replaced a 2,500-year-old tradition of secular monarchy with a theocracy which regards the glorification of that imperial tradition as hostile to the fundamental teachings of the Islamic Revolution.

*

On 29 October 2016, crowds numbering 15,000–30,000 people (precise figures are difficult to come by) swarmed around the tomb of Cyrus the Great in the usually quiet tourist destination of Pasargadae. They perambulated around its rectangular platform in the manner by which pilgrims circumnavigate the holy Kaaba in Mecca. And the crowds were vocal too: 'Iran is our country!' they shouted; 'Cyrus is our father! Clerical rule is tyranny!' These are dangerous words in the Islamic Republic of Iran, but ones which are highly symptomatic of the times.

Around 70 per cent of the Iranian population are below forty years of age. In fact, Iran has the youngest demographic on earth, the result of a government-fuelled fertility drive following the protracted and devastating Iran–Iraq war of the 1980s in which millions of soldiers and civilians died. Much of the youth of Iran are feeling increasingly remote from that war and from the Islamic Revolution which their grandparents had helped bring about and which changed the face of Iran so drastically. The mullahs who rule Iran no longer represent the vibrancy of the Iranian youth, and Islam has little or no appeal to the majority of the young people to flock to live in the cities and towns of Iran. For a theocracy, Iran has an overwhelmingly secular population. Devotion to Islam is being replaced, in fact, with a revitalisation of Iran's pre-Islamic identity. This is demonstrated in many ways: there is, for instance, an increasing trend in displays of nationalism among the general population that can be witnessed in a spike in the registration of pre-Islamic Persian names (Cyrus, Darius, Anahita) for new-born babies (in place of Muslim names like Hussain, Ali, and Fatemeh) and the use of the ever-present *farvahar* symbol, the Zoroastrian sign of Ahuramazda, which is sported on jewellery, T-shirts, tattoos, and bumper stickers. The pre-Islamic Persian past has been awakened in contemporary Iranian consciousness and its effect is galvanising Iranians to criticise the ruling regime.

Cyrus the Great and other Achaemenid successor kings have been regarded by Iranians as heroic figures for centuries, as men who created an empire built on (as far as the Iranians are concerned) tolerance and respect for all. This pseudo-history (for that is what it surely is) has provided a rich fodder of heroic stories of Great Kings and Shahs, upon which is founded national pride. Cyrus stands head and shoulders above all other kings when it comes to national mythmaking and his (invented) 'portrait' (we have no likeness of him from antiquity) is appearing in increasing numbers throughout Iran, on wall posters, mobile-phone covers, window stickers, and T-shirts. Yet in spite of his popular presence in Iranian society, given that pre-Islamic Persian history is only superficially taught in Iran's schools, Iranians are relatively naïve about the realities of Cyrus' empire-building (bloodshed and all). But even deprived of the facts, it is clear that they nevertheless remain deeply proud of their ancient heritage and of the leading role Cyrus had in it. For many Iranians, Cyrus was a freedom fighter and a human-rights activist. The last Shah enthusiastically lauded Cyrus in this way, claiming that he created the first ever Bill of Human Rights. This arose out of the Shah's long-held misunderstanding of the text of the Cyrus Cylinder, where a single line spoke of the invader's treatment of the inhabitants of Babylon: 'I relieved their weariness and freed them from their service.' It was hardly a declaration to end human suffering. That Cyrus subsequently liberated the Jews from their Babylonian captivity (and gained the title 'messiah') and allowed some (not all) of them to return to their homeland, augmented his reputation as a human-rights champion. The Shah used the Cyrus Cylinder as the official icon of his 1971 celebrations and plastered it on banknotes and coins. To tell the world that he was Cyrus reborn, a facsimile of the Cylinder was gifted by the Shah to the United Nations, where it remains to this day in a glass case in the New York lobby.

In more recent times, in the wake of the disputed presidential election in 2009, Iran's controversial president, Mahmoud Ahmadinejad, hoping to regain a measure of legitimacy, began to recast himself as a nationalist leading a struggle against foreign foes. He achieved something of a diplomatic triumph when the British Museum agreed to lend the National Museum of Iran the actual Cylinder for a special exhibition on Cyrus and his legacy. Thousands of Iranians flocked to Tehran for the once-in-a-lifetime chance to view a Babylonian-made document written in Akkadian and directed towards a Mesopotamian audience, which they nevertheless hailed as an icon of 'Iranianness'. As he placed a medal of honour onto the chest of an actor dressed in a colourful Cyrus the Great costume, at a ceremony in Tehran, President Ahmadinejad stated that 'Talking about Iran is not like talking about a geographical entity or race, talking about Iran is tantamount to talking about culture, human values, justice, love and sacrifice'.

Iranians may be relatively naïve about the realities of ancient Persian empire-building and of the content of the text of the Cyrus Cylinder, but that has not stopped the Cyrus craze from growing exponentially. Azadeh Moaveni, an Iranian American journalist and writer, echoes the feelings of many: 'Cyrus and the Achaemenid kings, who built their majestic capital at Persepolis, were exceptionally munificent for their time. They wrote the world's earliest recorded human rights declaration, and were opposed to slavery.' Much of this bogus understanding of the document arises from a plethora of fake translations which have been appearing on the internet for decades. One of the most high-profile victims of the Cylinder scam was Shirin Ebadi, who, in accepting the Nobel Peace Prize in 2003, quoted what she believed were Cyrus' genuine words:

I announce that I will respect the traditions, customs and religions of the nations of my empire and never let any of my governors and subordinates look down on or insult them as long as I shall live. From now on . . . I will impose my monarchy on no nation. Each is free to accept it, and if any one of them rejects it, I shall never resolve on war to reign.

Ebadi was, allegedly, mortified when she discovered the gaff.

The latest development in the tale, then, was the mass activation of the image of Cyrus which came to a head at his tomb in 2016. Today 29 October is celebrated annually by Iranians as an unofficial holiday; it is 'Cyrus the Great Day'. The Islamic government does not recognise its existence. In fact, the regime is befuddled, bewildered, and angered at its popularity. One venerable octogenarian mullah, Ayatollah Nouri-Hamedani, raged against the events at Pasargadae and dredged up the old Shah's misguided love of antiquity:

The Shah used to say, 'O Cyrus, sleep in peace as we are awake.' Now, a group of people have gathered around the tomb of Cyrus and they are circumambulating it and have taken their handkerchiefs out and cry [as they do for the Shiite Imam Hussein] . . . These [people] are counter-revolutionaries. I am amazed that these people get together around the tomb of Cyrus. Who in power has been so negligent to allow these people to gather? We are in a revolutionary and Islamic country, and this revolution is the continuation of the actions of the Prophet and the Imams.

Where will this movement go? Who knows? In the last sixty years Cyrus the Great has been used by two regimes to strengthen their power grip over Iran and its people. The Shah endorsed Pahlavi rulership as a natural continuation of Cyrus' policy of tolerance, yet Pahlavi rule was anything but tolerant. Ahmadinejad was willing to overlook the fact that Cyrus was a pagan in order to activate a much-needed nationalism to take focus away from his disputed election; in fact, he made Cyrus a sort of Shia saint. Now the young people of Iran have claimed Cyrus as their very own – separating him from shahs and mullahs, they are taking him into the streets in their iPhones and iPads. The myth of Cyrus is increasing, his cult is growing. Fact is displaced by a need to cast Cyrus as a new liberator, and that is a very powerful use of history. Antiquity is not dead; it is alive and vital. In Iran, the current use of the Achaemenid Persian past by the young and the restless might be the catalyst which drives Iran into a new age.

*

Why is it that in world history some empires lasted for centuries while others collapsed within a couple of generations? What, in a final analysis, may we make of the Persian empire and of the Achaemenid Great Kings who ruled it? That it was one of the world's most significant empires can no longer be in doubt, for despite some serious upheavals it experienced as a consequence of the rapidity of its growth, it nonetheless survived for over two centuries. Darius I and Xerxes were unsuccessful in their attempts to add European territories to the realm, but while they failed to impose lasting direct control in Greece, throughout its history the empire suffered no substantial territorial loss whatsoever. When Egypt broke away from Persian rule it was reconquered and resettled into the imperial structure. In the maintenance of the empire, the Persians were remarkably forward thinking and allowed the different areas to continue with traditional practices of rule, those which best suited them. The Persians did not change the tried-and-tested methods of governance and they imposed nothing of themselves onto conquered peoples and were sensitive to the cultures they vanquished. There was no forceful adoption of the Persian language, or Persian gods, or of a Persian 'system'. The Achaemenid kings were content to receive the tribute of the provinces, and while the wealth of empire flowed into the central administration, they remained placid masters. Variations in forms of Achaemenid rulership must not be taken as signs of imperial weakness. On the contrary, the varieties of political interaction experienced by the Persians and the elastic approach to governing which they practised is a great positive. It proves that there was another model for empire. It is all the more tragic then that the mode of empire adopted by later civilisations of the West – chiefly the Romans, the British, and the other imperial powers of the industrialised world – chose to ignore the Persian Version. Empire is never a happy state of being, it is not a good thing for subjected peoples, but an enlightened empire run on Persian lines would be preferable to the brutality of Roman rule and its aggressive adherence to a policy of Romanisation. The white-supremacist ideology that was brought to bear on the conquered peoples of Africa, India, the Middle East, and South Asia by powerful industrialist European imperialists was the antithesis of that of the Persian empire. Had the Persian Version of history been taught in the European equivalents of Eton and Sandhurst, with less emphasis placed on Rome as the model for empire, who knows, maybe the experience of millions of people around the globe might have been at least more dignified.

The kings of the Achaemenid dynasty ruled absolutely. They were unchallenged by outside forces and maintained their exclusive hold on the throne. They were weakened not by outside shows of strength, but by internal family strife. Their inability to set in motion an organised system of primogeniture meant that the dynasty's weaknesses were exposed with each death of a monarch and with every succession crisis which almost inevitably followed. The relationships between fathers and sons were often fraught with tensions while relationships between brothers could be bitter and, often, bloody. Had the Achaemenids managed to stop the infighting and to work as a harmonious unit, the empire might have outlasted Alexander's attack, for despite the trials and tribulations of the family itself, the Achaemenid empire was strong and functioning well at the time of its conquest by Macedon. The traditional 'rise and fall' scenario does not match what happened to Persia. Vigorous and vital to the end, the Persian empire was assaulted by Alexander, who held it to ransom for a short time while he toyed with it, debating if he wanted to be a Great King or a Macedonian warlord. Eventually he killed it with one swift slash to the throat. As it bled out, Alexander was convinced that he was the man who could not just restore the grandeur of the old realm of Darius the Great, but would enlarge it and make it a kingdom of everlasting fame. Yet just seven years after reducing Persepolis to rubble and ash, in 323 BCE Alexander lay dead in Babylon. His final years of life saw him turn to heavy drink, good living, and very poor leadership. His dreams of empire died with him and ultimately he failed in his mission to outstrip the long-lived glories of Cyrus, Darius, and Xerxes.

*

Abul-Qâsem Ferdowsi was a very wise man. He knew the value of evoking Iran's ancient past and he took great pride in its legacy, writing in *Shahnameh* that:

> The ancient kings who came before us here
> Were paid with foreign tribute every year.
> Once we were mighty, and in everything
> The Greek realm bowed before the Persian king.

Ferdowsi was also a realist. He knew that Iran would suffer further wars and incursions. It was a rich country, ripe for invasion. He was correct. Numerous world powers, on their own journeys of empire-building, have attempted to control Iran; they have attempted to crush its culture and destroy its identity. Yet the foreign powers who invaded Iran across many successive centuries – the Arabs, Mongols, and Turks – eventually ended up being conquered by the culture they aimed to destroy. The sheer force of Persian civilisation, its deep historical legacy, overpowered them as they became thoroughly 'Persianised'. Who knows what threats Iran will face next, or how its ancient history will be reactivated. Even in the midst of international threats to Iran's liberty, the scaremongering so beloved by Western media, and the difficulties Iranians face in their day-to-day lives, there is no danger that the Persian past will be forgotten again. Cyrus and the ancient Great Kings are figures of enormous pride, and perhaps even of ambition, because today they represent what it means to be Iranian, to be Persian. Long may the Great Kings reign.

Dramatis Personae

> Persian names, which express the nature of some bodily or mental excellence, all end with the same letter – that which is called *San* by the Dorians, and *Sigma* by the Ionians. Anyone who examines will find that the Persian names, one and all without exception, end with this letter.
>
> – Herodotus 1.139

Old Persian is an inflected language and so, like the Ionic Greek that Herodotus spoke, the suffix – that is, the part at the end of a word – would change depending on its case. What Herodotus observed was most likely the nominative form of Persian names, which, in Old Persian, can end in -*sh*, which is close to but not the same as the -*s* denoted by the Dorian *San* or Ionian *Sigma*. This is just one example of the many observable mistakes in Greek renderings of Persian names, and – more often than not – these names have passed through a number of mutations by the time that they reach us. Here, you will find the names belonging to the main characters of this book, some of which are attested in Old Persian or have been reconstructed into their original language from their Greek and foreign renderings.

The Great Kings

Achaemenes (Greek, *Achaiménēs*; Old Persian, *Haxāmanish* – 'Having a friend's mind'; *c.* late 8th to early 7th cent. BCE): Legendary founder of the Achaemenid dynasty.

Artaxerxes I (Greek, *Artaxérxēs* or *Makrókheir* – 'long-handed'; Old Persian, *Artaxshaça* – 'Whose rule is through deified truth'; r.465–424 BCE): Son of Xerxes I.

Artaxerxes II (Greek (birthname), *Arsicas* or *Arsēs*; Old Persian (reginal name), *Artaxshaça* – 'Whose rule is through deified truth'; r.404–358 BCE): The son of Darius II and the influential Parysatis; Artaxerxes' reign was initially contested through a bloody civil war with his younger brother, Cyrus the Younger.

Artaxerxes III (Greek (birthname), *Ōchos*; Babylonian (birthname), *Úmakush*; Old Persian (reginal name), *Artaxshaça* – 'Whose rule is through deified truth'; r.358–338 BCE): Ascended to the throne after a series of executions and plots against his elder brothers; Artaxerxes' reign oversaw a turbulent period in Persia's history.

Artaxerxes IV (Greek, *Arsēs*; Old Persian (birthname), *Arshaka* – 'Manly'; Old Persian (reginal name), *Artaxshaça* – 'Whose rule is through deified truth'; r.338–336 BCE): Son of Artaxerxes III, Arses ascended to the Persian throne after the murder of his father, but, like father, like son, was soon poisoned.

Bardiya (Greek, *Smerdis*; Old Persian, *Bardīya* – 'Lofty' or *Gaumāta*; r.522 BCE): As the youngest son of Cyrus the Great, Bardiya ascended to the Persian throne after the death of his half-brother, Cambyses II. Darius I, however, staged a coup d'état in the same year, claiming that Bardiya was none other than a Magus named Gaumāta who had murdered and usurped the throne from the true Bardiya.

Cambyses I (Old Persian, *Kambūjiya*; Akkadian, *Kambuziya*; r. *c.*600–559 BCE): King of Anshan and the son of Cyrus I; father to Cyrus the Great.

Cambyses II (Old Persian, *Kambūjiya*; Akkadian, *Kambuziya*; r.530–522 BCE): Inheriting the throne from his father, Cyrus the Great, Cambyses is best known for the Persian annexation of Egypt.

Cyrus I (Greek, *Kûros*; Old Persian, *Kûrush* – 'Humiliator of the Enemy'; r. *c.*600–580 BCE): Son of Teispes, Cyrus inherited the throne of Anshan and fathered Cambyses I.

Cyrus II (the Great) (Greek, *Kûros*; Old Persian, *Kûrush* – 'Humiliator of the Enemy'; *c.*590–530 BCE): King of Kings, King of the World, the Great King, Cyrus the Great, embarked on a series of military campaigns which founded the Persian empire.

Darius I (the Great) (Greek, *Dareîos*; Old Persian, *Dārayavaush* – 'Holding firm the good'; r. September 522–October 486 BCE): Eldest son of Hystaspes and Irdabama, Darius came to power through a coup d'état against Bardiya.

Darius II (Greek, *Nothos* – 'Bastard'; Greek (birthname), *Ôchos*; Old Persian (birthname), *Vauka* or *Vaush*; Old Persian (reginal name), *Dārayavaush* – 'Holding firm the good'; r. February 423–March 403 BCE): Son of Artaxerxes I and a Babylonian concubine, Darius ascended to the Persian throne in contest with his half-brother, Sogdianus.

Darius III (Latin, *Codomannus*; Old Persian (birthname), *Artashiyāta* – 'Happy in truth'; Old Persian (regnal name), *Dārayavaush* – 'Holding firm the good'; r.336–330 BCE): The last of the Achaemenid kings, Darius ascended to the Persian throne after the murder of his predecessor, Artaxerxes IV, and his heirs.

Sogdianus (Old Persian, *Sughudash* – 'The Sogdian'; r.424–423 BCE): Short-reigned son of Artaxerxes I.

Tishpish (Greek, *Teispes*; Old Persian, *Cishpish*; Babylonian, *Shîshpîsh*; r.675–640 BCE): King of the Teispid dynasty of Anshan in Persia.

Xerxes I (Old Persian, *Xshayarashā* – 'Ruling over heroes'; r.486–465 BCE): Succeeding his father, Darius I, to the Persian throne, Xerxes, having spent the early years of his reign suppressing revolts in Egypt and Babylonia, waged a series of successive campaigns across the Greek mainland.

Persian Nobility

Achaemenes (Greek, *Achaiménēs*; Old Persian, *Haxāmanish* – 'Having a friend's mind'; d. 460–50 BCE): Son of Darius I, satrap in Egypt at the time of Inarus' uprising.

Arsames (Old Persian, *Arshāma* – 'Having a hero's strength'; c.520 BCE): Son of Ariaramnes, father of Hystaspes, and loyal follower of Cyrus the Great.

Arshama (Old Persian, *Arshāma* – 'Having a hero's strength'; Greek, *Arsámēs*; r. c.454–407 BCE): Satrap of Egypt, Arshama was a loyal follower of Darius II, helping him overthrow his brother, Sogdianus, in 423 BCE.

Artabanus (Old Persian, *Artasūra* – 'Powerful [through the] deified truth'; Elamite, *Irdashura*; mid-6th to early 5th cent. BCE): Brother of Darius I and uncle to Xerxes I.

Artabanus of Hyrcania (Old Persian, *Artabānush* – 'The glory of the truth'; *fl.*): The commander of the Persian royal guard who, with the help of the eunuch Aspamitres, murdered Xerxes I.

Artobazanes (Old Persian, *Artabarzana* – 'Exalting truth'; c.530–470 BCE): As the firstborn son of Darius I, Artobazanes claimed the Persian throne until mounting pressure from his brother, Xerxes I, eventually forced him to abandon his aspirations.

Artabazus II (Elamite, *Irdumasda*; Old Iranian, *Artavazdā* – 'Persevering [through] truth'; *fl. c.*390–325 BCE): Satrap of Phrygia under Darius III.

Aspathines (Old Persian, *Aspačanā* – 'Delighting in horses'; *c.* mid-6th to mid-5th cent. BCE): Member of the Gang of Seven and bow-bearer of Darius I.

Bessus (Greek (birthname), *Bessos*; Old Persian (reginal name), *Artaxshaça* – 'Whose rule is through deified truth'; r.330–329 BCE): A prominent satrap of Bactria who hastily proclaimed himself Great King in a coup against Darius III.

Cyrus the Younger (Greek, *Kūros*; Old Persian, *Kūrush* – 'Humiliator of the enemy'; c.423–401 BCE): Second son of Darius II and brother to

Artaxerxes II; led an unsuccessful revolt against his newly crowned brother in 404 BCE.

Dariaios (Greek, *Dareîos*; Old Persian, *Dārayavaush* – 'Holding firm the good'; d.465 BCE): The son and crown prince of Xerxes I, Dariaios maintained a rather tenuous relationship with his family. His wife, Artyantē, was his father's mistress.

Gobryas (Greek, *Gobryas*; Old Persian, *Gaubaruva* – 'Cattle-baron'; c.6th cent. BCE): Leader of the Patischorian tribe of Pārs and one of the seven conspirators who killed Gaumāta.

Harpagus (Greek, *Arpagos*; Babylonian, *Arbaku*; c.6th cent. BCE): Median general credited with helping Cyrus the Great to the throne.

Hydarnes I (Old Persian, *Vidarna* – 'He who knows'; r. c.521–480 BCE): Member of the Gang of Seven; satrap of Media.

Hystaspes (Greek, *Histáspēs*; Old Persian, *Vishtāspa* – 'Whose horses are set loose' c.550 BCE): Satrap in Bactria and then Persia; father of Darius I.

Intaphernes (Old Persian, *Vindafarnā* – 'He who finds *Farr*'; c. mid- to late 6th cent. BCE): One of the Gang of Seven; put to death by Darius I.

Mardonius (Greek, *Mardonios*; Old Persian, *Marduniya* – 'He who is mild'; d.479 BCE): The son of Gobryas; leading general of the Persian army throughout the Greco-Persian wars; killed at the battle of Plataea.

Masistes (Greek, *Masistēs*; Old Iranian, *Masishta*; Old Persian, *Mathishta* – 'The greatest'. d.478 BCE): Son of Darius I and brother to Xerxes I, Masistes was the satrap of Bactria during his brother's reign.

Megabyzus I (the Elder) (Old Persian, *Bagabuxsha* – 'God-saved'; c. mid-6th to early 5th cent. BCE): One of the Gang of Seven.

Megabyzus II (Old Persian, *Bagabuxsha* – 'God-saved'; *fl.* 485–440 BCE): Grandson of Megabyzus I, son of Zopyrus; Persian general who participated in a number of military campaigns across Greece and Egypt.

Orentes (Old Persian, *Arvanta* – 'Swift'; c.401–344 BCE): Armenian satrap of Bactrian origins.

Otanes (Old Persian, *Utāna* – 'Having good descendants'; c. late 6th cent. BCE): A member of the Gang of Seven.

Pharnabazus (Greek, *Pharnábazos*; Old Persian, *Parnavazdā*; *c*.422–387 BCE): Satrap of Phrygia until the conquests of Alexander.

Pissoúthnēs (Old Persian, *Pishishyaothna*; *fl.* late 5th cent. BCE): Lydian satrap who instigated an unsuccessful revolt in Sardis with the help of the Greek general Lycon.

Sataspes (Old Persian, *Satāspa* – 'Having hundreds of horses'; Babylonian, *Shatashpa*; early to mid-5th cent. BCE): After raping the daughter of Zopyrus, Sataspes escaped execution when pardoned by Xerxes I. Eventually brought to justice and killed.

Terituchmes (*fl.* late 5th cent. BCE): Descendant of Hydarnes; husband of Amestris II; satrap of Armenia.

Tiribazus (Old Persian, *Tīrivazdā* – 'Persevering [through the god] Tir'; *c*.440–370 BCE): Satrap of Armenia and, later, Lydia; executed.

Tissaphernes (Old Persian, *Čiçrafarnah* – 'With shining *Farr*'; 445–395 BCE): Grandson of Hydarnes I; satrap of Sardis.

Ugbrau (Old Persian, *Gaubaruva* – 'Cattle-baron'; Greek, *Gobryas*; *c*.6th cent. BCE): Babylonian nobleman who assisted Cyrus the Great in toppling the Neo-Babylonian king, Nabonidus.

Persian Women

Amestris (Old Persian, *Amāstris* – 'Strength'; Greek, *Ámēstris*; d. *c*.424 BCE): Wife of Xerxes I and mother of Artaxerxes I.

Amytis I (Old Persian, *Umati* – 'Having good thoughts'; *c*.630–565 BCE): Daughter of the Median king and wife to Nebuchadnezzar II of Babylon.

Amytis II (Old Persian, *Umati* – 'Having good thoughts'; early 5th cent. BCE): Daughter of Xerxes I and wife of Megabyzus I.

Artayntē (mid 5th cent. BCE): Daughter of Masistes and wife to the crown prince, Dariaios.

Artazostre (Avestan, *Ashazaothra* – 'Offering to the deified truth'; late 6th to early 5th cent. BCE): Daughter of Darius I and wife to Mardonius, her cousin.

Artystone (Elamite, *Irtashduna*; Old Persian, *Artastūnā* – 'Pillar of the deified Truth'; *c*.6th cent. BCE): Daughter of Cyrus the Great, sister to Bardiya, and wife to her brother's usurper, Darius I.

Atossa (Old Persian, *Utautha* – 'Well-granting'; Avestan, *Hutaosā*; Elamite, *Udusana*; *c.*550–475 BCE): Daughter of Cyrus the Great and sister-wife to Cambyses II. After the death of her husband, she later remarried to Darius I and bore him the royal heir, Xerxes I.

Cassandane (Greek, *Kassandanē*; *c.*6th cent. BCE): Daughter of Pharnaspes; mother of Cambyses II and Bardiya; wife to Cyrus the Great.

Damaspia (Old Persian, *Jāmāspī*; Greek, *Damáspiā*; d. *c.*424 BCE): Wife of Artaxerxes I and mother to his heir, Xerxes II.

Gigis (d. *c.*332 BCE): Handmaiden of Parysatis; executed for conspiracy to murder.

Irdabama (*fl.* early 5th cent. BCE): Mother of Darius I; landholder.

Mandane (Old Iranian, *Mandanā* – 'delightful; 'cheerful'): Daughter of Astyages of Media and wife of Cambyses I of Anshan; mother of Cyrus the Great.

Mania (Greek, *Manía* – raging; *c.*440–399 BCE): Widow of Zenis, a client king of Dardanus in Asia Minor; female governor under the Persian satrap, Pharnabazus.

Parmys (Old Persian, *Uparmiya* – 'Abiding'; *c.* late 6th to mid-5th cent. BCE): Daughter of Bardiya and wife to his usurper, Darius I.

Parysatis (Old Persian, *Parushyātish*; *c.*5th cent. BCE): Daughter of Artaxerxes I who married her half-brother, Darius II; mother of Artaxerxes II and Cyrus the Younger.

Phaidyme (Old Persian, *Upandush*; *c.* late 6th cent. BCE): Daughter of Otanes and wife of Cambyses II and Bardiya.

Phratagoune (*fl.* early 5th cent. BCE): Daughter of Artanes and wife of Darius I.

Rhodogyne (*fl.* early 4th cent. BCE): Daughter of Artaxerxes II and Stateira I; wife of Orentes.

Rhoxane (Old Persian, *Rhauxshnā* – 'Shining one'; *c.* early to mid-6th cent. BCE): Sister-wife of Cambyses II.

Stateira I (*c.*370–332 BCE): Daughter of the influential *khān* Hydarnes III, and sister of Terituchmes; wife of Artaxerxes II; murdered by Parysatis.

Stateira II (d. *c.*332 BCE): The wife of Darius III; captured by Alexander the Great; died in childbirth giving birth to Alexander's child.

Stateira III (d. *c.*323 BCE): Daughter of Darius III and Stateira II; wife of Alexander the Great.

Courtiers and Administrators

Apollonides of Cos (Greek, *Apollōnidēs* – 'Son of Apollo'; *fl.* early 4th cent. BCE) A Greek physician at the court of Artaxerxes I.

Artasyras (Old Persian, *Artasūra* – 'Powerful through the deified truth'; Elamite, *Irdashura*; 6th cent. BCE): A Hyrcanian courtier under Cambyses II, Artasyras helped Darius I overthrow Bardiya and seize the throne.

Artoxares (Old Persian, *Artaxshara*; 5th cent. BCE): A Paphlagonian eunuch who, having returned from exile in Armenia, was said to have plotted against the newly seated king, Darius II, and was consequently executed.

Aspamitres (Old Persian, *Aspamitra* – 'Having horses by covenant'; *fl.* 5th cent. BCE): Eunuch who assisted in the murder of Xerxes I.

Bagapates (Old Persian, *Bagapāta* – 'Protected by the gods'; *c.*6th to early 5th cent. BCE): The king's chief steward and eunuch who betrayed Bardiya.

Bagoas (Old Persian, *Bagui*; Greek, *Bagōas*; d.336 BCE): A prominent eunuch and courtier within the Achaemenid court who poisoned two consecutive kings, Artaxerxes III and IV, before he was himself tricked into drinking his own poison by Darius III.

Parnakka (Greek, *Pharnákēs*; Elamite, *Parnakka*; *c.*565–497 BCE): Director of the Persepolis civil service; as a son of Arsames and brother to Hystaspes, was an uncle to Darius I.

Rashda (*fl.* early 5th cent. BCE): Chief of staff to Darius I's mother, Irdabama.

Teridates (Old Persian, *Tīridāta* – 'Given by [the god] Tir; *fl.* early 4th cent. BCE): Favourite eunuch of Artaxerxes III.

Zishshawish (Elamite, *Zishshawish*; Old Persian, *Ciçavahu* – 'Of good lineage'; *fl. c.*504–496 BCE): Deputy to Parnakka; in charge of recording ration orders at Persepolis.

Non-Persians

Alexander I (Greek, *Aléxandros* – 'Protector of man'; r. *c.*498–454 BCE): Macedonian vassal of the Achaemenid kings.

Alexander III (the Great) (Greek, *Aléxandros* – 'Protector of man'; r.336–323 BCE): Ascending to the throne of Macedon after the assassination of his father, Philip II, Alexander launched a series of infamous military campaigns across the Persian empire.

Artemisia II (Greek, *Artemīsíā* – 'Wormwood'; r.353–351 BCE): Member of the Hecatomnid dynasty, ruler of Caria.

Aspasia of Phocis (Greek, *Aspasia* – 'Welcome embrace'; *c.*450–380 BCE): Greek concubine of Cyrus the Younger.

Astyages (Babylonian, *Ištumegu*; Old Iranian, *Rishti Vaiga* – 'Swinging the spear, lance-hurler'; r. *c.*585–550 BCE): The last king of Media, defeated by Cyrus the Great.

Cyaraxes (Akkadian, *Umakishtar*; Old Iranian, *Uvaxshtra* – 'Good ruler'; r.625–585 BCE): King of Media and father of Astyages.

Gimillu (Babylonian, *Gimillu* – 'Favour-seeker'; *fl. c.*540–520 BCE): Petty criminal, thief, conman, and thug.

Inarus (d. *c.*454 BCE): A Libyan noble who led an Egyptian revolt against the Persians in 460 BCE.

Nectanebo II (Egyptian, *Nahkt-hor-hebit* – 'Strong is Horus [the god] of Hebit'; r.360–342 BCE): Third pharaoh of the Thirtieth Dynasty; the last native ruler of Egypt before it was reoccupied by Artaxerxes III.

Philip II (Greek, *Philippos* – 'Fond of horses'; r.359–336 BCE): King of Macedon until his assassination in 336 BCE.

Themistocles (Greek, *Themistoklēs* – 'Glory of the law'; *c.*524–459 BCE): Athenian politician and general.

Tomyris (Scythian, *Tahmirih* – 'Brave'; *c.* mid- to late 6th cent. BCE): Queen of the Massagetai who defeated Cyrus the Great in battle.

Udjahorresnet (*c.* late 6th cent. BCE): Egyptian courtier who served Cambyses II and his successor, Darius I.

Further Reading

The following bibliography is very selective and reflects mainly the English-language scholarship I have drawn on directly. I have tried to make this selection helpful for readers who wish to pursue their enquiries further and in a more scholarly form. To that end, I have annotated each entry with a comment on why I find the work useful.

One book warrants special attention:

Kuhrt, Amélie. 2007. *The Persian Empire. A Corpus of Sources from the Achaemenid Period*. London. This is an indispensable collection of source materials – Achaemenid inscriptions, Aramaic, demotic, Greek and Latin texts, as well as art and archaeology. Kuhrt, a leading expert in the field of Near Eastern Studies, supports her translated materials with fine commentaries. For anyone who wishes to take their study of Achaemenid history further, then this book is a must-have.

Allen, Lindsay. 2005. *The Persian Empire*. London. A nicely illustrated, well-constructed overview of Achaemenid history.
——. 2005. 'Le Roi Imaginaire. An Audience with the Achaemenid King', in O. Hekster and R. Fowler (eds.), *Imaginary Kings. Royal Images in the Ancient Near East, Greece and Rome*. Munich. 39–62. An excellent study of the perception and protocol of the royal audience.
Álvarez-Mon, Javier. 2020. *The Art of Elam*. London. Up-to-date study of Elamite material culture.

Asheri, David, Alan Lloyd, and Aldo Corcella. 2007. *A Commentary on Herodotus Books I–IV*. Oxford. A first-rate commentary on the early books of Herodotus' *Histories*. It includes much of value on Herodorus' views on Persia, Cyrus II, Cambyses II, and Darius I.

Balcer, J. M. 1987. *Herodotus and Bisitun. Problems in Ancient Persian Historiography.* Stuttgart. Sadly, long out of print, but well worth searching for a copy.

Boardman, John. 2000. *Persia and the West. An Archaeological Investigation of the Genesis of Achaemenid Art.* London. A well-illustrated overview of the art of Achaemenid Iran.

Briant, Pierre. 2002. *From Cyrus to Alexander. A History of the Persian Empire.* Winona Lake. The masterwork on the history of the Achaemenid empire; sometimes unwieldy and somewhat baroque, but always scholarly.

Briant, Pierre, Wouter Henkleman, and Matt Stolper (eds.). 2008. *L'Archive des fortifications de Persépolis.* Paris. Full of up-to-date analysis of the Persepolis cuneiform documents; many chapters are in English.

Brosius, Maria. 1996. *Women in Ancient Persia (559–331 BC).* Oxford. The only available monograph on Achaemenid women and to that end useful, but it is sadly blinkered in its approach to the subject and is fast becoming very dated.

Bullough, Vern L. 2002. 'Eunuchs in History and Society', in S. Tougher (ed.), *Eunuchs in Antiquity and Beyond.* Swansea and London. 1–17. A very engaging (and eye-watering), perceptive account of the process of becoming a eunuch.

Canepa, Matthew. 2018. *The Iranian Expanse. Transforming Royal Identity through Architecture, Landscape, and the Built Environment, 550 BCE–642 CE.* Berkeley. An exciting study of the *longue durée* of archaeological sites in Iran; simply excellent.

Colburn, Henry. 2019. *The Archaeology of Empire in Achaemenid Egypt.* Edinburgh. A fine new account of Egypt under Persian control, looking at art and archaeology.

Collon, Dominique. 1987. *First Impressions. Cylinder Seals in the Ancient Near East.* London. An excellent study of the use of seal imagery in the ancient Near East.

Cook, John M. 1983. *The Persian Empire.* London. A very fine narrative of the Persian empire's history written by an inquisitive Classicist at a time when Classics was being separated from Persian history.

Curtis, John. 2013. *The Cyrus Cylinder and Ancient Persia*. London. A useful synthesis of current thoughts on this important piece of Persian propaganda.

Curtis, John, and St John Simpson (eds.). 2010. *The World of Achaemenid Persia.* London. A very fine collection of scholarly articles drawn from the British Museum's *Forgotten Empire* symposium.

Curtis, John, and Nigel Tallis (eds.). 2005. *Forgotten Empire. The World of Ancient Persia.* London. Exhibition catalogue, full of great photographs.

Curtis, Vesta Sarkhosh. 1993. *Persian Myths.* London. A useful and interesting beginner's book.

Daryaee, Touraj (ed.). 2017. *King of the Seven Climes. A History of the Ancient Iranian World (3000 BCE–651 CE).* Irvine. A very readable series of scholarly essays covering the pre-Islamic history of Iran.

Davis, Dick. 2006. *Shahnameh. The Persian Book of Kings.* New York and London. A masterful (abbreviated) translation of Ferdowsi's great epic poem. A must-read.

Dusinberre, Elspeth R. M. 2003. *Aspects of Empire in Achaemenid Sardis.* Cambridge. A fascinating investigation of the Persian presence in Asia Minor.

Edelman, Diana, Anne Fizpatrick-McKinley, and Philippe Guillaume (eds.). 2016. *Religion in the Achaemenid Persian Empire*. Stuttgart. An excellent, up-to-date collection of thought-provoking essays.

Finkel, Irving L. 2013. *The Cyrus Cylinder. The Great Persian Edict from Babylon.* London. An excellent study which includes a new translation of the Babylonian text.

Finkel, Irving L., and Michael J. Seymour. (eds.). 2008. *Babylon*. London. A well-illustrated exhibition catalogue from the British Museum.

Frye, Richard N. 1962. *The Heritage of Persia.* London. A beautifully written love letter to Persia from a scholar whose soul was Iranian.

Garland, Robert. 2017. *Athens Burning. The Persian Invasion of Greece and the Evacuation of Attica.* Baltimore. A gripping account of Xerxes' conquest of Athens.

Hallock, Richard T. 1969. *Persepolis Fortification Tablets*. Chicago. Still the best collection of Persepolitan cuneiform tablets available. English translations throughout.

Harper, Prudence O., Joan Aruz, and Françoise Tallon (eds.). 1992. *The Royal City of Susa. Ancient Near Eastern Treasures in the Louvre*. New York. A fine study of the long history of Susa with many illustrations.

Harrison, Thomas. 2010. *Writing Ancient Persia*. London. An intriguing, thoughtful critique of modern Achaemenid historiography.

Head, Duncan. 1992. *The Achaemenid Persian Army*. Stockport. Well worth the read, a solid study of the nature of the Persian army, looking especially at equipment.

Heckel, Waldemar. 2020. *In the Path of Conquest. Resistance to Alexander the Great*. Oxford. A sweeping account of Alexander's campaigns by one of the best Alexander historians.

Henkelman, Wouter F. M. 2008. *The Other Gods Who Are. Studies in Elamite-Iranian Acculturation Based on the Persepolis Fortification Texts*. Achaemenid History XIV. Leiden. A groundbreaking study of Achaemenid-period religion.

Jacobs, Bruno, and Robert Rollinger (eds). 2021. *Blackwell Companion to the Achaemenid Persian Empire*. Oxford. A two-volume compendium of essays by leading scholars on all aspects of the Achaememids and their empire.

Kaptan, Denize. 2002. *The Daskyleion Bullae. Seal Images from the Western Achaemenid Empire*. 2 vols. Leiden. A revealing study of how seal imagery can be used to understand the Persian empire.

Khatchadourian, Lori. 2016. *Imperial Matter. Ancient Persia and the Archaeology of Empires*. Irvine. A challenging and bold approach to the archaeological evidence for the Persian empire.

Lincoln, Bruce. 2007. *Religion, Empire and Torture. The Case of Achaemenid Persia, with a Postscript on Abu Ghraib*. Chicago. A thought-provoking and controversial look at the Persian empire.

Llewellyn-Jones, Lloyd. 2012. 'The Great Kings of the Fourth Century and the Greek Memory of the Persian Past', in J. Marincola, L. Llewellyn-Jones and C. Maciver (eds.), *Greek Notions of the Past in the Archaic and Classical Eras. History Without Historians*. Edinburgh.

317–46. An exploration of what the Greeks thought about the
Persians in the late classical period.

Llewellyn-Jones, Lloyd, and James Robson. 2010. *Ctesias' History of Persia.
Tales of the Orient*. London. An English translation of Ctesias' insider
Persian history, with a historical introduction.

Manning, Sean. 2020. *Armed Force in the Teispid–Achaemenid Empire. Past
Approaches, Future Prospects*. Stuttgart. A much-needed new analysis
of the Achaemenid military. Highly recommended.

Morgan, Janett. 2016. *Greek Perspectives on the Achaemenid Empire. Persia
through the Looking Glass*. Edinburgh. An imaginative and innovative
take on Greco-Persian interactions. Very readable.

Mousavi, Ali. 2012. *Persepolis. Discovery and Afterlife of a World Wonder*.
Berlin. The best study of the archaeology of Persepolis.

Olmstead, A. T. 1948. *History of the Persian Empire*. Chicago. A dated, but
still very readable history by one of the greats of Persian historical
scholarship.

Perrot, Jean. 2013. *The Palace of Darius at Susa. The Great Royal Residence
of Achaemenid Persia*. London. Packed with colour photographs, this
is a masterful work on the archaeology of Susa.

Potts, Daniel T. 1999. *The Archaeology of Elam. Formation and
Transformation of an Ancient Iranian State*. Cambridge. A solid
account of the archaeology of the Elamites.

—— (ed.). 2013. *The Oxford Handbook of Ancient Iran*. Oxford and New
York. A great collection of academic papers on all things Iranian in
the pre-Islamic period.

Root, Margaret Cool. 1979. *The King and Kingship in Achaemenid
Art. Essays on the Creation of an Iconography of Empire*. Leiden. A
masterpiece of Persian studies.

Shayegan, M. Rahim. 2008. *Aspects of History and Epic in Ancient
Iran. From Gaumāta to Wahnām*. Cambridge, Mass. Intriguing
reinterpretation of Darius' Bisitun Inscription.

Stoneman, Richard. 2015. *Xerxes. A Persian Life*. New Haven. A highly
readable account of Persia's most notorious Great King.

Strassler, Robert B. (ed.). 2007. *The Landmark Herodotus*. New York.
Not only a great translation of the *Histories*, but also packed full of
introductory materials and commentaries.

Stronach, David. 1978. *Parsagade*. Oxford. The very best study of the palace and garden of Cyrus the Great.

Waters, Matt. 2014. *Ancient Persia. A Concise History of the Achaemenid Empire, 550–330 BC*. Cambridge. A very useful textbook, easy to digest.

Wiesehöfer, Josef. 1996. *Ancient Persia from 550 BC to 650 AD*. London and New York. An excellent introduction to the Achaemenid, Parthian, and Sasanian Persians.

Wilber, Donald N. 1969. *Persepolis. The Archaeology of Parsa, Seat of the Persian Kings*. Princeton. A well-illustrated guide to the history and archaeology of Persepolis.

Zaghamee, Reza. 2018. *Discovering Cyrus. The Persian Conqueror astride the Ancient World*. Los Angeles. A delightful, energetic study of Cyrus the Great.

Internet Resources

The following sites provide links to a wide range of Achaemenid-related resources and are well worth exploring:

Gateways

http://www.achemenet.com/
http://www.iranicaonline.org/
http://www.cais-soas.com/index.htm
http://www.livius.org/persia.html

An excellent selection of Persian-related books and materials for downloading is available at:
http://oi.uchicago.edu/research/pubs/catalog/persia.html

For more on Persian history and culture visit the website of the British Institute of Persian Studies (membership benefits are very well worth the small yearly charge); available at:
British Institute of Persian Studies (bips.ac.uk)

Royal Inscriptions and Old Persian Language
http://www.livius.org/aa-ac/achaemenians/inscriptions.html
http://www.fas.harvard.edu/~iranian/OldPersian/index.html

Achaemenid Aramaic and the Arshama Dossier
http://arshama.classics.ox.ac.uk/

Persepolis
http://www.persepolis3d.com/

Notes on Abbreviations

I have attempted to aid the reader who may be unfamiliar with standardised academic abbreviations by citing references to ancient authors (where known) and the titles of their works in full. This applies to both classical and Near Eastern texts. But there are, nevertheless, systems of abbreviating references which might prove useful to the reader seeking further study:

For Achaemenid royal inscriptions:

A^1 – Artaxerxes I
A^2 – Artaxerxes II
A^3 – Artaxerxes III
C – Cyrus
D – Darius I
D^2 – Darius II
X – Xerxes
B – Babylon (for the Cyrus Cylinder)
B – Bisitun (for the inscription of Darius I)
E – Elvend
H – Hamadan
M – Parsagade
N – Naqšh-i Rustam
P – Persepolis
S – Susa
V – Van (Lake Van, Armenia)
Z – Suez

SC – Seal
VS – Vase
W – Weight

A³Pa is therefore: Artaxerxes III's Persepolis inscription a.
D²Sb means: Darius II's Susa inscription b.

Texts from Persepolis:

PFT – Persepolis Fortification Tablets
PF – siglum for Persepolis Fortification tablets published by Hallock 1969
PFa – further Persepolis Fortification tablets published by Hallock 1978
PF-NN – siglum for Persepolis Fortification tablets transliterated by Hallock, but as yet unpublished
PFS – Persepolis Fortification seal (cylinder seal)
PFS* – Inscribed Persepolis Fortification seal (cylinder seal)
PFs – Persepolis Fortification stamp seal
PFS-N – Persepolis Fortification seal only attested on PFa tablets

Acknowledgements

For the last thirty years or so, the study of ancient Persia has developed into a rigorous academic discipline and it has become an integral aspect of research in the fields of Ancient History and Archaeology. Enthusiasm for knowing more about Persia and the Persians is steadily growing among the public. There is an appetite for Persian history. This book, I hope, helps to feed the interest and to promote further investigation.

I have written this book out of the passion I have for the study and dissemination of Persian history. I have also written it as a declaration of love to the people of Iran, for I am deeply enamoured of Iran and the Iranians. And yet it seems that hardly a week passes by when Iran is not in the news – always, it seems, for negative reasons. Iran is vilified by the Western media as a harbinger of terrorism, the home of fundamentalism, intolerance, and hatred and, as an extension, the centre of the threat to world peace. I cannot deny the difficulties the West faces in interacting with the Islamicist regime which rules Iran, having been swept to power in a surge of popularism in the Islamic Revolution of 1979. But the jingoistic image that the West has created of Iran underplays the fact that for many Iranians, life in Iran is difficult – restrictive, claustrophobic, frustrating, even frightening. Western Iranophobia means that we look at Iran through blinkered eyes. It means that we bypass the rich cultural heritage of the country, its deep and proud history, and the diversity of its social institutions. Western media also does an injustice to the people of Iran who are, in my experience of travelling to that country over many years, the warmest, most welcoming, and most cultured of peoples. The Iranians are intensely aware of – and rightly proud of – their ancient heritage. It is a fact that I have learned from my numerous visits to Hamadan, Persepolis,

Shiraz, Susa, Isfahan, Yazd, Kashan, Tehran, and many other cities, towns, and villages throughout this beautiful country. The welcome, kindness, and courtesy I have encountered on my visits has been overwhelming and I want to return the warmth I have experienced during my time among the Persians. And so, I thank my Iranian friends and colleagues for all that they bring to me. In particular I want to express my sincere good wishes to Farnaz, Forough, Mahmoud, Armin, Moji, Leily, Nacim, Kourosh, Kami, and Parvaneh.

In preparing this book, I have encountered people who have been wonderfully helpful to me, reading drafts, offering advice, and making me think harder and better and clearer. Thanks go to Eve MacDonald, Rhian Morgan, and Clare Parry. I especially wish to express my gratitude to my wonderful and committed PhD student, Jack Neighbour, who carefully read through each version of the manuscript, and offered invaluable advice and common sense. He also put together the *Dramatis Personae* – a real labour of love. I am grateful to Sabir Amiri Parian, Keivan Mahmoudi, Pejman Abarzareh, and Laurent Galbrun for giving me permission to use their beautiful photographs, and to the wonderful Farnaz Mohsenpour for creating the stunning piece of *nastaliq* calligraphy of the Hafez verse which opens this book. My colleagues in the department of Ancient History at Cardiff University have cut me the slack when I needed it most, and I am grateful for their camaraderie. Alex Clarke at Wildfire Books and Brian Distelberg at Basic Books have both been supportive and encouraging throughout the time this book has been in the making. Their comments and recommendations were always spot on and much appreciated, and I thank them warmly and sincerely for everything they have done to bring this work to fruition. An enormous debt of gratitude goes to my literary agent, the visionary Adam Gauntlett.

My greatest thanks go to family and friends: to David Pineau, my amazing husband, and to my ever-kind parents Gillian and William. Thanks also to Jean-Yves and Dominique Pineau for bringing me into your family (and driving me to Versailles so often). And finally, to Rhian, Aled, Ifan, and Mabon for being my most loving second family: *diolch o galon am bopeth*.

Lloyd Llewellyn-Jones
Cardiff, May 2021

Index

Page numbers in **bold** refer to illustrations.